Post-Specimen Encounters Between Art, Science and Curating

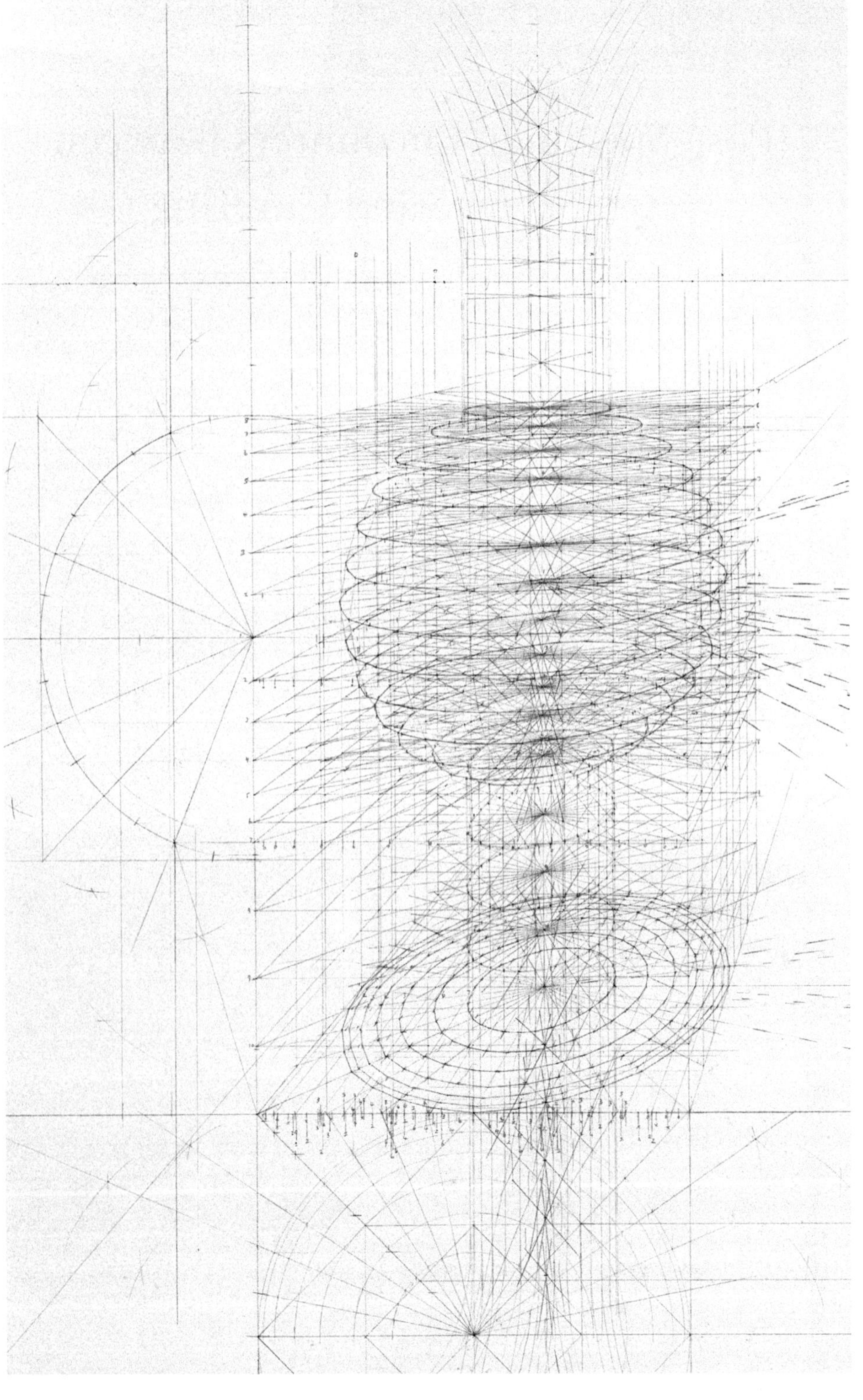

Post-Specimen Encounters Between Art, Science and Curating

Rethinking Art Practice and Objecthood through Scientific Collections

EDITED BY

Edward Juler & Alistair Robinson

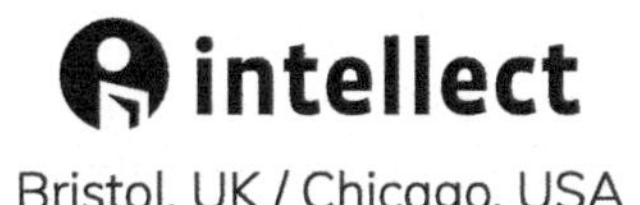

Bristol, UK / Chicago, USA

First published in the UK in 2020 by
Intellect, The Mill, Parnall Road, Fishponds, Bristol, BS16 3JG, UK

First published in the USA in 2020 by
Intellect, The University of Chicago Press, 1427 E. 60th Street,
Chicago, IL 60637, USA

A catalogue record for this book is available from
the British Library.

Cover designer: Aleksandra Szumlas
Cover image: Edward Juler, *Vitrine*, 2017. Photograph taken at the
Anatomy Museum of the Faculty of Medicine/University of Montpellier.
Frontispiece image: Richard Talbot, *Point, Line, Plane, Solid* (2017).
Pencil on paper. Detail.
Copy editor: Newgen KnowledgeWorks
Production manager: Mareike Wehner
Typesetting: Newgen KnowledgeWorks

Print ISBN 9781789383119
ePDF ISBN 9781789383126
ePub ISBN 9781789383133

Printed and bound by Severn, UK.

To find out about all our publications, please visit
www.intellectbooks.com
There you can subscribe to our e-newsletter,
browse or download our current catalogue,
and buy any titles that are in print.

This is a peer-reviewed publication.

Contents

Acknowledgements

This book has been made possible through the support of a number of individuals and institutions who have, over the past three years, been willing to provide help, both financial and intellectual, to the project. The editors would particularly like to thank Newcastle University for its support, most especially in the form of a generous subvention which assisted with the overall costs of publication. Special thanks are due to Wolfgang Weileder who helped to secure vital funding for the project. The volume germinated from a two-day interdisciplinary conference hosted by the University of Montpellier in 2016 on the occasion of the exhibition, *A Scientific Encounter: Inter-Objectivity*. Since then, the University of Montpellier has been wonderfully accommodating to the needs of the project, helping to nurture it during its early stages and providing access to its collections whenever needed. Caroline Ducourau, Hélène Lorblanchet and Véronique Bourgade, in particular, have been tremendously kind in offering their time and expertise. The editors would also like to thank M. Phillipe Augé, President of the University of Montpellier, M. Michel Mondain, the Dean of the Faculty of Medicine at Montpellier, as well as Hélène Palouzié, of the Heritage Department of Occitanie. Katie Evans, formerly of Intellect, helped to steer the manuscript at an early point in its development; as has Mareike Wehner, whose guidance and support throughout the publication process has helped to considerably lessen editorial anxieties. Maria Kostoglou and Kate Sloan offered sagacious feedback on the manuscript in ways that positively informed the final shaping of the text. We would especially like to thank Ludmilla Jordanova for generously agreeing to write the afterword to this volume as well as Christine Borland for her enthusiastic support of the project. Edward Juler would like to thank family and friends for their love and patience, most especially Arielle Juler, Paul Juler, and Emily and Richard Moon. Alistair Robinson would like to give especial thanks to Elpida Hadzi-Vasileva, Daniel Brown, Keith Brown, Kelly Richardson, Bettina Dittlmann, Rosalind McLachlan, Murray Ballard; and to Caroline McDonald and the team at the Great North Museum, Newcastle-upon-Tyne.

Introduction

Edward Juler and Alistair Robinson

What or who is a specimen? By what means or powers of authority is an object rendered into a specimen, and as such a particular kind of 'thing'? The term 'specimen' habitually carries connotations of scientific neutrality or objectivity, as though it were an overarching and timeless concept rather than a historical construct, characteristic of a distinctive idea of 'modernity'. One might go so far as to say that the specimen itself is slippery, mercurial; less an example of objecthood disinterestedly beheld than the product of changeable praxes and shifting discursive regimes; a thing riven by taxonomy. Indeed, how can one begin defining an idea that not only spans disciplines but is peculiarly redolent of scientific practice? We suggest that a specimen might be understood, to borrow the term coined by Sherry Turkle, as an 'evocative object'; an object which acts as a companion 'to our emotional lives or as provocations to thought'.[1] Certainly, how could a specimen be anything *but* evocative, given its metaphorical embeddedness within scientific practice as exemplar, as evidence and as epistemological locus?

In its classification of the word, the *Oxford English Dictionary* lists two, now obsolete, definitions: 'A means of discovering or finding out; an experiment' and 'a pattern or model'. Yet these empirical and indeed diagrammatic meanings resonate still within those more commonplace, contemporary definitions that provide the specimen with its scientific connotations and symbolic richness. It is both a

> single thing selected or regarded as typical of its class; a part or piece *of* something taken as representative of the whole [as well as an] animal, plant, or mineral, a part or portion of some substance or organism, etc., serving as an example of the thing in question for purposes of investigation or scientific study.[2]

In this sense, 'the specimen' constitutes the empiric bedrock of scientific enquiry; it can be, in its various guises: an investigative object, material evidence of a scientific theory as well as an epistemological paradigm. Above all, it is a particular way of *knowing*; a means of ordering and making sense of the world through the objects that constitute it.[3]

From the refrigerated human tissue sample to the crystal housed in the natural history museum, specimens might be understood to have an exemplary *materiality*, quite aside from any abstract values they may be seen to possess. For even if the object itself, such as a geometrical diagram, appears to the casual observer intangible or theoretical, its representation enjoys a 'facture': a material form over and above the object it describes (even if that form is but a single line drawn on paper or pixels flickering on a screen). Indeed, the epistemological weddedness of concept and material representation in science is perhaps nowhere better evinced than in the specimen itself, whose status as paradigm depends upon it embodying in some way the very properties it purports to illustrate. Thus, it is the ontology of the specimen which makes it an evocative object precisely because it represents a materiality wrought in the crucible of scientific thought, whose episteme is the product of a range of philosophical, cultural, ethical and sociopolitical concerns.[4]

This volume is about specimens; or rather, it is about what happens to objects when they become 'specimens', which is to say when they enter a museum or other collections as items of classification and comparison.[5] It is also concerned with how specimens can be reimagined both by the academy and by visual artists. And it leads us to ask if art objects, too, may be properly seen as 'specimens', or indeed as *post*-specimens: things freed from the limits of curatorial narrative or the narrow constraints of historical time. In particular, the chapters that follow take that most paradigmatic of specimens—the object stored or displayed in the science and medical museum—and ask how creative practice, whether written or artistic, can interrogate its scientific thingness, its epistemic objectivity, its ideological valence. This volume approaches the relationship between museums, their specimens and collections, and visual art practice as a form of what the artist Mark Dion has termed 'epistemological critique'.[6] In a broad sense, this type of critique might be seen to exhume and question those historical epistemic values that, over the centuries, have become embedded in the fabric of the science or natural history museum so that the 'truth' which such institutions attempt to convey about their specimens is revealed, in the words of Marion Endt-Jones, 'as a constructed fiction, as a distinctly anthropocentric narrative influenced by a plethora of discourses, ideologies and interests'.[7]

David Edwards has coined the term 'artscience' to describe the purposeful combination of aesthetic and scientific methods. This neologism was, in part, inspired by Edwards's dissatisfaction with the lamentable state of contemporary interdisciplinarity and how, more often than not, both art and scientific institutions err on the side of caution by disseminating values that reaffirm disciplinary autonomy and traditional cultural hierarchies. He argues that the 'challenge of the cultural institution is to realise its mission while not letting it become an obstacle to the kind of innovation that opens up meaningful dialogue with contemporary science'.[8] Edwards's theorization of the divide between art and science (and how artscience modes of thinking might bridge this disciplinary chasm) is, in some ways, a contemporary if timely rearticulation of C. P. Snow's, now rather infamous, 'Two Cultures' paradigm. Delivered as a Rede Lecture in 1959, Snow's thesis postulated that 'the whole of western society is increasingly being split into two polar groups'; at the one side are the 'literary intellectuals' and other artistic elites, and 'at the other scientists'.[9] Although Snow's account addressed the problem of the relations between the disciplines as they were then broadly conceived, the issue that most preoccupied him was the apparent and wanton ignorance of science displayed by post-war arts practitioners and those connected to the cultural establishment. 'It is bizarre', he marvelled, 'how very little of twentieth century science has been assimilated into twentieth century art'.[10] But if Snow's hypothesis revealed an implicit bias towards the physical sciences which inferred that the arts must, in effect, be instrumentalized towards scientific ends, then Edwards imagines something very different: the cultural institution as a shared disciplinary space wherein artscience emerges as a hybrid, innovative form of practice.

It has become routine in art history and cultural studies to criticize the theoretical shortcomings of Snow's thesis, not least because nothing better demonstrates its rhetorical redundancy than contemporary art's fascination with curating, rearranging and intervening in the science museum.[11] And Snow's disinterest in public engagement with science disqualified from his thesis those very types of cultural institution which currently seem to offer the most opportune grounds for developing what Georgina Born and Andrew Barry have described elsewhere as the 'heterogeneous space of overlapping interdisciplinary practices at the intersection of the arts, sciences and technologies'.[12] Yet the need for this kind of space, be it the 'studio-lab' in which mongrel practices are innovated or else the contemporary museum as a zone of artscience encounter, paradoxically only underscores the cogency of Snow's account, at least in terms of how science tends to view its representations as a means to an end rather than as objects of aesthetic interest in their own right. Ken Arnold, the former head of public programmes at the Wellcome Collection, has remarked on the 'unbridgeable and enduring gap [which] exists between image-makers in science and those in the arts'. He notes that the

> aims of scientific image-makers are entirely coterminous with the rest of their professional colleagues who use different methods of presenting data. And though the images they produce are undoubtedly aesthetically attractive, they will continue to be seen by scientists who make them as data and tools and not prized objects in themselves.[13]

So it is with the specimen also, which, quite aside from any aesthetic qualities it might possess, is comprehended as an objective if tacit representation of instrumentalized scientific knowledge.

If the scientific status of the object or specimen epitomizes the polarization hypothesized by Snow, then the museum potentially troubles these discursive boundaries through subjecting the specimen to a radical reframing which interrogates its agential function and de-territorializes disciplinary domains. As Clementine Deliss has explained, collections contain 'epistemic objects' that are inherently performative; they act as 'knowledge generators' which are 'able to infer into different narratives, to engineer combinatory interpretations'. Like all specimens, such museum-bound objects intimate pan-historicity while, in actuality, 'their performativity offers an understanding of trans-historicity on the fluid, horizontal plane of synchronicity rather than linear progress [...], a collection is about the friction between coding a thing and feeling encoded through the agency of objects'.[14] This tension between predetermined epistemology and free agency allows museum specimens to become 'boundary objects' *par excellence*: things which spontaneously enter into discursive interplay with other objects, publics and cultural domains in ways often starkly unrelated to their original fashioning or purpose.[15] At their most straightforward, such encounters could be seen to obey the laws of an 'alien phenomenology' in which, as the philosopher Ian Bogost has described, 'objects try to make sense of each other through the qualities and logics they possess'.[16] Or to put it another way, it is the unexpected spark which flares through the specimen as it comes into contact with other things that enriches its objecthood and illuminates, uneasily perhaps, its fraught status as paradigm within competing networks of cultural affinity. Surveyed from this angle, the museum, and the plurality of relations it enables, can be seen, to paraphrase Timothy Morton's thinking on the subject, as a kind of 'hyperobject' whose occupation of space and agency serve to dissolve any coherent sense of what an entity or object might be.[17]

As Megan Halpern has observed, the complexity of boundary objects stems from their place at the very heart of the Two Cultures debate: they offer points of dialogue or interchange between disciplines, publics and cultures and, in so being, 'provide a way to begin to untangle the complex relationship between interdisciplinary work in art and science, and science communication'.[18] Through confronting the specimen head-on, as it were, within the contemporary museum, art, science and curating proffer new pathways by which we might negotiate and know the material world. Such concerns are powerfully articulated in the chapters by Alistair Robinson, Marion Endt-Jones and John Mack. Robinson discusses how objecthood can be reanimated somehow through curating strategies which bring artworks into dialogue with scientific artefacts. Drawing on object-oriented ontology and Latourian philosophy, he argues that 'interobjective' colloquy bestows upon objects an agential capacity that transcends the mute segregation imposed by disciplinary and museological categories. Placed in juxtaposition, contemporary art and scientific objects thus 'socialize' with each other in unexpected ways, generating provocative and dissolute couplings which dramatically reconfigure their epistemology. What does it mean, after all, Robinson asks, to think of a specimen aesthetically; or else, an artwork scientifically? How might the museum or even the very objecthood of these things be transformed by such interobjective encounters? The influence of artist-led 'wonder-museums' on recent curatorial trends in natural history museum displays is the subject of Endt-Jones's chapter. Apropos of the curator Nicolas Bourriaud's suggestion that such venues—formed as they are upon seemingly anachronistic and hermetic values that are traditionally associated with seventeenth-century cabinets of curiosity—induce a state of passivity in the observer, Endt-Jones questions if such curiosity museums can still be understood as interpersonal, collaborative and socially engaged spaces. Might not the contemporary Wunderkammer, in taking inspiration from the artist-envisioned relational wonder museum, instil astonishment and curiosity in the eyes of the visitor through the sheer abundance or breathtaking variety of scientific objects on show? The uneasy relationship between the agential function of specimens and museum display is also examined in John Mack's chapter. Focusing upon the complex array of meanings to which Kongo figures have been subjected in Western museums, Mack maintains that while such objects have been a staple of ethnographic displays since the nineteenth century, they have continued to 'defy easy or singular classification'. Indeed, so he argues, the mercurial nature of the figures themselves, whose unfinished aesthetic retains an agential potential that defies the curatorial etiquette of the collections in which they are placed, makes them potent boundary objects which influence their emergence as objects of the contemporary artistic imaginary.

Our use of the prefix 'post' in our title signifies a particular problem. At the broadest level, it is employed to suggest a reconsideration of what a specimen might be, when analysed in the light of contemporary arts practice and the recent turn towards more self-reflexive and experimental forms of art writing in the humanities. More specifically, the sense of 'post-specimen' that we want to outline echoes that employed by the philosopher of art Peter Osborne in his coinage 'post-conceptual', and in his understanding of the idea of the 'postmodern' in relation to the modern. For Osborne, the 'postmodern' is precisely the 'revival, deepening, multiplication and complication of discourses of the modern' itself, rather than its inversion or complete transcendence.[19] Osborne's use of the prefix does *not* designate a successor in a historical linear sequence. Rather, it designates a stage of development by which new thinking has *internalized* the legacy of previous positions staked out. The term 'post-specimen' here is therefore intended to recognize the legacy of the orthodox understanding of artefacts as specimens in museum collections, under Enlightenment and modernist systems of knowledge. In Osborne's terms, a curatorial practice that thinks in terms of 'post-specimens' must be one that emerges *from within* the logic of the specimen in order to outgrow it.

As the museologist Alan Wallach argued, at their outset museum displays were intended to create a 'world arranged with taxonomic order and precision [ordered through] the collection, description, classification, and systematic display' of artefacts.[20] In Wallach's scheme, the idea of the 'museum object' is all but interchangeable with that of a 'specimen', whatever its disciplinary affiliation. These terms imply a *transparent* form of representation. That is something almost all academic disciplines across the humanities and sciences alike now accept as problematic. This is what must be outgrown.

We also draw on a second aspect of Osborne's thinking. He has made the fundamental observation that 'modernity is a qualitative, not a chronological, category'.[21] This is crucial here, given that the condition of possibility for a 'specimen' to exist is the order of knowledge that developed in Europe in the eighteenth century. A 'specimen' is, fundamentally, a *representative* object with a fixed place within a regime of disciplinary knowledge. To simplify the matter enormously, that regime of knowledge, as museums have portrayed it, is one which not only exemplifies but constitutes European modernity. The 'specimen' is therefore a product of the enthronement of the scientific method as the sole defining legitimate means of instituting knowledge—which links the 'teaching and research' model shared by the academy and the museum. Certainly, as Mary Winsor argues, it was the development of the natural history museum in the period leading up to 1800 which facilitated the emergence of the modern scientific method precisely through presenting specimens as instruments of systematic comparison and analysis.[22] In the Weberian bureaucracies of both academy and museum, the means of knowledge production are only legitimate if peer-reviewed and if they partake of a scientific or quasi-scientific method. And, of course, this modern, scientistic attitude applies not only to science museums, but to museums in the widest sense of the term, ranging from history and folk museums to collections of fine art. Many museologists (including Donald Preziosi perhaps most prominently) have convincingly argued that the museum itself *exemplifies* this very modernity and its contradictions. In modernity, only the museum provides an authoritative and universal means of conveying knowledge to the entire public, through its 'exhibitionary complex'.[23] In modernity, museums are or were charged with constructing a universal, totalizing, single history and a falsifiable account of their field of knowledge.

We argue that orthodox museum artefacts are objects of exemplification and this process makes them quasi-specimens by definition. The actual mechanics of existing forms of 'exemplification' are varied, but often consistent. Even within individual collections, there are multiple forms of exemplification at work in curatorial labour. There are those that articulate the relations between artefacts typologically, in relation to a wider genus or species of objects. There are those which speculatively see material things as the vehicles for manifesting abstract or philosophical concepts, or points in intellectual or cultural history. And there are those that reveal objects' positions within a particular socio-historical formation. And indeed, there are those that simply make hierarchical status claims of historical significance—in the case of art objects, characteristically that those objects are the 'representative art of the moment'.[24]

We are using the term 'specimen' here for its metonymic capacities, in full awareness of the conceptual burden it is being asked to bear. The idea of a *post-specimen* suggests that an entire mode of museum practice may now be facing its terminal point or moment of crisis. It may, even, be taken to signify an epistemological shift or rupture. Has the age of the museum object reached its end? And, if so, what might replace it? One indication of this is that whereas 'knowledge' was a term used strictly in the singular, we find it habitually pluralized in academic discourse—but not yet in museum practice. Both these ideas are related to the proposition that the idea of a 'specimen', like that of 'modernity', should be seen as (in Osborne's phrase) a 'qualitative' term: namely, one that carries a style of thinking within it. The idea of a 'specimen' contains a particular character of thought about objects within it, and it is, as we suggest, an 'evocative' idea. The peculiar redolence of the specimen is thus examined by Rahma Khazam in her contribution to this volume. Reconsidering the specimen in light of contemporary bio-art practice and transhumanist theory, Khazam contests the ideological foundations upon which not only the specimen but also modern science and contemporary art are based. So might the specimen then, in its metonymic and cultural richness, allow for a critique of the 'museum' and those knowledges that are ideologically indebted to its praxes and episteme.

To also suggest that specimens are *evocative* objects means that we must re-evaluate their very nature. Certainly, the specimen is traditionally understood to be a discrete yet paradigmatic entity. It is something that is ontologically unitary, even as it is expected to speak for entire classes of objects or else furnish information from which whole data sets might be extrapolated. The chapters which follow disrupt such normative understandings. They open up the idea of the object as specimen to alternative readings that undermine epistemological certainties and place museological hierarchies into doubt. In this task, we take seriously Elizabeth Ermarth's questioning of orthodox epistemologies. Her questions have as yet been unanswered in museum practice and certainly in science and natural history museums, which rest upon an established empiricism. We are proposing that the kinds of experimental writing that have begun to appear in art and art history may be productive even in the sciences. As James Elkins has observed in relation to art writing, while art historians, theorists and critics 'cite poststructuralist philosophers on the idea of writing [...] [their] own writing continues to be restricted by disciplinary expectations. The few authors who permit their writing to become more experimental tend to have their texts viewed as sources for art history, rather than examples of art history'.[25] This is, perhaps, the pre-eminent challenge that has entered academic life across the last 40 years: that writing both in the humanities and sciences must go beyond realism or transparency and incorporate self-reflexivity. We might say that in academic history, texts such as Hayden White's *Metahistory* (1973) exemplify the beginnings of this process; Reinhart Kosseleck's work is not unrelated. In art history, parallel revolutions have not been forthcoming—yet.

One of the central concerns of this volume is that the narrative conventions of realist writing within the humanities demonstrate a commitment to those quasi-scientific ideologies of rationality, objectivity and empiricism that 'the specimen' itself might be seen to represent.[26] Yet such a position exemplifies something of a paradox: that an object can only be meaningfully analysed through the language of its own discursive ideation. And in the case of modern and contemporary art, as Gavin Parkinson acknowledges, to 'think and write about these through the realist and rationalist means that constitute academic art writing is to drag them into the very forms of knowledge that such art repudiates, criticizes, questions, seeks to overthrow, or at least considers limited'.[27] The challenge is to begin to accept subjective reflexivity, indeterminacy, relationality and narratological diversity in both academic and museum practice.

These alternative analytical strategies can generate genuinely novel interpretative models. These in turn can illuminate the lacunae of existing discursive structures. Such an approach might therefore be seen as particularly apposite when questioning the epistemological character of the specimen through creative practice. As Ermarth claims,

> discursive critique subverts the metaphysic that posits essences like stable, self-identical, non-discursive identities and the transcendental 'laws' that operate 'in' them. Such a metaphysic simply becomes inadequate in the discourse where essence or identity is multiplied because it is always *situated*, and where the situation is always discursive, which is to say always constructed by systems of signs whose function is differential.[28]

A number of chapters in this volume directly draw upon traditions of 'experimental' and creative writing from both within and beyond the discipline of art history. Such writing, to quote the art historian Catherine Grant, is 'self-conscious of its own process, foregrounding form as much as content'.[29] Edward Juler's chapter thus foregrounds a psychogeographical approach to art historical writing through weaving a peripatetic narrative around the specimens in the anatomy museum at the University of Montpellier. By turns subjective and analytical, and moving between different rhetorical registers which range from the self-reflective to the critical, Juler's text considers the strange, suppressed agency of the anatomical specimens in the context of Christine Borland's photographic investigation of the collection in 1996. By contrast, Gavin Parkinson's contribution presents two parallel texts—one historiographical, and one poetic—which, read jointly, investigate the use-value of mathematical objects within surrealism. Shifting between a realistic mode of writing which follows the rationalist priorities of academic discourse and an improvised, subjective text which echoes surrealist poetics, Parkinson seeks to unite form and content while acknowledging that knowledge itself is often the product of serendipity.

Insofar as *Post-Specimen Encounters* examines the relationship between specimens, collections, museums and art practice, it also provides alternative methodologies for interdisciplinary research. These range from poetico-critical forms of analysis (as in the case of Christy Ducker's poetic response to the Wohl Pathology Museum) to imaginary dialogues with botanical objects (in her text, Nadia Lichtig imagines the cultural history of the lotus flower from the perspective of the plant itself). These approaches are intended to provoke new forms of cross-disciplinarity, by weaving subjective threads into the language of art history, into the history of science and medicine, into museology and art writing. Although not all of the chapters in this volume self-consciously experiment with narrative style in the manner envisaged by figures like Ermarth, rhetorical criticality is nonetheless present in varied ways. These include speculative forms of interdisciplinarity and first-person accounts of the process of artistic production alike. The chapters by Richard Talbot, Gemma Anderson, Irene Brown and Jane Wildgoose each present very different practice-led perspectives on the 'post-specimen', whether that be through considering 'object biographies' as stimuli for art-making or the creation of artist-led curiosity museums as vehicles for rethinking object histories. By foregrounding critical reflection, *Post-Specimen* therefore echoes Grant's belief that by 'attending to the act of writing, the desires of the [researcher] can be brought back into focus' to address 'questions of authorship, authority and history'.[30]

It is, of course, a commonplace that the object of research and the subjectivity of the researcher are impossible to ultimately disentangle. Indeed, across various disciplines, the idea of 'entanglement' has long been useful in describing the complex, affective relationships and discontinuities between different systems.[31] Such an understanding of interobjective relations considers the agential interactivity between things as their primary epistemological condition. Objects, in other words, can only meaningfully exist when comprehended in dynamic interaction with other objects.[32] This framework is not unrelated to the propositions put forward in the last decade about objects and objecthood. 'The object' has had its return, or revenge both in philosophy and art practice. Materiality, the implacable unknowability of materials, and the otherness of things have become dominant in recent discourse around art practice. These are directly relevant to the idea of the 'specimen' and complicate it considerably.

Graham Harman has argued that these ideas first reached a public stage in 2007.[33] The principal protagonists, in his scheme, are far from united in their ideas. As Harman outlines, the association of object-oriented thinking with figures as diverse as Bruno Latour, Quentin Meillassoux, Levi Bryant, Ray Brassier, Iain Hamilton Grant, Ian Bogost and Timothy Morton among others divided early-on into two fundamental movements—which he (tendentiously) names 'speculative materialism' and 'object-oriented' thought.[34] For Harman, the differences can be identified upon their responses to the question of whether 'things-in-themselves [are] *directly* accessible to humans or not? Simply put, the answer of speculative materialism is yes, while the answer of object-oriented ontology is no'.[35] There is a common denominator, though. This is the rejection of an a priori privilege given to human perspectives above 'non-human' ones, such that there is a 'levelling' of importance between human and non-human objects. The logical implications of this are that the category of the specimen is either dissolved, or enlarged vastly. The idea that we can 'know' the 'natural' or material world by collecting and ordering it systematically is put into doubt again by object-oriented thought.

On the other hand, the opposition to anthropocentrism that characterizes some object-oriented thought could be easily read as an attempt to stake out a thoroughly 'scientific' form of thinking when humankind's place in the world is in direct question, if the 'sixth great extinction' that some scientists predict, comes to pass. And such thinking might help us examine the existing use of scientific images or figures in creative practice. Lia Carreira has argued that the idea of 'the exhibition space as a laboratory' has been the dominant image by which modernist artwork has been characterized.[36] As she puts it, 'The laboratory as an institutionalized space for experiments in science has been adopted for by the arts as a key concept and structure' throughout the history of modern art.[37] The questions arising from this might be these: how far can scientific models of thought genuinely inform artistic and curatorial behaviours and thinking? Conversely, can ideas from art practice help us rethink the order of knowledge that has privileged the scientific method above all others—but led us to the brink of mass extinction? Such ideas are foremost in Andrew Patrizio's mind as his chapter considers the post-human sensibility of Christine Borland's practice from the standpoint of her work with botanical, mineral and zoological specimens. Her penchant for using such diverse materials, Patrizio maintains, demonstrates an 'ecology of practices' that transcends narrow speciesism and disrupts anthropocentric narratives by subtly repositioning the human in relation to the non-human, so that these two poles of being might become more contiguous and mutually respectful.

Another reason for our interest in the specimen character of objects is the degree to which artists have internalized object-oriented thinking; it is difficult to overstate how astonishingly influential object-oriented philosophy has become in artistic and curatorial practice alike in the space of a decade. It has become effectively canonized as what we might call 'the artistic dominant' (to paraphrase Fredric Jameson).[38] In our understanding, this process was cemented by Carolyn Christov-Bakargiev in *dOCUMENTA 13* in 2012, which as the most prestigious, most costly and arguably the largest single exhibition in the world, enjoys a unique position of influence.[39]

Subsequent projects such as the *British Art Show* of 2015 followed in its wake, but *dOCUMENTA 13*, exerted a special influence in presenting both artefacts and artworks as quasi-'specimens'. It presented both historical art objects and non-art objects together in a single space titled the 'Brain', creating a kind of 'master-collection': a museum of everything, we might say, in which all kinds of 'things', scientific and artistic, historical and contemporary, could intermingle. In the 'Brain', 'stone miniatures from Central Asia dating from about 2000BC converged with such works as photographs of Adolf Hitler's bathtub by Lee Miller [...] and photos of bomb-crater lakes in Vietnam'.[40] *dOCUMENTA 13* was one of the first major exhibitions to give curatorial shape to Bruno Latour's understanding of *all* objects as enmeshed in human/non-human 'assemblages', all of which are merely conducting or inhabiting different 'modes of existence'.[41] It asked the question: Can we see objects, and specimens, through either the 'flat ontology' proposed by Manuel deLanda, or the 'ontological pluralism' forwarded by Bruno Latour?[42]

To approach objects and museum specimens through these problematics is also to reiterate the criticism of science museums that they have treated specimens as little more than 'pure objects': as 'object[s] pushed onto an aesthetic plane that no longer belongs to the practical and tangible space of functionality'.[43] Latour's imperative, of following chains of agency in relation to objects, decentres specimens from their prime position in museums as forms of evidence; they become 'actants', as if they are tools with an operational value rather than having fixed locations in a field of knowledge.

In Latour's scheme, interobjectivity is where 'each actor's every action is interfered with by others' such that we need to 'take into account a large number of variables at the same time'.[44] Objects' 'behaviours' are not determined solely by their own characteristics, in other words, but by their capacities or affordances, and their dependencies. Such an account is related to the idea of plotting the 'social life of objects' as Arjun Appadurai's advocated. Appadurai asked of objects: 'The definitional question is: in *what does their sociality consist?*'.[45] He also noted that 'No social analysis of things can avoid a minimum of what might be [a] called methodological fetishism [...] [thus r]eturning attention to objects themselves'.[46] The starting point here is precisely the ways in which 'objects in themselves' have returned to the centre stage of artistic and intellectual attention. Through a Latourian methodology, or rather, a Latourian museology, we can start to gauge objects' potential agency and capacities in the world.

These ideas in turn derive from the philosophy and the anthropology of science associated with Michel Serres. We argue that Serres, Latour, Harman and Appadurai's ideas *do* allow the idea of a 'post-specimen' to now make sense in museum practice. Serres famously coined the image that a ball is a thing that creates a community by gathering subjects around it: 'the body is the object of the ball [...] the ball isn't there for the body; the exact contrary is true: the body is the object of the ball; playing is nothing else but making oneself the attribute of the ball'.[47] If we take this seriously, for museums' collections and specimens, therefore, objects are not only of interest in terms of their capacity to act representationally. Art, in particular, allows a way out of this impasse. As Harman says: 'Art is something that seemingly lets us see the "impossible depth of objects"'.[48]

This volume therefore draws together developments in thought around objects, collecting and epistemology. One common denominator among several of the chapters, including those by Irene Brown and Alistair Robinson, is how far it is possible or productive to reanimate historical modes of understanding specimens. The museologist Steven Conn has called the nineteenth-century model of museum display an 'object-based epistemology'.[49] In this understanding, objects are not *merely* aids for learning, that is, 'specimens'—but themselves *embody* knowledge in their very materiality as beings. Conn's work suggests we might see museum collections both as 'libraries' of non-human things where knowledge is stored, and as spaces where knowledge is made palpable, is 'felt': where knowledge has its own kinds of affect.

Recent research into the origins and genealogy of modern museums is relevant to our thinking here. William Poole has recently argued that a small number of core questions have traditionally preoccupied museologists and curators. These are concerned with the development of the modern museum as an institutional form, with its responsibilities, the relations between the forms of knowledge production in the academy, the museum and the creative arts. One core question concerns how knowledge became disaggregated into discrete disciplines, each with its own institutions, methodologies and protocols.[50] As this history of disaggregation has been so thoroughly researched in recent years, Poole argues that a 'potentially more interesting discussion [is] "what are the origins of the teaching-and-research-model?"'.[51] Recent museological thinking suggests that the histories of universities, museums, and indeed art galleries, are even more intimately connected or entangled than was previously imagined, even at relatively late dates. Poole notes that in the earliest museum-type institution in England, in particular, there was 'an intellectual ambiguity at the heart of the [museum] collection', such that contemporaries observed many of its objects 'do not belong at all [in] a [...] museum, but would be much more suitable to an art gallery'.[52] The connections between aesthetics, academic knowledge and scientific investigation were once intimate. In a world where specimens, art objects and teaching resources overlap, there is room for speculation about what objects and specimens are for, and can do or be.

Poole notes that England's first museum was 'in what is today [part] of the Bodleian Library', and that the preservation of objects and their embodied knowledge should be described as a 'three body problem' between 'library [...] school and museum'.[53] Might collections of specimens yet be reconceived by reasserting the early 'museum's transitional status between [...] "museum", "art gallery"' and library?[54] Might this 'ambiguity' between institutional types—and therefore between types of object—still be present but latent or suppressed? Might the classificatory logic of the science museum be treated as a historical artefact in its own right and its objects and taxonomic arrangements actually be at odds with the epistemological order its staff imagine it imposes?[55] This much would require any researcher to reconsider 'the [entire] distribution of knowledge' not only between disciplines and classes of object, but between types of institution.[56] The contributors here invite us to imagine how artists, curators and academics might approach such alternative distributions of knowledge and deal with objects and specimens subject to them.

As Lorraine Daston tells us, things talk; 'they do not merely repeat'.[57] But what of the thing that does not merely soliloquize, or whisper into the ear of the obliging historian but, rather, engages in conversation with other objects and disciplines? Such is the question *Post-Specimen Encounters* asks of those things which exist at the interstices of art and science. Here, specimens critically participate in an ongoing discourse between disciplines. The complexity of interdisciplinary dialogue, in which objects and their agents shape and are, in turn, shaped by discursive interrelations might be thought of as a kind of assemblage or an 'uneven topography'; a living confederation of emergent properties whose 'gelling endures alongside energies and factions that fly out from it and disturb it from within'.[58] Or perhaps such an interchange might be considered a type of discursive entanglement; a space where disciplines and discourses intertwine. Such a 'knotting', as Tim Ingold tells us, should not be thought of as a kind of closure, but rather an infinite looping that enriches the correspondence between things. Interobjective dialogue envisaged in this way is a kind of meshwork-in-process whose

> parts are not elementary components but ever-extending lines, and its harmonies reside in the way each strand as it issues forth, coils around the others and is coiled in its turn, in a counter-valence of equal and opposite twists which hold it together and prevent it from unravelling.[59]

The philosophical and affective potential of both scientific and artistic artefacts are live problems in contemporary thought. But there are differences between how contemporary scientific objects and historical ones 'live' in museums. For art historians like Georges Didi-Huberman, Alexander Nagel and Christopher S. Wood, these differences are arguably far greater in scope than those between historical art objects and contemporary ones, which have been mitigated by an emphasis upon the positive value of anachronistic interpretation.[60] The museologist Alan Wallach quoting Stephen Conn argues that 'unlike collections of natural history specimens or anthropological artifacts, [historical] works of fine art even today "continue to function successfully as objects", in part because "art history and art museums enjoy a close intellectual relationship"' and in part because of their temporality as aesthetic objects.[61] As Griselda Pollock argues, art objects belong to *two* worlds at once: that of the present in which we encounter them and in which they 'live' alongside us, and that of their birth.[62] By contrast, the specimen in the science museum (and less frequently the natural history museum) can suffer a fate worse than death: being consigned to storage in perpetuity. As historical paradigms of scientific knowledge must be definitively superseded by the hypotheses that supported them being falsified, their objects become not only redundant, but effectively invisible. As the speculative realist Robin Mackay has written, 'The most radical philosophical problematics [of our time include] the status of the scientific object [in the light of the] revival of speculative realism'.[63] We may need what the art historian Michael Baxandall called a 'period eye' to have the historical imagination to make older art objects 'live', but they can be imaginatively revisited, even if we can never recapture or inhabit the world of their making, or recuperate the worldview of their first viewers.[64] Many specimens, on the other hand, are destined to be forgotten or consigned to oblivion.

The obvious questions that logically follow are these. First, whether art objects can or should be re-understood as 'specimens'. Second, if scientific or natural history 'specimens' can 'live' in two worlds at once, as art history's objects (are imagined to) do. As the curator Teresa Gleadowe outlines, curating is 'a discipline whose [very] purpose is to exemplify'.[65] If this is true then the idea of a museum of 'post-specimens' is an outright contradiction in terms. But as she also argues (if referring to contemporary art specifically): the dominant 'understanding of contemporary curating is based on the now orthodox assumption that since the late 1960s [...] [that] curating has shifted from a caring, meditative [...] activity to one [that is] [...] performative'.[66] If, as Sarah Mengler and Fiona Cameron insist, what museums have been fundamentally concerned with is 'the conceptualization and performance of knowledge', then all curatorship is always already performative.[67] Two of the intriguing possibilities that this volume holds out for curators, artists and others, are museums whose objects do not exemplify; another is institutions might yet make clear that they 'perform' their knowledge and therefore do so as a subjective construction.

In art museums, at least, such ideas have become far more commonplace. To take one example: a decade ago, The Museum of Modern Art in New York announced to the world that it had 'acquired' the '@' symbol. Not a 'specimen' of the symbol like a computer keyboard; nor a typographer or designer's drawing of a version of the symbol prior to production; nor any comparative examples of the symbol whether at the design stage or in published texts. In Paola Antonelli's words, the museum acquired the symbol *itself*:

> We have acquired the design act in itself [...] Being in the public realm [...] it is immaterial and synthetic, and therefore does not add unnecessary 'weight' to the world [...] MoMA curators' [...] acquisition of '@' takes one more step. It relies on the assumption that physical possession of an object as a requirement for an acquisition is no longer necessary, and therefore it sets curators free to [acquire things that] are in the air and belong to everybody and to no one, like the '@' as art objects befitting MoMA's collection.[68]

Might we see Antonelli's 'act' as providing a model for 'post-specimen' curatorial practice? Perhaps so; the curatorial manoeuvre of acquiring a creative 'act', making museum objects akin to J. L. Austin's 'speech acts' or works of performance art, is a provocative one.[69] It undermines the idea of the museum object as 'specimen'; as typical of its class or representative of the whole. To acquire an *idea* is to acquire a 'class' in its entirety by proxy; this logic would ultimately result in a museum collection without specimens. The interest of Antonelli's proposition here lies in what constitutes the 'exemplarity' of museum objects—or rather, how far they must *behave* as 'specimens' once in a collection. In curatorial thought, Beryl Graham and Sarah Cook argue that 'The traditional art museum has a set of categories determined by medium, geography, and chronology [...] [but we] define [...] media as a set of *behaviours* not as a medium'.[70] In their scheme, curators must think in terms of objects' *behaviours* rather than their technical or formal characteristics. Their project also upends the very idea of objects as specimens, examined by an omniscient researcher, or interpreted by a nineteenth-century realist author—an omniscient narrator.

Antonelli's is, however, only one model, of what a 'post-specimen' museum might be and perhaps an already outmoded one. Antonelli's account figures the museum curator's work as symptomatic of a brave new world of digital immateriality commensurate with texts such as Joasia Krysa's 2006 volume *Curating Immateriality*, where museums and galleries could work with virtual space, independently of objects entirely.[71] The return to objects in object-oriented thinking and art practice since c. 2007 has rendered this idea archaic.

Such an account is related to the idea of plotting the 'social life of objects' as Arjun Appadurai has advocated.[72] A Latourian or Appadurian museum would follow actors' agency in the world. Even the '@' sign is more than a symbol of deterritorialized, globalized (but American-led) digital culture; it is an 'object' in the Latourian sense that has multiple 'lives' beyond being reducible to a 'specimen' of a culture of design circa 2010. Its career in the world echoes the spirit of adventurous writing here. In Greek it is called a 'little duck'; in Russian, a 'dog'; in Swedish, it is 'snabel-a' (an 'a' attached to an elephant's trunk), or a 'kanelbulle' (a spiral-like pastry); in Norwegian it is a 'kroellalfa' (a curled 'a', recalling an ammonite); in Germany it is a 'klammerraffe': a monkey clinging to a tree with an arm extended; in Brazil, it is an 'arroba': an archaic weight measurement; in Italy, it's a 'chiocciolina': a small snail; in Hungary it is a 'kukatsz': a little worm wandering; in Finland it is a 'miukumauku': a cat curled up fast asleep.[73]

A museum of post-specimens might be a Latourian space of 'encounters' where new relations are set in play. But Graham Harman has argued that 'The true chasm [...] lies not between humans and the world, but between objects and relations'.[74] An object-oriented museum of post-specimens might be a Harmanian place where relations themselves are problematized or made opaque and objects plainly utter their otherness to us. Harman suggests that such a museum would be 'a world packed full of ghostly real objects signalling to each other from inscrutable depths, unable to touch one another fully'.[75] All of these propositions act as fundamental challenges to the idea of the specimen and the regime of knowledge it is integral to. Put another way: what, when we talk about specimens, do we avoid talking about? The objects? The mysterious gulfs between them? Or, maybe, just maybe, ourselves?

NOTES

1. Sherry Turkle, 'Introduction: The Things That Matter', in *Evocative Objects: Things We Think With*, ed. S. Turkle (Cambridge, MA: MIT Press, 2007), 5.

2. 'specimen, n.'. *OED Online*. June 2018. Oxford University Press, [online] available at http://www.oed.com/view/Entry/186018?redirectedFrom=specimen (accessed 12 June 2018) (original emphasis).

3. In this way, the specimen might align with John Pickstone's 'ways of knowing' which, at their simplest, encompass 'the activity of describing and classifying, along with allied activities such as collecting, storing and displaying'. Pickstone makes the distinction that this kind of sorting is 'not restricted to objects or to records of objects, but can include observations of processes and happenings, or the results of interventions or experiments'. J. V. Pickstone, 'A Brief Introduction to Ways of Knowing and Ways of Working'. *History of Science* 49, no. 3 (2011): 237, https://doi.org/10.1177/007327531104900301.

4. For instance, the animated ethical and legal debate that surrounds the current usage of human biological samples for biomedical research underscores the potential epistemological complexity of the specimen, at least in relation to contemporary biomedicine. See: Suzanne M. Rivera, Barbara E. Bierer, Glenn Cohen and Holly Lynch, 'Introduction', in *Specimen Science: Ethics and Policy Implications*, ed. H. F. Lynch, B. Bierer, G. Cohen and S. Rivera (Cambridge, MA: MIT Press, 2017), 1–9.

5. As Mary P. Winsor demonstrates, the history of the science museum and the wider history of science are closely related, not least because the science museum provided science with objects to systematically compare and classify. See: M. P. Winsor, 'Museums', in *The Cambridge History of Science*, ed. P. Bowler and J. Pickstone (Cambridge: Cambridge University Press, 2009), 60–75, 60, https://doi.org/10.1017/CHOL9780521572019.005.

6. Mark Dion quoted in Marion Endt-Jones, 'Beyond Institutional Critique: Mark Dion's Surrealist Wunderkammer at the Manchester Museum', *Museum and Society*, 5, no. 1 (2007): 2, ISSN 1479–8360, [online] available at https://journals.le.ac.uk/ojs1/index.php/mas/article/view/89/104 (accessed 7 June 2018).

7. Marion Endt-Jones. 'Beyond Institutional Critique: Mark Dion's Surrealist Wunderkammer at the Manchester Museum'. *Museum and Society*, 5, no. 1 (2007), p. 2. ISSN 1479–8360, [online] available at https://journals.le.ac.uk/ojs1/index.php/mas/article/view/89/104 (accessed 7 June 2018).

8. David Edwards, *Artscience: Creativity in the Post-Google Generation* (Cambridge: Harvard University Press, 2008), 41–42.

9. Charles Percy Snow, *The Two Cultures and the Scientific Revolution* (Cambridge: Cambridge University Press, 1961), 4.

10. Ibid., 17.

11. See: Sian Ede, 'The Scientist's Mind, The Artist's Temperament', in *Strange and Charmed: Science and the Contemporary Visual Arts*, ed. Sian Ede (London: Calouste Gulbenkian Foundation, 2000), 28–49, 36.

12. Georgina Born and Andrew Barry, 'Art-Science', *Journal of Cultural Economy* 3, no. 1 (March 2010): 104.

13. Ken Arnold, 'Between Explanation and Inspiration: Images in Science', in *Strange and Charmed: Science and the Contemporary Visual Arts*, ed. Sian Ede (London: Calouste Gulbenkian Foundation, 2000), 68–83, 74.

14. Clementine Deliss, 'Dark Venues', in *How Institutions Think: Between Contemporary Art and Curatorial Discourse*, ed. Paul O'Neill, Lucy Steeds and Mick Wilson (London: MIT Press, 2017), 49–53, 52.

15. See: Megan K. Halpern, 'Across the Great Divide: Boundaries and Boundary Objects in Art and Science', *Public Understanding of Science* 21, no. 8 (2011): 922–37, 924.

16. Ian Bogost, *Alien Phenomenology, or What It's Like to Be a Thing* (Minneapolis: University of Minnesota Press, 2012), 66.

17. See: Timothy Morton, *Hyperobjects: Philosophy and Ecology after the End of the World* (Minneapolis: University of Minnesota Press, 2013). While hyperobjects, in Morton's view, are stupefying precisely because of their incalculable timescales and the sheer vastness of their physical magnitude, such qualities, though more readily apparent within ecologies or planetary structures, are nonetheless present within the pan-historical diversity of museum collections and the abundance of the relational networks they propagate. The specimens housed within the museum form an epistemological ecosystem of infinite complexity.

18. Ibid., 925.

19. Peter Osborne, 'The Postconceptual Condition; Or, the Cultural Logic of High Capitalism Today', *Radical Philosophy*, no. 184 (March/April 2014), [online] available at https://www.radicalphilosophy.com/article/the-postconceptual-condition (accessed 20 February 2020).

20. Alan Wallach and Carol Duncan, 'The Universal Survey Museum', *Art History* 3, no. 4 (December 1980): 448–69.

21. Peter Osborne, 'Modernity Is a Qualitative, Not a Chronological, Category', *New Left Review* I / 192, (March–April 1992): 65–84, [online] available at https://newleftreview.org/I/192/peter-osborne-modernity-is-a-qualitative-not-a-chronological-category (accessed 19 February 2020).

22. M. P. Winsor, 'Museums', 60–75.

23. Outlined in Tony Bennett, 'The Exhibitionary Complex', *New Formations*, no. 4 (Spring 1988): 77–102.

24. Laura Cumming, 'Thinking Inside the Box', *The Observer: The New Review*, 22 July 2018, 40–41, reference 41.

25. James Elkins, *What Is Interesting Writing in Art History* (Edinburgh: University of Edinburgh Press, 2014), 15.

26. On this topic see: Gavin Parkinson, '(Blind Summit) Art Writing, Narrative, Middle Voice'. *Art History*, 34, no. 2 (April 2011): 269–71.

27. Ibid., 270.

28. Elizabeth Deeds Ermarth, *Sequel to History: Postmodernism and the Crisis of Representational Time* (Princeton: Princeton University Press, 1992), 11.

29. Catherine Grant, 'A Narrative of What Wishes What It Wishes It to Be': An Introduction to "Creative Writing and Art History"', *Art History* 34 (2011): 230–43, https://doi.org/10.1111/j.1467-8365.2011.00817.x.

30. Ibid., 9–10.

31. Felicity Callard and Des Fitzgerald, 'Entangling the Medical Humanities', in *The Edinburgh Companion to the Critical Medical Humanities*, ed. A. Whitehead and A. Woods (Edinburgh: Edinburgh University Press, 2016), 35–49.

32. Here we follow the interdisciplinary position outlined in recent work in the Medical Humanities: W. Viney, F. Callard and A. Woods, 'Critical Medical Humanities: Embracing Entanglement, Taking Risks', *Medical Humanities* 41 (2015): 2–7, http://dx.doi.org.libproxy.ncl.ac.uk/10.1136/medhum-2015–010692.

33. Graham Harman, 'The Road to Objects', *continent* 1, no. 3 (2011): 171–79, reference 176, [online] available at http://continentcontinent.cc/index.php/continent/article/view/48 (accessed 23 July 2018).

34. Ibid., 171.

35. Ibid., 171.

36. Lia Carreira, 'The Exhibition Space as a Laboratory', *continent* 7, no. 1 (2018): 17–21, [online] available at http://www.continentcontinent.cc/index.php/continent/article/view/313 (accessed 10 August 2018).

37. Ibid., 17.

38. Fredric Jameson, *Postmodernism or the Cultural Logic of Late Capitalism* (London: Verso, 1989), xii.

39. The budget for *dOCUMENTA 13* was, according to the project's website, over thirty million Euros and it received nearly a million visitors: see https://www.documenta.de/en/retrospective/documenta_13 (accessed 10 August 2018).

40. *dOCUMENTA 13* website [online] available at https://www.documenta.de/en/retrospective/documenta_13 (accessed 10 August 2018).

41. Bruno Latour, *An Inquiry into Modes of Existence: An Anthropology of the Moderns*, trans. Catherine Porter (Cambridge, MA: Harvard University Press, 2013).

42. Manuel DeLanda, *Intensive Science & Virtual Philosophy* (London: Bloomsbury, 2013) ('[…] while an ontology based on relations between general types and particular instances is *hierarchical*, each level representing a different ontological category (organism, species, genera), an approach in terms of interacting parts and emergent wholes leads to a *flat ontology*, one made exclusively of unique, singular individuals, differing in spatio-temporal scale but not in ontological status', 47). Latour, 182.

43. Jean-François Gauvin, 'Functionless: Science Museums and the Display of "Pure Objects"', *Science Museum Group Journal* (Spring 2016), (unpaginated), http://dx.doi.org/10.15180/160506. For an alternative take on the chief points associated with the new philosophical

school of object-oriented ontology, see: Thomas Lemke, 'Materialism Without Matter: The Recurrence of Subjectivism in Object-oriented Ontology', *Distinktion, Journal of Social Theory* 18, no. 2 (2017): 133–52, https://doi.org/10.1080/1600910X.2017.1373686.

44. Bruno Latour, 'On Interobjectivity', *Mind, Culture, and Activity* 3, no. 4 (1996): 228–45, reference 228.

45. Arjun Appadurai, *The Social Lives of Objects: Commodities in Cultural Perspective*, (Cambridge: Cambridge University Press, 1988), 6 (emphasis added).

46. Ibid., 5.

47. Michel Serres, *The Parasite*, trans. Lawrence R. Schehr (Baltimore: John Hopkins University, 1982). As we suggested earlier, it is a commonplace of museological discourse that museum spaces are crucibles in which subjectivities are forged: Serres writes that objects per se perform this function, but this holds open the possibility that museum objects are privileged ones in which we *attend to* the process of our own subject-formation by attending to the subject-formation of the object. In Serres's words, a 'quasi-object is not an object, but it is one nevertheless, since it is not a subject, since it is in the world; it is also a quasi-subject, since it marks or designates a subject who, without it, would not be a subject'. The logic is that we can only *experience* subjectification when acknowledging the privileged positions objects hold as quasi-objects, not just because of our position in the object-world. Ibid., 225.

48. Graham Harman, *Guerilla Metaphysics* (Peru, IK: Open Court, 2005), 105.

49. Steven Conn, *Museums and American Intellectual Life*, 1876–1926 (Chicago: University of Chicago, 1988), reference 24. See also Steven Conn, *Do Museums Still Need Objects?* (Philadelphia: University of Pennsylvania Press, 2010).

50. See for example Christopher Whitehead, *Museums and the Construction of Disciplines: Art and Archaeology in Nineteenth-Century Britain* (London: Duckworth, 2009).

51. William Poole, 'Skeletons, Crocodiles, Human Skin', *Times Literary Supplement*, 7 June 2017, [online] available at https://www.the-tls.co.uk/articles/private/first-british-musuem/ (accessed 23 July 2018).

52. Ibid., n.p.

53. Ibid., n.p.

54. Ibid., n.p.

55. On Hiller's critique of Sigmund Freud's collection, see: Joanne Morra, 'Not-Archaeology: Freud and Hiller as Collectors', in *In Focus: From the Freud Museum 1991–6 by Susan Hiller*, ed. Alexandra Kokoli (London: Tate Research Publication, 2017).

56. Poole, 'Skeletons, Crocodiles, Human Skin', n.p.

57. Lorraine Daston, 'Introduction: Speechless', in *Things That Talk: Object Lessons from Art and Science*, ed. Lorraine Daston (New York: Zone Books, 2004), 11.

58. Jane Bennett, 'What Is an Assemblage?', in *Networks*, ed. L. B. Larsen (London: Whitechapel Gallery, 2014), 84.

59. Tim Ingold, *The Life of Lines* (London: Routledge, 2015), 11.

60. See Georges Didi-Huberman, *Devant le temps: History de l'arte et anachronisme des images* (Paris: Editions de Minuit, 2000); Alexander Nagel and Christopher S. Wood, *Anachronic Renaissance* (New York: Zone Books, 2010); Alexander Nagel, *Medieval Modern: Art Out of Time* (London: Thames & Hudson, 2012).

61. Alan Wallach, 'Reviews—Steven Conn: Museums and American Intellectual Life, 1876–1926', *College Art Association* reviews 22 June 1999, [online] available at http://www.caareviews.org/reviews/218#.W2RIQIUzpaQ (accessed 3 August 2018).

62. Griselda Pollock, 'Whither Art History?' *The Art Bulletin* 96, no. 1 (2014): 9–23.

63. Robin Mackay, 'Introduction', in *Collapse II at Urbanomic*, [online] available at https://www.urbanomic.com/book/collapse-2/ (accessed 16 August 2018).

64. The phrase is from Michael Baxandall, *Painting and Experience in Fifteenth-Century Italy: A Primer in the Social History of Pictorial Style* (Oxford: Oxford University Press, 1974), 29.

65. Teresa Gleadowe, 'Reviews: Thinking Contemporary Curating: The Culture of Curating and the Curating of Culture', *Art Monthly*, no. 368 (July–August 2013), [online] available at https://www.questia.com/magazine/1G1-337620760/thinking-contemporary-curating-the-culture-of-curating (accessed 19 July 2018).

66. Ibid., n.p.

67. Sarah Menlger and Fiona Cameron, 'Complexity, Transdisciplinarity and Museum Collections Documentation: Emergent Metaphors for a Complex World', *Journal of Material Culture*, 14, no. 2 (2009): 189–218.

68. Paola Antonelli, '@ at MoMA', (New York: MoMA: 2010) [online] available at https://www.moma.org/explore/inside_out/2010/03/22/at-moma/ (accessed 1 May 2020).

69. J. L. Austin, *How to Do Things with Words* (Oxford: Oxford University Press, 1962).

70. Beryl Graham and Sarah Cook, *Rethinking Curating* (Cambridge, MA: MIT Press, 2012), 4–5.

71. Joasia Krysa, *Curating Immateriality: The Work of the Curator in the Age of Network Systems* (New York: Autonomedia, 2006).

72. Appadurai, *The Social Lives of Objects*, 6.

73. *The Guardian*, 'Notes and Queries: Semantic Enigmas—Does the Symbol @ Have a Name', *The Guardian* (2011), [online] available at https://www.theguardian.com/notesandqueries/query/0,5753,-1773,00.html (accessed 19 July 2018).

74. Graham Harman, *Tool-Being: Heidegger and the Metaphysics of Objects* (Chicago: Open Court, 2002), 2.

75. Graham Harman, 'On Vicarious Causation', in *Collapse II*, ed. Robin Mackay, at *Urbanomic*, (2007) 171–206, [online] available at https://www.urbanomic.com/chapter/collapse-ii-graham-harman-on-vicarious-causation/ (accessed 16 August 2018).

REFERENCES

Appadurai, Arjun. *The Social Lives of Objects: Commodities in Cultural Perspective*. Cambridge: Cambridge University Press, 1988.

Arnold, Ken. 'Between Explanation and Inspiration: Images in Science'. In *Strange and Charmed: Science and the Contemporary Visual Arts*, ed. Sian Ede. London: Calouste Gulbenkian Foundation, 2000.

Austin, J. L. *How to Do Things with Words*. Oxford: Oxford University Press, 1962.

Baxandall, Michael. *Painting and Experience in Fifteenth-Century Italy: A Primer in the Social History of Pictorial Style*. Oxford: Oxford University Press, 1974.

Bennett, Jane. 'What Is an Assemblage?'. In *Networks*, ed. L. B. Larsen, 84–85. London: Whitechapel Gallery, 2014.

Bennett, Tony. 'The Exhibitionary Complex'. *New Formations*, no. 4 (Spring 1988): 77–102.

Bogost, Ian. *Alien Phenomenology, or What It's Like to Be a Thing*. Minneapolis: University of Minnesota Press, 2012.

Born, Georgina, and Andrew Barry. 'Art-Science'. *Journal of Cultural Economy* 3, no.1 (March 2010): 104.

Callard, Felicity, and Des Fitzgerald. 'Entangling the Medical Humanities'. In *The Edinburgh Companion to the Critical Medical Humanities*, ed. A. Whitehead and A. Woods. Edinburgh: Edinburgh University Press, 2016.

Carreira, Lia. 'The Exhibition Space as a Laboratory'. *continent*, no. 7.1 (2018): 17–21. Available at http://www.continentcontinent.cc/index.php/continent/article/view/313 (accessed 10 August 2018).

Conn, Steven. *Museums and American Intellectual Life, 1876–1926*. Chicago: University of Chicago, 1988.

Cumming, Laura. 'Thinking Inside the Box'. *The Observer: The New Review*, 22 July 2018, 40–41.

DeLanda, Manuel. *Intensive Science & Virtual Philosophy*. London: Bloomsbury, 2013.

Deliss, Clementine. 'Dark Venues'. In *How Institutions Think: Between Contemporary Art and Curatorial Discourse*, ed. Paul O'Neill, Lucy Steeds and Mick Wilson. London: MIT Press, 2017.

Didi-Huberman, Georges. *Devant le temps: History de l'arte et anachronisme des images*. Paris: Editions de Minuit, 2000.

dOCUMENTA 13. 'Website'. [online] available at https://www.documenta.de/en/retrospective/documenta_13 (accessed 10 August 2018).

Ede, Sian. 'The Scientist's Mind, The Artist's Temperament'. In *Strange and Charmed: Science and the Contemporary Visual Arts*, ed. Sian Ede. London: Calouste Gulbenkian Foundation, 2000.

Edwards, David. *Artscience: Creativity in the Post-Google Generation*. Cambridge: Harvard University Press, 2008.

Elkins, James. *What Is Interesting Writing in Art History*. Edinburgh: University of Edinburgh, 2014.

Endt-Jones, Marion. 'Beyond Institutional Critique: Mark Dion's Surrealist Wunderkammer at the Manchester Museum'. *Museum and Society*, 5, no. 1 (2007), 1–14. Available at: https://journals.le.ac.uk/ojs1/index.php/mas/article/view/89/104 (accessed 7 June 2018).

Ermarth, Elizabeth Deeds. *Sequel to History: Postmodernism and the Crisis of Representational Time*. Princeton: Princeton University Press, 1992.

Gauvin, Jean-François. 'Functionless: Science Museums and the Display of "Pure Objects"'. *Science Museum Group Journal* (Spring 2016): n.p. http://dx.doi.org/10.15180/160506.

Gleadowe, Teresa. 'Reviews: Thinking Contemporary Curating: The Culture of Curating and the Curating of Culture'. *Art Monthly* no. 368 (July–August 2013). Available at https://www.questia.com/magazine/1G1-337620760/thinking-contemporary-curating-the-culture-of-curating (accessed 19 July 2018).

Graham, Beryl, and Sarah Cook. *Rethinking Curating*. Cambridge, MA: MIT Press, 2012.

Grant, Catherine. "A Narrative of What Wishes What It Wishes It to Be": An Introduction to "Creative Writing and Art History"'. *Art History* 34 (2011): 230–43. doi:10.1111/j.1467-8365.2011.00817.x.

The Guardian. 'Notes and Queries: Semantic Enigmas—Does the Symbol @ Have a Name'. *The Guardian* (2011). Available at https://www.theguardian.com/notesandqueries/query/0,5753,-1773,00.html (accessed 19 July 2018).

Halpern, Megan K. 'Across the Great Divide: Boundaries and Boundary Objects in Art and Science'. *Public Understanding of Science* 21, no. 8 (2011): 922–37.

Harman, Graham. *Tool-Being: Heidegger and the Metaphysics of Objects*. Chicago: Open Court, 2002.

Harman, Graham. *Guerilla Metaphysics*. Peru, IK: Open Court, 2005.

Harman, Graham. 'On Vicarious Causation'. In *Collapse II*, ed. Robin Mackay. 2007. Available at https://www.urbanomic.com/chapter/collapse-ii-graham-harman-on-vicarious-causation/ (accessed 16 August 2018).

Harman, Graham. 'The Road to Objects'. *continent* 1, no. 3 (2011): 171–79, reference 176. Available at http://continentcontinent.cc/index.php/continent/article/view/48 (accessed 23 July 2018).

Ingold, Tim. *The Life of Lines*. London: Routledge, 2015.

Jameson, Fredric. *Postmodernism or the Cultural Logic of Late Capitalism*. London: Verso, 1989.

Krysa, Joasia. *Curating Immateriality: The Work of the Curator in the Age of Network Systems*. New York: Autonomedia, 2006.

Latour, Bruno. 'On Interobjectivity'. *Mind, Culture, and Activity* 3, no. 4 (1996): 228–45.

Latour, Bruno. *An Inquiry into Modes of Existence: An Anthropology of the Moderns*, trans. Catherine Porter. Cambridge, MA: Harvard University Press, 2013.

Lemke, Thomas. 'Materialism Without Matter: The Recurrence of Subjectivism in Object-oriented Ontology'. *Distinktion: Journal of Social Theory* 18, no. 2 (2017): 133–52. https://doi.org/10.1080/1600910X.2017.1373686.

Mackay, Robin. 'Introduction'. In *Collapse II*. Available at https://www.urbanomic.com/book/collapse-2/ (accessed 16 August 2018).

Menlger, Sarah, and Fiona Cameron. 'Complexity, Transdsciplinarity and Museum Collections Documentation: Emergent Metaphors for a Complex World'. *Journal of Material Culture*. 14, no. 2 (2009): 189–218.

Morra, Joanne. 'Not-Archaeology: Freud and Hiller as Collectors'. In *In Focus: From the Freud Museum 1991–6 by Susan Hiller*, ed. Alexandra Kokoli. London: Tate Research Publication, 2017. Available at https://www.tate.org.uk/research/publicatoins/in-focus/from-the-freud-museum-susan-hiller/freud-hiller-as-collectors (accessed 19 February 2020).

Morton, Timothy. *Hyperobjects: Philosophy and Ecology after the End of the World*. Minneapolis: University of Minnesota Press, 2013.

Nagel, Alexander. *Medieval Modern: Art Out of Time*. London: Thames & Hudson, 2012.

Nagel, Alexander, and Christopher S. Wood. *Anachronic Renaissance*. New York: Zone Books, 2010.

Osborne, Peter. 'Modernity Is a Qualitative, Not a Chronological, Category'. *New Left Review* I / 192, (March–April 1992): 65–84. Available at https://newleftreview.org/I/192/peter-osborne-modernity-is-a-qualitative-not-a-chronological-category (accessed 4 May 2020).

Osborne, Peter. 'The Postconceptual Condition; Or, the Cultural Logic of High Capitalism Today'. *Radical Philosophy* no. 184 (March / April 2014). Available at https://www.radicalphilosophy.com/article/the-postconceptual-condition (accessed 19 February 2020).

Parkinson, Gavin. '(Blind Summit) Art Writing, Narrative, Middle Voice'. *Art History*, 34, no. 2 (April 2011): 269–71.

Pickstone, J. V. 'A Brief Introduction to Ways of Knowing and Ways of Working'. *History of Science* 49, no. 3 (2011): 237. https://doi.org/10.1177/007327531104900301.

Pollock, Griselda. 'Whither Art History?'. *The Art Bulletin* 96, no. 1 (2014): 9–23.

Poole, William. 'Skeletons, Crocodiles, Human Skin'. *Times Literary Supplement*, 7 June 2017. Available at https://www.the-tls.co.uk/articles/private/first-british-musuem/ (accessed 23 July 2018).

Rivera, Suzanne M., Barbara E. Bierer, Glenn Cohen, and Holly Lynch. 'Introduction'. In *Specimen Science: Ethics and Policy Implications*, ed. H. F. Lynch, B. Bierer, G. Cohen and S. Rivera, 1–9. Cambridge, MA: MIT Press, 2017.

Serres, Michel. *The Parasite*, trans. Lawrence R. Schehr. Baltimore: John Hopkins University, 1982.

Snow, Charles Percy. *The Two Cultures and the Scientific Revolution*. Cambridge: Cambridge University Press, 1961.

Turkle, Sherry. 'Introduction: The Things That Matter'. In *Evocative Objects: Things We Think With*, ed. S. Turkle, 3–11. Cambridge, MA: MIT Press, 2007.

Viney, W., F. Callard, and A. Woods. 'Critical Medical Humanities: Embracing Entanglement, Taking Risks'. *Medical Humanities* 41 (2015): 2–7. http://dx.doi.org.libproxy.ncl.ac.uk/10.1136/medhum-2015–010692.

Wallach, Alan, and Carol Duncan. 'The Universal Survey Museum'. *Art History* 3, no. 4 (December 1980): 448–69.

Wallach, Alan. 'Reviews—Steven Conn: Museums and American Intellectual Life, 1876–1926', *College Art Association* reviews 22 June 1999. Available at http://www.caareviews.org/reviews/218#.W2RIQIUzpaQ (accessed 3 August 2018).

Whitehead, Christopher. *Museums and the Construction of Disciplines: Art and Archaeology in Nineteenth-Century Britain*. London: Duckworth, 2009.

Winsor, M. P. 'Museums', in *The Cambridge History of Science*, ed. P. Bowler and J. Pickstone. Cambridge: Cambridge University Press, 2009. https://doi:10.1017/CHOL9780521572019.005.

1

Narratives of the 'Fetish'

John Mack

Abstract

Kongo figures have provoked more discussion and the attribution of a greater diversity of significance than any other object from Africa in Western museums. In London at present there are examples on display in the Royal Geographical Society, the Wellcome Collections, the British Museum and (until removed recently for a gallery refurbishment) the Science Museum. There they are displayed variously as trophy, as medical object, as ethnography and as magical technology. Other examples are prominent parts of permanent galleries in Manchester, Liverpool, Bristol, Exeter and elsewhere with a similar range of interpretation. They have also been taken as inspiration by contemporary artists in the Congo itself, by African American artists (like Renée Stout) and in Britain by artists like Grayson Perry and the Chapman Brothers, the supposed purposes of the figures at once indulged and exoticized. They have appeared in New Yorker *cartoons. Kongo figures are, thus, suggestive of innumerable tropes, but in no case has their agency been presented as unequivocally aesthetic. Though present in museum displays since the nineteenth century, they have continued to defy easy or singular classification. Originally described as 'fetishes', in contemporary language they are 'power objects' rather than 'art objects'. This chapter explores the source of this enduring facility for provocation relating it to the historical trajectory of other tropes—about the 'primitive', about the unconscious and so forth. Yet, it will be argued, the object itself with its protruding nails, mirrors and bundles of substances is so obviously not a finished product that it resists the idea that in a museum collection it is in retirement. As displayed in a museum it is readily imagined to retain its potential and agency in defiance of museum protocols, a perception that makes it ripe for the imaginary.*

During 1914–15, with the financial implications of the war effort impacting on government coffers, the German Empire (as it then was) embarked on a 'men of iron' project. A series of wooden sculptures of heroic figures were set up in major cities. For an appropriate donation, citizens could purchase a nail and hammer it into the plinths of the memorials, recording their contribution to the national cause. The most dramatic example was a 42-foot (12.8 metre) wood sculpture of the popular war leader Field Marshal Paul von Hindenburg by the sculptor Georg Marschall erected in the Königsplatz next to the Reichstag in the Prussian capital of Berlin (Fig. 1.1). It was inaugurated in September 1915. Different levels of donations were recorded by the materials of which the nails were made: iron nails (5 deutschsmarks each), silver (10 deutschsmarks) and gold (for higher sums).

Several things were different about this commission. First, Hindenburg was a living war hero, thus breaking with the tradition of only commemorating the heroic dead. He had led the German forces in the successful battle of Tannenberg defeating the Russians in the opening year of the war. Second, unlike the similar 'men of iron' elsewhere, scaffolding was erected as the nails began to cover the lower levels of the vast sculpture and spread upwards from the plinth onto the figure itself. Donors were thereby permitted access to the upper levels where they would mark their backing of the war effort with a nail on the body of the sculpture. Though the process of nailing seems to have stopped when the coverage approached the head, the fact that the bulk of the sculpture should have been treated in this manner at all attracted a certain amount of criticism in Germany itself from those with more traditional artistic tastes.[1]

Outside Germany, the Hindenburg statue was a gift to wartime publicity. On Christmas Day, 1915, the *Illustrated London News* devoted a double-page spread to the nailing craze, adapting a German newspaper article with appropriate illustration and adding its own editorial comment. Quoting one of its correspondents, the paper remarks:

> The inner meaning of this strange performance and the nature of the satisfaction derived by the operator, are a trifle obscure. We can hardly see in the new custom a revival of the magical practices of an earlier date, when, to the accompaniment of appropriate incantations, waxen figures were stuck with pins and otherwise maltreated; for in the latter case it was believed that bodily harm was caused to the individual whom the effigy represented.[2]

The answer to the riddle was 'furnished by a wooden idol in the British Museum'. Illustrations show a nailed figure in the British Museum and originally from the Kongo people who occupy the coastal region of what is now Angola, the Democratic Republic of Congo (DRC) and the Republic of Congo. Alongside the British Museum piece is a similar example from the Royal Geographical Society described in its nineteen-century accession details and in the title of a watercolour by the Victorian painter Thomas Baines of its 'capture', as a 'war fetish'. The nailing, it is suggested, is not in fact a perverse attempt to do harm to a national hero—least

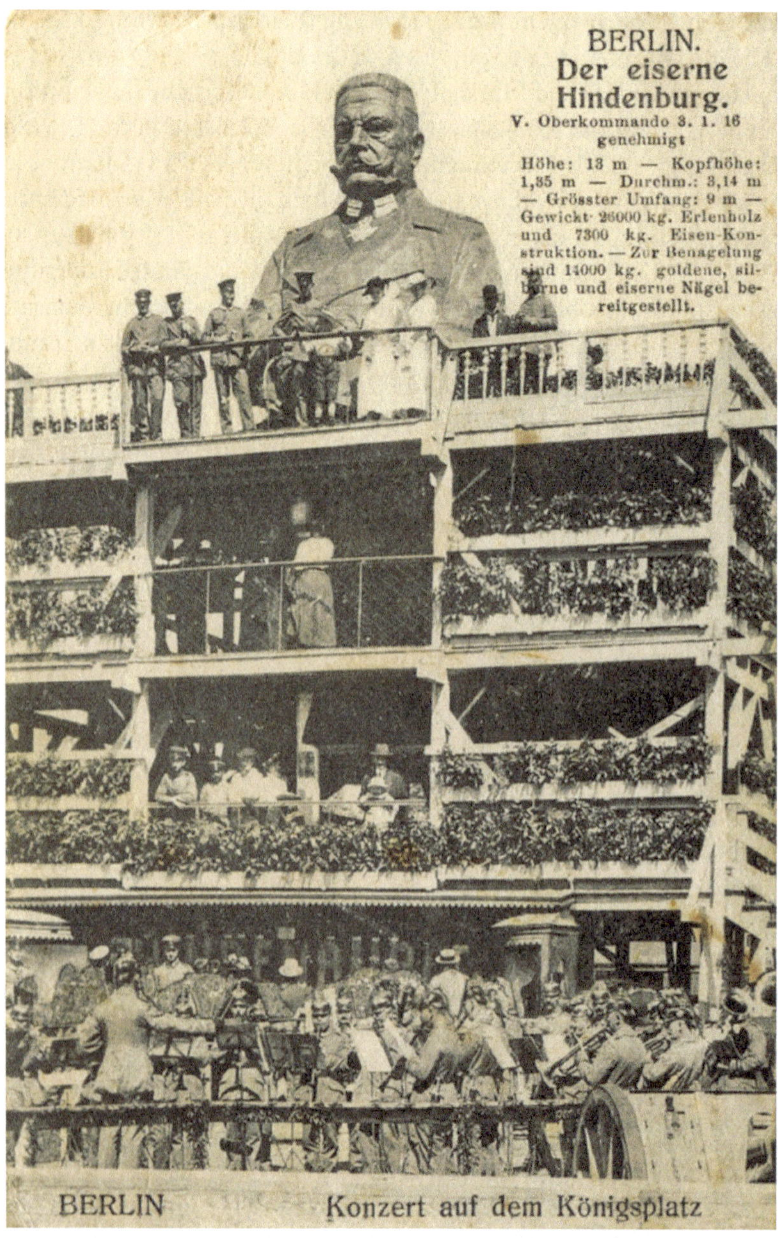

FIGURE 1.1. Georg Marschall, 'Der eiserne Hindenberg' ('The Iron Hindenberg'), c. 1915–16. Postcard.

of all, to a living one—though that is how it was seen by critics in Germany. Rather, the newspaper article argues, it represents a misguided appeal to a great military leader to confront the wrongs inflicted on fellow countrymen by a hated foe, just as driving a nail into a Kongo figure is—in one understanding—a means of identifying and killing a witch.[3]

Though there is no reason to think that in Germany an association of the Hindenberg statue with Congolese nailing practices was commonly taken up, the point was developed in Britain. In an accompanying comment, the German psyche and '*kultur*' are openly ridiculed for not having yet evolved to the level of 'the more advanced natives of West Africa'. The racial stereotyping is echoed in a wartime pamphlet entitled *The Wooden Idol of Berlin* where the comparison led to the conclusion that the Germans are 'white negroes'—a version of an allegation which was often made against German expressionist artists in Germany itself, some of whom—Ernst Kirchener, for example—were not discouraged by being described as 'primitives'. This is, further, an instance of a common propaganda description of German acts of wartime destruction as indicative of inherent barbarism, such as the 'deliberate' shelling of Reims Cathedral in 1914.[4] The Hindenburg statue is described as a 'monstrous pin-cushion' in front of which, the parody continues, 'the chief men of the tribe, adorned with their best feathers' parade 'executing a sort of religious dance which they curiously call "the Goose Step" '.[5]

Beyond the war of words, the 'men of iron' initiative was also lampooned in satirical reconstructions of the nailing process itself. At a charity event in Stepney in London a version of the Hindenburg monument was put up and nurses from the nearby Mile End Hospital were photographed on a ladder hammering nails directly into the head of the crudely constructed adaptation. Their purpose was also to raise war funds, this time for British 'brave and wounded soldiers'. But, clearly, in this case the intention in knocking nails into an image was to mock the entire rationale behind the project and, by implication, reverse German intentions and do harm to its living subject, Hindenburg himself—and by extension his countrymen.[6]

That the 'men of iron' project was capable of being inflected in divergent ways is inextricably linked to the idea of 'the fetish'—of which Kongo nailed figures were a classic example—being deeply embedded in European thought. While the term has come under a great deal of scrutiny and been subject to revision or replacement in a number of contexts, there have also been arguments for its retention as a viable description of the agency attributed to certain objects and the responses to them. In exploring how such objects have been understood in academic and curatorial circles, the focus in this chapter will principally be on Kongo *minkisi* (sing. *nkisi*) a generic category of which the nailed figures, *minkondi* (sing. *nkondi*), are one example. In museums and catalogues, the way of referring to *minkisi* has gradually slipped into the use of a different vocabulary as they have been more fully understood. Even so, they retain a significance which still resonates with contemporary visual artists if—like Congolese or African American painters, sculptors and conceptual artists—they have some sense of direct linkage. For other artists with no connection, referencing *minkisi* is still a way of invoking a particular cultural or psychological condition which, in reality, may have little to do with the original intentions of their makers, operators and clients. The work of William Pietz, in particular, has exposed both the longevity and the tenacity of the fetish idea which, he argues, has roots in the encounters between Europeans and Africans along the western Atlantic littoral in the sixteenth and seventeenth centuries.[7] Indeed, his contention is that the association of the idea with certain classes of objects derives precisely from the character of these coastal interactions. The disjunctions between the things that were valued by Europeans and by the African intermediaries with whom they conducted commercial relationships was a source of much conjecture. Gold was highly valued by all sides, yet it could be acquired for goods that Europeans regarded as trinkets. Likewise, the apparent attribution of active spiritual and healing properties to materials and objects apparently assembled randomly implied a mistaken appreciation of the properties of things. As described by Pietz, the idea of the fetish emerges from a combination of these characteristics: a seeming inconsistency or ineptitude in the attributing of value and a radical misunderstanding of the principles of causality. 'The fetish' is a tendril that weaves its way back and forth through different crevices in European thought, something at times perverse and menacing, at times finding fertile soil in Western imaginings.

In the latter part of the nineteenth century, the pioneering anthropologist E. B. Tylor discussed fetishism as a development of the concept of animism, an idea which has since been extended to explore the attribution of an inherent 'personhood' and 'agency' to certain classes of object.[8] From there attention focused on a language of obsession, desire, idolatry and worship. As such, the term found its way into the vocabulary of Marxist economics, Freudian psychoanalysis,[9] and early anthropological and art historical writing. Marxists adopt the term 'commodity fetish' to characterize the ascription of value to an object in virtue of the labour expended in its production rather than its inherent properties; Freudians talk of 'sexual fetishism' to reference the displacement onto an object of the fears of castration in childhood (indeed of boyhood). It was used by missionaries and colonizers in a derogatory sense to promote their projects of conversion and control as improvements on what was portrayed as an otherwise degenerate condition. Later, it would be adopted by surrealist writers and artists with a subversive intention. Thus, at the time the French authorities organized a major colonial exhibition in Paris in 1931, an alliance of communists and surrealists mounted an alternative anti-colonial display including a display case devoted to '*Fétishes*

Européens'. This featured an image of the Virgin and Child alongside a charity box in the form of a black child with a basket marked '*merci*' to attract donations.[10]

By contrast, European modernist artists and collectors, though embracing an enlarged perspective and interested in ethnographic objects, often largely avoided so-called fetishes. To take one example, the collections made by Sir Robert and Lady Sainsbury (and subsequently donated to the University of East Anglia) include major sculptures from Africa, the Pacific and the ancient cultures of Asia, Egypt and the Americas together with works by Henry Moore, Francis Bacon, Alberto Giacometti and other major European artists of the early and mid-twentieth century. Yet, although the published catalogue runs to three volumes (two of which are devoted to non-European artworks), they include very few works which would have fallen into the 'fetish' category.[11]

Beyond that, a practice of 'cleaning up' Kongo *minkisi* is evident in a number of collections, instigated in some cases, it seems, by dealers to better align their stock with prevalent aesthetic expectation—though there is significant evidence that the makers and operators of *nkisi, banganga* (sing. *nganga*) might also disarm them if disposing of them whether under duress or otherwise.[12] One instance from the Sainsbury collections of 'improving' them is a figure on which the materials added to the object have been polished over to give the appearance of being part of its original conception. Other examples include objects where the assembled materials have been almost entirely scrapped off to reveal the original sculpted form, as occurred with the Royal Geographical Society 'war fetish' once brought to London. Another such figure, stripped back to its carved prototype, was cast in copper alloy to be sold in multiples in Britain in the mid-twentieth century. In other cases, the reverse process seems to have happened, as in an example in the Pitt Rivers Museum, Oxford, whose facial markings have been overpainted subsequent to its original acquisition by the Victorian traveller Mary Kingsley, apparently to make it more menacing.

The comparison of the Iron Hindenburg with Kongo *minkisi* turns on a common challenge that they seemed to pose to received ideas. In both cases their status as 'art' was impaired—indeed, denied—in the act of nailing. Once created, it was argued, they were immediately 'disfigured' by having other materials applied and not necessarily by the same hands as those of the original maker. Indeed, it is likely that, in many cases, blanks were carved at ateliers of the sculptors and subsequently had the active materials added by an *nganga* which was what rendered them potent and significant objects, particularly in the case of the largest and most impressive examples known as 'Mangaaka'.[13] That said, they could not be 'art' in early-twentieth-century terms because the distance between object and viewer had been violated. The 'fetish' in these terms characteristically fused creator and creation, subject and object, collapsing expectations of aesthetic distance in the act of altering its original state in a manner more readily associated with iconoclasm. Rather than exclusively the sculptor, the *nganga* (or the donor to the German war effort) became the maker. To remake it as 'art', it had to be returned to its first state as originally carved. The model was at war with the modality; art was antithetical to ethnography.

The idea of the fetish image has thus provoked a rich historical array of contrasting narratives, mostly negative, and very few concerned to move beyond the persistent characterization of them as degenerate and unsettling. Among these, Kongo nail figures and other assemblages from the same region incorporating mirrors, pieces of white ceramic, mica, bits of cloth and bundles of various materials identified as *bilongo* (medicines) were archetypical. Such objects were the brunt of many early disparaging accounts. They were 'devil images', 'scarecrows', 'ferocious' or 'frankly obscene'.[14] These are somewhat ironic descriptions if, following Pietz, they are applied to objects that were created in the same intercultural climate of exchange and interaction as the idea of the fetish itself. In that context, European intervention could be interpreted not as a benign but as a morbid influence. Some Europeans, though, did try and to understand *minkisi* on their own terms.

In his autobiographical reflections published in 1900, the Baptist missionary William Holman Bentley, with extensive experience in the Congo region, provides a more informed account of the kinds of content a Kongo 'fetish' might assemble. He writes:

> The fetish itself may be very various. The power may be contained in a rag, stone, water, pipeclay or rubbish of all kinds; the more singular and uncanny the better. It may be red camwood powder mixed with pepper, ochrous earth, a snake's head or fang, the beak of a fowl or any bird, a bird's claw, a twisted root, the foot of a crocodile or monitor (Varana) lizard, a bead, or a piece of copal.[15]

There are a number of features of this description that are notable. First, there is a strong emphasis on materiality which stands in contrast to the attention that might be given to the figures as visual objects. Indeed, the materials listed are not only associated with figures but may be brought together in other forms of *minkisi*: contained in shells, baskets or bundles of cloth. The essence of the *nkisi* is identified with the empowering materials, rather than with the figure or container. Second, the bewildering range of elements which may be incorporated appear to have no functional implication—their impact lies in their mysterious capacity to surprise. From this comes a third feature: the apparent irrationality of the whole construction. And, finally, Bentley identifies the combination of these elements as a source of undefined 'power', using the term which re-emerges in later descriptions as a preferred alternative to the word 'fetish' which came to be an embarrassment as a category.

Many such assemblages found their way into the public domain in Europe through missionaries and travellers, often collected originally as evidence of the kinds of societies in which evangelization was thought to have particular urgency. Others came through various channels subsequent to having been confiscated by colonial authorities, particularly the powerful *minkisi* Mangaata seen as restricting commercial activity along the coast in the late nineteenth century (Fig. 1.2).[16]

In that context, *minkisi* came to stand for a wider regressive condition seen to obtain in much of Africa and used to justify both colonization and exploitation. When they found their way into museum collections, as many ultimately did, they were readily thought of as 'specimens' in evolutionary terms in the same way as

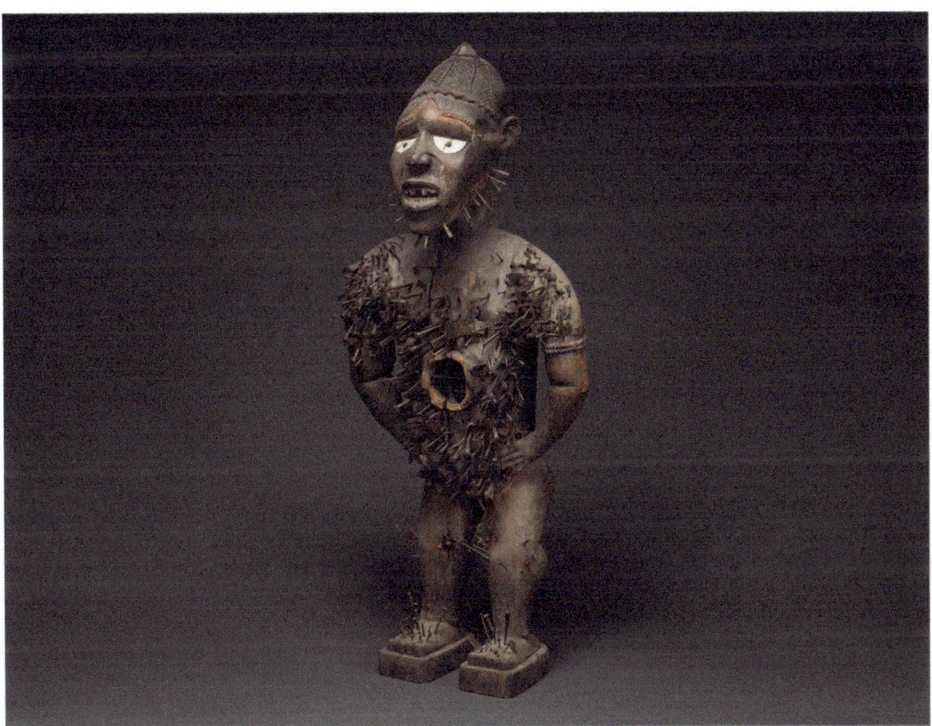

FIGURE 1.2. Power Figure (*Mangaaka*), Kongo, Democratic Republic of the Congo, Republic of the Congo, or Cabinda, Angola, 19th century. Wood, iron, resin, ceramic, plant fibre, textile, pigment. H. 46 1/2 in. (118 cm), W. 19 1/2 in. (49.5 cm), D. 15 1/2 in. (39.4 cm). The Metropolitan Museum of Art, New York; Purchase Lila Acheson Wallace, Drs Daniel and Marian Malcolm, Laura G. and James J. Ross, Jeffrey B. Soref, The Robert T. Wall Family, Dr and Mrs. Sidney G. Clyman, and Steven Kossak Gifts.

natural history collections were. In the British Museum, the use of a terminology that implied a natural history approach to objects in the collection is no surprise. Natural history had been an important part of the British Museum from its inception in the mid-eighteenth century, until that department was moved out to form what is now the Natural History Museum which opened in 1881.

This was a terminology and approach that persisted well into the twentieth century. In the anthropological world, the idea of specimens and of type series of objects that might illustrate particular cultural—and especially social Darwinian—themes, was well established by the late nineteenth century. *Notes and Queries on Anthropology*, the guide-book to collectors of information and objects in 'the field' (i.e. the areas overseas where examples might be acquired for ethnographic departments in British museums) had sections written or edited by British Museum curators including both A. W. Franks and his successor C. H. Read. The 1912 edition included a section specifically entitled 'General Note on the Collection of Specimens'. There, the researcher is advised that 'to collect specimens of native work merely because they are pretty and without ample notes to identify and explain them is useless'.[17] In ethnographic collections of the period the idea of 'the specimen' encompassed two parallel ideas: one was that of examples of types of objects assembled in different categories (as, for example in the Pitt-Rivers Museum in Oxford); the other was that of the collection as illustrating the material conditions of a society (as in the British Museum). In both cases the typical and the everyday trumped the atypical and unique. From the other side of the spectrum, ethnography was, indeed, antithetical to art.

But, while the language of 'specimens' implied types of objects where diversity was downplayed and duplicates could be confidently identified, subsequent in-depth historical and anthropological study has revealed the much greater complexity that Bentley's observation of the 'singularity' of individual *nkisi* signals. Each, he says, is 'a bundle of mysteries'.[18] Indeed, the appropriateness of the idea of the fetish in historical descriptions of *minkisi* has itself come to be nuanced and questioned as knowledge of their construction and context of use have increased. This has led to much greater scepticism about the notions of irrationality and corresponding appreciation of the nature of the power that *minkisi* are attributed. Many of the materials that are applied to them are now understood to be far from arbitrary but have qualities which—metaphorically or metonymically—are significant in a local context. Thus, the white ceramic eyes, shells and a paint derived from white clay use a colour associated with the dead. A metaphoric reference is to the skin which lightens in death; a metonymic one is to the white clay which comes from the bed of a stream and is known by the same name as the word for 'cemetery' and 'land of the dead' (*mpemba*). Other materials—a strongly scented herb, a twisted root, types of resin and so forth—might be included in recognition of their association in Kongo thought (and language) with certain appropriate abstract properties.[19]

All the elements incorporated in *minkisi* are implicated in this semantic circuitry. For instance, imported European mirrors, a popular item of trade, had an altered significance when used as part of a power object. Their reflective surface reproduces that of the water across which the dead are conceived as travelling on their way to the 'other world', whether a river, a lake or the ocean itself across which slaves were transported in previous centuries to die, literally, overseas. In denying the viewer visual access to the interior of the *nkisi*, it conceals what lies within, just as what lies beneath the surface of water is hidden: not simply, in this case, the composition of the materials (*bilongo*) but the world of the dead which gives the object its power to transform human circumstances.

It is through such detailed analysis that a more refined understanding of the status of *minkisi* has been arrived at. It is 'irreducibly material'; unlike the Hindenburg statute and other 'men of iron', it does not represent any other entity but rather provides a local habitation for such an entity. In that sense 'an *nkisi* was a spiritual entity, a personality from the world of the dead, present in a material body, but not restricted to that body'.[20] As habitation, each *nkisi* might have its own name, its own repertoire and reputation. When the German ethnographer Adolf Bastian described his encounter with one on a stopover, he saw it in remarkably human terms:

> When I was taking a walk, I met Mangaka, the chief fetish of the town, who is well-known and feared in the whole town. He was being carried by a slave of the ganga or priest to the home of Manuel Punha who was in a serious condition due to a lengthy illness. Normally this idol travels only in a hammock but in this case something had gone wrong with arrangements and it had to make do on the back of a native.[21]

However, having an agency which is ultimately dependent on the materials of which it is composed, it is not an object of worship as earlier European commentators supposed—and as Bastian implied by describing it as an idol. Indeed, the reverse was sometimes the case: they might be ridiculed and insulted to coax them into more rigorous and targeted response if they were judged to be less effective than expected. In the specific case of the *nkisi nkondi*, driving a nail into the body of the object is another means of inciting it to action, violating its interiority physically, and made all the more specific by the nail having some of the clothing, sweat or spittle of the client/patient on it.

That Kongo *minkisi* have agency in a local context is not in doubt. Nor, it could be argued, is it inherently irrational to believe this is so, and submit to processes of healing and retribution that it is held to enable. It can be shown that the assemblage which *minkisi* comprise, while containing diverse materials rather than following any single formula, is none the less intentional. But Cartesian ideas of rationality are not the real issue, for the focus is not on some abstract idea of causality but on the efficiency of the object in an operational context. If it appears to work from the evidence of positive results achieved that is sufficient to confirm the object possesses effective agency. In discussing the idea of the fetish, Bruno Latour has remarked:

> It is this truth that we should redeem, without believing in either the rantings of a psychological subject lost in fantasy, or the exterior existence of cold and ahistorical objects said to fall into laboratories as if from the sky.[22]

To highlight this perspective Latour suggests the term 'factish', an invented word which grants the fetish the same status as the word 'fact'.

While working in the relevant department of the British Museum several decades ago, I vividly recall several occasions on which Kongo objects were brought in by members of the public as potential additions to the collections. In each case, the donors reported a run of misfortune triggering the decision to rid themselves of an object suspected of exercising a malign influence over them and their families. The objects themselves with their protruding nails, mirrors and bundles of substances were so obviously not neutralized that they resisted the idea that on a family mantlepiece they were in retirement. Their agency was imagined to remain undiminished despite the distance—physically and culturally—from the context of their original conception and use.[23] They proved ripe material for the imaginary.

In the museum world, there have been significant developments evident since the last decades of the twentieth century in the display of objects from Africa in general, and a curatorial response to analyses of Kongo *minkisi* figures in particular. For present purposes, two exhibitions on Kongo art in the United States demonstrating different emergent directions can be cited. The earliest is *Astonishment and Power: Kongo Minkisi and the Art of Renée Stout* at the Smithsonian's National Museum of African Art in Washington, DC, in 1993/1994. What was distinctive about this exhibition was a major display of Kongo objects with a rigorous commentary by Wyatt MacGaffey alongside work of an African American artist, Renée Stout (b. 1958), inspired by *minkisi*.[24] The title itself was grounded in new understandings of the impact of *minkisi*. The 'astonishment' refers to the captivating virtuosity with which the different elements have been brought together on the objects by an *nganga*—enchantment, as Alfred Gell has called it.[25] The 'power' of the title lies in the animate qualities of an *nkisi* that enables it to change circumstances.

Recently, at the Metropolitan Museum of Art in New York a major scholarly catalogue and exhibition, *Kongo: Power and Majesty* (2015–16), adopted a similar vocabulary in reassessing Kongo art and history. The range of the project was wider than that at the Smithsonian, revisiting early historical sources and reconsidering a corpus of work that extended well beyond the so-called fetishes. The approach itself definitively contested earlier characterizations of the Kongo world that had been based on a restricted perspective and its recurrent misrepresenting of *minkisi*, in so far as it was still necessary. To achieve this, the exhibition first took the visitor on a historicized journey through the impressive textiles, ivories, mother-and-child sculptures and other examples of the refined qualities of Kongo workmanship that had adorned prestigious collections in Europe from the Renaissance onwards. Given the expectation raised by the venue, visual qualities were an important consideration. A dramatic finale was provided by a darkened room displaying 15 of the 20 known examples of monumental *minkisi* Mangaaka. Each was displayed in its own case, confronting the viewer face to face with staring white eyes, some with bared teeth and arms akimbo to create a similarly challenging impact to that which they had on the inhabitants of the coastal areas of the Congo from which they came: individual, imposing, inherently formidable. The objects are not portrayed as 'beautiful' in a conventional sense, but exude a commanding presence which contributed to what the organizers aptly termed a 'culturally distinct vernacular of power' – apt because the original intentions of the object are translated into its effects on the visiting public within the museum space.[26] In this case, what is presented is not an overt division but a carefully contrived example of art and ethnographic understanding working together.

Outside of such institutions—and apart from *banganga* themselves, who continue to construct *minkisi* in various formats in the Congo region—the closest in terms of referencing many of the esoteric elements that characterize Kongo imagery is not the work of Congolese or other African artists, but that of a number of their African American counterparts. African American modernists were already engaging with African art from the 1920s.[27] Their successors have continued this practice, doing so in a way which often adopts performance and conceptual strategies that are familiar in an international context but is distinctive in its echoes of African-inspired or -derived allusions. One of the most discussed of contemporary exemplars working in this area is Renée Stout, whose work came to prominence in the *Astonishment and Power* exhibition. Her art has a distinctive autobiographical character going back to her first sighting of a Kongo *nkisi nkondi* in the Carnegie Museum in Pittsburg at the age of ten. In a statement she recalls:

> I saw a piece there that had all these nails in it. And when I saw that one it was
> as if I was drawn to it. I don't know why […]. Even when I go home, I still go

back to that piece and look at it each time because I feel like I'm coming back with a little more knowledge each time.[28]

Stout's art has a strongly narrative, often autobiographical form, drawing on her own experiences and upbringing in a tightly knit working-class family—and often incorporating her own hair, nail clippings, photographs and other memorabilia. Where other artists have assembled discarded objects from unknown sources to create sculptural collages, Stout's art has a highly personalized quality.[29]

A work exhibited in *Astonishment and Power* is a sculpture representing her own body, 'naked' in the mode of an initiate submitting to transformative ritual process, rather than 'nude' as in conventional Western artistic representations. It is one of a series she terms *Fetish #* with no overt sense of irony (Fig. 1.3 and Fig. 1.4).

By incorporating elements of her own personhood in the manner of *minkisi* her work achieves an intensely engaged aspect: she is at once subject and object, breaking down aesthetic barriers in the manner German critics of the 'men of iron' project found so disruptive. It is *her* body that is in search of healing in the larger sense of physical and psychological restoration and, by extension, those of other African Americans. She is not creating post-specimen work in the external reflective way of other artists discussed later on and of examples cited by other contributors to this volume. In a complex web, her practice is in one sense a reversion to the processes of making exemplified by *banganga* with the assemblage of significant but hidden bundles and objects. In subsequent work the connection is less direct. A multimedia installation, *Master of the Universe* (2011–12), brings together an adapted Victorian cast timepiece in the form of a slave with the clock face repurposed as a mirror on the stomach and carrying with both hands medicine bundles on chains.[30] It sits on a glass-topped table inside which are a series of obscure objects assembled in the manner of a curiosity cabinet or one of Joseph Cornell's boxes. The whole ensemble evokes the sense of hidden sources of power; but it is clearly now a cultural analogue, a reinvention rather than a reversion in the manner of *Fetish #*. She has become her own *nganga*, a 'conjure woman'.[31]

It is interesting that Stout trained as a graphic artist and her early professional works were in the photo-realist style associated (by her) with Edward Hopper. When turning to explore Africa-inspired imagery she, like many African American artists, adopted a sculptural format in closer conformity with *minkisi*. Congolese artists, by contrast, have largely adopted two-dimensional means of reference in their work. Postcolonialism and the experience of urban modernity in Africa are common themes. In the *Digi-Nsiki* (Lost Tribe) series, Steve Bandoma (b. 1981 and from the DRC) deploys *minkisi* as a motif in contexts suggestive of African traditional culture as a whole. Figures shown nailed and de-nailed, often with medicine box protrusions from the stomach area and mirror-like screens, are deployed as

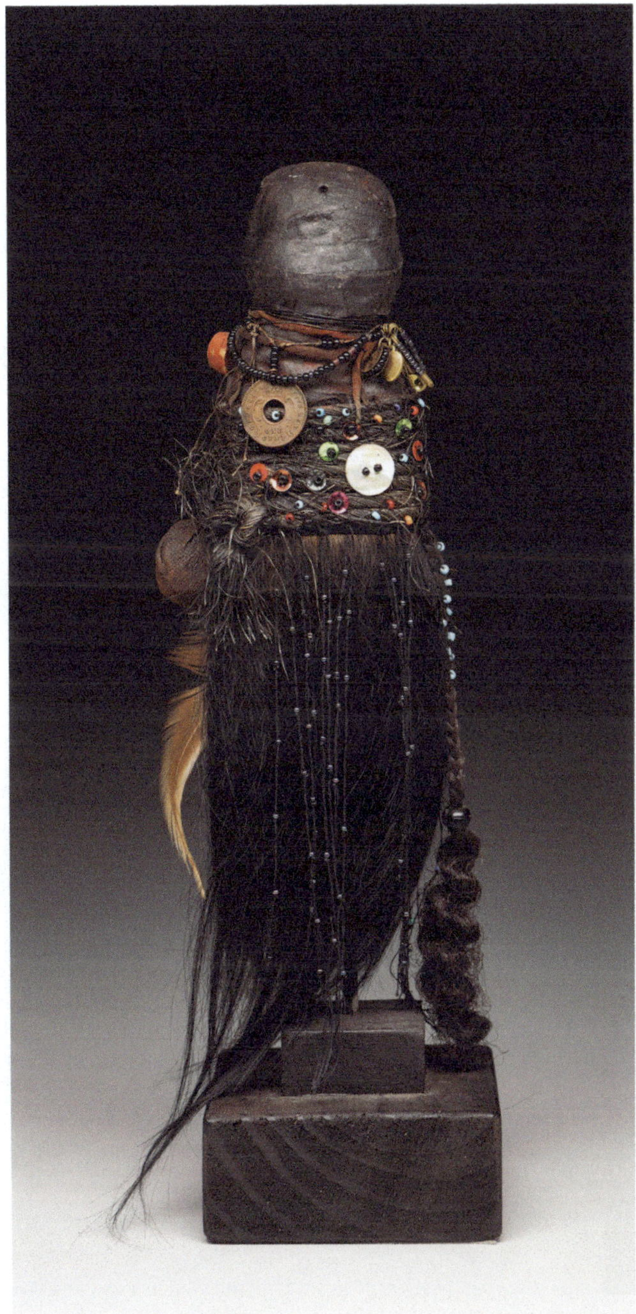

FIGURE 1.3. Renée Stout, *Fetish #1*, 1987, monkey hair, nails, beads, cowrie shells and coins, 12 1/8 x 3 ½ x 3 3/8 in., Dallas Museum of Art Gift of Roslyn and Brooks Fitch, Gary Houston, Pamela Ice, Sharon and Lazette Jackson, Maureen McKenna, Aaronetta and Joseph Pierce, Matilda and Hugh Robinson, and Rosalyn Story in honour of Virginia Wardlaw.

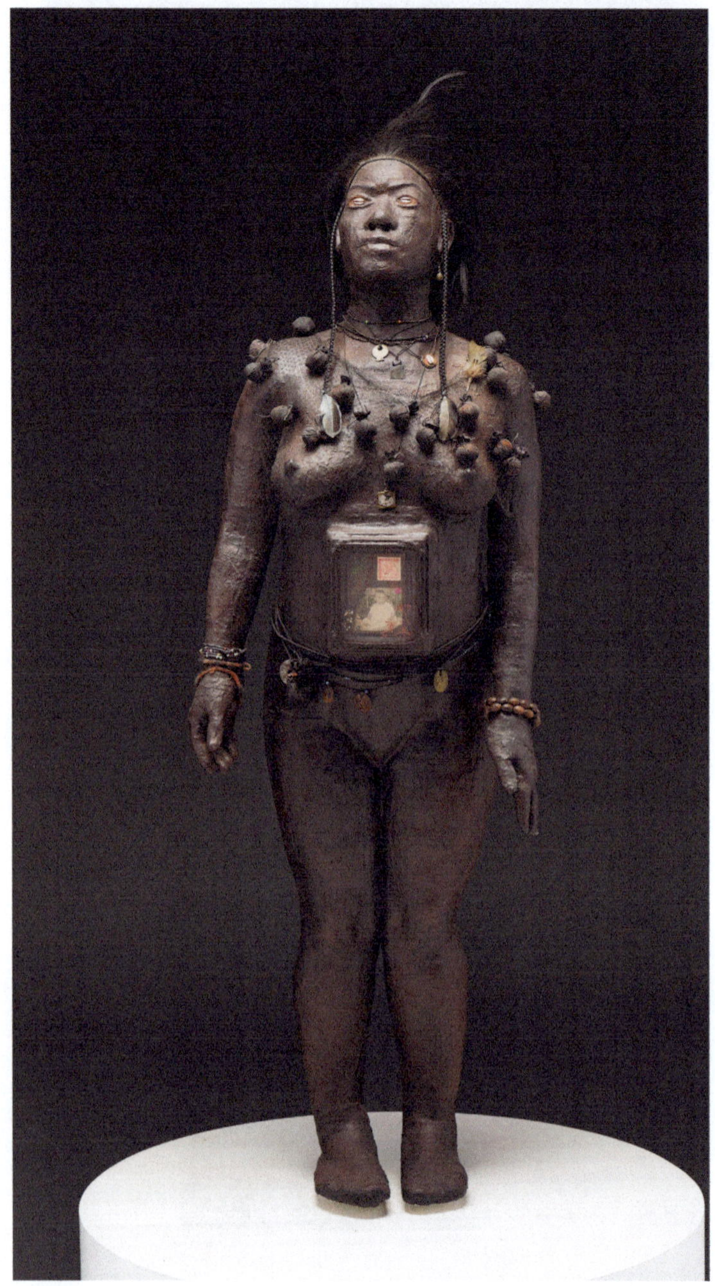

FIGURE 1.4. Renée Stout, *Fetish #2*, 1988, mixed media (plaster body cast), 64 in. (1 m 62.56 cm), Dallas Museum of Art Metropolitan Life Foundation Purchase Grant.

part of a complex visual commentary. His work *Trésor Oublié* (2011), a painted image with multiple collage hands cut out from fashion magazines protruding from the body, has explicit references to decolonization.[32] The hands appear to have yanked the nails from the body of the figure and are shown tumbling towards the ground. The image has a strong narrative construction, conflating the idea of decolonization with that of de-fetishization: the nails have been pulled out, the cavity in the stomach is empty and the *nkisi*, now furnished with red lipstick, is being unceremoniously ripped from its plinth by other unseen hands tugging on bright red ropes. The plinth itself shows the period that had been commemorated 1848–1960.[33] The image of the *nkisi* portrays a fundamental act of iconoclasm: it is feminized by the lipstick when *minkisi* are almost always masculine and the *nganga* themselves are almost always male; it has been decommissioned with the removal of its activating parts; and, finally, it is deposed by being toppled. An image of a European monument of a winged victory, sword in hand appears on a smaller scale in the bottom of the picture, diminished in size by comparison with the *nkisi*, but still triumphantly intact.

In other of Bandoma's pictures the mirrors on the stomach become screens on which other images of modernity appear (the Facebook logo, for instance) or the mirror is represented as a torch illuminating a rifle, a plane, a car, a dollar, euro symbol and so forth in its yellow light. In conception it recalls an earlier work by another Congolese artist (from the Republic of Congo rather than the DRC), Trigo Piula (b. 1953), which explores a similar range of implications in terms of contemporary consumerism. His work *Ta Télé* (1988) has been illustrated and exhibited a number of times.[34] The painting shows what we assume to be a Congolese audience seated in an auditorium and facing a larger than human-scale *nkisi* which is portrayed wearing a form of feathered headdress. In its stomach area it has a television screen where the mirror would be. Electrical wires connect it to devices behind it. On the wall are a series of 14 other screens showing a range of images as if from television programmes being broadcast simultaneously. These include an amorous white couple, a car, the Eiffel tower, a footballer and a satellite image of Africa. Other motifs appear on the back of the heads of the viewers suggestive of their own desires excited by watching the *nkisi*: clothing, food, drink, a car and a heart-shaped image.

Interpretations of the picture have focussed on the consumerism depicted with the implication that the fetishism associated with the *nkisi* is replicated in the Western obsession with consumer goods which in their turn have been exported—like the televisions themselves—to Africa. Yet there is an interplay of 'gazes' at work. The audience depicted in the auditorium watch an *nkisi* which in a modern context is portrayed as still capable of realizing wants and desires. But, where it was consulted on a wide range of personal issues in the past from making a vow to acts of healing and enacting retribution against a wrong-doer, its techno-logical descendant is approached to realize largely consumer-driven aspirations. The enlarged *nkisi* figure is itself potentially also one of these, able to respond to desires in local conception but, in Western eyes, reconfigured into a consumer good in its own right—enlarged, perhaps, to reflect the central place it had come to occupy in external understandings of 'traditional' Africa. As viewers of the picture, western audiences are challenged to consider how this perspective also influences their own assumptions.

However, there is another 'gaze' to consider: the painting displays a close-up image of the head of the *nkisi* itself replete with feathered headdress on the screen which is being watched by its audiences. It is the *nkisi* which is looking at the viewers, rather than reflecting back the image of its audience: the observer is also being observed. Like the *nkisi* in use by *nganga*, the screen continues to conceal what lies behind in the cavity. In the game of mirrors within the picture, the *nkisi*—electrically charged, as it is portrayed—maintains the hidden source of its agency.

In cases such as these, the *nkisi* remains ambiguous, capable of several readings. Such subtlety is less evident in some of the works *minkisi* have inspired amongst artists who reference them despite having no direct personal connection to Kongo culture. In such contemporary spin-offs, the original object is stripped of any pretence of the kind of magico-medicinal agency that some African and African American artists—Renée Stout in particular—look to achieve. A whole installation of artworks by the Chapman Brothers (b. 1962 and b. 1966) was devoted to the theme with a series of 34 wood sculptures said to be the family's collection of ethnographic works of art assembled over 70 years. First exhibited at the White Cube Gallery, London, in 2002 it has since been acquired as a whole by the Tate Gallery, London. The White Cube press release gave the alleged provenance: the 'extraordinary assemblage of rare ethnographic and reliquary fetish objects' had been brought together from the former colonial regions of Camgib, Seirf and Ekoc. In conformity with museum practice, each had its individual acquisition number—CFC76311561 and so forth. Included was an example of a Kozo, a type of Kongo *nkisi* in the form of a double-headed dog with a version of its medico-magical pack in the middle of the back. Other figures also involve wood representations of (at first sight) nails protruding from the body. On exhibition, the objects were displayed in a typical modernist setting: spotlit on their own plinths in a darkened space. They are, the advertising assured potential visitors, 'an embodiment of skilful control that demonstrates that the divine manipulation of spiritual power is one of the principle functions of ethnographic art'.[35]

But this, of course, is all an elaborate spoof, as the purported colonial sources of the objects already imply. Among the objects is a version of a Cameroonian figure carrying a takeaway with the unmistakeable logo of McDonalds. A copy of a Songye figure from the Congo and wearing a tunic with the same distinctive logo has nails in the hair which turn out to be french fries, while the medicine pack on Kozo's back represents not *bilongo* but a burger. The regions from which the objects purportedly come are part of the McDonalds's menu read backwards and the acquisition detail conveniently gives the phone numbers of various London branches of the fast-food chain.[36] And the letters CFC in the collection registration detail, though presumably referencing the Chapman family, also suggest (fortuitously or otherwise) a McDonalds' competitor—KFC. The pun on the word 'fetish' in the advertising materials is thereby exploited to the full.

By indulging, then undermining, the tropes of appropriation implicit in the distinction of the primitive and the modern, of the local and the global, the intention is to provoke questions and a subtler self-awareness by those steeped in art-historical and gallery-visiting practices.[37] The exhibition layout itself plays on the same paradigms. The lighting and the environment deliberately replicate the regimes of wonder which decontextualized modernist display typically deploy. A year after the opening of the aestheticized Sainsbury African Gallery in the British Museum in London, which some interpreted as an example of a return to modernist techniques and expectation,[38] the subterfuge was compounded. Spotlit as if on stage, like Piula's *nkisi*, the effect is to suggest that the objects as 'fetishes' provide—in and of themselves—a means of access to an Indiana Jones-like world of different, potentially meaningful, spiritual experience.

However, it is not just playing on the labelling of *minkisi* as 'fetish' that is exploited in contemporary Western art contexts. Two other contrasting examples show how *minkisi* have become so pervasive an image that they have been deployed at opposite ends of the aesthetic spectrum. Grayson Perry's (b. 1960) sculpture *The King of Nowhere* (2015) was created as a result of the experience of making and presenting a TV documentary on the divisions within modern British society. The wood figure with baseball cap and white button eyes represents a gangster. It is stabbed with knife blades, scissors and syringes and stands on a plinth with bottles of alcohol and other apparently discarded objects. The tab off a beer can hangs from one ear. The presence on the plinth of candles suggests a shrine-like composition. But the title of the work implies that it is about self-delusion, while the figure itself is an abject image of urban chaos cast in terms of an object of a kind familiar in 'ethnographic' collections. The assemblage of objects recalls an *nkisi*, even if aspects of the form seem to model a figure of Papua New Guinea origin.

At the other end of the spectrum are highly accomplished aesthetic depictions of mostly West African subjects produced by the European–Brazilian artist Alexis

Peskine (b. 1979). In form they bear little resemblance to Kongo or other African 'traditional' work. Yet, the use of nails as a medium is deliberate, reconfiguring a usage in what has otherwise been seen as a perverse way to create disciplined portraits by innovative means. The background of the works are wooden boards which have been stained a coffee colour. Into these nails with heads of different sizes are driven at different depths creating the contours of the face. This is then highlighted by covering the nail heads with gold and silver leaf to realize an elegant portrait. Where the nails on the Hindenburg figure covered up the sculpture, here, as in a Pointillist painting, the dots on the nail heads are what makes the portrait. If Perry's image reverts to an older narrative embodied in the western response to *minkisi*, Peskine reinvents it for a totally different purpose: to produce images of technical assuredness by unconventional means, depicting not so much self-delusion as self-possession. A 2017 exhibition of his work (at the October Gallery in London) made the link to *minkisi* explicit both in the associated literature and in the exhibition subtitle, *Power Figures*.[39]

What all these examples have in common is that they are created in a transactional context. A link to commercial operations and to processes of commodification is central. The most striking example is that of the nailed figures which attained a major status in civil and commercial affairs in the complex and chaotic world of the late nineteenth-century coastal towns of the Congo region. As personalities in their own right, these figures were consulted on the well-being of individuals, exercised a judicial function and, in effect, regulated trade and commerce for a decade and more. Their seizure and removal to Europe was part of a strategy to regain commercial as much as administrative control. Since then, they have been sold at auctions, acquired by museums, illustrated in expensive catalogues and have inspired both exhibitions and artists within and beyond Africa. Throughout, they have retained their capacity to provoke and as such they have been open to use as an intellectual and artistic strategy producing multiple different narratives, at once playful and subversive, reversions or reinventions. Versions of them created by artists within and beyond the Congo have been represented as icons of the very process of consumerism to which, ironically, they themselves have been susceptible. Their fate was to themselves become fetishized. Their own capital in commercial and cultural terms has soared from the days when they were denigrated as trophies of degenerate cultural practice. They are no longer specimens of some arcane pseudo-religious belief system, as the changing language around them testifies.

But it would be wrong to ascribe primacy in this process to any one form of intervention. Has artistic engagement altered the way Kongo objects are seen in museums? Has curatorial practice influenced their emergence as objects of artistic value? Arguably, the realignments that have been taking place in different arenas are the result of a combination of the deeper understanding of their original significance, curatorial interventions, exhibitions and artistic engagement. *Minkisi* have ceased to be classic specimens of the category 'fetish' and emerged as powerful objects in their own right.

Acknowledgements

I am grateful to the editors of this volume for the invitation to contribute and to Ed Juler in particular for his suggestions on the text. I am also indebted to Simon Dell and to Lisa Madigan Newby for valuable comment on an earlier draft. Some of the material discussed was presented at the conference 'Representing Africa in British Museums', organized by Timothy Insoll and Tony Eccles through the University of Exeter and the Royal Albert Memorial Museum in June 2018. The ideas were further developed in the Von Hugel Lecture I gave at the University of Cambridge later in the same month. The responses to both presentations have helped inform the narrative developed here. I also thank James Green for his assistance in tracking down a number of contemporary resonances of the *nkisi* phenomenon and for his informed comments on the article itself.

NOTES

1. The definitive study of this phenomenon is Sherwood Simmons, 'Men of Nails: Expressionism, Fetishes, Dadaism', *RES: Anthropology and Aesthetics* 40 (Autumn 2001): 211–38.

2. Anon., 'For Germans to Drive Nails into! War Memorials—and Congo Cases of Nailing', *Illustrated London News* (London), 25 December 1915, 842–43.

3. The description of the Royal Geographical Society nailed figure as a 'war fetish' is accurate only to the extent that it could be used to fight witchcraft. Nailed figures of this type do not otherwise seem to have been used for warfare in the sense implied here. There were other types of objects for that purpose; see Wyatt MacGaffey, 'Commodore Wilmot encounters Kongo art, 1865', *African Arts* 43, no. 2 (Summer 2010): 53; Alisa Lagamma, 'Mangaaka', in *Kongo: Power and Majesty*, ed. Alisa LaGamma (New York: Metropolitan Museum of Art, 2015), 222–23.

4. See Nicola Lambourne, 'Production versus Destruction: Art, World War I and Art History', *Art History* 22, no. 3 (September 1999): 350–52.

5. Anon., *The Wooden Idol of Berlin* (London: Eyre and Spottiswoode, c.1915).

6. Anon., 'Stepney's Iron Hindenburg', *Illustrated War News* (London), 27 September 1916, 31.

7. William Pietz, 'The Problem of the Fetish, I', *RES: Anthropology and Aesthetic* 9 (Spring 1985): 5–17; 'The Problem of the Fetish, II: The Origin of the Fetish', *RES: Anthropology and Aesthetics* 13 (Spring 1987): 23–45; 'The Problem of the Fetish, IIIa: Bosman's

Guinea and the Enlightenment Theory of Fetishism', *RES: Anthropology and Aesthetics* 16 (Autumn 1988): 105–24; Emily Apter and William Pietz, eds, *Fetishism as Cultural Discourse* (Ithaca, NY: Cornell University Press, 1993).

8.   E. B. Tylor, *Primitive Culture: Researches into the Development of Mythology, Philosophy, Religion, Art and Custom* 2 vols (London: John Murray, 1871). See also the differently nuanced arguments developed by Phillippe Descola, *Beyond Nature and Culture*, trans. Janet Lloyd (Chicago: University of Chicago Press, 2013); Tim Ingold, 'Totemism, Animism and the Depiction of Animals', in *The Perception of the Environment: Essays in Livelihood, Dwelling and Skill*, ed. Tim Ingold (London: Routledge, 2000), 111–31; and Alfred Gell, *Art and Agency: An Anthropological Theory* (Oxford: Clarendon Press, 1998).

9.   In fact, Freud was not the first to discuss fetishism as a psycho-sexual phenomenon. Freud's famous 1927 article was preceded by an analysis by Alfred Binet 40 years earlier; see Dawn Ades, 'Surrealism: Fetishism's Job', in *Fetishism: Visualising Power and Desire*, ed. Anthony Shelton (London: Lund Humphries, 1995), 70–71.

10.   Ibid., 68–69. See also Adam Jolles, *The Curatorial Avant-garde: Surrealism and Exhibition Practice, 1925–1941* (Philadelphia: Penn State University Press, 2013).

11.   Steven Hooper, ed., *Robert and Lisa Sainsbury Collection*, 3 vols (New Haven, CT: Yale University Press, 1997).

12.   LaGamma, *Kongo*, 264–65.

13.   Wyatt MacGaffey, 'Franchising *Minkisi* in Loango: Questions of Form and Function', *RES: Anthropology and Aesthetics* 65/66 (2014/15): 148–57; LaGamma, *Kongo*, 222.

14.   Zdenka Volavkova, 'Nkisi Figures of the Lower Congo', *African Arts* 5, no. 2 (Summer, 1972): 52.

15.   W. Holman Bentley, *Pioneering on the Congo* (London: Religious Tract Society, 1900), 256.

16.   LaGamma, *Kongo*, 226–42.

17.   *Notes and Queries on Anthropology* (London: Royal Anthropological Institute,1912), 27.

18.   Bentley, *Pioneering*, 256.

19.   Wyatt MacGaffey, 'African Objects and the Idea of the Fetish', *RES: Anthropology and Aesthetics* 25 (Spring 1994): 123–31.

20.   Ibid., 125.

21.   As quoted in Phyllis M. Martin, 'The Kingdom of Loango', in *Kongo: Power and Majesty* ed. Alisa LaGamma (New York: Metropolitan Museum of Art, 2015), 85.

22.   As translated and quoted in Anne-Marie Bouttiaux, 'The Porosity of Objects', in *Fetish Modernity*, ed. Anne-Marie Bouttiaux and Anna Seiderer (Tervuren, Belgium: Royal Museum for Central Africa, 2011), 156.

23.   I recall visiting a prominent British artist at his house in South London in an area prone to burglaries. As a security device, he had confected his own version of an *nkisi nkondi*, positioned on a table just inside the front door in the expectation that anyone foolish enough

to look through the letterbox flap—or worse, break in—would immediately turn tail on seeing it for fear of its malign potential.

24. Wyatt MacGaffey, 'The Eyes of Understanding: Kongo *Minkisi*', in *Astonishment and Power*, ed. Wyatt MacGaffey and Michael D. Harris (Washington, DC: Smithsonian Institution Press, 1993), 18–103; Michael D. Harris, 'Resonance, Transformation and Rhyme: The Art of Renée Stout', in *Astonishment and Power*, ed. Wyatt MacGaffey and Michael D. Harris, 106–56. Washington, DC: Smithsonian Institution Press, 1993.

25. Wyatt MacGaffey, 'Astonishment and Stickiness in Kongo art: A Theoretical Advance', *RES: Anthropology and Aesthetics* 39 (Spring 2001): 141; MacGaffey, 156; Alfred Gell, 'The Technology of Enchantment and the Enchantment of Technology', in *Anthropology, Art and Aesthetics*, eds Jeremy Coote and Anthony Shelton (Oxford: Clarendon Press, 1992), 40–67; *Art and Agency: An Anthropological Theory* (Oxford: Clarendon Press, 1998), 68–72.

26. https://www.metmuseum.org/press/exhibitions/2015/kongo (accessed 1 May 2020).

27. For a useful recent summary of this history see Tobias Wofford, 'Feedback: Between American Art and African Art History', *Nka, Journal of Contemporary African Art* 41 (2017): 154–64.

28. As quoted in Harris, *Astonishment*, 111.

29. Although no direct inspiration from Kongo is documented, an interesting parallel is the African American female artist Adrian Piper's evolving piece 'What will become of me' in the Museum of Modern Art, New York, which consists of a shelf of glass jars in which Piper places her own nail and hair clippings, adding to the bottles as more exuviae assemble. The final bottle will be her own cremated remains.

30. Susan Cooksey, 'Renée Stout', in *Kongo across the Waters*, ed. Susan Cooksey, Robin Poynor and Hein Vanhee (Gainesville: University Press of Florida, 2013), 396–97.

31. Mark Sloane, ed., *Tales of the Conjure Woman: Renée Stout* (Charleston, SC: Halsey Institute Press, 2013).

32. Susan Cooksey, 'Steve Bandoma', in *Kongo across the Waters*, ed. Susan Cooksey, Robin Poynor and Hein Vanhee (Gainesville: University Press of Florida, 2013), 406–09.

33. It would seem likely that the period intended is that of colonialism starting in 1884, the date of the Berlin conference (otherwise known as the Congo conference) which divided Africa into domains under the control of various European countries. 1848, however, could refer to the date of the European revolutions or of the second French legislative challenge to slavery.

34. Shelton, *Fetishism*, 48; Nicholas Mirzoeff, *Introduction to Visual Culture* (London: Routledge, 2009), 152–53; Bouttiaux and Seiderer, 229; Susan Mullin Vogel, *Africa Explores: 20th Century African Art* (New York: Center for African Art, 1991), 229.

35. http://whitecube.com/exhibitions/exhibition/jake_and_dinos_chapman_hoxton_square_2002 (accessed 1 May 2020).

36. Helen Delaney, 'Jake Chapman, Dinos Chapman: The Chapman family collection 2002', [online] available at https://www.tate.org.uk/art/artworks/chapman-the-chapman-family-collection-t12755. (accessed 22 July 2018).

37. Michael Archer, 'Jake and Dino Chapman', *ArtForum* 41, no. 9 (May 2003): 182.
38. Ruth Phillips, 'Where Is "Africa"? Re-viewing Art and Artifact in the Age of Globalization', *American Anthropologist* 104, no. 3 (September 2002): 944–52.
39. http://www.octobergallery.co.uk/exhibitions/2017pes/ (accessed 1 May 2020).

REFERENCES

Ades, Dawn. 'Surrealism: Fetishism's Job'. In *Fetishism: Visualising Power and Desire*, ed. Anthony Shelton, 66–87. London: Lund Humphries, 1995.

Anon. 'For Germans to Drive Nails into! Enemy War Memorials—and Congo Cases of Nailing'. *Illustrated London News*, 25 December 1915.

Anon. *The Wooden Idol of Berlin*. London: Eyre and Spottiswoode, c. 1915.

Anon. 'Stepney's Iron Hindenburg'. *Illustrated War News*, 27 September 1916.

Apter, Emily, and William Pietz, eds. *Fetishism as Cultural Discourse*. Ithaca, NY: Cornell University Press, 1993.

Archer, Michael. 'Jake and Dino Chapman'. *ArtForum* 41, no. 9 (May 2003): 182.

Bentley, W. Holman. *Pioneering on the Congo*, 2 vols. London: Religious Tract Society, 1900.

Bouttiaux, Anne-Marie. 'The Porosity of Objects'. In *Fetish Modernity*, ed. Anne-Marie Bouttiaux and Anna Seiderer, 53–57. Tervuren, Belgium: Royal Museum for Central Africa, 2011.

Bouttiaux, Anne-Marie, and Anna Seiderer, eds. *Fetish Modernity*. Tervuren, Belgium: Royal Museum for Central Africa, 2011.

Cooksey, Susan, Robin Poynor and Hein Vanhee, eds. *Kongo across the Waters*. Gainesville: University Press of Florida, 2013.

Cooksey, Susan, and Robin Poynor. 'Kongo Inspiration in Contemporary World Art'. In *Kongo across the Waters*, ed. Susan Cooksey, Robin Poynor and Hein Vanhee, 355–66. Gainesville: University Press of Florida, 2013.

Cooksey, Susan. 'Renée Stout'. In *Kongo across the Waters*, ed. Susan Cooksey, Robin Poynor and Hein Vanhee, 396–97. Gainesville: University Press of Florida, 2013a.

Cooksey, Susan. 'Steve Bandoma'. In *Kongo across the Waters*, ed. Susan Cooksey, Robin Poynor and Hein Vanhee, 406–09. Gainesville: University Press of Florida, 2013b .

Delaney, Helen. 'Jake Chapman, Dinos Chapman: The Chapman Family Collection 2002'. (2009). Available at https://www.tate.org.uk/art/artworks/chapman-the-chapman-family-collection-t12755 (accessed 22 July 2018).

Descola, Phillippe. *Beyond Nature and Culture*, trans. Janet Lloyd. Chicago: University of Chicago Press, 2013.

Gell, Alfred. 'The Technology of Enchantment and the Enchantment of Technology'. In *Anthropology, Art and Aesthetics*, ed. Jeremy Coote and Anthony Shelton, 40–67. Oxford: Clarendon Press, 1992.

Gell, Alfred. *Art and Agency: An Anthropological Theory*. Oxford: Clarendon Press, 1998.

Harris, Michael D. 'Resonance, Transformation and Rhyme: The Art of Renée Stout'. In *Astonishment and Power*, ed. Wyatt MacGaffey and Michael D. Harris, 106–56. Washington, DC: Smithsonian Institution Press, 1993.

Harris, Michael D. 'Kongo Squared: The Art of Renée Stout'. In *Kongo across the Waters*, ed. Susan Cooksey, Robin Poynor and Hein Vanhee, 370–76. Gainesville: University Press of Florida, 2013 .

Hooper, Steven, ed. *Robert and Lisa Sainsbury Collection*, 3 vols. New Haven, CT: Yale University Press, 1997.

Ingold, Tim. 'Totemism, Animism and the Depiction of Animals'. In *The Perception of the Environment: Essays in Livelihood, Dwelling and Skill*, ed. Tim Ingold, 111–31. London: Routledge, 2000.

Jolles, Adam. *The Curatorial Avant-garde: Surrealism and Exhibition Practice, 1925–1941*. Philadelphia: Penn State University Press, 2013.

LaGamma, Alisa, ed. *Kongo: Power and Majesty*. New York: Metropolitan Museum of Art, 2015.

LaGamma, Alisa, ed. 'Mangaaka'. In *Kongo: Power and Majesty*, ed. Alisa LaGamma, 221–65. New York: Metropolitan Museum of Art, 2015.

Lambourne, Nicola, 'Production versus Destruction: Art, World War I and Art History'. *Art History* 22, no. 3 (September 1999): 347–63.

MacGaffey, Wyatt, and Michael D. Harris. *Astonishment and Power*. Washington DC: Smithsonian Institution Press, 1993.

MacGaffey, Wyatt. 'Fetishism Revisited: Kongo *nkisi* in Sociological Perspective', *Africa* 47, no. 2 (1977): 172–84.

MacGaffey, Wyatt. 'The Eyes of Understanding: Kongo *Minkisi*'. In *Astonishment and Power*, ed. Wyatt MacGaffey and Michael D. Harris, 18–103. Washington, DC: Smithsonian Institution Press, 1993.

MacGaffey, Wyatt. 'African Objects and the Idea of the Fetish'. *RES: Anthropology and Aesthetics* 25 (Spring 1994): 123–31.

MacGaffey, Wyatt. 'Astonishment and Stickiness in Kongo Art: A Theoretical Advance'. *RES: Anthropology and Aesthetics* 39 (Spring 2001): 137–50.

MacGaffey, Wyatt. 'Commodore Wilmot Encounters Kongo Art, 1865'. *African Arts* 43, no. 2 (Summer 2010): 52–53.

MacGaffey, Wyatt. 'Franchising *Minkisi* in Loango: Questions of Form and Function'. *RES: Anthropology and Aesthetics* 65/66 (2014/15): 148–57.

Mack, John. 'Fetish? Magic Figures in Central Africa'. In *Fetishism, Visualising Power and Desire*, ed. Anthony Shelton, 52–65. London: Lund Humphries, 1995.

Martin, Phyllis M. 'The Kingdom of Loango'. In *Kongo: Power and Majesty*, ed. Alisa LaGamma, 47–85. New York: Metropolitan Museum of Art, 2015.

Mirzoeff, Nicholas. *Introduction to Visual Culture*. London: Routledge, 2009.

Notes and Queries on Anthropology. London: Royal Anthropological Institute, 1912.

Phillips, Ruth. 'Where Is "Africa"? Re-viewing Art and Artifact in the Age of Globalization'. *American Anthropologist* 104, no. 3 (September 2002): 944–52.

Pietz, William. 'The Problem of the Fetish, I'. *RES: Anthropology and Aesthetics* 9 (Spring 1985): 5–17.

Pietz, William. 'The Problem of the Fetish, II: The Origin of the Fetish'. *RES: Anthropology and Aesthetics* 15, (Spring 1987): 23–45.

Pietz, William. 'The Problem of the Fetish, IIIa: Bosman's Guinea and the Enlightenment Theory of Fetishism'. *RES: Anthropology and Aesthetics* 16 (Autumn 1988): 105–23.

Shelton, Anthony. 'Introduction' and 'The Chameleon Body: Power, Mutilation and Sexuality'. In *Fetishism, Visualising Power and Desire*, ed. Anthony Shelton, 7–9, 10–32. London: Lund Humphries, 1995.

Simmons, Sherwood. 'Men of Nails: Expressionism, Fetishes, Dadaism'. *RES: Anthropology and Aesthetics* 40 (Autumn 2001): 211–38.

Sloane, Mark, ed. *Tales of the Conjure Woman: Renée Stout*. Charleston, SC: Halsey Institute Press, 2013.

Thompson, Carol. '*Minkisi* and *dikenga* in the Art of Radcliffe Bailey: Multiplied Exponentially'. In *Kongo across the Waters*, ed. Susan Cooksey, Robin Poynor, and Hein Vanhee, 377–84. Gainesville: University Press of Florida, 2013.

Thompson, Robert Farris. *Flash of the Spirit: African and Afro-American Art and Philosophy*. New York: Random House, 1983.

Tylor, E. B. *Primitive Culture: Researches into the Development of Mythology, Philosophy, Religion, Art and Custom*, 2 vols. London: John Murray, 1871.

Vogel, Susan Mullin. *Africa Explores: 20th Century African Art*. New York: Center for African Art, 1991.

Volavkova, Zdenka. 'Nkisi Figures of the Lower Congo'. *African Arts* 5, no. 2 (Summer 1972): 52–59.

Wofford, Tobias. 'Feedback: Between American Art and African Art History'. *Nka, Journal of Contemporary African Art* 41 (2017): 154–64.

Websites:

http://www.octobergallery.co.uk/exhibitions/2017pes/ (accessed 20 May 2018).

http://whitecube.com/exhibitions/exhibition/jake_and_dinos_chapman_hoxton_square_2002 (accessed 21 June 20018).

https://www.metmuseum.org/press/exhibitions/2015/kongo (accessed 28 July 2018).

2

Curating Interobjectively in Museums

Alistair Robinson

Abstract

Robinson, as a curator of contemporary art, examines a particular case study exhibition realized in 2016, which set out to 'reanimate' scientific artefacts, archival objects from natural history collections and little-seen artworks from the archives of Montpellier University. The exhibition, A Scientific Encounter: On Interobjectivity, *juxtaposed new works by a dozen artists from across Europe with objects from these three collections, setting them into 'dialogue'. A trio of examples are outlined to suggest how we might think about objects and objecthood in new ways, in the light of the ideas that have originated from the philosophical movement variously known as 'speculative realism' or 'object-oriented ontology', among other titles. Drawing specifically upon Bruno Latour's idea of 'interobjectivity', which grants objects a parallel kind of agency to humans, Robinson asks what kind of 'encounters' museums can generate between artefacts—and more provocatively, what kinds of encounters they can create between human objects and non-human ones.*

'A Scientific Encounter': Envisaging the Myth of the Museum

This chapter examines a particular exhibition project as a case study of how artistic and scientific concerns might collide, and where artefacts from both artistic and scientific collections could be set 'into dialogue' with works by contemporary artists. The title of the project was *A Scientific Encounter: On Interobjectivity*. The exhibition asked these questions, common to many curatorial experiments: How far can we rethink our existing categories of object; and how far can we accept new or unexpected relationships between objects through curatorial 'remediations'? Can we know the vast range of things that we, as a public, collectively own? The title was intended to direct attention onto two issues. First of these was that the exhibition was a kind of meeting both between objects and one between disciplines. The phrasing of the title also suggested a second issue: that we might think of the 'encounters' between objects as a scientific event, or rather, understand art objects in scientific terms. Can we see art objects in terms of the history of scientific thought, or even its potential future?

The theoretical armature for the project drew upon three sets of ideas. First, Donald Preziosi's conception of museum collections as being possessed of a novelistic imaginary; second, Arjun Appadurai's idea of the 'social lives' of objects; and third and most importantly, Bruno Latour's concept of "interobjectivity" where objects are addressed as having an agency akin to that of human subjects. What might it be to curate 'interobjectively'? What might a Latourian museum look like? The case study suggested that a Latourian curatorial method might involve a strategic confusion between 'non-human and human' domains.[1] In a Latourian curatorial practice, we might not see museum objects as inert 'specimens' subject to a rule of human law, but as if a community of thoroughly 'socialized' individuals, each occupying a highly particular and localized milieu. These ideas reinforce the hypothesis that museum collections are complex 'social' entities: micro-societies of their own, in effect. In this scheme, much like social or political bodies of persons, museum collections are both a labour of the imagination—a world view built by assembling a world-in-miniature for preservation—and localized 'societies' of objects in their own right. Many museums, including that in the case study, have accumulated millions upon millions of individual objects, in which there are a few élite artefacts subject to a disproportionate amount of attention; a small proportion believed to be of some note; and a larger mass of unloved, invisible specimens, held in storage. In the 2012 American election, the Republican candidate Mitt Romney announced that 'corporations are people, too', extolling the theory of corporate personhood; if we can imagine museum collections are 'corporate' bodies that extend across time, then museum objects are (akin to) people, too.[2]

A Scientific Encounter: On Interobjectivity was created from the multiple museum collections of Montpellier University, which include the most comprehensive collection of medical artefacts in Europe. The final exhibition was staged in a highly unusual setting: its thirteenth-century former medical libraries. This trio of spaces was never intended to be galleries, though they are dignified, high spaces, with exposed stone walls and vaulted ceilings. They have the mathematically defined proportions of medieval architecture.[3] These rooms could be described as strange spaces in which to display contemporary art or museum objects. But most curators would suggest there has been no point in modern European history since their foundation in which museums have *not* been strange places. This is true whether we see museums through Michel Foucault's idea of a 'heterotopia', or through Donald Preziosi's concept that museums are essentially fictions and akin to nineteenth-century novels, in their dual commitments to act as encyclopaedic surveys of the whole world, and to be transparent and 'realist' modes of representation.[4]

In a gesture of extraordinary intellectual generosity, Montpellier University granted full access to all of its collections which range across natural history, the history of medicine and the history of European art alike. *A Scientific Encounter* was able to draw upon several hundred years of institutional collecting: Montpellier was one of the first universities to teach and study medicine and, indeed, was one of Europe's earliest universities. The offer of unprecedented access to even the most fragile, valuable and rare materials across multiple collections of many millions of artefacts gave the project its focus, perhaps unexpectedly. Put another way, the university's role as the principal institutional collections in the city across half a millennium provided a particular frame by which we could proceed. Many commentators have made comparisons between the functions of academy and the museum, and here the academy itself encompasses multiple museums including the *Musée et Conservatoire d'Anatomie*; the *Jardin de Plantes de Montpellier*; and the *Musée Atger*, covering medicine, botany and natural history, and European art history respectively.

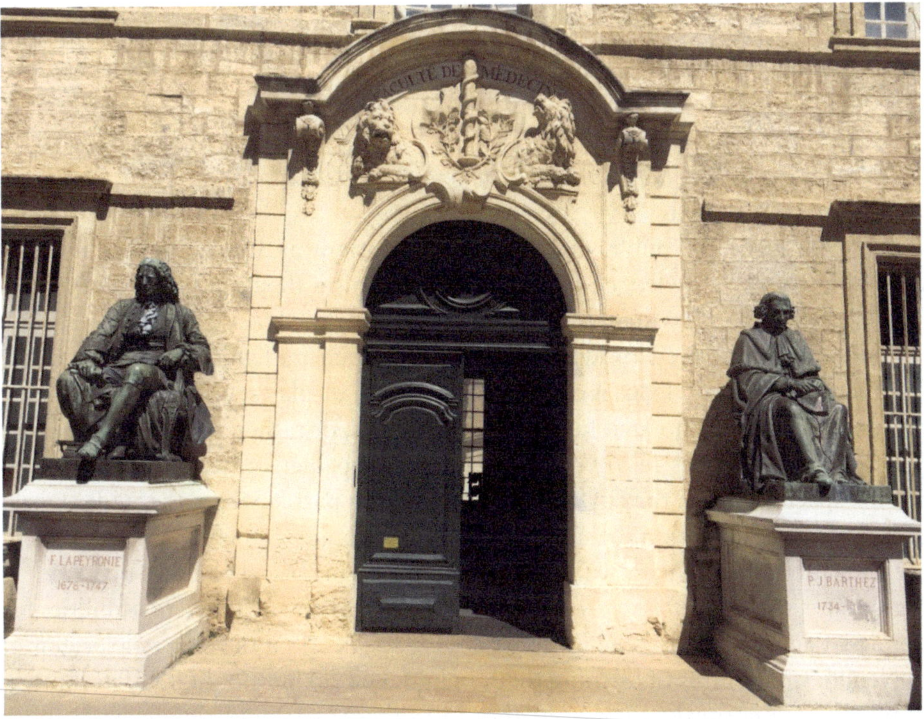

FIGURE 2.1. Main entrance to the medical school, University of Montpellier. Photograph © the author.

The Museum's Omniscience

To summarize, therefore: Montpellier University's collections include tens of millions of objects that have been acquired across half a millennium. Donald Preziosi posits that in modernity, museums must encompass *everything* and survey all possible fields of knowledge to have the universality that is their signature, their distinguishing feature.[5] This logic became a starting point, given the apparent impossibility of selecting a tiny number of 'representative' objects from such vast collections. If the museum's job is precisely to attempt the impossible, then a project concerned with museumhood and the institutionality of the 'museum object' should do exactly the same.

A Scientific Encounter therefore attempted to enlist objects from all possible sources into its remit. The scale of the collections prompted the thought experiment of what a single museum that could encompass them all at once might be. What would a kind of museum-of-all-museums be? Or more realistically, what might a single exhibition look like that could function as a microcosmic museum of all the university's collections? In what possible way could one speak about such monumental bodies of knowledge? A kind of museum-of-museums, then, could be one solution: a collection-of-all-collections. But even this kind of assembly, to be a collection of its own, needs to have a founding logic and an esprit de corps, rather than becoming merely heterodox.

Presenting Objects in the Academy: The Poetics of Academic Space

The academy and the public museum are institutions authorized to lay claim to what constitutes 'knowledge'. In both instances, this is their unique distinguishing feature and what unites them. Put in a radically simplified form, libraries act as the storehouse of authorized knowledge, or rather as the paradigmatic place and space in which written knowledge is collected. Museums' display spaces act in parallel as the storehouse of authorized knowledge of objects, or rather, as the paradigmatic place in which objects *become* knowledge. Montpellier's three ancient libraries are the space in which the city founded its claim to participate in the wider world of knowledge production. Being re-employed as 'found' display spaces reoriented their function: though their walls remain lined with historical volumes no longer in regular use, the signs of its previous life are present. This suggested possibilities for our approach. The bare stone walls are able to speak about the monastic origins of universities, as centres of learning that are in the world but not quite *of* it. If medieval architecture speaks to us now about the almost unthinkable physical labour needed to make inhabited spaces before modern tools existed, it is also still clearly the embodiment of a world-picture. It is often all too tempting to see architecture as a transparent window onto a world view, but in Montpellier that sense is irresistible.

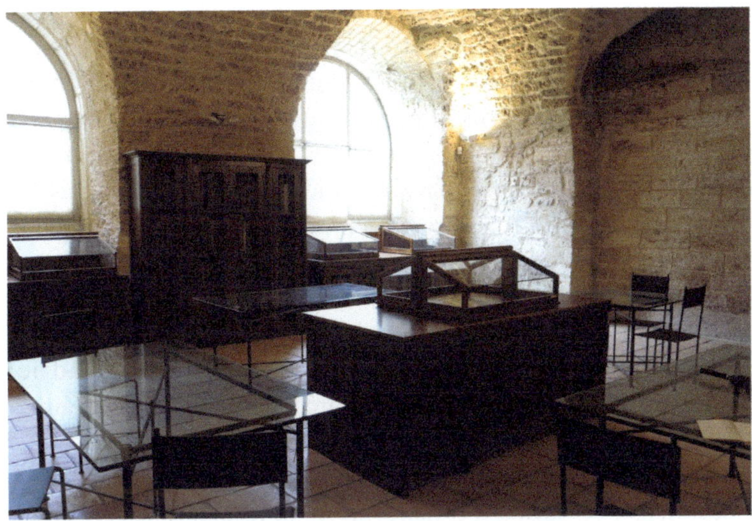

FIGURE 2.2. Medieval medical libraries, University of Montpellier. Photograph © the author.

Like modernist buildings, the libraries reveal their structure and means of construction, placing their structural materials in full view. Today, there is no decoration of any kind, leaving only exposed stone walls and stone ceiling. It is again, tempting to feel that the weight of labour invested in making the building is paralleled by that of building a body of knowledge and building a world view. The harmonic proportions of the spaces and the cabinets of monumental volumes invite visitors to see the three rooms as spaces where 'knowledge' is not only produced but seemingly made manifest and tangible (a Benjaminian idea).[6] In the museologist Donald Preziosi's scheme museums act as 'the brain of the earth's body'.[7] 'Knowledge' in the academy is often principally textual in its representation of the world. By contrast, we have to imagine museums' construction of their domains of knowledge as being embodied. Preziosi remarks that only museums permit an 'epistemological archaeology': an enquiry into what 'knowledge' itself once was and therefore might yet be.[8] Put another way, the experience of a conjunction (or disjunction) of times is only possible within the museum—not through textbooks. Only the physical presence of objects that have had long careers in the world can sustain the illusion of imaginatively empathizing with others across time and space. Only the museum allows the illusion of 'reaching' across time to access times and places where things are undertaken differently'.

Such an idea started to recall the virtues of an 'object-based epistemology' outlined in the introduction to this volume, where objects are not the receptacles of knowledge, but are knowledge themselves (however so construed). Within the three rooms, for conservation reasons, all objects new and old had to be displayed within a set of dark-wood vitrines. Our assembled collection of artefacts could possess an espirit de corps in part through its method of display. Objects of diverse ages, materials, disciplinary affinities and capacities could cohabit happily in such quarters, as formal equals as if under the law. Within this democratic milieu, objects could begin to address each other on equal terms and enter into imaginative 'dialogues' (rather than be subject to uneven dynamics of presence and power). And such a display could become something of a 'cabinet of curiosity', in which scientific and artistic artefacts would take their rightful place.

The display strategy could suggest that such modern divisions had not become formalized and objects not become disaggregated into their own meagre categories, or segregated into their own micro-social worlds.

Of course, placing objects into glass cases is also the pre-eminent way of presenting 'specimens'; or rather, it transforms all objects into specimens, whatever their natures. Placing artworks directly alongside them inside cases invited the question of which artefacts were artworks and which were museum objects. Combining scientific 'specimens' and works of art into single cases allowed for a programmatic as much as a merely 'poetic' approach to presentation. The aestheticizing gaze we employ to regard artworks could be shifted onto scientific objects; and the analytic scrutiny we deploy to view specimens might conceivably be transferred onto artists' productions. To use Graham Harman's Heideggerian term, this frame might allow visitors to see artworks in terms of their embodied 'tool-being' instead of through an aestheticizing lens alone.[9] It might allow us to see scientific artefacts not as merely passive 'specimens', as if patiently waiting for our examination, but as having agency in the world.

Towards an Interobjective Curatorial Practice: Exercises in Diplomacy

Bruno Latour defines the term 'interobjectivity' as being forms of 'interaction [between] [...] at least two actors; these two actors must be physically co-present; they must be linked by behaviour[s] [...] and finally, the behaviour of each must evolve as [...] there is an emergence of unexpected properties'.[10] This aptly describes the curatorial ambitions here. The aims were precisely to allow new, 'unexpected properties' of art objects and scientific objects to 'emerge', and to shift the 'behaviours' of both through new forms of 'interaction' in their 'co-presence'. Latour also posits that all intellectual labour is a form of "mediation" (although he also uses the term 'translation' elsewhere, relatedly).[11] If curating is mediation, then the factor of first importance in any successful project is the *manner* in which strategies of mediation are realized. To paraphrase Latour, the *manners* by which objects address each other are crucial in their interactions. Latour's own term is to suggest that any successful mediation involves a 'diplomacy' between parties (here, between objects).[12] If the curator is a diplomat: curatorship can be understood a form of 'object-oriented diplomacy'.[13] The works in *A Scientific Encounter* were invited to 'socialize' and engage with extraordinarily diverse new and unexpected colleagues.

As we also suggested in the introduction, one premise of recent thinking about objects has been that they are defined not by their intrinsic essences, but by their interactions with other objects, much as we are ourselves in the social world. Staging interactions, therefore, became our guiding principle. The phrase 'object encounters' should be seen here as both 'meetings' *between* objects, and between 'them' and 'us'. In each instance, the aim was to transform the 'behaviours' of each through the meeting. The curatorial structure, put simply, was a linear sequence of pairings: of temporary marriages between seemingly unsuitable partners who might learn from a new acquaintance with each other.

The Collection as Collectivity—'How to Redefine the Collectives?'

Latour's animating question in one recent volume is this: 'How to redefine the collectives'?[14] The museologist Susan Pearce has provided a concise definition of the primary criteria of what constitutes a museum collection and the type of labour that collections undertake. As she puts it,

> [T]he idea [is] that collections are essentially composed of objects which bear an intrinsic relation to each other in a sequential or representative sense [...] The significant point [is] that the collection is somehow more than the sum of its parts.[15]

A Latourian understanding of collections, by contrast, would be that they are entities whose value is constituted by the fact they are a *collectivity* of objects, just as any society is an imagined collectivity of humans. Any collectivity is built both through physical co-presence and the idea that it exists as an 'imagined community' in Benedict Anderson's terms.[16] In our imagined collection, historical or archaic objects can enter into new relationships with artworks new and old, in a way they would or could not elsewhere in the world. Scientific and artistic objects can become part of each other's temporary social circle. In total, 12 artists were paired with artefacts selected from across the entirety of Montpellier's collections. Working democratically, we chose four objects from the *Musée et Conservatoire d'Anatomie,* four from the *Jardin de Plantes de Montpellier* and four from the *Musée Atger*. The vignettes below are all concerned with those from the *Musée Atger*.

An 'interobjective' curatorial mode might register objects as inhabiting different 'modes of existence' instead of their disciplinary affiliation. This, in part, allows it to avoid the hazards of a merely 'interdisciplinary' approach instead of a "*trans*disciplinary" one, which figures like Mieke Bal a have outlined.[17] In the case of *A Scientific Encounter*, the opportunity to encompass artefacts from natural history collections, medical collections and European art history in each of the three rooms created a highly particular form of 'diplomacy'. In Latourian terms, it involved a 'diplomacy' between artefacts inhabiting distinct 'modes of existence', from artworks ('the beings of fiction'/ '[FIC]'), to those normally associated with what Latour calls the 'most difficult [domain] of all, the question of Science' (or, 'COR' for 'correspondence').[18]

Three Scenes from an Exhibition:

Object Encounter #1: Kelly Richardson and Annibale Carracci

The three examples of pairings outlined here are between contemporary art objects and art-historical ones; all three are intended to shape encounters with scientific precepts or ideas. As outlined earlier, Montpellier's collection of botanical specimens is truly extraordinary and built over centuries. They are barely able to be displayed, however; an alternative means to dwell upon their significance was required. A modest drawing by Annibale Carracci in the *Musée Atger* offered a way. The drawing was created just before the compulsion to collect the world became a kind of mania and was made possible through the colonial power of the larger European states, including France.

The Carracci drawing is an early picture of landscape as an independent subject, being made between 1602 and 1609. It can readily be taken to mark a momentous moment in the 'birth' of landscape in the European artistic imagination: not in the history of art-historical genre, but as an imaginary space in which fantasies about the history and trajectory of 'civilization' could be projected. The character of the drawing suggests its appealing modernity. It appears it may have been made in en plein air, in the manner adopted by the impressionists as the mark of their own modernity nearly 250 years later. Visitors were invited to 'inspect' the Carracci as akin to a document: as a record of the world-as-it-once-was. The implication was not that the picture 'represents' a landscape, but that we should imagine 'landscape' as being the very 'material' of which it is made—the intellectual materials, that is.

Carracci's gentle Italianate landscape is characterized by a tall, elegant, tree with fluttering leaves: it is a direct predecessor of Claude Lorrain's ink sketches. Claude set the model for subsequent classicizing landscapes across Europe and

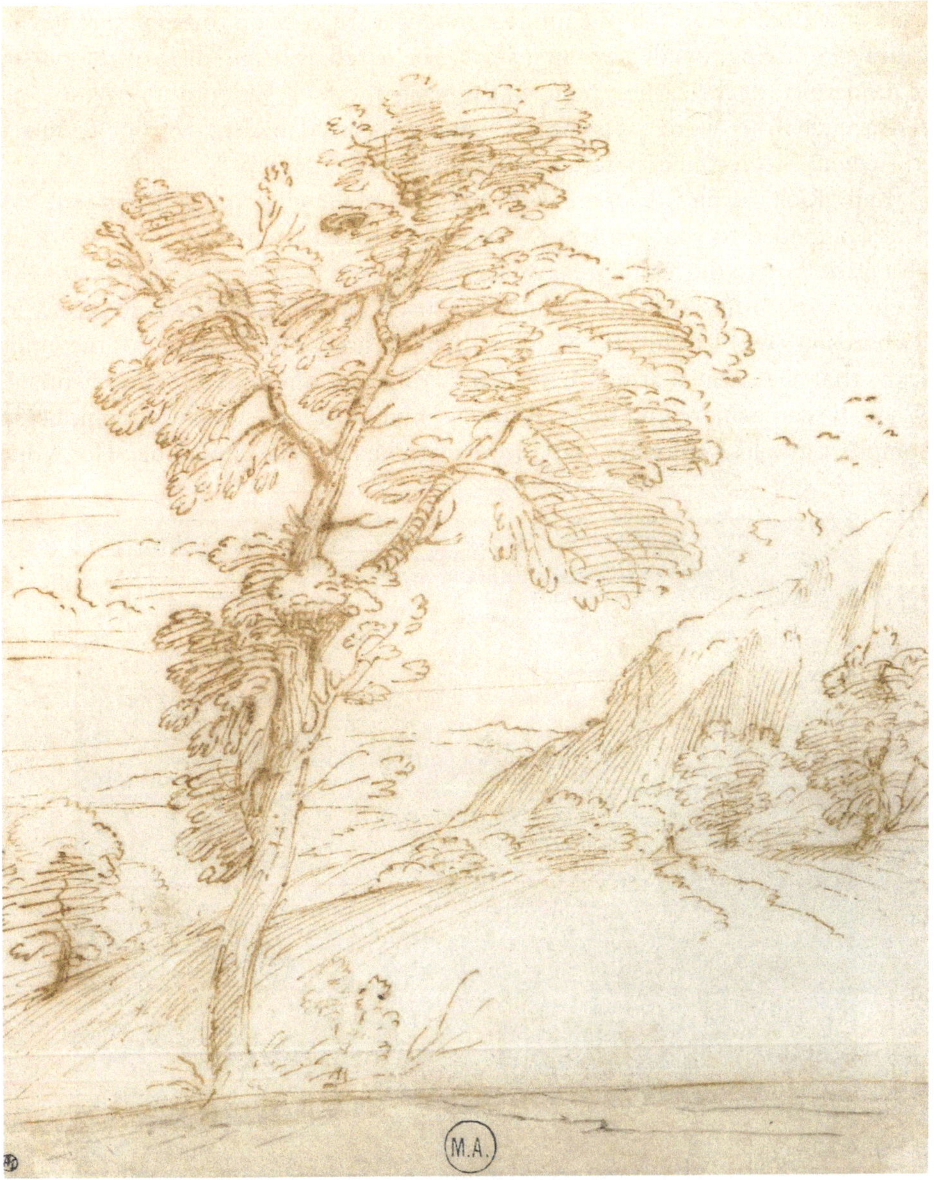

FIGURE 2.3. Annibale Carracci, known as *Landscape with a tree in front of a hill*, 1602–9, brown ink, © and collection of Musée Atget, Montpellier.

pictured the apex and fall of classical civilization. It is easy to read the Carracci drawing in this light. It is also easy to connect the idea of landscape as the space in which 'civilization' can be imagined to contemporary artists' concerns. In their work, the decline and fall of capitalist modernity can begin to be pictured. The Carracci drawing, by all accounts, should be dated as being made at the outset of modernity: at the earliest point in the 'early modern' period of the West. The Carracci, in other words, is an object that has survived modernity from its outset to—what?—its terminal point in the Anthropocene, perhaps.[19]

Kelly Richardson's *Pillars of Dawn* is not only iconographically similar, but is also intended to bear *witness* to landscape. Richardson intends her work to be a *testimony* to the 'sixth great extinction' that some scientists forecast for the twenty-first century: the end of landscape 'itself', in other words, as we know it. Richardson's work is directly based on hypotheses about the future of the landscape that she gathers at first hand from conversations with climate scientists. What she can achieve and they cannot is to painstakingly visualize them, using computer graphics software that allows us to imagine the impossible. Her work

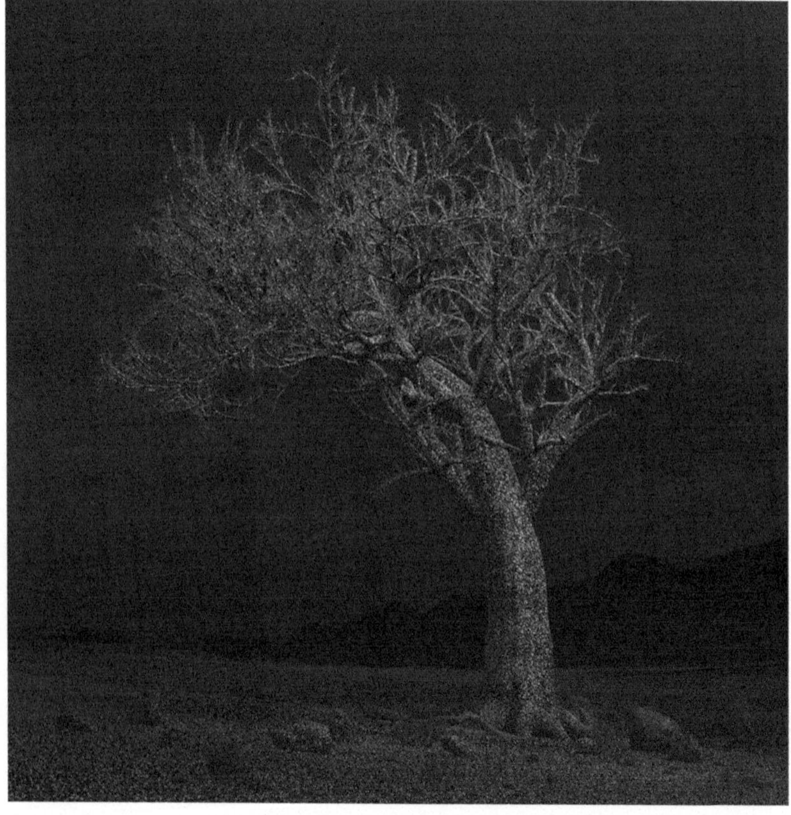

FIGURE 2.4. Kelly Richardson, *Pillars of Dawn*, 2015–18, digital C-type, 100 x 100 cm, © the artist.

invites a 'speculative' future history of the coming century. It is perhaps no accident that speculative-realist and object-oriented thinkers have posed very similar questions to her. Richardson's work echoes Quentin Meillassoux: 'speculative realism asks: can we imagine or access an "ancestral" realm *before humans*, (or after, or without?)'[20] In this Richardson's work is closely aligned to speculative realism in its enthusiasm for the experiments of science fiction. In Robin Mackay's words,

> science fiction [...] is so important to speculative realism. Because [artists are] those [...] who create scenarios that allow us to imagine for a moment what it would be like to actually inhabit a reality where [...] we would soon be destroyed by solar catastrophe [...] What [...] if we were able to live this reality?[21]

Each image in the series *Pillars of Dawn* is populated by an impossible *multitude* of individual objects and pictures several million sculptural crystals. There is, roughly, one crystal in each picture for every species still extant at the time of production—according to some estimates. Richardson acts, in other words, as if the encyclopaedic ambitions of the museum could be condensed into a single artwork. It pictures a kind of inverted Noah's Ark, in which all of the species have been transformed into carbon crystals rather than 'saved' from the oncoming apocalyptic wave of extinctions. If our ambition was to create a museum-of-museums, Richardson's work outstripped this by creating a micro-museum of all life forms, crystallized into carbon. If the museum collections of the past were built through all-encompassing accumulation, Richardson pictures a kind of museum-of-the-dead, in which all species are present in their absence. The work is a kind of memento mori for modernity itself. If this work is like a biblical ark, then so is Montpellier's reserve collection, preserving dead examples of species.

The relationship between Carracci and Richardson is, in short, that they bookend ideas of 'landscape' and modernity, allowing us to glimpse both the *promise* that landscape offered and the sense of *threat* that it now labours under. It is perhaps no accident that object-oriented thinkers including both Latour and Timothy Morton have focused squarely upon the landscape under climate change in their most recent volumes.[22] Famously, Latour posits that the fundamental mark of modernity is that it instituted an imagined division between 'nature' and human 'culture'.[23] His conception of modernity rests on the idea that it was falsely constituted by the imagined, false separation of the world into human (cultural) objects and non-human (natural) ones. For Latour, this distinction has led to, or legitimated destructive behaviours that threaten to obliterate us. Richardson pictures this with extraordinary vividness. Seeing the Carracci drawing in this light—as a participant in and witness to a momentous event in cultural history and in the story of modernity—allows us to suggest that it is *both* speculative *and* evidentiary in character.

Object Encounter #2: Murray Ballard and Anon.

The final work of the entire exhibition was a deliberately perverse choice, in the context of an institution dedicated to the pursuit of scientific knowledge. This work was a photograph by the artist Murray Ballard, who travelled the world for a full ten years documenting the pseudo-science of 'cryonics'. Ballard's resulting body of work was titled as the series *The Prospect of Immortality*. In Ballard's own words, cryonics involves 'the process of freezing a human body after death in the hope that scientific advances might one day restore life'.[24]

Richardson's experiments with historical time also prompted reflection on the hazards or possibilities of seeing museum collections in terms of speculative realist ideas. For Graham Harman, for example, in 'the object-oriented model only the present exists [...] time does not exist simply because only the present ever exists'.[25] By contrast, other figures such as Ian Bogost believe that 'Time is on the *inside* of objects' (rather than being merely meaningfully evidenced by the seductive patina of their surfaces).[26] For curators, such competing claims have high stakes. If museums to take Harman's claim that as 'only the present' exists, they would become unmanageable or logical impossibilities. Harman's 'rejection of everyday common sense' nevertheless served as a spur to the thought experiments here.[27] In particular, Harman's provocations framed another dialogue between a contemporary artist's experiments with the Heideggerian idea of 'being-in-time', and the life cycle of museum objects. If one thing defines all museum objects across disciplines, it is their ability to exist *in perpetuity* well beyond individual human lifetimes.[28]

Ballard's work allowed us to reflect upon the nature and fate of the museum object. Ballard's object presents a human body as if a 'museum object': one preserved in perpetuity, in deep freeze. The work was the sole photograph in the exhibition: the only 'documentary' artwork and the only indexical object. The pairing generated spoke about the potential both of human objects and museum artefacts to survive transhistorically. For cultural historian Andreas Huyssen, the myth of permanence can only be imaginatively satisfied by the 'object encounter'. It is 'the materiality of [museum] objects themselves [that] seems to function like a guarantee' against our own mortality: 'the need for auratic objects, for permanent *embodiments* [...] [for] objects that have lasted through the ages' is an understandable, even logical reaction to the transience of modernity.[29]

The photograph from Ballard's series that was included is titled 'Patient Day Care (dewar being filled with liquid nitrogen)' from October 2006. It was taken at the Alcor Life Extension Foundation in Scottsdale, Arizona. Ballard's work pictures the deep-freeze tank used to preserve a single human corpse 'in perpetuity'. Or at least until 'the manifest destiny of science [is] realized' in the founder of cryonics Robert C. W. Ettinger's words.[30] This belief—this faith, we should say—in the ultimate destination of 'science' has been one of the long-standing leitmotifs of an extreme form of belief in 'modernity'. In Ballard's work, the dead person is never seen as an object; it is the 'scientific' apparatus that holds subjectivity and which is almost fetishized, filling the frame.

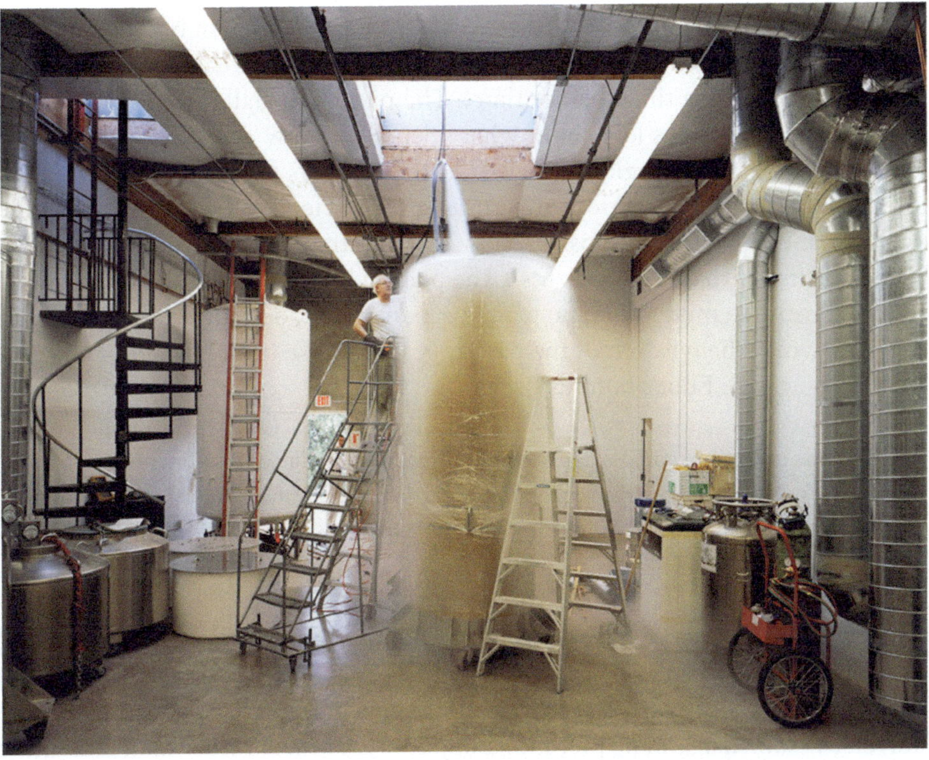

FIGURE 2.5. Murray Ballard, 'Patient day care (Dewar being filled with liquid nitrogen)' from the series The Prospect of Immortality, 2006–16, digital C-type, 100 x 70 cm, © the artist.

As might be imagined, the pairing of Ballard's artwork required some tact—'diplomacy' in Latour's sense, as not to render such a macabre subject as comic or tragic. The object selected was, in the end, a seventeenth-century Baroque sculpture: a miniature carved from black granite barely 9 inches tall. The first oddity is that this artwork is preserved as part of the collections of the *Musée et Conservatoire d'Anatomie* rather than the art collections of the *Musée Atger*. It is ordinarily displayed among thousands of medical specimens, tools and jars of human remains. More oddly still given the skill and labour involved, no documentation or attribution about the object exists. Not only has the undoubtedly gifted sculptor of this object been long forgotten, but the life history of the object prior to its entrance into the museum has been lost entirely. Its career in the world is a matter of speculative enquiry.

As a carved miniature this sculpture's delicacy is beguiling. It combines two motifs. First, it depicts an exquisite domed funerary temple. But in the centre of this temple is a carving of a foetus: a human object, but one that appears somewhat other than human. If Ballard conceals from us the human body in the time immediately after its life has ended, then this sculpture reveals the time before life should begin: the time 'before time'. The pairing of Ballard's work and this anonymous sculpture is less about what science can now accomplish than what we *desire* of it, at an imaginative level. As Ballard puts it, one fantasy that even infected political life at various junctures is that 'science' can simply solve 'the problem of death'.[31] Ballard asks simply whether the 'moderns' are more sound in their attitudes than the 'ancients'. The pairing here tried to untie the intuitive equation between modernity and progress many make, on Latourian grounds. In Ballard's work, the wisdom of the past appears to have been mislaid by the present, echoing T. S. Eliot's famous lines:

> Endless invention, endless experiment / Brings knowledge of motion, but not of stillness / Knowledge of speech, but not of silence [...] Where is the wisdom we have lost in knowledge? Where is the knowledge we have lost in information?[32]

Object Encounter #3: Daniel Brown and Jan Breughel

A third pairing also invited reflection on the natural history collections of the university—albeit again, by presenting objects *about* them rather than presenting those artefacts themselves. As outlined, the most extensive archives are those of dried plant species, collected across continents and centuries. For many years, these have been of relatively finite use scientifically, acting as a reserve collection. However, as forecasts of the changes to the planet become ever more alarming, artists' attention has turned to the idea of alternative ways of either preserving or remaking species. Some recent estimates suggest that up to 80 per cent of all biomass is flora rather than fauna.[33] This is where object-oriented thinking has begun to impact on artists' understandings. If we were to see 'life' on earth *quantitatively*—rather than imagine ourselves as the sole species occupying the apex of a quasi-medieval 'great chain of being'—then we might also be to act differently.

Despite humans' disproportionate impact on planetary atmospheric systems, if the biomass on planet earth is principally plant life, then it should not be surprising that artists have turned to thinking about the objecthood of plants and flowers. A third pairing began with the artwork *On Growth and Form* by the digital artist Daniel Brown, a version of which is held by the Victoria & Albert Museum (V&A), London. Brown's work is one of the very few in the V&A to be described as "software": in other words it is an app.[34] For Brown, the calculating power of twenty-first century computers has enabled machines to generate an infinite range of objects from a finite range of variables, just as evolution has.

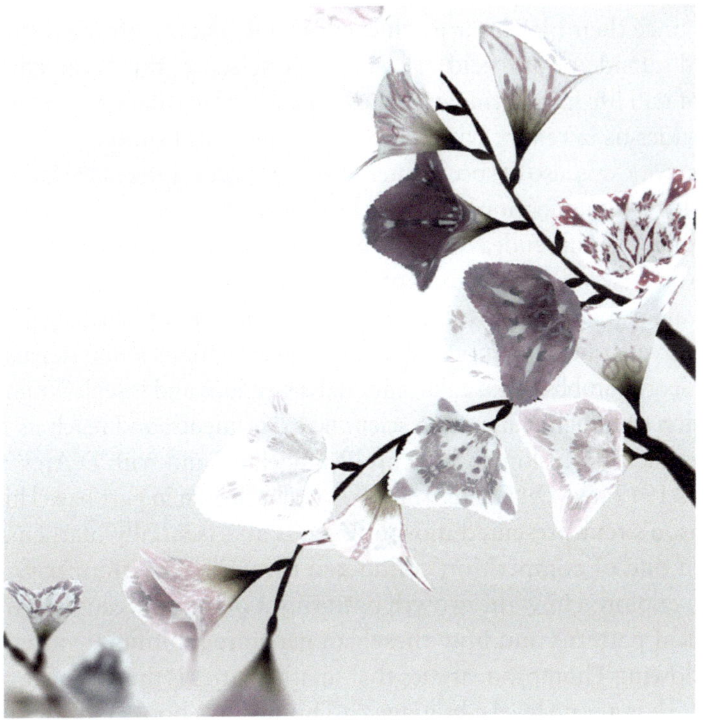

FIGURE 2.6. Daniel Brown, *On Growth and Form*, 1999–2013, computer programme, display size variable, © the artist.

In *On Growth and Form*, Brown creates multiple new 'species' of flower, each of which employs complex mathematical algorithms in order to continuously animate and grow new petals (Fig. 2.6). Each and every flower seems to explode into a permanent state of bloom. These objects exist as sculptural three-dimensional objects in virtual space. Each has what we might call an independent life of its own, mutating through random combinations of variables. The artist does not predetermine these combinations but allows them to be generated anew, continually. Brown's work exemplifies the idea that 'the scientific' and 'the artistic' are no longer separate or separable. It also exemplifies the idea that the 'human' and the 'virtual' are not readily separable.

Put in other terms, Brown's flowers in *On Growth and Form* are a never-ending continuous flow of animate 'life' that defy the laws of mortality that affect all ordinary living things. Each new individual flowering is, just like its organic counterpart, a unique configuration of patterns that is never-to-be-repeated. Each is unique, like a snowflake, being composed from algorithms whose variables effectively allow for an effectively infinite range of permutations and possible outcomes. But Brown's flowers never visibly 'die': they remain frozen in suspended animation once their blooms are achieved, merely sliding off the bottom of their screens and outside of our field of vision. In one sense, this is the entire basis of the genre of still life in painting: to keep in a state of permanent preservation that which provides us in reality with a fleeting moment of beauty.

Brown's work was also of special interest to *A Scientific Encounter* because it can be read as the logical culmination of one art historical narrative: that which plots artists' relationship to scientific endeavour. It is easy to imagine a history of quasi-'scientific' attempts to understand the structures of flora and fauna through European art history. Such a genealogy might begin with Leonardo da Vinci's and Michelangelo's dissection studies at the very outset of 'modern' medical investigations in the Renaissance; continue with George Stubbs's painstaking animal dissections and Joseph Wright of Derby's dramatization of Enlightenment-era scientific experiments; and reach its full fruition with figures such as Ruskin and the pre-Raphaelites, and with D'Arcy Wentworth Thompson's 1917 text *On Growth and Form* that Brown in part based his work on.

Thompson's text presented morphology as an essentially mathematical issue rather than one of competition conducted through evolution, *contra* Darwin. Thompson explored how the growth patterns of plants and animals are based on mathematical patterns and how these can generate an infinite variety of forms. Brown, following Thompson, argues that 'mathematics is the language of nature'.[35] Brown's work is at one level a homage to Thompson's book: it draws upon attention to the peculiar career of the text in both scientific-technological and artistic circles. The film-maker Patrick Keiller has recently described Thompson's text as central to the history of twentieth-century modern art and architecture and as having a role even in the history of technology. In Keiller's words, Thompson's

> scientific successor was Alan Turing, who had read the book when, in 1941, at Bletchley Park, he and Joan Clarke began discussing the appearance of the Fibonacci series in diaries. Turing studied morphogenesis increasingly after about 1950, using the Manchester computer.[36]

The evidence is that Turing engaged with the book deeply—that 'in 1954, he had developed equations that could account for some of the simpler patterns found in monocellular Radiolaria, the subjects of one of the most striking illustrations in Thompson's book'.[37]

Thompson's text was undoubtedly a key point of reference for modern artists as diverse as Jackson Pollock, Henry Moore, Richard Hamilton, Nigel Henderson, Eduardo Paolozzi, William Turnbull Victor Pasmore, Naum Gabo and Laszlo Moholy-Nagy; and an inspiration for canonical modern movement architects including Mies van der Rohe, Leslie Martin and Jørn Utzon.[38] Keiller's recent thesis suggests that Thompson's *On Growth and Form* might even be described as the single most important text in the development of European modernism from the 1920s to the 1950s. If so, this places Brown's work both as a successor to canonical modernism and to the intellectual developments that Thompson helped unleash. Thompson's work has also been reviewed as anticipating object-oriented thought. As Keiller has noted: 'Thompson blurred the distinction between living and non-living things, in opposition to the early twentieth-century view among many scientists and others that living organisms were animated by a "vital force" somehow exempted from the laws of physics'.[39] This is not a bad summation of the achievements of object-oriented thought.

The pairing of Brown's work was with a rare, unfinished Jan Brueghel water-colour sketch from the *Musée Atget*. The sketch reveals a burgeoning collection of fruit and flowers: a still-life painting created as a private study rather than a public presentation. Breughel's work is filled with supersaturated, brightly coloured fruits and flora, testifying to the abundance of 'nature' by adapting the classical imagery of the burgeoning garland. This unites Brown's work with Breughel's. In the latter's work, every object is in luscious, tantalizing bloom, as if at the very moment of its peak ripeness or fertility. This much is not unusual; but the remarkable aspect of Breughel's private study is that it is left unfinished, as if in a permanent state of becoming. The 2016 exhibition at the Metropolitan Museum, New York, titled *Unfinished: Thoughts Left Visible*, placed our thoughts into focus.[40] As the title implies, such 'unfinished' works 'give insight into the process of their creation' far more than finished canvases and even 'extend [...] the boundaries of art into both space and time'.[41] Brown's work is 'unfinished' in that it is permanently in motion—in a perpetual state of becoming. His series is 'crafted' through complex mathematics with sufficient variables that however long the work runs, the precise shapes of each flower is unique: despite only lasting for seconds, no two flower-ings will ever be the same.

As mentioned, in Latour's recent writings, the core question at stake is what we might call the nature of 'nature', when the human species faces a threat to its very existence, and the extinction of other species is historically unprecedented. Brown's

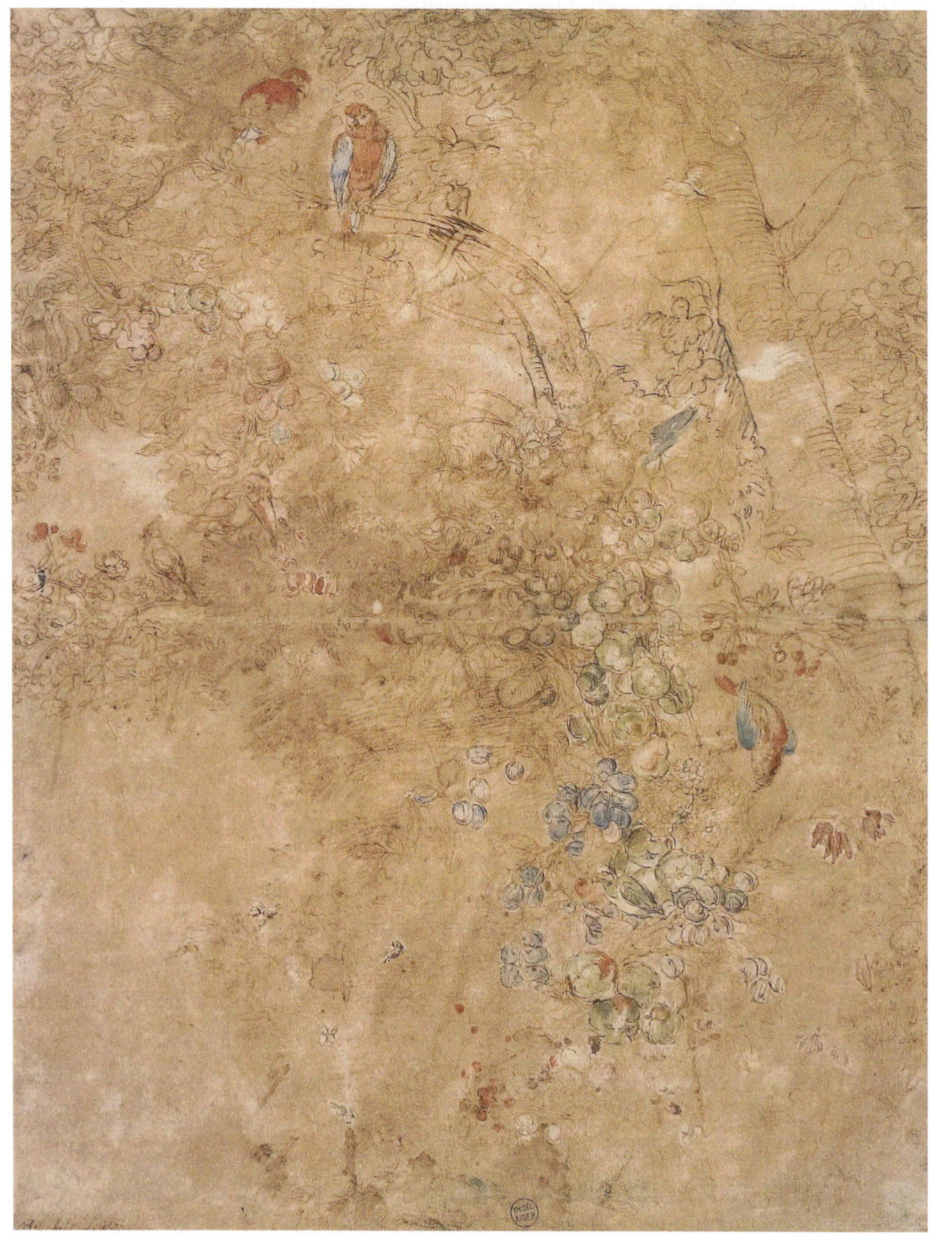

FIGURE 2.7. Jan Breughel, known as *Flowers, fruits, trees and birds*, date unknown, 48.7 × 38.4 cm, © and collection of Musée Atget, Montpellier.

work offers a 'second', parallel nature in virtual space that is its own, independent reality, forever changing. Rather than inquisitorial or adversarial, Brown's is a genuinely *speculative* enquiry into what nature might be if remade from scratch. One of Brown's achievements is to forge a compelling image of a 'new' suite of non-human species that are 'independent' of 'us'—and to do so through the very means of twenty-first-century technological and material 'progress'.

Brown's works are ordinarily animations that *model* of the endless patterns of growth that exist in the natural world. But instead of being pale imitations of 'real' flowers, his works might be seen as performing magical transformations, creating teeming life from inanimate code. As the art critic Clement Greenberg remarked, 'The avant-garde poet or artist tries in effect to imitate God by creating something *valid solely on its own terms, in the way nature itself is valid* [...] something *given*, increate, independent of meanings, similars, or originals'.[42] Brown's work, in its endlessness and its infinite variety, offered visitors an alternative reality for us to inhabit: a nature that is not consolatory, but exists *in itself*, quite independent of us. This much is a reality that, if the sixth great extinction does come to pass, we will have to face in a rather different way.

To conclude: the 'object encounters' generated here were experimental attempts to both treat artworks as artefacts or specimens: as objects that we see in terms of their 'tool-being' rather than as disinterested, ahistorical aesthetic productions. Elsewhere in the exhibition, the reverse strategy was applied to 'ordinary' objects whose tool-status and functionality were downplayed in favour of their specifically visual interest. This strategic attempt to generate apparent category errors in viewers' imaginations should be seen as related to the broader dissolution or confusion between human and non-human, or animate and inanimate that speculative realism has fostered in art practice. Richard Grusin has diagnosed a 'nonhuman turn' in the humanities in which 'decentering the human [is undertaken] in favour of a turn toward and concern for the nonhuman, understood variously in terms of animals [...] organic and geophysical systems, materiality or technologies'.[43] And the context for this, here, should be seen as one where, as Peter Osborne argues, artworks are the only category of object ordinarily allowed to possess a kind of quasi-human subjectivity. In this sense, artworks have finally become 'decentred' themselves in the object world, and become recognized as both special types of production and as 'non-human' rather than merely surrogates for their human creators. This means that they can no longer be merely readily assimilated into our consciousness as extensions of ourselves, or enjoyed as if harmless aids to our own psychic fulfilment or completion. It means, instead, that their full strangeness and alien-ness must begin to be acknowledged—just as that of other parts of the material world must be, in their own ways.

NOTES

1. Bruno Latour, *We Have Never Been Modern* (Cambridge, MA: Harvard University Press, 1993), 96.

2. Mitt Romney reported on BBC News website, 12 August 2011 [online] available at https://www.bbc.co.uk/news/av/world-us-canada-14511692/mitt-romney-corporations-are-people (accessed 22 September 2018).

3. A list of participants and summary information are available at the website http://www.ngca.co.uk/exhibs/default.asp?id=238&prnt=18 (no longer available).

4. Michel Foucault, 'Of Other Spaces: Utopias and Heterotopias', *Architecture/Mouvement/Continuité*, October, 1984; first published as 'Des Espace Autres', March 1967, trans. Jay Miskowiec. (Foucault concludes his definition of heterotopias by arguing that 'in civilisations without [...] heterotopias [...] dreams dry up'.); D. Preziosi, 'Epilogue: The Art of Art History', in *The Art of Art History*, ed. D. Preziosi, (Oxford: Oxford University Press, 2009), 488–503.

5. Ibid.

6. Walter Benjamin's phrase in *The Arcades Project*, Volute 1053, translated by Rolf Tiedemann in the passage *'palpable knowledge'* (gefühltes Wissen), which is 'not only nurtured by what appears sensorily before the eyes, but which is also able to assimilate mere knowledge'. In Rolf Tiedemann, 'Dialectics at a Standstill: Approaches to the Passagen-Werk', in *Walter Benjamin: Critical Evaluations in Cultural Theory: Volume 1 – Philosophy*, ed. Peter Osborne, (Abingdon: Routledge, 2005), 232–56, reference 239.

7. Donald Preziosi, *The Brain of the Earth's Body* (Minnesota: University of Minnesota Press, 2003).

8. Ibid., 1.

9. Graham Harman, *Tool-Being: Heidegger and the Metaphysics of Objects* (Chicago IL: Open Court Publishing, 2002).

10. Latour, *We Have Never Been Modern*, 229.

11. Bruno Latour, *An Inquiry into Modes of Existence: An Anthropology of the Moderns*, trans. Cathy Porter (Cambridge, MA: Harvard University Press, 2013), 78.

12. Ibid., 78.

13. Bruno Latour, *Reassembling the Social: An Introduction to Actor-network-theory* (Oxford: Oxford University Press, 2005), 237.

14. Latour, *An Inquiry into Modes of Existence*, 42.

15. Susan Pearce, *On Collecting: An Investigation into Collecting in the European Tradition* (Abingdon: Routledge, 1995), 20, 21.

16. Benedict Anderson, *Imagined Communities: Reflections on the Origin and Spread of Nationalism* (London: Verso, 1983).

17. In the introductory chapter of Mieke Bal, *Travelling Concepts in the Humanities: A Rough Guide* (Toronto: University of Toronto Press, 2002), 10.

18. Latour, *An Inquiry into Modes of Existence*, 295; 70, 233.

19. This coinage was used by ecologist Eugene F. Stoermer in the 1980s, and given widespread currency by scientist Paul J. Crutzen in articles form 2000 and 2002, namely, Paul J. Crutzen, 'Geology of Mankind', *Nature* 415 (6867): 23, 3 January 2002, [online] available at https://www.nature.com/articles/415023a (accessed 6 July 2018); J. Paul, Crutzen and Eugene F. Stoermer, *IGBP Global Change Newsletter* 41 (Stockholm: Royal Swedish Academy of Sciences, 2000), [online] available at http://www.igbp.net/globalchange/anthropocene.4.1b8ae20512db692f2a680009238.html (accessed 6 July 2018).

20. Quentin Meillassoux, *After Finitude: An Essay on the Necessity of Contingency*, trans. Ray Brassier (London: Bloomsbury, 2010), 10.

21. Robin Mackay, 'The Real Thing: Panel Discussion', (London: Tate Britain, 3 September 2010), [online] available at https://www.urbanomic.com/document/the-real-thing-panel-discussion/ (accessed 6 August 2018).

22. Bruno Latour's most recent two books at the time of writing are *Down to Earth: Politics in the New Climatic Regime*, trans. Cathy Porter (Cambridge: Polity, 2018), and *Facing Gaia: Eight Lectures on the New Climatic Regime*, trans. Cathy Porter (Cambridge: Polity, 2017). Morton's volumes include *Being Ecological* (London: Pelican, 2018); *Dark Ecology: For a Logic of Future Coexistence* (New York: Colombia University Press, 2016); *The Ecological Thought* (Cambridge, MA: Harvard University Press, 2010); and *Ecology Without Nature: Rethinking Environmental Aesthetics* (Cambridge, MA: Harvard University Press, 2007).

23. Latour, *We Have Never Been Modern*, trans. Catherine Porter (Cambridge, MA: Harvard University Press, 1993). Originally published in French as *Nous n'avons jamais été modernes: Essai d'anthropologie symétrique* (Paris: La Découverte, 1991).

24. Murray Ballard at his website http://murrayballard.com/work/the-prospect-of-immortality/ (accessed 23 July 2018).

25. Graham Harman, 'The Road to Objects', *continent.* 1, no. 3 (2011): 171–79, reference 176, [online] available at http://continentcontinent.cc/index.php/continent/article/view/48 (accessed 23 July 2018).

26. Peter Gratton, 'Bogost on Time and OOO': *Philosophy in a Time of Error* (2012) [online] available at https://philosophyinatimeoferror.com/2012/07/05/bogost-on-time-and-ooo/ (accessed 23 July 2018) (emphasis added).

27. Harman, 'The Road to Objects', 171.

28. Martin Heidegger, *Being and Time* (New York: State University of New York Press, [1927] 2010).

29. Andreas Huyssen, *Twilight Memories: Marking Time in a Culture of Amnesia* (London: Routledge, 1995), 33.

30. Murray Ballard, *The Prospect of Immortality*, [online] available at http://murrayballard.com/work/the-prospect-of-immortality/ (accessed 1 May 2020).

31. Ibid.

32. T. S. Eliot, *The Rock* (New York: Harcourt, Brace, 1934), 7.

33. Yinon M. Bar-On, Rob Phillips, Ron Milo, *Proceedings of the National Academy of Sciences*, no. 115, 25 (2018): 6506–11; [online] available at http://www.pnas.org/content/115/25/6506 (accessed 5 November 2018).

34. See http://collections.vam.ac.uk/item/O1247182/on-growth-and-form-digital-artwork-brown-daniel/ (accessed 29 August 2018).

35. Interview with the author, 14 July 2018.

36. Patrick Keiller, 'The Shape of Things to Come', *Tate Etc* no. 30 (Spring 2014): 88–95.

37. Ibid., 93.

38. Ibid., 88, 92.

39. Ibid., 92.

40. See https://www.metmuseum.org/exhibitions/listings/2016/unfinished (accessed 1 May 2020).

41. Ibid.

42. Clement Greenberg, 'Avant Garde and Kitsch', in *Art and Culture: Critical Essays* (Boston: Beacon Press, 1989), 6 (emphasis added).

43. Richard Grusin, 'Introduction', in *The Nonhuman Turn*, ed. R. Grusin (Minneapolis: University of Minnesota Press, 2015), vii.

3

'A Readiness to Find What Surrounds Us Strange and Odd': Objects in the Alternative Curiosity Museum

Marion Endt-Jones

Abstract

To begin with, this chapter compares recent 'alternative curiosity museums' and collection interventions modelled on visual and epistemological practices of the sixteenth- and seventeenth-century cabinet of curiosities—either conceived by artists as alternative natural history or anthropology displays or originating in private natural history and anthropological collections—in the light of French curator and critic Nicolas Bourriaud's critique of cabinets of curiosities as passivity-inducing, hermetic environments reserved for insiders. Examining narrative strategies of display and interpretation, and considering the concept of 'wild museum' (Angela Jannelli) and a 'return to curiosity' (Stephen Bann), I ask if museum projects such as the Museum of Jurassic Technology (Los Angeles), Museum der Unerhörten Dinge (Berlin), Musée de la Chasse et de la Nature (Paris) and Château d'Oiron (western France) succeed in avoiding passivity and exclusivity.

Next, this chapter analyses two contrasting tendencies in recent natural history museum display: towards an aestheticized accumulation of specimens behind enormous glass screens reminiscent of both art installations and shop window displays (as exemplified by Manchester Museum's 'Living Worlds' gallery and Museum für Naturkunde Berlin's 'Biodiversity Wall') on the one hand, and towards a 'spotlight on single specimens' type arrangement as employed by the Natural History Museum's 'Treasures' exhibition in the Cadogan Gallery on the other. Whether through dazzling abundance or extraordinary rarity, both aim to instil wonder and curiosity in visitors.

This chapter argues that modelling contemporary museum displays on the sixteenth- and seventeenth-century cabinet of curiosities turns museum objects and specimens into curious objects, with powerful implications for the visitor's museum experience and reception of objects. Relieved from its pressure to signify and to act as evidence for scientific facts and historical chronology, the specimen's materiality and subjective value come to the fore, allowing the affective responses of curiosity and wonder. This effect is augmented when specimens are juxtaposed with contemporary artworks, as in the Musée de la Chasse et de la Nature. In their double sense of astonishment on the one hand and desire to know more on the other, curiosity and wonder encourage an in-depth engagement with pressing contemporary issues ranging from post-truth politics to environmental degradation.

Interspersed throughout the discussion are alternative dictionary entries for relevant key concepts, such as 'curiosity', 'classification' and 'museum'. Peppered with references to popular culture, humour, personal preference and other subjective elements and idiosyncrasies, they take inspiration from the alternative curiosity museum's strategies of questioning the Western reliance, post-Enlightenment, on academic rigour, scientific fact and historical accuracy.

Specimen: 1. Object imbued with scientific authority. 2. A pickled one, a pinned one and a stuffed one meet in a museum [...] 3. Often dead in jars, display cases, dioramas, cabinets, frames and boxes, on mounts and stands. 4. In vitro, alcoholic, dusty or online.[1]

'I dream of a new age of curiosity', the French philosopher Michel Foucault declared in an interview with the newspaper *Le Monde* in 1980.[2] While, according to Foucault, we witness at present an overabundance of things to be known accompanied by a profound desire to know them, society lacks appropriate means of processing and distributing information and knowledge. In order to overcome this problem of inadequate mediation, Foucault envisions stripping curiosity from traces of stigmatization by the Church, philosophy and certain strands of science throughout the centuries—and ultimately to proclaim 'a new age of curiosity' characterized by care, passion and readiness to embrace the unexpected.[3]

Several developments in the contemporary art and museum world suggest that the new age of curiosity that Foucault called for almost 40 years ago is well upon us. Compiling a list of recent Wunderkammer-inspired shows and related publications, one quickly realizes that the new age of curiosity is, fundamentally, a phenomenon carried by specific exhibition and display strategies, by museum and gallery practice.[4] The recent spate of academic scholarship on curiosity and the Wunderkammer[5] was in fact preceded by two major exhibitions organized in the last two decades of the twentieth century: the 'Wunderkammer' section of the Venice Biennale under the overriding topic of 'Art and Science', curated by art historian Adalgisa Lugli in 1986; and *Wunderkammer des Abendlandes* at the Kunst- und Ausstellungshalle der Bundesrepublik Deutschland in Bonn of 1994–95. Interestingly, both shows established a lineage between the sixteenth- and seventeenth-century 'age of curiosity',[6] the French surrealist group's concerns with taxonomy and classification, and contemporary art and museum practice.[7]

I argue that the revival of interest in cabinets of curiosities is not only inspired by a critical re-evaluation of the legacies of surrealism,[8] but also by artists practicing 'institutional critique'[9] from the 1960s onwards: artists whose questioning of institutional authority involves archival methods and processes of collecting and juxtaposition; artists who probe ways in which institutions produce knowledge by engaging with dilettantism and protocols of natural history; and artists for whom the interdisciplinary, subversive impulse of the cabinet of curiosities—as propounded by the surrealists—has emerged as a critical tool, both visually and epistemologically (the American artist Mark Dion is certainly one of the key figures in this respect).[10] In a similar vein, a number of what I call 'alternative curiosity museums', conceived by artists, amateurs and curators with explicit reference to the sixteenth- and seventeenth-century cabinet of curiosities, challenge the foundations of the modernist 'white cube' gallery and museum[11] by deliberately blurring the boundary between museum, laboratory and permanent art installation. Examples include David Wilson's Museum of Jurassic Technology in Culver City, Los Angeles (opened in 1988); Roland Albrecht's Museum der Unerhörten Dinge in Schöneberg, Berlin (founded in 1998); Reinhard Zabka's Lügenmuseum in Radebeul near Dresden (opened in 2012); The Viktor Wynd Museum of Curiosities, Fine Art & Natural History in Hackney, London (established in 2014); Joanna Ebenstein's Morbid Anatomy Museum in Brooklyn, New York (2014–16); the Seafoam Palace Museum, run by an artist collective in Detroit since 2015; *Curios & Mirabilia*, curated by Jean-Hubert Martin at Château d'Oiron in the region of Poitou-Charentes in France (and permanently installed there since 1993); and the Musée de la Chasse et de la Nature in Paris, conceived by head curator Claude d'Anthenaise between 1998 and 2007.[12]

Arguably, however, the supposedly ideology-laden modernist white cube museum and gallery has in recent years, not least owing to artists' interventions, changed into a more open organism prepared for self-scrutiny—the kind of institution that museologist Duncan Grewcock describes as 'connected, plural, distributed, multi-vocal, affective, material, embodied, experiential, political, performative and participatory'.[13] In light of this 'relational turn'[14] in museum studies and practice, I discuss four case studies (Museum of Jurassic Technology, Museum der Unerhörten Dinge, Musée de la Chasse et de la Nature and Château d'Oiron) to consider the unique contribution the alternative curiosity museum offers to the museum landscape. Do objects and specimens signify differently when they become *curious* objects, released from institutional instrumentalization and from the pressure to substantiate historical narrative and scientific knowledge? What exactly is the nature of the affective responses and experiences these objects and displays elicit from the visitor? Does the alternative curiosity museum merely present a nostalgic nod to the sixteenth- and seventeenth-century cabinet of curiosities, or does it encourage a more profound epistemological engagement with the historical model of the Wunderkammer? And finally, what is the alternative curiosity museum's critical, political potential?

Museums: Laboratories of the Marvellous?

Museum: 1. Shrine of the muses. 2. Findlen, Paula (1989), 'The Museum: Its Classical Etymology and Renaissance Genealogy', Journal of the History of Collections, *1:1, pp. 59–78. 3. Where to go on a rainy day.*

According to Mark Dion, the ideal museum resembles a laboratory of the marvellous, a place stirring curiosity and imagination, 'a kind of visually and intellectually exciting space'.[15] Rather than answering questions via labels, information sheets and lengthy wall panels, the display should, by letting the objects speak for themselves, encourage learning by stimulating thought-provoking questions: 'I'm interested in how knowledge is generated through objects, through things that I can be in a certain space with. So I find that that's part of my passion for museums: you get to see the thing'.[16] A recent issue of the magazine of ICOM, the International Council of Museums, describes the expectations of museum visitors in similar terms:

> For most visitors, the best museums are those which are capable of surprising, impressing and enchanting them. They go there to see in real life what screens aren't able to deliver, to take part in a collective experience of the museum as concrete space and to deepen their knowledge. If all of these elements are present, the visitor will have an inspiring, powerful, *unexpected* experience.[17]

Anthropologist Nicholas Thomas places a return to curiosity at the heart of the current 'museum boom' and visitor experience. He argues that, although curiosity and curious objects became suspect with the onset of the Enlightenment, deemed by the political philosopher Edmund Burke 'the most superficial of all the affections' in 1757,[18] curiosity—'marked by an eagerness to encounter what is new or unfamiliar, an openness to difference and perhaps a willingness to suspend judgement'—allows museum-goers to make 'unexpected discoveries […] that enable you to know something new or that take you somewhere you have not previously been'.[19] Or, in the words of Mark Elliott, Senior Curator of Anthropology at the Museum of Archaeology and Anthropology in Cambridge: 'That's why I go to museums: because they are where the unexpected happens'.[20] Envisaging a similar approach to curating art exhibitions, curator and critic Ralph Rugoff concurs:

> The most thrilling moments in any exhibition are when the art catches us off-guard, takes us by surprise and launches us into moments of unpredictable insight, wonder and pleasure. [...] The most compelling adventures in contemporary curating set out [...] to re-engage viewers by catching them unawares.[21]

Surprise and the unexpected—or curiosity, wonder and the marvellous—are the very affects the alternative curiosity museum capitalizes on. Thus the Seafoam Palace defines itself as 'a museum of absurdity [...] designed to stimulate a sense of playfulness and wonder' and entices prospective exhibition visitors and event participants with the following message: 'We invite you on a journey to the strangely hued edges of your imagination, to the outlandish and perplexing, and look forward to leaving you inspired and confused',[22] and the Musée de la Chasse et de la Nature acknowledges in accompanying interpretative materials that the nature of its displays requires visitors to remain constantly on their toes—their 'senses on the alert',[23] prepared for 'an emotional experience', 'experimentation', 'humour', 'discovery', 'ambiguity', 'uncertainty', 'play', 'surprise' and 'magic'.[24]

Cabinets of Curiosities: 'Boudoirs Earmarked for Experts'?

Wunderkammer: 1. Cabinet of curiosities, kunstkammer, theatrum mundi, memory theatre, studiolo, treasury, workshop, library, encyclopaedic structure, cornucopia, archive, microcosm, alchemist's lair, laboratory, apothecary. 2. Kunstschrank. 3. Catch-all term for disorderly, unruly collections. 4. Where wonders never cease.

One might acknowledge that this relentless readiness to be surprised and amazed requires an exceptionally engaged, committed viewer prone to this kind of stimulation, for in order to truly interact with the exhibition, he or she must overcome several intellectual and actual barriers; and the inability, or reluctance, to do so could lead to passivity and frustration. A charge historically brought forward against wonder is, in fact, the risk of political capitulation and intellectual passivity it entails: countering Aristotelian and Cartesian notions of wonder as a catalyst of human enquiry, the origin of all philosophy and learning, seventeenth-century Dutch philosopher Baruch Spinoza, among others, argued that wonder represented an epistemological cop-out and intellectual shutdown. According to Spinoza, we passively marvel at a stunning object instead of acting or attempting to know, because its absolute novelty does not recall anything else with which our mind could establish connections; as a result, it simply shuts down.[25] Referring to this passive inclination, the philosopher of science Isabelle Stengers marks 'wonder' 'a dangerous term, […] because of its association with mysticism, bowing down in front of what cannot be understood'.[26]

And what, indeed, if our mind began to stall and break down even at an earlier stage? The possibility that an installation such as the Museum of Jurassic Technology might become a hermetic environment reserved for insiders is considered by French curator and critic Nicolas Bourriaud, who claims in his book *Relational Aesthetics* of 1998, polemically, that 'the spread of "curiosity cabinets", which we have been witnessing for some time, but also the elitist attitudes of certain people in art circles, attest to an absolute loathing of the public place and shared aesthetic experimentation, in favour of boudoirs earmarked for experts'.[27] Bourriaud regards the cabinet of curiosities as an exclusive, restricted space diametrically opposed to the relational, interactive, collaborative, participatory and socially engaged artistic practices he identifies as characteristic of contemporary production. I would argue that this proposition presumes a somewhat limited notion of the curiosity cabinet; although it is certainly true that historical cabinets of curiosities were accessible only to a select few, recent scholarship in art history and the history of science has convincingly established that assembling and maintaining a collection of curiosities involved a rich set of diverse, relational activities, including travelling, exploring, experimenting, writing, publishing, exchanging and interacting with the scientific community and institutions.[28] Moreover, Samuel Quiccheberg's *Inscriptiones vel Tituli Theatri Amplissimi* of 1565—a manual written for Duke Albrecht V of Bavaria which is often considered the first museological treatise—lays out an expanded notion of *Kunstkammer*, which includes research spaces and workshops forming a hub of related activities, among them a library, print shop, wood turnery, foundry, mint and laboratory ('theatrum sapientiae').[29] Devising a similarly all-encompassing, encyclopaedic model around 1700, the German philosopher and mathematician Gottfried Wilhelm Leibniz envisaged a 'theatrum naturae et artis', a cabinet of curiosities accompanied by a menagerie, gardens, grottos, an anatomical theatre, workshops, laboratories, a concert hall, a library and more.[30]

Museum of Jurassic Technology: A Detective Challenge

> *Collector: 1. Someone who is passionate about things. 2. Usually combines a compulsive love of objects with an impossible desire for totality. 3. Was Noah the first?*

However, since curiosity and wonder are affective and cognitive responses varying considerably from individual to individual, the possibility of a limited reception of museum objects cannot be ruled out. Audience interactions at two alternative curiosity museums, the Museum of Jurassic Technology and the Museum der Unerhörten Dinge, serve to illustrate this point. In the former, a small, dimly lit storefront space situated on a large boulevard in West Los Angeles, film producer David Wilson exhibits Wunderkammer objects, such as a fruit stone carving similar to the cherry stone carved with 185 human faces and heads on display in Dresden's Green Vault[31] and a human horn allegedly originating from Tradescant's Ark, a collection of rarities assembled by John Tradescant, both the Elder and Younger, during the seventeenth century, which later formed the nucleus of the Ashmolean Museum in Oxford;[32] and objects belonging to other areas of natural history, anthropology and the history of science, such as an African ant growing a proboscis from fungal spores and a South American bat supposedly capable of flying through solid surfaces.[33] Combining the intimacy of a house museum with the narrative possibilities of a three-dimensional storytelling device, the display fosters uncertainty about the truthfulness of the stories being told. Rugoff argues that 'one way curators can reanimate our curiosity is by instilling doubt about what it is we're looking at, and what rules or criteria we should be using to examine it'.[34] Indeed, visitors and commentators often spend their time at the museum trying to establish whether the exhibits are authentic and the stories behind them are true; they turn into determined detectives on a hunt for clues and on a quest to solve a riddle.[35] This kind of either/or response suggests that the display's objective of overruling ways of thinking in binary categories—entrenched in Western culture and philosophy since the Enlightenment—such as fact versus fiction, reality versus imagination, or historical versus contemporary,[36] fails spectacularly.

Museum der Unerhörten Dinge: 'A Literary Wunderkammer'

Curator: 1. Someone who cares (Lat. cura—care). 2. Everybody who has something 'bespoke', an Instagram feed, a playlist, or simply lunch, if one believes the hipsters.

Roland Albrecht, photographer and artist with a medical background and founder of the Museum der Unerhörten Dinge in Berlin, takes a slightly different approach. The museum title plays on the triple entendre of the word 'unerhört', which can mean 'unheard' and 'unheard of', but also 'outrageous' and 'incredible'.[37] Like the exhibits of the Museum of Jurassic Technology, the objects displayed in the Museum der Unerhörten Dinge are unusual things one would not come across in a more official, mainstream or scientific institution; and both curators quote the discipline-defying impetus of the Wunderkammer as their most important historical point of reference.[38] But unlike Wilson, Albrecht does not even pretend that objects such as the fur of a Japanese bonsai stag or the fossilized skeleton of a 'Havling', a hermaphrodite 'missing link' between amphibian and reptile found in Scandinavia, might really exist. In the mission statement of his museum, he explains that he collects—in fact, the term he prefers is 'find', which brings to mind the surrealist practices of objective chance and *objet trouvé*—overlooked and unnoticed objects in order to lend them his voice. Since museum objects and specimens are often dismissed as dead matter, Albrecht's idea is to bring them to life through stories. The resulting narratives are made up of 'outrageous stories, unbelievable experiences, improbable events'.[39] 'The objects don't always tell the truth', Albrecht warns his museum visitors; 'they boast, exaggerate and present themselves in a better light, even tell lies'.[40]

With the object biographies exposed as fictional, their fascination resides in the variety of fields, topics and references included in the stories and documentation, ranging from nautical history to natural history, literary cult, oenology, film, philosophy, music, art, religion and popular science. Thus, visitors who are prepared to engage with the object narratives on a deeper level might be rewarded with a collective reading experience which cultural historian Winfried Pauleit compares to moments of quasi-religious transcendence:

> But it is also fascinating to observe the other visitors reading in this museum; sometimes they appear spellbound for hours. On these occasions, one can witness individual secular acts of absorbed reading, which can turn into communal reading experiences: a worldly form of meditation during which smiles and expressions of amazement alternate, condensed into a palpable atmosphere transferred from one visitor to another.[41]

Acknowledging a similarly exhilarating experience, Albrecht refers to 'moments of happiness' on the rare occasions when previously mute museum objects begin to reveal their stories:

> Sometimes only, very rarely—one can never force it—the objects talk and talk and talk, they talk to scientists and academics, talk to visitors, talk to everybody who listens, and they keep talking; these are true moments of happiness for all museum people.[42]

This dependence on object narratives, labels and literary devices, however, creates another problem in a museum context: if visitors do not take the time or afford the patience to read the double-sided information sheets accompanying each of the 20-odd items on display (Fig. 3.1), the exhibits remain obscure—rather common, everyday objects such as reindeer antlers, a bottle of wine and a matchbox car.[43]

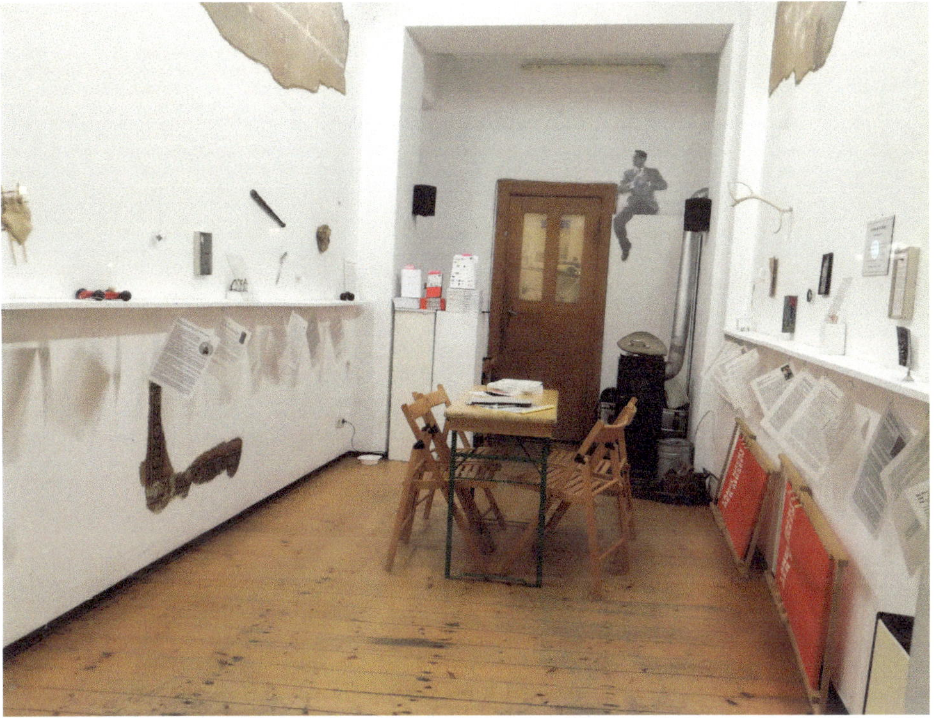

FIGURE 3.1. Museum der Unerhörten Dinge, Berlin, main exhibition gallery. Photo: Roland Albrecht. Courtesy of Museum der Unerhörten Dinge.

As Albrecht admits, without the possibilities of discovering new things, experiencing wonder and encountering the unexpected, the museum becomes 'a place of emptiness'.[44]

One could argue, in this light, that the artist's book accompanying the project provides a more appropriate home to the object stories. Albrecht recognizes this disparity between the narrative and the visual himself when describing his museum as 'a literary Wunderkammer'.[45]

I would also suggest that the museum's storeroom, where a bewildering array of objects are grouped and juxtaposed according to their respective weight (Fig. 3.2), presents a more interesting and evocative display. Mark Dion goes as far as calling for a reversal of the museum's exhibition and storage/research spaces: 'So I say freeze the museum's front rooms as a time capsule and open up the laboratories and storerooms to reveal art and science as the dynamic processes that they are'.[46] Implicated in this statement is the assumption that front rooms often attempt to tell an official story of Objectivity, Truth and Beauty—Weschler refers to 'the Voice of Institutional Authority'[47]—whereas backrooms have the potential to provide more powerful and meaningful

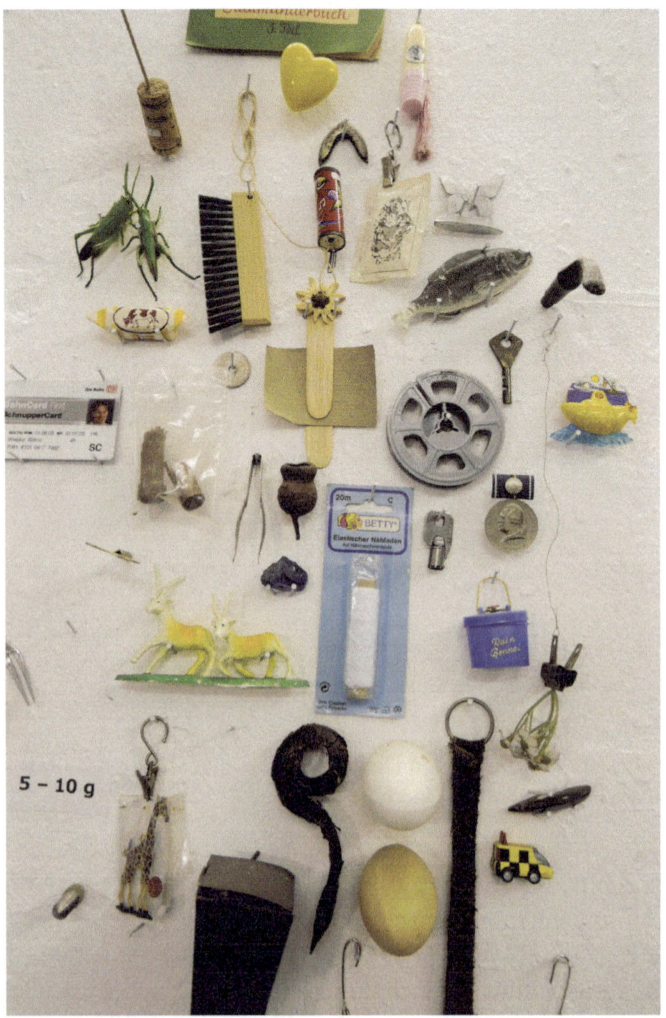

FIGURE 3.2. 'Depot', Museum der Unerhörten Dinge, Berlin. Photo: Roland Albrecht. Courtesy of Museum der Unerhörten Dinge.

insights and connections, because they favour the irrational and overlooked—objects that have fallen through the cracks of institutional consciousness—and thus mark a 'return of the repressed'.[48] According to Dion, museum storerooms are the rightful heirs to cabinets of curiosities, because, like 'flea markets and dusty old museums [they] challenge cultural boundaries and generate questions today'.[49]

Wonder in the Face of Abundance or Wonder in the Face of Rarity?

Curiosity: 1. What kills the cat and makes Alice go through the looking-glass and down the rabbit hole. 2. A rare or novel object, or knick-knack.

Interestingly, a number of major museums and big institutions have begun in recent years to subscribe to the concept of 'open' or 'visible' storage by either making research collections accessible to the public and allowing contact with scientists (the Natural History Museum's Darwin Centre, which opened in 2009, is the most prominent example) or by punctuating their exhibition spaces with what historian of science and curator Anke te Heesen calls 'the display of the infinite amount'.[50] Staying with the example of the Natural History Museum in London, displays which single out extraordinary objects and specimens accompanied by both conventional labels and digitized content—the 'Treasures' display in the Cadogan Gallery is a case in point—are juxtaposed with glass display cases showing masses of barely distinguishable specimens of the same kind—birds or minerals or corals—accompanied by little, or at most generic, interpretation. While the rarity of the 'Treasures' appeals to visitors' curiosity, encouraging an in-depth cognitive and affective engagement with the objects—among them Hans Sloane's nautilus shell, Charles Darwin's pigeons, Alfred Russel Wallace's butterflies, the first ever found Archaeopteryx fossil and three Blaschka glass models of sea creatures—the mass displays inspire wonder in the face of dazzling abundance. One might argue that the 'Treasures' display is modelled on inventories and catalogues accompanying collections of curious objects in the sixteenth and seventeenth centuries, which embedded the objects into a narrative of acquisition and display, whereas the showcasing of a wealth of specimens calls to mind the aim of the collector of curious objects to achieve a representation of the whole world in miniature at a single glance, 'A World of Wonders in one closet shut', according to John Tradescant's epitaph.[51] However, the reality of living in the Information Age, where knowledge seemingly has no limits, bestows a whole new quality on the display of the infinite amount: it becomes a metaphor for 'the unending quantity of objects'[52] of mass production and consumer culture, ironically the very mechanisms and phenomena that play a major role in threatening the survival of many species on display at the Natural History Museum. For all their differences, both modes of display—the spotlight on the extraordinary object and the aestheticized accumulation of specimens—seem to aim at what art historian Stephen Bann calls the 'typological exuberance' of the object:[53] taking a sporadic, episodic, punctual and thematic approach unhinges the objects from the shackles of an overriding historical master narrative and opens them up to visitors' curiosity; likewise, presenting the aestheticizing spectacle of the infinite amount to the dazzled gaze of the visitor frees the single specimen from the obligation to signify and draws attention to larger issues of classification and epistemology. The viewer is left to wonder in both senses of the word, marvelling and desiring to know more. As I have argued elsewhere, both modes of reception and engagement with objects and specimens, curiosity and wonder in the face of the difficult-to-classify, can lead to an ethical or ecological sensibility in museum and exhibition visitors;[54] wonder and curiosity can be activated and harnessed to raise awareness of pressing contemporary issues ranging from biodiversity loss and habitat destruction (pertinent in the case of the Natural History Museum) to the omnipresence of fake news and alternative facts in media and politics (relevant in the case of the Museum of Jurassic Technology and the Museum der Unerhörten Dinge).

The Alternative Curiosity Museum as 'Wild Museum'

Laboratory: 1. Where experiments happen. 2. Of Mice and Men.

Considering the importance of individual object narratives and the attempts to encourage alternative, non-scientific ways of engagement with objects in both the Museum of Jurassic Technology and the Museum der Unerhörten Dinge, cultural anthropologist Angela Jannelli's concept of the 'wild museum' proves a fruitful lens through which to examine alternative curiosity museums.[55] Departing from Claude Lévi-Strauss's notion of *pensée sauvage*, Jannelli identifies the proliferation of small, provincial and offbeat museums as 'wild' museums, distinguishing them from scientific or academic museums. In opposition to more official institutions, 'wild' museums are often founded by amateurs and run by communities and clubs; they are characterized by object-rich displays and a lack of labelling, wall texts or other forms of formal interpretation; and, following Lévi-Strauss's idea of a 'science of the concrete', they place an emphasis on magic, symbolic and figurative modes of knowledge-making that are based on analogy and correspondence rather than abstract thought processes.[56] According to Jannelli, the wild museum's 'aim is not to explain abstract facts such as industrialization, structural change or "grand history"; it is rather [...] a space for negotiating experiences which are directly related to the objects in the collection'.[57]

Consequently—and this is where David Wilson's and Roland Albrecht's strategies of constructing oblique object biographies and stories become important—wild museums resist slotting their objects into a grand, totalizing, coherent and chronological historical master narrative; rather, following Lévi-Strauss's remarks on 'history and dialectic', they rely on a view of history as non-linear, discontinuous, fragmentary and complex.[58] Therefore, the alternative curiosity museum as a form of 'wild museum' tends to weave a web of small stories around exhibits, which can take the shape of anecdotes, biographical sketches, myths, legends, rumours and even lies. Blurring the distinction between fact and fiction, the rational and irrational, and imagination and fabrication, these stories put pressure on any totalizing institutional perspective or pre-packaged narrative that propagates a view of history as bound by progress and linear advancement. Ultimately, these narratives contribute to a spontaneous, immediate and affective engagement with objects, favouring a form of active, experiential, material knowledge over passive, didactic and abstract learning.[59]

Observing a similar anti-historicist tendency in contemporary art and museum display, Stephen Bann has proposed to consider artworks and museum objects from the perspective of a return to the epistemological regime of curiosity: 'Curiosity has the valuable role of signalling to us that the object on display is invariably a nexus of interrelated meanings—which may be quite discordant—rather than a staging post on a well trodden route through history.'[60] In Bann's interpretation, curiosity is a specific historical phenomenon with roots in sixteenth- and seventeenth-century discourses and practices of collecting—but forming an underlying stratum in Western cultural consciousness and resurfacing at certain moments in time as a counter-discourse to academic tradition and other dominant cultural phenomena—on the one hand, and a motivating concept, a certain way of seeing and perceiving works of art and objects on the other. Seen as a curiosity, the object acts as a point of intersection for several conflicting discourses, each attributing to it a certain identity, status and value; at the same time, its insistent, almost obstinate materiality grates against these discourses and unravels meanings we might have taken for granted. With the emphasis placed on materiality, heightened attention, analogy, correspondence, agency and interaction, the object—'emancipated, through the creation of new meanings, from the paranoia of an all-embracing system'[61]—answers back.

Musée de la Chasse et de la Nature: Wonder and Critical Awareness

Amateur: 1. Lover of curiosities. 2. Someone who is motivated by passion, pleasure and desire. 3. Well-meaning dilettante.

As the examples of unresponsive visitors at the Museum of Jurassic Technology and the Museum der Unerhörten Dinge have shown, the possibility of affective failure vis-à-vis the 'curious' object or display remains. A closer look at the Musée de la Chasse et de la Nature and Château d'Oiron suggests that, compared to these two alternative curiosity museums led by artists and amateur curators, the cooperation between artist and institution offers more creative and fruitful ways of mediation between viewer and installation. The Musée de la Chasse et de la Nature originates from the private collection of hunting-related art, weaponry and taxidermy amassed by nature enthusiasts François and Jacqueline Sommer. Part of a foundation which aims to promote ethical hunting and the conservation of wildlife, the museum opened its doors to the public in 1967 and underwent a major process of modernization between 1998 and 2007 under the leadership of Claude d'Anthenaise. In order to augment the private collection's relevance to the urban community, d'Anthenaise invited contemporary artists to create works in response to the objects and setting, and which at the same time reflect on wider themes, such as the relationships between art and nature and human and animal, and the increasing need for habitat protection and conservation. The museum's location in two adjacent 'hôtels particuliers', private mansions in the Marais, coupled with the ambiguous and often humorous nature of the displays, result in an unusual museum experience.[62] The design, scenography and arrangement of the artworks and objects are subtly orchestrated to unsettle the visitor. Thus the placement of furniture and objects of decorative art in most rooms, alongside names such as 'Salon Bleu', prompt us to imagine we are taking a stroll through the private residence of a hunter-collector. Elsewhere in the museum, galleries like the 'Cabinet of the Unicorn' suggest a recreated historical cabinet of curiosities. However, what should we then make of the contemporary artworks interspersed with historical paintings and hunting trophies? Considering the whole setting as an elaborate backdrop to works by Jan Fabre, Jeff Koons, Oleg Kulik, Karen Knorr, Rebecca Horn and Mark Dion, among others, one might be forgiven if one asks whether the Musée de la Chasse et de la Nature is not rather a gigantic piece of contemporary installation art?

In addition to instilling doubt and uncertainty in visitors by blurring the boundaries between the private home of a noble hunter-collector, historic house museum, cabinet of curiosities and art installation, a number of curatorial devices are aimed at heightening the audience's affective response. Thus labelling is sparse—in the case of the contemporary artworks as good as absent—and often has to be actively retrieved by lifting flaps or peering inside drawers. Although general information about objects and artworks is available via removable gallery information plates hanging on the walls, visitors are handed the option to ignore any official institutional explanation provided. As Rugoff states, the omission of labels lends objects 'a slightly mysterious aspect that invite[s] scrutiny and encourage[s] acts of individual discovery'.[63] Similarly, no accompanying interpretative leaflets or signage exist to prescribe any particular route through the museum; like a hunter in the forest, visitors are encouraged to follow their instincts and inclinations. The forest-like feel of the installation is enhanced by the use of lighting, which stages an opposition between dark spaces like the 'Room of the Boar' and brighter galleries like the 'Salon of the Dogs' in order to imitate the transition from dark and wild undergrowth to light and airy clearings in the forest. The analogy between visitor and hunter is employed profusely in various books and pamphlets available in the museum shop: visitors are encouraged to remain constantly alert and 'on the prowl', senses sharpened and mind wide open, as if tracking wolves or stalking deer.[64]

If visitors are attentive and dedicated enough to join in the game, the risk remains, as it does in the Museum of Jurassic Technology, that they spend their time hunting for clues and the museum experience therefore degenerates into a sport, compromising the display's potential to act as a springboard for the imagination and to provoke a deeper engagement with the issues at stake, which range from colonialism to the ethics of hunting, human conceptions of the animal and the deterioration of natural habitats. Opposing a reductive view of wonder as associated with mysticism and irrationality, Stengers reminds us of the double meaning of the verb 'to wonder' in the English language as 'both to be surprised and to entertain questions. It thus may refer to [...] being affected, troubled, surprised, but also being forced to think and question'.[65] What distinguishes the Musée de la Chasse et de la Nature from the Museum of Jurassic Technology—and what contributes to inspiring both astonishment and critical awareness—is that visitors encounter a plethora of multisensory stimuli, such as hands-on cabinets, optical devices and olfactory triggers; but most importantly, the contemporary artworks, along with temporary exhibitions organized periodically on the premises, provide audiences with an extra level of appreciation and analysis; shining a reflective light on the Sommers's collection, they activate wonder in both senses of the word and ultimately prevent the displays from becoming overly didactic, static or inferential.

Château d'Oiron: Curiosity and Multisensory Engagement

Wonder: 1. The first of all the passions (René Descartes), a sudden surprise of the soul (Descartes again), a constriction and suspension of the heart (Albertus Magnus), and a fleeting return to childlike excitement about life (Jane Bennett). 2. Critical reflection often resulting in squinting and a furrowed brow. 3. Can refer to singer (Stevie) or superhero (Woman).

Another alternative curiosity museum, Château d'Oiron, which was the seat of the powerful Gouffier family in the Renaissance period, has been housing, since 1993, the permanent collection *Curios & Mirabilia*, an installation of works by

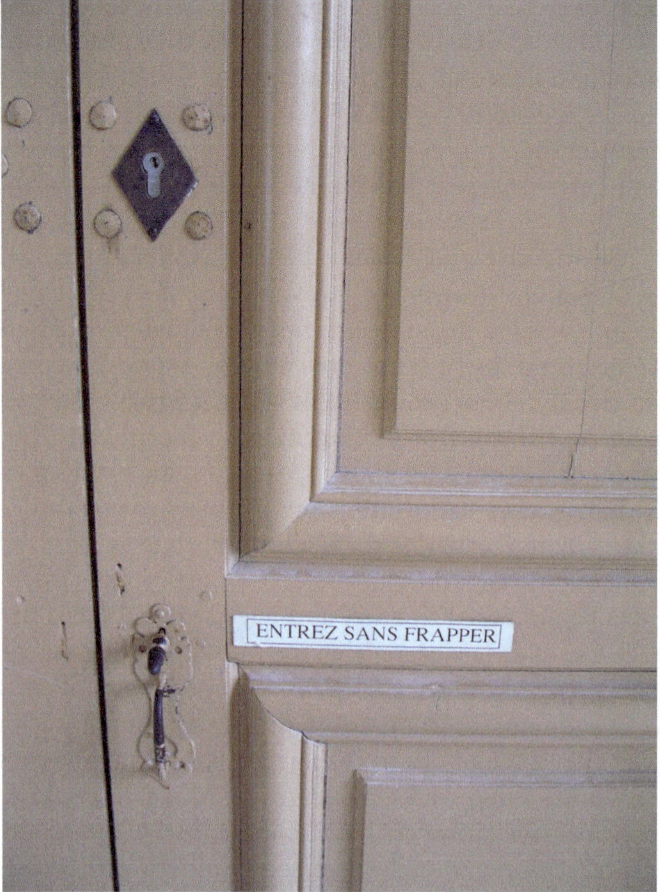

FIGURE 3.3. 'Enter without knocking'. Signage at Château d'Oiron, France. Photo: Marion Endt-Jones. Courtesy of Centre des monuments nationaux, Paris.

over 70 contemporary artists, which establish links with the historic site. Curator Jean-Hubert Martin, who is also well known for organizing the influential but contested exhibition *Magiciens de la Terre* at the Centre Pompidou and Parc de la Villette in 1989, commissioned works from a number of artists—among them Daniel Spoerri, Christian Boltanski, Thomas Grünfeld, Ian Hamilton Finlay and Hubert Duprat—whose contributions were to reflect on Claude Gouffier, the theme of collecting and the cabinet of curiosities in different ways.

Conceived as an alternative museum—it might be referred to as 'anti-Beaubourg', an antithesis to the cultural factory of the Museum of Contemporary Art at the Centre Pompidou in Paris—Château d'Oiron invites the visitor to explore the collection at his or her own pace. Like at the Musée de la Chasse et de la Nature, the lack of signage and near absence of museum guards encourage viewers to embark on a voyage of discovery. Upon entry, visitors are handed a floor plan featuring a brief description of the main exhibition rooms, but are strongly advised to abandon prescribed routes, to let chance and curiosity guide them and to randomly follow sounds and smells, push closed doors and enter semi-hidden passageways (Fig. 3.3). For museum-goers who are accustomed to period rooms, wall panels and well laid out, systematic or chronological itineraries, the lack of signage can be an utterly perplexing experience. Approaching the castle from the courtyard, it is impossible to identify the main entrance; visitors push doors and stumble upon artworks and installations almost at random.

Each of the works on display evokes the practice of early modern collectors of curious objects, corresponding with the historical site on the one hand and with a related sixteenth- or seventeenth-century engraving chosen by historian and designer Laurent Joubert on the other. The black-and-white engravings defy the imperative that museum labels have to be of textual nature; here, an image adds a further layer of meaning and creates multiple associations.

Since the artworks include different genres, media and materials, all of the visitor's senses are constantly challenged. Anamorphoses and optical illusions test our sense of vision and we often have to look twice, take a closer look or peer through optical devices such as lenses, mirrors or microscopes. Proceeding through the exhibition spaces, we are greeted by a variety of sounds. These range from the cry of the 'cocatrix', an imaginary, hybrid, hermaphrodite creature that—as Spanish artist Joan Fontcuberta tries to convince us through his elaborate pseudo-scientific display—has purportedly lived on the castle grounds for centuries, to the snoring of a (taxidermied) bear which lies—again, no label or wall text give any warning—peacefully asleep in a dungeon. A clue as to its origin is provided by a pamphlet available at the museum shop, entitled *Mark Dion presents Dungeon of the Sleeping Bear, the Phantom Forest, the Birds of Guam and Other Fables of Ecological Mischief*, the product of the artist's residency at the Atelier Calder in 2005.

But it is above all our olfactory receptors that are continuously aroused. Thus an intense smell of wine prompts visitors to climb a narrow wooden staircase to the mezzanine floor where, at the end of the corridor, they happen upon *Small Glass Pouring Light* by New Zealand artist Bill Culbert, a huge white Formica-topped table on which 25 glasses filled with red wine placed underneath three suspended lamps project the reflections of light bulbs. Located in one of the towers, *Paroi*, an immense wall consisting of beeswax designed by the German sculptor Wolfgang Laib emits a strong scent; and the stench greeting visitors in front of Mark Dion's bear dungeon suggests that a real, rather than taxidermied, bear has taken up quarters there. The further one advances, the more Château d'Oiron appears like a marvellously orchestrated Gesamtkunstwerk comprising all artistic genres and challenging all of the visitor's senses.

Curiosity as a Way of Seeing, Thinking and Caring

Classification: (1) Results from collecting, naming, labelling and pigeonholing things. (2) 'Arbitrary' (Jorge Luis Borges) and 'oppressive' (Roland Barthes) attempt 'to tame the wild profusion of existing things' (Michel Foucault). (3) Animals are divided into (a) belonging to the zoo, (b) taxidermied, (c) cuddly, (d) factory-farmed pigs, (e) corals, (f) extinct, (g) show dogs, (h) included in the present classification, (i) rabid, (j) Disneyfied, (k) photographed with a very expensive smartphone, (l) et cetera, (m) having just knocked over the wine bottle, (n) that from a long way off look like hippos.

Of the examples I have discussed, Musée de la Chasse and Château d'Oiron seem to me the more creative, imaginative realizations of an alternative, relational curiosity museum. Their multisensory, multilayered displays convincingly suggest that the historical paradigm of curiosity has profound repercussions in contemporary artistic and curatorial practice, clearly transcending a nostalgic act of recovery that is based on a purely visual, aesthetic attraction. The epistemological revitalization of curiosity is consequential in a museological context, because wonder and curiosity present a vital immediate response to the objects on display, upon which any further engagement with historical or political themes hinges. As Rugoff puts it,

> what is needed are strategies that create a psychological space for the critical first phase of our encounter with art works, which occurs on an emotional and experiential level. [...] You cannot expect viewers to explore the discursive and theoretical issues at stake in a show if the work itself is presented in a way that stifles their curiosity and gives no value to visceral response.[66]

What makes the case studies I have discussed interesting in this respect is, first, the fact that they all originate from private collections, whether real or imaginary, historical or contemporary. By emphasizing rather than masking the idiosyncratic nature of the exhibits, the collectors' passion is transferred onto the viewer. Personal idiosyncrasies are played up rather than glossed over, resulting in thought-provoking and varied displays that do not attempt to present any single coherent or totalizing perspective and thus provide a wealth of stimuli for visitors to latch onto. Acknowledging—even deliberately highlighting—that the object's history and status are firmly linked with the collector's and curator's identity causes a subtle shift in the object's value system: 'What is private and idiosyncratic is normally outside the vision of the social sciences, but it seems important to recognize that artefacts can have peculiarly personal value arising from some association with an individual's autobiography'.[67] Instead of deriving the object's value from its ability to support a coherent, chronological historical narrative and gaining authority from institutional hierarchy and the Objectivity of History, an authored display represents 'a subjective act of enunciation'[68]—a narrative riddled with idiosyncrasies, gaps and discrepancies. This shift in value is reflected in the epistemological status of the object: according to Bann, curiosity 'always takes for granted a kind of secondary revision of value, with the object being tied to something immaterial like a story or a personal association, as well as asserting its own materiality in animal, vegetable or mineral terms'.[69]

Second, my readings of the Musée de la Chasse et de la Nature and Château d'Oiron suggest that, for the cabinet of curiosities to remain relevant today, there are worse strategies to enlist than the playfulness, humour, multiple materialities and political resonances granted by contemporary artworks.[70] If we prefer a creative, dynamic revaluation, which remains sensitive to the historical context, to a purely nostalgic, artificial, static or sterile recreation,[71] the open, interdisciplinary and multifaceted input of artists seems a good place to start. Wonder, curiosity, curious objects and the Wunderkammer are historical phenomena that are anchored in the epistemological reality of the sixteenth and seventeenth centuries; but they also emerge as critical concepts that resurge at specific times in history: with surrealism and again in contemporary art and museum display, where they find their most pointed form of expression in the alternative curiosity museum. Exploring the meaning of the word 'curiosity', Foucault suggests that

> it evokes 'care'; it evokes the care one takes of what exists and what might exist; a sharpened sense of reality, but one that is never immobilized before it; a readiness to find what surrounds us strange and odd; a certain determination to throw off familiar ways of thought and to look at the same things in a different way; a passion for seizing what is happening now and what is disappearing; a lack of respect for the traditional hierarchies of what is important and fundamental.[72]

In an era characterized by post-truth politics, globalization, the omnipresence of the virtual, the perpetual onslaught of images and information, the challenges of interdisciplinarity, postcolonialism and the ecological crisis, practicing curiosity as a critical, attentive and passionate way of seeing, thinking and engaging with objects, subjects and ideas seems like a vital task. Against this contemporary backdrop, the alternative curiosity museum acts as an experimental space in which curiosity can be cultivated, probed and played out.

NOTES

1. My glossary entries are inspired by Mark Dion, 'The Lexicon of Relevant Terms', in *Natural History and Other Fictions: An Exhibition by Mark Dion* (Birmingham: Ikon Gallery, 1997), 53–77 and Mark Dion, Petra Lange-Berndt and Dietmar Rübel et al., 'Glossary: A Boundless Accumulation of Commonplaces to Describe the State of Things', in *Mark Dion: The Academy of Things*, ed. Petra Lange-Berndt and Dietmar Rübel (Cologne: Verlag der Buchhandlung Walther König, 2015), 217–38.

2. Michel Foucault, 'The Masked Philosopher', in *Michel Foucault, Ethics: Subjectivity and Truth, The Essential Works of Michel Foucault 1954–1984*, vol. 1, ed. Paul Rabinow and trans. Robert Hurley et al. (New York: New Press, 1997), 325.

3. Ibid., 325–26.

4. Noteworthy recent exhibition catalogues include Nike Bätzner, ed., *Assoziationsraum Wunderkammer. Zeitgenössische Künste zur Kunst- und Naturalienkammer der Franckeschen Stiftungen zu Halle* (Wiesbaden: Harrassowitz, 2015); Horst Bredekamp, Jochen Brüning and Cornelia Weber, eds., *Theater der Natur und Kunst – Theatrum naturae et artis. Wunderkammern des Wissens an der Humboldt-Universität zu Berlin* (Berlin: Henschel, 2000); Brian Dillon, ed., *Curiosity: Art and the Pleasures of Knowing* (London: Hayward Publishing, 2013); Michel-Édouard Leclerc, Laurent Le Bon and Patrick Mauriès, eds., *Cabinets de Curiosités* (Landerneau: Fonds Hélène & Édouard Leclerc pour la Culture, 2019); and Barbara Maria Stafford and Frances Terpak, *Devices of Wonder: From the World in a Box to Images on a Screen* (Los Angeles: Getty Research Institute, 2001). For a more detailed evaluation of museological Wunderkammer manifestations, ranging from historical cabinets of curiosities being reopened and museums redisplaying their collections according to a Wunderkammer rationale, to permanent and temporary Wunderkammer-inspired exhibitions, see Marion Endt, 'Reopening the Cabinet of Curiosities: Nature and the Marvellous in Surrealism and Contemporary Art', PhD diss., The University of Manchester, 2008, 11–14 and 18.

5. Recent examples include Stephen Bann, 'The Return to Curiosity: Shifting Paradigms in Contemporary Museum Display', in *Art and its Publics: Museum Studies at the Millennium*, ed. Andrew McClellan (Malden, Oxford: Blackwell Publishing, 2003), 116–30; Stephen Bann, *Ways around Modernism* (New York: Routledge, 2007); Gabriele Beßler, *Wunderkammern: Weltmodelle von der Renaissance bis zur Kunst der Gegenwart* (Berlin: Reimer, 2012); Horst Bredekamp, 'Die Renaissance der Kunstkammer', in *Macht. Wissen. Teilhabe. Sammlungsinstitutionen im 21. Jahrhundert*, ed. Katharina Hoins and Felicitas von Mallinckrodt (Bielefeld: transcript Verlag, 2015), 45–61; Dominik Collet, *Die Welt in der Stube: Begegnungen mit Außereuropa in Kunstkammern der Frühen Neuzeit* (Göttingen: Vandenhoeck & Ruprecht, 2007); Christine Davenne, *Modernité du cabinet des curiosités* (Paris: L'Harmattan, 2004); Robert J. W. Evans and Alexander Marr, eds., *Curiosity and Wonder from the Renaissance to the Enlightenment* (Aldershot: Ashgate, 2006); Robert Felfe, 'Die Kunstkammer – und warum ihre Zeit

erst kommen wird', *Kunstchronik* 67, no. 7 (2014): 342–52; Arthur MacGregor, *Curiosity and Enlightenment: Collectors and Collections from the Sixteenth to the Nineteenth Century* (New Haven: Yale University Press, 2007); and Lisa Skogh and Earle Havens, eds., *A Field Guide to Curiosity: A Mark Dion Project* (London: V&A, 2019), https://www.vam.ac.uk/articles/a-field-guide-to-curiosity-a-mark-dion-project. For a more extensive literature review and assessment, see Endt, 'Reopening the Cabinet of Curiosities', 14–17.

6. Krzysztof Pomian, *Collectors and Curiosities: Paris and Venice, 1500–1800*, trans. Elizabeth Wiles-Portier (Cambridge: Polity Press, 1990), 45–64.

7. See Endt, 'Reopening the Cabinet of Curiosities'.

8. See ibid. and Marion Endt-Jones, 'Between *Wunderkammer* and Shop Window: Surrealist *Naturalia* Cabinets', in *Sculpture and the Vitrine*, ed. John C. Welchman (Farnham: Ashgate, 2013), 95–120.

9. See Alexander Alberro and Blake Stimson, eds., *Institutional Critique: An Anthology of Artists' Writings* (Cambridge, MA: MIT Press, 2009).

10. See Marion Endt-Jones, 'Beyond Institutional Critique: Mark Dion's Surrealist Wunderkammer at the Manchester Museum', *Museum and Society* 5, no. 1 (2007): 1–14, https://journals.le.ac.uk/ojs1/index.php/mas/article/view/89.

11. See Brian O'Doherty, *Inside the White Cube: The Ideology of the Gallery Space* (Berkeley: University of California Press, 1986).

12. Closely related phenomena are artist collectives and experimental communal, interdisciplinary research, work and exhibition spaces, such as Mildred's Lane, founded by J. Morgan Puett and Mark Dion in Pennsylvania in 1998, and Pioneer Works, set up by Dustin Yellin in Brooklyn in 2012.

13. Duncan Grewcock, *Doing Museology Differently* (New York: Routledge, 2014), 5.

14. Ibid., 2–16.

15. Mark Dion, Anna Dezeuze, Julia Kelly and David Lomas, 'Mark Dion in Conversation with Anna Dezeuze, Julia Kelly and David Lomas'. *Papers of Surrealism* 4 (2005): 6, https://www.research.manchester.ac.uk/portal/files/63517388/surrealism_issue_4.pdf (accessed 4 May 2020).

16. Ibid., 6.

17. Nick O'Flaherty, 'Les attentes des visiteurs', *Les Nouvelles de l'ICOM* 67, no. 4 (2014): 10 (my translation; original emphasis).

18. Quoted in Nicholas Thomas, *The Return of Curiosity: What Museums Are Good for in the 21st Century* (London: Reaktion Books, 2016), 12.

19. Ibid., 15.

20. O'Flaherty, 'Les attentes des visiteurs', 11 (my translation).

21. Ralph Rugoff, 'Rules of the Game', *frieze* 44 (1999), https://frieze.com/article/rules-game-0. (accessed 4 May 2020).

22. Seafoam Palace Museum Website (accessed 26 July 2019) http://seafoampalace.org (accessed 4 May 2020).

23. Claude d'Anthenaise, ed., *Un musée singulier* (Paris: Musée de la Chasse et de la Nature, 2010), 8 and 11 (my translation).

24. Claude d'Anthenaise, *Le Cabinet de Diane au Musée de la Chasse et de la Nature* (Paris: Editions Citadelles & Mazenod, 2007), 74, 216, 229, 250 and 254 (my translation).

25. See Philip Fisher, 'The Poetics of Wonder', in *Meaning in the Visual Arts: Views from the Outside. A Centennial Commemoration of Erwin Panofsky (1892–1968)*, ed. Irving Lavin (Princeton: Institute for Advanced Study, 1995), 176.

26. Isabelle Stengers, 'Wondering about Materialism', in *The Speculative Turn: Continental Materialism and Realism*, ed. Levi Bryant, Nick Srnicek and Graham Harman (Melbourne: re.press, 2011), 374.

27. Nicolas Bourriaud, *Relational Aesthetics*, trans. Simon Pleasance and Fronza Woods (Dijon: Les presses du réel, 2002), 58.

28. See for example Paula Findlen, *Possessing Nature: Museums, Collecting, and Scientific Culture in Early Modern Italy* (Berkeley: University of California Press, 1994).

29. Samuel Quiccheberg, *The First Treatise on Museums: Samuel Quiccheberg's* Inscriptiones *1565*, trans. Mark A. Meadow and Bruce Robertson (Los Angeles: Getty Research Institute, 2013), 25–29.

30. Bredekamp, Brüning and Weber, *Theater der Natur und Kunst*, 12–19.

31. Staatliche Kunstsammlungen Dresden Online Collection, https://skd-online-collection.skd.museum/Details/Index/117609 (accessed 17 July 2018).

32. Lawrence Weschler, *Mr. Wilson's Cabinet of Wonder* (New York: Vintage Books, 1996), 55–57 and 90–97.

33. Ibid., 3–10.

34. Rugoff, 'Rules of the Game'.

35. Examples of this approach include Weschler, *Mr. Wilson's Cabinet of Wonder*, and Susan A. Crane, 'Curious Cabinets and Imaginary Museums', in *Museums and Memory*, ed. Susan. A. Crane (Stanford: Stanford University Press, 2000), 60–90.

36. David Wilson remains famously vague on the Museum of Jurassic Technology's mission: 'Part of the assigned task […] is to reintegrate people to wonder' (quoted in Weschler, *Mr. Wilson's Cabinet of Wonder*, 60).

37. *Duden Online*, s.v. 'unerhört', https://www.duden.de/rechtschreibung/unerhoert_unglaublich_besonders (accessed 4 May 2020) (my translation).

38. Roland Albrecht, *Museum der Unerhörten Dinge* (Berlin: Verlag Klaus Wagenbach, 2004), 113 and Weschler, *Mr. Wilson's Cabinet of Wonder*, 26–30 and 75–97.

39. Ibid., 113 (my translation).

40. Ibid., 113 (my translation).

41. Museum der Unerhörten Dinge Website https://www.museumderunerhoertendinge.de/museum_de/museum/museum.html (accessed 9 July 2018) (my translation).

42. Roland Albrecht, 'Betrachtungen über das Museum im Allgemeinen und über das Museum der Unerhörten Dinge im Besonderen', in *Kunst – Museum – Kontexte: Perspektiven der Kunst- und Kulturvermittlung*, ed. Viktor Kittlausz and Winfried Pauleit (Bielefeld: transcript Verlag, 2006), 34 (my translation).

43. A small number of one-star reviews online provide a snapshot of some visitors' frustration: 'Sorry, but this was definitely too trivial: someone hanging a few objects taken from their own scrapbook, and one has to consult long-winded explanations to know why. I did not feel touched, I feel ripped off' (Bruno Müller on Google reviews, August 2017, https://goo.gl/maps/zVvZcCsVJN32 [accessed 23 July 2018] [my translation]).

44. Albrecht, 'Betrachtungen über das Museum', 30 (my translation).

45. Museum der Unerhörten Dinge Website (my translation).

46. Mark Dion, 'Miwon Kwon in Conversation with Mark Dion', in *Mark Dion*, ed. Lisa Graziose Corrin, Miwon Kwon and Norman Bryson (London: Phaidon, 1997), 19.

47. Weschler, *Mr. Wilson's Cabinet of Wonder*, 101–4.

48. See Rosamond Wolff Purcell and Stephen Jay Gould, *Illuminations: A Bestiary* (New York: W. W. Norton, 1986).

49. Dion, 'Miwon Kwon in Conversation with Mark Dion', 18.

50. Anke te Heesen, 'The Unending Quantity of Objects: An Observation on Museums and Their Presentation Modes', in *Aesthetics of Universal Knowledge*, ed. Simon Schaffer, John Tresch and Pasquale Gagliardi (Cham: Palgrave Macmillan, 2017), 119. Other notable examples of aestheticized mass displays include the Museum für Naturkunde Berlin's 'Biodiversity Wall', which opened in 2007 as part of the 'Evolution in Action' display, the 'Wet Collections', also in the Museum für Naturkunde, for which one million specimens preserved in glass jars were made visible to museum visitors in the reconstructed East Wing in 2010, and Manchester Museum's 'Living Worlds' gallery, which replaced the old zoology displays in 2011.

51. Findlen, *Possessing Nature*, 17.

52. te Heesen, 'The Unending Quantity of Objects', 115.

53. Bann, 'The Return to Curiosity', 125.

54. Marion Endt-Jones, 'Coral Fishing and Pearl Diving: Curatorial Approaches to Doubt and Wonder', in *Wonder in Contemporary Artistic Practice*, eds. Christian Mieves and Irene Brown (New York: Routledge, 2017), 177–93.

55. Fiona Candlin's analysis of 'micromuseums' is also relevant in this context: Fiona Candlin, *Micromuseology: An Analysis of Small Independent Museums* (London: Bloomsbury, 2016).

56. Angela Jannelli, *Wilde Museen: Zur Museologie des Amateurmuseums* (Bielefeld: transcript Verlag, 2002), 21–33.

57. Ibid., 28 (my translation).

58. Ibid., 33–34.

59. Jannelli acknowledges that the predominance of intuitive, often unconsciously formed knowledge which is gleaned from objects embedded in a narrative based on the identities, sensibilities and experiences of an individual – the (amateur) collector and curator – involves the risk of visitors simply not understanding and remaining on the outside (Angela Jannelli, 'Wilde Museen: Das Amateurmuseum als partizipative Graswurzelbewegung', in *Das partizipative Museum: Zwischen Teilhabe und User Generated Content. Neue Anforderungen an kulturhistorische Ausstellungen*, ed. Susanne Gessner, Martin Handschin, Angela Jannelli and Sibylle Lichtensteiger [Bielefeld: transcript Verlag, 2002], 169). This corresponds with my observation that, for many visitors, the objects on display at the Museum of Jurassic Technology and the Museum der Unerhörten Dinge do not elicit an affective response. In these cases, the object encounter and narrative devices fail to trigger wonder or curiosity; the objects remain mute.

60. Bann, 'The Return to Curiosity', 120.

61. Stephen Bann, *The Clothing of Clio: A Study of the Representation of History in Nineteenth-century Britain and France* (Cambridge: Cambridge University Press, 1984), 78.

62. A virtual tour of the entire museum is available at https://tourmkr.com/t5rAwBqGLZ/4581186p,163000m,105.04h,90.00t (accessed 26 July 2019).

63. Rugoff, 'Rules of the Game'.

64. d'Anthenaise, *Un musée singulier*, 8 and d'Anthenaise, *Le Cabinet de Diane*, 13 and 250.

65. Stengers, 'Wondering about Materialism', 374.

66. Rugoff, 'Rules of the Game'.

67. Nicholas Thomas, *Entangled Objects: Exchange, Material Culture, and Colonialism in the Pacific* (Cambridge, MA: Harvard University Press, 1991), 30.

68. Bann, 'The Return to Curiosity', 123.

69. Ibid., 125.

70. It is interesting to note in this context that the aforementioned 'Treasures' exhibition in the Cadogan Gallery of the Natural History Museum features the only work of art permanently installed at the Museum, Tania Kovats's *TREE*, which was commissioned in 2009 to mark the bicentenary of Charles Darwin's birth.

71. See Bann, 'The Return to Curiosity', 119.

72. Foucault, 'The Masked Philosopher', 325.

REFERENCES

Alberro, Alexander, and Blake Stimson, eds. *Institutional Critique: An Anthology of Artists' Writings*. Cambridge, MA: MIT Press, 2009.

Albrecht, Roland. *Museum der Unerhörten Dinge*. Berlin: Verlag Klaus Wagenbach, 2004.

Albrecht, Roland. 'Betrachtungen über das Museum im Allgemeinen und über das Museum der Unerhörten Dinge im Besonderen'. In *Kunst—Museum—Kontexte: Perspektiven der*

Kunst- und Kulturvermittlung, ed. Viktor Kittlausz and Winfried Pauleit, 25–35. Bielefeld: transcript Verlag, 2006.

d'Anthenaise, Claude. *Le Cabinet de Diane au Musée de la Chasse et de la Nature*. Paris: Éditions Citadelles & Mazenod, 2007.

d'Anthenaise, Claude, ed. *Un musée singulier*. Paris: Musée de la Chasse et de la Nature, 2010.

Bann, Stephen. *The Clothing of Clio: A Study of the Representation of History in Nineteenth-century Britain and France*. Cambridge: Cambridge University Press, 1984.

Bann, Stephen. 'The Return to Curiosity: Shifting Paradigms in Contemporary Museum Display'. In *Art and its Publics: Museum Studies at the Millennium*, ed. Andrew McClellan, 116–30. Malden, Oxford: Blackwell Publishing, 2003.

Bann, Stephen. *Ways around Modernism*. New York: Routledge, 2007.

Bätzner, Nike, ed. *Assoziationsraum Wunderkammer. Zeitgenössische Künste zur Kunst- und Naturalienkammer der Franckeschen Stiftungen zu Halle*. Wiesbaden: Harrassowitz, 2015.

Beßler, Gabriele. *Wunderkammern. Weltmodelle von der Renaissance bis zur Kunst der Gegenwart*. Berlin: Reimer, 2012.

Bourriaud, Nicolas. *Relational Aesthetics*, trans. Simon Pleasance and Fronza Woods. Dijon: Les presses du réel, 2002.

Bredekamp, Horst. 'Die Renaissance der Kunstkammer'. In *Macht. Wissen. Teilhabe. Sammlungsinstitutionen im 21. Jahrhundert*, ed. Katharina Hoins and Felicitas von Mallinckrodt, 45–61. Bielefeld: transcript Verlag, 2015.

Bredekamp, Horst, Jochen Brüning, and Cornelia Weber, eds. *Theater der Natur und Kunst—Theatrum naturae et artis. Wunderkammern des Wissens an der Humboldt-Universität zu Berlin*. Berlin: Henschel, 2000.

Candlin, Fiona. *Micromuseology: An Analysis of Small Independent Museums*. London: Bloomsbury, 2016.

Collet, Dominik. *Die Welt in der Stube: Begegnungen mit Außereuropa in Kunstkammern der Frühen Neuzeit*. Göttingen: Vandenhoeck & Ruprecht, 2007.

Crane, Susan A. 'Curious Cabinets and Imaginary Museums'. In *Museums and Memory*, ed. Susan. A. Crane, 60–90. Stanford: Stanford University Press, 2000.

Davenne, Christine. *Modernité du cabinet des curiosités*. Paris: L'Harmattan, 2004.

Dillon, Brian, ed. *Curiosity: Art and the Pleasures of Knowing*. London: Hayward Publishing, 2013.

Dion, Mark. 'The Lexicon of Relevant Terms'. In *Natural History and Other Fictions: An Exhibition by Mark Dion*, 53–77. Birmingham: Ikon Gallery, 1997.

Dion, Mark. 'Miwon Kwon in Conversation with Mark Dion'. In *Mark Dion*, ed. Lisa Graziose Corrin, Miwon Kwon and Norman Bryson, 7–33. London: Phaidon, 1997.

Dion, Mark, Anna Dezeuze, Julia Kelly, and David Lomas. 'Mark Dion in Conversation with Anna Dezeuze, Julia Kelly and David Lomas'. *Papers of Surrealism* 4 (2005). Available at https://www.research.manchester.ac.uk/portal/files/63517388/surrealism_issue_4.pdf (accessed 11 July 2018).

Dion, Mark, Petra Lange-Berndt, Dietmar Rübel, et al. 'Glossary: A Boundless Accumulation of Commonplaces to Describe the State of Things'. In *Mark Dion: The Academy of Things*, ed. Petra Lange-Berndt and Dietmar Rübel, 217–38. Cologne: Verlag der Buchhandlung Walther König, 2015.

Duden Online. S.v. 'unerhört'. Available at https://www.duden.de/rechtschreibung/unerhoert_unglaublich_besonders (accessed 11 July 2018).

Endt-Jones, Marion. 'Beyond institutional critique: Mark Dion's surrealist wunderkammer at the Manchester Museum'. *Museum and Society* 5, no. 1 (2007): 1–14. Available at https://journals.le.ac.uk/ojs1/index.php/mas/article/view/89 (accessed 11 July 2018).

Endt- Jones, Marion. 'Reopening the Cabinet of Curiosities: Nature and the Marvellous in Surrealism and Contemporary Art'. PhD diss., University of Manchester, 2008.

Endt-Jones, Marion. 'Between *Wunderkammer* and Shop Window: Surrealist *Naturalia* Cabinets'. In *Sculpture and the Vitrine*, ed. John C. Welchman, 95–120. Farnham: Ashgate, 2013.

Endt-Jones, Marion. 'Coral Fishing and Pearl Diving: Curatorial Approaches to Doubt and Wonder'. In *Wonder in Contemporary Artistic Practice*, ed. Christian Mieves and Irene Brown, 177–93. New York: Routledge, 2017.

Evans, Robert J. W., and Alexander Marr, eds. *Curiosity and Wonder from the Renaissance to the Enlightenment*. Aldershot: Ashgate, 2006.

Felfe, Robert. 'Die Kunstkammer—und warum ihre Zeit erst kommen wird'. *Kunstchronik* 67, no. 7 (2014): 342–52.

Findlen, Paula. *Possessing Nature: Museums, Collecting, and Scientific Culture in Early Modern Italy*. Berkeley: University of California Press, 1994.

Fisher, Philip. 'The Poetics of Wonder'. In *Meaning in the Visual Arts: Views from the Outside. A Centennial Commemoration of Erwin Panofsky (1892–1968)*, ed. Irving Lavin, 175–93. Princeton: Institute for Advanced Study, 1995.

Foucault, Michel. 'The Masked Philosopher'. In *Michel Foucault, Ethics: Subjectivity and Truth, The Essential Works of Michel Foucault 1954–1984*, vol. 1, ed. Paul Rabinow and trans. Robert Hurley et al., 321–28. New York: New Press, 1997.

Grewcock, Duncan. *Doing Museology Differently*. New York: Routledge, 2014.

Heesen, Anke te. 'The Unending Quantity of Objects: An Observation on Museums and Their Presentation Modes'. In *Aesthetics of Universal Knowledge*, ed. Simon Schaffer, John Tresch and Pasquale Gagliardi, 115–34. Cham: Palgrave Macmillan, 2017.

Jannelli, Angela. 'Wilde Museen: Das Amateurmuseum als partizipative Graswurzelbewegung'. In *Das partizipative Museum: Zwischen Teilhabe und User Generated Content. Neue Anforderungen an kulturhistorische Ausstellungen*, ed. Susanne Gessner, Martin Handschin, Angela Jannelli and Sibylle Lichtensteiger, 164–73. Bielefeld: transcript Verlag, 2002.

Jannelli, Angela. *Wilde Museen: Zur Museologie des Amateurmuseums*. Bielefeld: transcript Verlag, 2002.

Leclerc, Michel-Édouard, Laurent Le Bon and Patrick Mauriès, eds. *Cabinets de Curiosités*. Landerneau: Fonds Hélène & Édouard Leclerc pour la Culture, 2019.

MacGregor, Arthur. *Curiosity and Enlightenment: Collectors and Collections from the Sixteenth to the Nineteenth Century*. New Haven: Yale University Press, 2007.

Museum der Unerhörten Dinge Website. Available at https://www.museumderunerhoertendinge. de (accessed 9 July 2018).

O'Doherty, Brian. *Inside the White Cube: The Ideology of the Gallery Space*. Berkeley: University of California Press, 1986.

O'Flaherty, Nick. 'Les attentes des visiteurs'. *Les Nouvelles de l'ICOM* 67, no. 4 (2014): 10–11.

Pomian, Krzysztof. *Collectors and Curiosities: Paris and Venice, 1500–1800*, trans. Elizabeth Wiles-Portier. Cambridge: Polity Press, 1990.

Purcell, Rosamond Wolff, and Stephen Jay Gould. *Illuminations: A Bestiary*. New York: W. W. Norton, 1986.

Quiccheberg, Samuel. *The First Treatise on Museums: Samuel Quiccheberg's* Inscriptiones *1565*, trans. Mark A. Meadow and Bruce Robertson. Los Angeles: Getty Research Institute, 2013.

Rugoff, Ralph. 'Rules of the Game'. *frieze* 44 (1999). Available at https://frieze.com/article/ rules-game-0 (accessed 11 July 2018).

Seafoam Palace Museum Website. Available at http://seafoampalace.org (accessed 26 July 2019).

Skogh, Lisa, and Earle Havens, eds. *A Field Guide to Curiosity: A Mark Dion Project*. London: V&A, 2019, https://www.vam.ac.uk/articles/a-field-guide-to-curiosity-a-mark-dion-project (accessed 26 July 2019).

Staatliche Kunstsammlungen Dresden Online Collection. Available at https://skd-online-collection.skd.museum/Details/Index/117609 (accessed 17 July 2018).

Stafford, Barbara Maria, and Frances Terpak. *Devices of Wonder: From the World in a Box to Images on a Screen*. Los Angeles: Getty Research Institute, 2001.

Stengers, Isabelle. 'Wondering about Materialism'. In *The Speculative Turn: Continental Materialism and Realism*, ed. Levi Bryant, Nick Srnicek and Graham Harman, 368–80. Melbourne: re.press, 2011.

Thomas, Nicholas. *Entangled Objects: Exchange, Material Culture, and Colonialism in the Pacific*. Cambridge, MA: Harvard University Press, 1991.

Thomas, Nicholas. *The Return of Curiosity: What Museums Are Good for in the 21st Century*. London: Reaktion Books, 2016.

Weschler, Lawrence. *Mr. Wilson's Cabinet of Wonder*. New York: Vintage Books, 1996.

4

Art, Science and the Mutant Object

Rahma Khazam

Abstract

Khazam takes stock of new approaches to the specimen—or what we might call the post-specimen—showing how it challenges and unravels many of the long-standing assumptions on which contemporary art and modern science are based. She discusses artists such as Pinar Yoldas, whose speculative hybrid organisms based on research in gene therapy map the future of transhumanism, raising a number of pressing questions. What is their status with respect to art history? How are we to apprehend them: as artworks of sorts, as examples of material culture or as scientific experiments? Or should they rather be viewed as constituting a new artistic genre combining all these aspects at once? In the first part of this chapter, 'The Live Specimen', Khazam looks at how artists are working with live specimens, in collaboration with biologists and using laboratory techniques: this practice known as bio art questions the distinction between science and art. In the second part, 'Mutant Objects', the development of the 3D-printed specimen invites reconsideration of the human/technology binary. The third part, 'Neither Animal, Nor Vegetable Nor Mineral' examines the blurring of the divisions between animal, vegetable and mineral specimens, showing how it leads to the breakdown of further binaries, such as human/non-human, life/non-life.

In contemporary art, the specimen is more often than not an inert object held in a museum collection and represented by artists in paintings, sculptures or drawings. Take Nancy Graves's *Variability of Similar Forms* (1970), consisting of 36 sculpted camel leg bones based on drawings that Graves made of Pleistocene camel skeletons, or Geoffrey Harrison's paintings of a heart, brain, hands and feet inspired by the eighteenth- to twentieth-century anatomical specimens held in Barts Pathology Museum, where they were shown in 2013. In recent years, however, a new generation of artists has been putting the specimen to very different ends: no longer dead, inert and encased in a vitrine, it has, so to speak, leapt out of its display case to become an artistic material in itself. We might also note the emergence of the 3D printed specimen, which looks set to enjoy a bright technological future. Finally, the specimen need no longer be confined within the three kingdoms of animal, vegetable and mineral—for these boundaries are becoming obsolete. This chapter will take stock of these new approaches to the specimen—or what we might call the *post-specimen*, to borrow the title of this book—showing how it challenges many of the long-standing assumptions on which contemporary thinking is based.

As I will endeavour to show, the post-specimen unravels such key dichotomies in Western thought as art/science, human/non-human, thereby reflecting the increasing interest in undoing these oppositions characterizing contemporary culture at large. In the first part, I show that the live specimen explored with the help of biologists and using laboratory techniques is giving rise to an art form known as bio art, which questions the distinction between science and art. The second part highlights the emergence of the 3D printed specimen, inviting us to reflect on the human/technology binary. Finally, I will examine the new and constantly shifting taxonomy to which the post-specimen gives rise: as I will show in the third part, it not only breaks down the divisions between animal, vegetable and mineral, but also challenges the dividing lines between human and non-human, life and non-life.

My method will consist of outlining—through a combination of theoretical considerations and examples of artworks—each of these three stages in the life of the post-specimen: the first part explores the specimen as an artistic material; the second as a conduit for technological innovation; and the third, as the basis for a new conception of life.

The Live Specimen

Historically, scientists and artists have approached the specimen in very different ways: scientists have been interested in the specimen as such for purposes of study and display, whereas artists have for the most part represented specimens in paintings, drawings or sculpture, often with scant concern for verisimilitude. In recent years however, the emergence of bio art, that is, an art form exploring live tissue and life processes, whether by manipulating genes, cells or other living matter, or by creating interspecies hybrids,[1] has turned these concerns on their head: bio art is not in thrall to representation but takes its cue from science, with bio artists transforming or manipulating the specimen itself for purposes of study or display. Rather than representing it, they present the real thing, initiating new artistic methods and practices that overlap with the scientific or experimental approach. In the first part of my essay, I will examine this new approach to the specimen: I will show how it differs from the older tradition of the taxidermy specimen, before going on to demonstrate how it is also showing up the inadequacies of existing practices of specimen-based art.

I will start by pointing out that bio art, as the art of live specimens, contests the principles underlying taxidermy: it displays live specimens as opposed to dead ones, and privileges ephemeral life processes over preservation and conservation. At the same time however, the ethical problems it raises are similar to those confronting taxidermy, which has to contend with the long, albeit rarely acknowledged, history of exploitation and violence that brought it into the museum in the first place. Springer and Turpin look back over the largely unacknowledged history of taxidermy specimens in their article 'Necroaesthetics: Denaturalising the Collection'. Commenting on their seeming neutrality when exhibited in natural history museums, and on the lack of anxiety felt by the viewer as to their provenance and the acts of violence they underwent, they write: 'In their *reanimation* as natural history collection objects, the specimens on view declare their neutrality, which makes it difficult to connect their presence to the political, colonial, or ecological sites of struggle from which they were extracted.'[2] Yet connected they are, in the same way as bio art is often charged with violating Western humanist ethics and infringing animal rights. Even more to the point, some of the tactics Springer and Turpin summon to decipher the contemporary necroaesthetic strategies that perpetuate the fiction of specimen displays,[3] could also be used to decode bio art. They locate such decoding tactics in Donna Haraway's essay 'Teddy Bear Patriarchy: Taxidermy in the Garden of Eden, New York City, 1908–1936' (1989). Citing Haraway, they point out for instance that exhibitions produce permanence, thereby arresting decay.[4] The practice of exhibition-making thus reinforces the desire for permanence inherent in taxidermy while paradoxically contradicting bio art's desire to explore the ephemerality of life. Haraway also highlights the role of human exceptionalism in our treatment of taxidermy and the hierarchies we construct around it.[5] In the same way, our treatment of the live specimen is the product of human exceptionalism—even though the latter is called into question by bio art's human–animal hybrids. Bio art is thus a hybrid form that has rid itself of some, although not all, of taxidermy's failings, while also provoking criticism on account of its intermediate position between art and science: in addition to raising the same kind of ethical problems as science often does, it is generally regarded by the art world as nothing more than a means of generating public interest in science.

Yet even though bio art suffers from these associations, it nonetheless shows up the inadequacies of existing forms of specimen-based art as well as the artistic discourse accompanying them. By 'existing forms of specimen-based art' I refer to the work of artists like Mark Dion, who describes himself as a dilettante with regard to science and seeks to engage artistically with taxidermy specimens rather than living specimens, as in bio art.[6] Working in a similarly representational vein, the Danish Icelandic artist Olafur Eliasson points out: 'I look for inspiration from science, but I do not translate scientific ideas or theories into artworks. I rather begin from a feeling or intuition and develop the work pragmatically through the process of working on it'.[7]

Eliasson's work is thus on his own admission intuitive, arguably even more so than that of many other artists whose names are not as readily associated with science. As Christian Mieves points out, Eliasson's approximate emulation of a natural specimen, the sun, in *Weather Project* (2003) stands in marked contrast to such works as John Constable's landscape paintings, in which the representation of the clouds epitomizes fidelity to scientific observation of nature.[8] The intuitive approach favoured by Eliasson and Dion stands in marked contrast to the perspective of the bio artists, who work directly on the specimen itself and whose use of cells and DNA as artistic materials calls for close collaboration with scientists. In other words, the bio artists' work does not address the specimen on the level of emulation and representation but as a material and end point.

There is yet another key difference between bio art and the work of artists such as Dion and Eliasson, in that bio art asks us to reconsider the idea that art is solely intended for the viewer. This was particularly obvious in Pierre Huyghe's eponymous exhibition at the Pompidou Centre in 2013, which clearly illustrates my point, even though Huyghe's practice does not pursue the same goals as bio art. In the Pompidou Centre, bees and a dog cohabited with a spider, a stream of ants, and various sea creatures housed in aquariums, offering a spectacle that continued after the museum's opening hours, at its own pace and rhythm, foregrounding the unpredictability of living things.[9] These traits—the relinquishment of control, unpredictability, the downplaying of the viewer, are very much present in the experimental set-ups of bio artists.

A final, even more conclusive difference between bio art and the work of Eliasson and Dion is that bio art promotes a new interpretation of science, one, I argue, that corresponds to sociologist and philosopher of science Andrew Pickering's vision of the discipline. Although Pickering does not specifically mention bio art in his article 'Art, Science and Experiment', he distinguishes between scientific experiments that are used to validate or falsify a theory and pure experimentation, without any particular aim. For Pickering, some forms of contemporary art belong in this latter mode, staging 'a sort of ontological theatre in which the artist himself has no definitive knowledge of how the work will behave and instead sets in motion processes of unpredictable emergence'.[10] Bio art can be said to belong in this category, insofar as bio artists stage indeterminate science-based processes whose outcome is unpredictable.

Indeed, Pickering goes so far as to advocate the establishment of a science and technology-based canon in contemporary art which would challenge the traditional sciences. Such artworks would correspond to Pickering's vision of an alternative science that functions in a similar way to art, reconciling art with science, and constituting 'an alternative art-science formation in which the arts and sciences of unknowability genuinely hang together'.[11] For Pickering, such works are not only art but also models of the world and of how we can engage with it: the examples he gives are based on the view that the task of the artist is not to create something new, for everything is already present in nature, but rather to create the conditions that will allow nature to become art.[12] For example, Chris Welsby's experimental works hand over control of the work to the wind or the weather. In the film *Seven Days* (1974), Welsby filmed a landscape in Wales over the course of a week, adjusting the camera so that it pointed upwards when the sun was concealed by clouds and downwards when the sun came out. As Pickering emphasizes, Welsby explored 'the liveliness and agency of nature in two ways: showing us images of the wind blowing and the rain falling, but [...] letting nature—here the sun and the clouds—control the camera-angles'.[13] We can connect Pickering's thesis of the unknowability of art as embodied by *Seven Days*, with the unknowability of bio art, which likewise foregrounds process, observation, experiment and the agency of nature itself. Bio art thus goes some way towards ridding specimen-based art of its necroaesthetic legacy, enabling it to enjoy a new lease of life in art exhibitions that literally celebrate not only the union of art and science but also the intricacies of life itself.

Take the exhibition *NatureCultures*, organized in 2016 at Alfred Ehrhardt Stiftung in Berlin. It featured among other artists Pinar Yoldas, an interdisciplinary artist-researcher who explores the relationship between nature and science. With *Regnum Alba* (2015), Yoldas addresses the use of artificially bred albino organisms by scientists, exposing their desire for purity at the expense of natural growth, while her *Designer Babies* series explores the implications of applying transhumanist thinking to the field of speculative design. Also featured in the exhibition was the work of artist and biologist Brandon Ballengée, who addresses the decline of amphibians through artworks that associate aesthetics with scientific tools. Ballengée uses the traditional chemical process of 'clearing and staining' specimens—whereby hard tissues are assigned bright colours and muscles rendered transparent—adapting it to deformed frogs. He thereby creates visually striking portraits of the frogs, which also serve scientific aims in that they help him understand the cause of their deformities.[14] The work of these two bio artists reflects Pickering's preoccupation with experimentation and research, while acknowledging contemporary art's critical and aesthetic concerns.

Nonetheless, the bio artists' practice of sharpening their understanding of biological processes through close collaboration with scientists can pose certain problems: when artists draw attention to controversial experiments that are normally conducted in the secrecy of laboratories, they often become the scapegoat for them.[15] In the same way, bio art, an emerging field going back only a few decades, generates considerable controversy in itself on account of its use of live human and animal tissue, raising questions that are as weighty, if not more, than those posed by taxidermy specimens. As writer and editor Olivia Solon confirms: 'So knotty is the area that very few galleries even show these works, and those that do tend to be large scientific institutions.'[16] However bio art also raises key theoretical issues, asking whether art can be an effective way of helping scientists to communicate with a wider audience and whether science can itself be considered a form of art. Following a discussion of these and other issues at the #postARTandSCIENCE symposium (Wellcome Collection, 22 September 2017), the conclusion was reached that bio art is a new and highly promising way of bringing art and science together: not only is it based on scientific collaboration, but it is ideally placed to problematize and critique the work that scientists do. In other words, rather than focusing on the controversies bio art arouses, we might regard it as an instrument of critique, a means of monitoring the excesses of science. As we shall see in the next part, we might also regard the 3D specimen as an instrument of critique: insofar as it is the result of technological innovation, it is ideally placed to problematize the human/technology relation.

Mutant Objects

As we saw in the first part of this essay, the live specimen can be used as an artistic material. However, specimens are also products that undergo technological development, as in the case of the 3D printed specimen, which I shall turn to now. In *The Inbetweenness of Things*, Paul Basu writes that we need to refrain from categorizing things using restrictive categories of place and purpose, for they are not particular things but many things at once. Adopting an object-centred approach, Basu looks at how things mediate between different worlds, whether cultural, geographic or temporal.[17] The 3D printed specimen can be described in these terms: it mediates between image and object, copy and original, but also between art and mass production. It also questions these long-standing binaries insofar as it can be unique, like an artwork, but nonetheless industrially produced. Furthermore, like live tissue, the 3D specimen is a new and radical development in the history of the specimen that triggers controversies of its own, challenging, as I will show, both our conception of the art object and our relation to technology, and thereby generating an inescapable unease whose whys and wherefores I will seek to ascertain.

From the point of view of art, first of all, 3D specimens challenge the distinction between image and object, insofar as they are three-dimensional images that recast the image as a material object.[18] The incomplete, imperfect materiality of 3D specimens, which are neither as material as objects, nor as immaterial as digital images, makes them hard to classify and as a result, they are usually not even regarded as art. They also contest another fundamental distinction in art, that between the copy and its original: in Matthew Plummer's *Digital Natives* series, for instance, everyday items such as a watering can are 3D scanned, subjected to distorting algorithms and then 3D printed in coloured resin or sandstone, thereby acquiring a kind of materiality, as well as constituting deformed 3D variants of the real thing, copies with no original, simulacra that have become real.[19] It is this constant vacillation between image and object and between copy and original that accounts for the skewed temporality and disturbing sense of lack they exude. Olivier Zeitoun describes them as tinged with melancholy and evoking a certain absence or incompleteness, as if they had not fully materialized.[20] Merleau-Ponty explores a similar kind of absence: '[T]he proper essence of the visible is to have a layer of invisibility in the strict sense, which it makes present as a certain absence'.[21] Perhaps the kind of absence to which Merleau-Ponty refers is more 'visible' in 3D objects, and that is why they appear wanting to us. In any case, invisibility, absence and incompleteness are all terms that we can readily associate with 3D objects and artworks. Examples of 3D printed artworks derived from specimens include Studio Swine's *Meteorite Shoes* (2014), which consist of high-heeled shoes designed to generate a sensation of lightness similar to that of a meteorite floating in space. With the help of a 3D scanner, the designers produced modelizations of meteorites from the collection of the Natural History Museum in London, using aluminium foam to simulate the lumps of rock. Gassing agents were injected into the metal while it was in a molten state, creating thousands of irregular cells. The solid foam—consisting of 90 per cent air—was then ground to give the shoe its uneven external shape, while the insides were covered with leather.[22] The shoes thus resemble meteorites but are nonetheless lacking substance and weight: midway between image and object, copy and original, they are as light as air.

Exuding a similarly evanescent materiality, are the rows of faces lined up in Heather Dewey-Hagborg's *Stranger Visions. Portraits and samples from New York* (2012). For this work, Dewey-Hagborg collected specimens of hair, chewed up gum and cigarette butts from the streets, public bathrooms and waiting rooms of New York City, and extracted DNA from them. Analysis of the DNA enabled the artist to identify certain physical characteristics of its owner, such as gender, eye colour, weight, and so on, and thus to generate 3D printed life-size faces possessing these characteristics. The project was intended to draw attention to the developing technology of DNA phenotyping and the problematics of biological surveillance. As the artist points out on her website, there are many potentially racist biases in the existing technology 'which I (and many scientists) do not consider accurate or impartial enough for use in criminal investigations'.[23] The vacant expressions of Dewey-Hagborg's lifelike faces bear witness not only to the distortions inherent in 3D printed imagery but also to its incompleteness, as does the paradoxical lightness of the meteorite shoes. Indeed, incompleteness or absence may well become one of the leitmotifs of the 3D post-specimen, which no longer consists of an actual specimen, but of an object derived from it, an object that is therefore incomplete with respect to the original and that succeeds or comes after it and therefore differs from it, as implied by the prefix 'post'.

More than just the fundamental distinctions on which art is based, the 3D printed object is also reshaping our relation to technology. Take the 3D printed models developed by the Center for Human Anatomy Education at Monash University: consisting of anatomical models created from CT and laser scans of real specimens that capture detail more efficiently than traditional techniques, they associate images and objects, virtuality and reality, custom and digital fabrication, constituting a key phase in the convergence of physical and computational matter.[24] They are also becoming a valuable tool in anatomy education, where they herald a future in which, as studies suggest, the accurate, manipulable, easy to use 3D printed model will increasingly be preferred to the real thing. Yet the ease and rapidity of 3D printing can prove disorientating for the consumer, in the same way as 3D art objects generate a sense of absence in the viewer. In other words, whether in the form of artworks or scientific objects, 3D printing is exacerbating our innate discomfort with technology, a discomfort that, I argue, resurfaces from time to time in our collective consciousness, only to be forgotten or repressed.

In order to get a better grasp of this sense of unease and how it ties in with the 3D printed specimen, we might go back in time to the exhibition *Les Immatériaux*, co-organized by Jean-François Lyotard at the Centre Pompidou in 1985. Its main aim, as John Rajchman points out, was precisely to make manifest the sense of unease that scientific progress was provoking in those years. As Rajchman writes:

> Lyotard was keen to insist that the aim of *Les Immatériaux* was not to display objects, but to make visible, even palpable […] a kind of 'post-industrial' techno-scientific condition […]. Far from the informational ideals of 'communication', *Les Immatériaux* presented a condition of unease, a sense of disarray.[25]

Just as the technosciences were generating unease in 1985, so, I claim, is the 3D printed specimen generating a similar sense of unease in this century, insofar as it is revolutionizing the significance, design and production of objects. In her analysis of *Les Immatériaux*, Isabelle Thomas-Fogiel expounds on the nature of the unease that the exhibition sought to elicit, an unease that is intimately related to our current discomfort:

> Its aim was initially to show how the technosciences had become […] our everyday 'reality,' and thus obscured […] originary, non-constructed reality. […] Because they are now programs or services (that is, internalized 'immaterials'), they appear as the very foundation and condition of our relationship with the world.[26]

In the years that have passed since 1985, we have become progressively more detached from non-constructed reality as the technosciences become the prime mediators of our relation to the world. The unease generated by the 3D printed post-specimen is a reminder that the issue of the encroachment of technology on our lives has yet to be resolved. At the same time however, the post-specimen merges art and technology, thereby gesturing towards a solution of sorts, namely that we cease to resist technology, and instead acknowledge our reliance on it. The post-specimen thereby reflects the approach of theorists such as N. Katherine Hayles, whose term 'nonconscious cognition' bridges human and technical cognition by locating them on a continuum.[27] I The new theorizations of the animal, plant or mineral specimen that I explore in the next part of this essay go in a similar direction, by redistributing agency between humans and non-humans, and thereby challenging anthropocentrism and the practices and beliefs to which it is linked.

Neither Animal, Nor Vegetable Nor Mineral

Although the two above-mentioned variants of the post-specimen—bio art and 3D printing technology—are key developments in their own right, they both gesture towards a third type of post-specimen, based on a non-dualist ethos of continuity. As has been pointed out, technology and the technosciences now appear as the very foundation of our relation to the world, or in other words as the means by which we connect ourselves to the world and establish continuity with it. In bio art, as the art historian and curator Jeanette Zwingenberger likewise points out, visitors establish connections between their body and the specimen on view, insofar as both the viewer and the viewed consist of living matter: 'The transformational processes and their temporal nature [...] no longer consist of the representation of a referent but of the presentation of a complex continuity.'[28] Finally, for Andrew Pickering, whose views echo, as we have seen, certain aspects of bio art, continuity is manifest in our connections with nonhuman agents, in the fact that we are all part of the same constantly transforming world. He contests what he describes as modernity's dualist Cartesian ontology, claiming that it attributes genuine agency to humans alone, and not to non-humans, which it considers passive and awaiting human intervention to give them shape.[29] For Pickering, the real world is non-dualist, 'an endlessly lively world of flux and becoming, that we are just a part of'.[30] By contesting human exceptionalism, he emphasizes our continuities and similarities with the rest of the world.

This third and last part will take an in-depth look at the notion of continuity, as manifest in particular in the shifting taxonomy of the specimen, which has undergone profound transformations since modern science declared eighteenth-century Swedish naturalist Carl Linnaeus's division of nature into the animal, plant and mineral kingdoms obsolete. Even the traces of these divisions that subsist in common parlance are disappearing in the wake of the far-ranging ongoing investigations—by anthropologists, artists, philosophers and cultural theorists—into the frontiers between life and non-life, human and non-human. This last part of my essay will explore our changing perception of animal, plant and mineral specimens, focusing on the ways the new approaches establish continuities between humans and non-humans, anthropocentric constraints.

Take for instance, Italian philosopher Emanuele Coccia, author of *La Vie des Plantes* ('The Life of Plants') (2016), who explores the similarities and differences between human and plants. Coccia points out on the one hand that plants are essential to human and animal life, providing us with oxygen and making the planet habitable. On the other hand, we feel closer to animals than to plants. For plants are immobile and privilege surface rather than volume in order to be as close as possible to the soil that nourishes them. Furthermore, plants are autonomous with respect to other living beings: whereas humans and animals are dependent on plants or other animals for their survival, plants need only soil, water, air and light and consequently are superior to us in this respect.[31] Yet despite these differences, we cannot but acknowledge that our lives have always been intertwined with plants: whereas today they supply us with many of the objects and tools we use in our daily lives (food, clothing, etc.), Aristotelianism in Antiquity and the Middle Ages went so far as to regard plants not just as a specific life form but as the principle by virtue of which all beings are alive.[32] The role of plants and their proximity to other forms of life are key themes in contemporary art, for example in Cécile Beau's exhibition *Hyle*. The French artist shows to what extent the vegetable, animal and mineral realms are intertwined and indistinguishable: what we take to be stalactites turn out to be tree trunks, while photographs of plants printed on aluminium plates acquire a shiny aspect that makes them look like minerals.

The mineral world is also being reconsidered, and in particular its exploitation by humans. T. J. Demos has commented on how artists and researchers 'are contesting the anthropocentric domination of the Earth and the assumption of the paramount role of human agents and supporting a more horizontal and sustainable approach to resource distribution, investigated via open-access media and aesthetic presentation'.[33] One of the artists he names is Ursula Biemann, whose video *Deep Weather* (2013) explores the effects of the tar sands mining operations in Northern Canada. Shots of the open pit extraction zone in Alberta give way to images of Bangladeshi flood victims constructing mud embankments, to protect themselves against global warming. *Deep Weather*'s disturbing imagery demonstrates the effects of environmental exploitation while also showing how the activity of non-human agents is affecting human behavioural patterns.

Ilana Halperin also draws attention to the incommensurate power and force of geological activity. In the photograph *Boiling Milk Solfataras* (1999), the artist can be seen heating up a saucepan of milk in a 100°C sulphur spring, thereby suggesting that geological activity dwarfs that of man. Meanwhile, her exhibition *Steine* (*Stones*) (2012) at the Berlin Museum of Medical History focused on the relation between body stones and geological phenomena. The work portrayed landmass formed both inside and outside the body, pointing up their differences in scale and impact.

Insofar as they explore our relation to geological phenomena, these works tie in with the writings of cultural theorist Monika Bakke, who investigates the co-evolution of biological and mineral species and the geological forces at work in all life, taking as her starting-point both the biological and the geological or deep-time perspectives and seeking to convey the complexity of the biological and mineral entanglements linking species. She addresses these questions via the concept of metabolism, noting that the terms 'nutrition' and 'metabolism' are now understood as 'self-organization'.[34] Bakke bases her concept of metabolism on Myra Hird's definition of the term, which is not restricted to organic activity or life, but also comprises non-life, and turns environment into organism and vice versa 'in various processes of recycling of matter contributing to the planetary cycles crucial for sustaining life'.[35]

Bakke gives the example of artist Michael Burton's *Astronomical Bodies* (2010), a project developed in collaboration with astrobiologist Terence Kee that investigates the minerals present in human bodies. It consists of a wearable apron fitted with chambers for storing urine and recovering the phosphorus in it through a process of crystallization. Phosphorus is one of the fundamental building blocks of carbon-based life, and a form of it is thought to have arrived on Earth through meteors and interstellar dust. Burton's aim is to transform phosphorus from the body into a man-made meteorite, to be sent into space in order to trigger life-forming processes on other planets.[36] By emphasizing the relation between the human body and minerals, his project recontextualizes the human species in a deep-time perspective, connecting it to this very different timescale and questioning the boundaries between life and non-life, the biological and the geological. As Bakke states, such multispecies alliances make us realize that 'the human experience of living on earth actually equals being earth'.[37] Or as Lynn Margulis and Dorion Sagan point out:

> People, for example, redistribute and concentrate oxygen, hydrogen, nitrogen, carbon, sulphur, phosphorus, and other elements of Earth's crust into two-legged, upright forms that have an amazing propensity to wander across, dig into, and in countless other ways alter Earth's surface. We are walking, talking minerals.[38]

Yet we refuse to acknowledge these numerous instances of continuity with the non-human world. One reason might be, as anthropologist Elizabeth Povinelli points out in her book *Geontologies* (2016), that we only take being (ontology) into account and not non-life (*geos*): 'Western ontologies are covert biontologies—Western metaphysics as a measure of all forms of existence by the qualities of one form of existence (*bios, zoe*)'.[39] Art projects such as Burton's take *geos* into account, displacing the human and blurring the boundaries between life and non-life, human and non-human agency.

As with plants and minerals, so with animals, where theorists are also disrupting conventional practices of power distribution, by showing how animals overstep the limits of the categories to which we assign them. *Dictionary of Now #12—ANIMAL*, a discussion held on 24 May 2018 at Haus der Kulturen der Welt in Berlin, insisted on the need to pay attention to animal agents, alongside human agents. The philosopher Rosi Braidotti pleaded in favour of dismantling hierarchical systems of exploitation and dominance of animals, while the anthropologist Philippe Descola advocated that we take into account our variegated relationships to non-human animals in order to forge a new self-understanding of humankind. Descola is known for his system of four ontologies, or systems of properties that humans ascribe to beings, which vary in accordance with whether or not intentionality or selfhood are ascribed to non-humans. These ontologies consist of animism, which postulates that humans and non-humans possess similar interiorities, naturalism, which makes a distinction between humans and non-humans, totemism, according to which certain groups of humans and non-humans share interior and physical attributes, and analogism, which claims that each entity is different and unique.[40] Only naturalism, the mode favoured by modern science, separates animals and other non-humans from humans, placing special emphasis on human agency.

Artists and curators are also exploring ways of giving animal agency its due. Take the series of symposia organized by the Serpentine Galleries under the title *The Shape of a Circle in the Mind of a Fish*, a reference to the activities of puffer fish, as explained in the programme: 'At the bottom of the sea, a small puffer fish performs a labour of love, making elaborate sand circles […] How to understand the movement that constitutes it as a language […] in an interspecies landscape'?[41] The first session on 28 May 2018 assembled artists, dancers, writers and scientists at the London Zoo to reflect on the intersections between cognition, language, affect, agency and sensibility. The event featured, among others, Rasmus Nielsen from the collective Superflex, who discussed biomimicry, translation and the sand circles traced by puffer fish, explaining how they inform the group's research into non-human agency.

Other artists go even further in their privileging of the animal and decentring of the human. As opposed to highlighting the parallels between animals and humans, the idea is to reverse the relations between them, as the following extract from a recent CFP points out:

> The focal point here is not so much about becoming animal or of turning the animal into a ventriloquist of humanity, according to what is in fact a classical concept, but rather about very recent practices based on relations of exchange or complete reversal.[42]

The CFP gives the example of a musical performance for the sheep, goats and pigs of a Peckham farm that took place in 2017 under the aegis of David Harradine, thereby recalling Laurie Anderson's low frequency concert for dogs (*Concert for dogs*, 2010), which was apparently audible only to canine listeners.

Yet although the examples of artworks I have given here go some way towards flattening the hierarchies between humans, animals, plants and minerals, they do not address the underlying problem that even reversing the relations between humans and animals remains a cosmetic gesture. Deploring what he describes as our dialectical efforts to reconcile distinct domains, Bruno Latour writes: 'Ecological thought has suffered just as much from attempts to 'recombine' the two artefacts of nature and society as from the older more violent history that forced the two realms—that of necessity and that of freedom—to bifurcate'.[43] As he points out, even the idea of drawing up a contract between two parties suggests that they are separate entities with conflicting interests. Problems likewise arise when the two parties are forcibly unified and both regarded as parts of nature—not because this would imply the objectification of humans, but because such a scientific world view does not do justice to the diversity of all that might be involved, from microbes and plate tectonics, through to engineers and politicians.[44] Latour resorts to the concepts of animation and de-animation, proposing that the real world is generally considered as made up of inanimate matter to which we refrain from adding a layer of animation, but that in fact it should not be de-animated in the first place. It is not a matter of animating inert matter but of refraining from de-animating everything we encounter.[45] We can likewise transpose this argument to the human/technology distinction, by suggesting that we abstain from continually de-animating technology, and, as N. Katherine Hayles proposes, grant it certain capacities in terms of agency.[46] Latour's solution is thus to refrain from reconciling opposites and instead redistribute agency in as differentiated a way as possible, to the point where the notions of object and subject both return to the ground from which we continually try to extricate them, whether by de-animating the object or over-animating the subject.[47] Yet this approach nonetheless poses the problem that the subject and object distinction does not completely disappear: it is the subject who de-animates, over-animates, or redistributes agency to the object.

The Swiss artist Pauline Julier addresses this very problem in artistic terms in her *Naturalis Historia* (2018),[48] an encyclopaedic book project exploring the relation between human and non-human agency. Its contents range from interviews with Philippe Descola and Bruno Latour, to a parable about nature and human hubris, images of volcanic landscapes, stills from the artist's video *Doha* (2017) on the Icelandic volcano that grounded European air traffic in 2010, and the story of Pliny the Elder, who died in AD 79 following the eruption of Mount Vesuvius, having authored the original *Historia Naturalis* (AD 77), an account of all the Romans knew about the natural world. The book does not discuss the specimen as such but recontextualizes it by focusing on the natural habitats from which it is extracted. By showing plants and rocks in their natural context, before they become specimens as it were, it emphasizes the extent to which the specimen is a human construct. Indeed, Julier's book is based around the idea that theorizations of the world, whether those of Pliny the Elder, geographers, artists or scientists, are mere constructs: they are incommensurate with the forces of nature, yielding no more than illusory, partial and incomplete glimpses of the world. As she notes, in order to navigate their environment, humans interpret and 'confine it with their categories of thought [...] I want to stress how much the concepts that are used to organize the diversity of the world are our own'.[49] For Julier, the act of imposing one's thoughts on the world implies slicing it up into categories and ridding it of its liveliness by making it coherent and understandable.

The concept of the post-specimen is a construct just as much as our other categories of thought, but it nonetheless contributes to the breakdown of the categories ordering the natural world. By emphasizing the continuities between human and non-human entities, it constitutes a first step towards undoing the confinement of the world within human thought—and looks set to continue doing so in the future.

The post-specimen plays an important role in contemporary thinking, insofar as it unsettles, dynamizes and rejuvenates the contemporary cultural and scientific landscape. I showed how the specimen has inspired a new art movement, I demonstrated that it has become a conduit for technological innovation, and I explored its capability to blur the dividing lines between animal, vegetable and mineral, between human and non-human, and between life and non-life.

NOTES

1. Frances Stracey: 'Bio-art: The ethics behind the aesthetics', *Nature Reviews. Molecular Cell Biology* 10, no. 7 (2009): 496-500. Available at https://www.nature.com/articles/nrm2699 (accessed 21 June 2020).

2. Anna-Sophie Springer and Etienne Turpin, 'Necroaesthetics: Denaturalising the Collection', *L'internationale,* (2016), http://www.internationaleonline.org/research/politics_of_life_and_death/73_necroaesthetics_denaturalising_the_collection (accessed 16 June 2018) (original emphasis).

3. Ibid., n.p.

4. Donna Haraway cited in Ibid., n.p.

5. The title mentioned above has been evaluated for inclusion in Scopus by the Content Selection & Advisory Board (CSAB). The review of this title is now complete and the CSAB has advised that the title will be accepted for inclusion in Scopus. For your information, the reviewer comments are copied below:

    + The journal consistently includes articles that are scientifically sound and relevant to an international academic or professional audience in this field.

    + In general, the content of the articles is consistent with the scope and aims of the journal.

    - Despite being published for quite some time, articles in this title have attracted few citations by other titles currently covered by Scopus.

    + Although the scope of this journal is narrow, it addresses the need of an important niche audience.

    Our Source Collection Management department will contact the publisher of this title within the next three months to initiate the indexing process for Scopus. A content coverage agreement needs to be in place before we can start adding the content to Scopus.com. If you are the publisher, please do not send us your content yet unless requested by our Source Collection Management department.

6. Daniel Neville, 'Classifying Mark Dion', *Nevolution*, (2010): 9, http://nevolution.typepad.com/theories/2010/06/mark-dion.html (accessed 12 June 2018).

7. Anthony King, Olafur Eliasson, 'Olafur Eliasson: Art, Science and Environmental Consciousness'. *Euroscientist* (2017), https://www.euroscientist.com/artist-olafur-eliasson-art-science-environmental-consciousness/ (accessed 16 June 2018).

8. Christian Mieves, 'From Nimbus Cloud to Cloud Canyon', in *Wonder in Contemporary Artistic Practice*, ed. C. Mieves and I. Brown, 105–20 (New: Routledge, 2017); ref. 113.

9. Rahma Khazam, 'Pierre Huyghe/Philippe Parreno', *Frieze*, (2013), https://frieze.com/article/pierre-huyghe-philippe-parreno (accessed 12 June 2018).

10. Andrew Pickering, 'Art, Science and Experiment', *MaHKUscript: Journal of Fine Art Research* 1, no. 1 (2016): 2, ref 4 (online) available at https://www.mahkuscript.com/articles/10.5334/mjfar.2/ (accessed 21 June 2020).

11. Ibid.

12. Andrew Pickering, 'Neo-Sigma: Art, Agency, and Revolution', *Leonardo Electronic Almanac* 22, no. 2 (2017): Cambridge, MA: LEA/MIT Press, (online) available at https://contemporaryarts.mit.edu/pub/neo-sigma/release/9 (accessed 21 June 2020).

13. Ibid., n.p.

14. *NatureCultures*, cur. Regine Rapp, Christian de Lutz, Alfred Ehrhardt Foundation, Berlin, 2 July–4 September 2016, [online] available at https://www.aestiftung.de/en/exhibitions/naturecultures-kuratiert-von-regine-rapp-christian-de-lutz/ (accessed 21 June 2020).

15. Olivia Solon, 'Bioart: The Ethics and Aesthetics of Using Living Tissue as a Medium', *Wired*, (2011) https://www.wired.com/2011/07/bioart/ (accessed 12 June 2018).

16. Ibid., n.p.

17. Paul Basu, (ed.), *The Inbetweenness of Things*, London: Bloomsbury, 2017.

18. Mitchell cited in Marie-Ange Brayer, 'La fin de la représentation?', in *Imprimer le Monde*, ed. M.-A. Brayer (Paris: Editions du Centre Pompidou, 2017), 84, (my translation).

19. Ibid., 84.

20. Olivier Zeitoun, 'Matière à penser' ('Matter for thought'), in *Imprimer le Monde*, ed. M.-A. Brayer (Paris: Editions du Centre Pompidou, 2017), 94.

21. Maurice Merleau-Ponty, 'Eye and Mind', in *Merleau-Ponty: The Primacy of Perception*, trans. James M.Edie (Evanston: Northwestern University Press, 1964), 187.

22. Dan Howarth, 'Studio Swine's Meteorite Shoes Simulate Space Debris', *dezeen*, (2015) https://www.dezeen.com/2015/01/09/studio-swine-meteorite-shoes-aluminium-foam/ (accessed 12 June 2018).

23. Heather Dewey-Hagborg, 'Stranger Visions', [online] available at http://deweyhagborg.com/projects/stranger-visions (accessed 12 June 2018).

24. Zeitoun, 'Matière à penser', 94.

25. John Rajchman, 'Les Immatériaux or How to Construct the History of Exhibitions', *Tate Papers*, no.12 (2009), [online] available at http://www.tate.org.uk/research/publications/tate-papers/12/les-immateriaux-or-how-to-construct-the-history-of-exhibitions (accessed 16 June 2018).

26. Isabelle Thomas-Fogiel, 'Isabelle Thomas-Fogiel interviewed by Rahma Khazam', in *Behavioral Objects/Behavioral Matter*, ed. S. Bianchini and E. Quinz, forthcoming; here quoting Jean-François Lyotard and Bernard Blistène, 'A Conversation with Jean-François Lyotard', *Flash Art* no. 121 (1985): 32–35, 33.

27. Katherine N. Hayles, *Unthought: The Power of the Cognitive Nonconscious* (Chicago: University of Chicago Press, 2017), 67.

28. Jeanette Zwingenberger, 'Les corps mutants des artistes. Bio-art', *Rue Descartes* 64, no. 2 (2009): n.p., https://www.cairn.info/revue-rue-descartes-2009-2-page-117.htm (accessed 21 June 2020) (my translation).

29. Pickering, 'Neo-Sigma', n.p.

30. Ibid.

31. Emanuele Coccia, *La vie des plantes* (Paris: Editions Payot & Rivages, 2016), 20.

32. Ibid., 22.

33. T. J. Demos, 'Contemporary Art and the Politics of Ecology', *Third Text* 27, no. 1 (2013): 1–9, 3, [online] available at https://www.tandfonline.com/doi/full/10.1080/09528822.2013.753187 (accessed 18 June 2018).

34. Mark Bedau cited in Monika Bakke, 'Art and Metabolic Force in Deep Time Environments', *Environmental Philosophy* 14, no. 1 (2017): 41–59, 41, [online] available at https://www.researchgate.net/publication/314717015_Art_and_Metabolic_Force_in_Deep_Time_Environments (accessed 3 February 2020).

35. Myra Hird cited in Bakke, 43.

36. Ibid., 45.

37. Bakke, 55.

38. Lynn Margulis and Dorian Sagan, *What Is Life?* (Berkeley: University of California Press, 2000), 49.

39. Elizabeth Povinelli, *Geontologies: A Requiem to Late Liberalism* (Durham: Duke University Press, 2016), 6.

40. Eduardo Kohn, 'A Conversation with Philippe Descola', *Tipití: Journal of the Society for the Anthropology of Lowland South America* 7, no. 2 (2009), Article 1, [online] available at https://digitalcommons.trinity.edu/tipiti/vol7/iss2/1 (accessed 12 June 2018).

41. Serpentine Galleries, 'The Shape of a Circle in the Mind of a Fish, Part 1', (2018) [online] available at https://www.serpentinegalleries.org/whats-on/symposium-shape-circle-mind-fish-part-1/ (accessed 21 June 2020).

42. Espace art actuel, 'Point de vue animal'. *ArtHist.net* no. 121, (2018), 15 May 2018, [online] available at https://arthist.net/archive/18134 (accessed 15 June 2018).

43. Bruno Latour, 'Agency at the Time of the Anthropocene', *New Literary History* 45 (2014): 1–18, 16, [online] available at http://www.bruno-latour.fr/sites/default/files/128-FELSKI-HOLBERG-NLH-FINAL.pdf (accessed 12 June 2018).

44. Ibid., 1–18, 16.

45. Ibid., 15.

46. Hayles, *Unthought*, 67.

47. Latour, 'Agency at the Time of the Anthropocene', 17.

48. Pauline Julier, *Naturalis Historia*, ed. J.-P. Felley and O. Kaeser (Paris: Centre Culturel Suisse Paris, 2018).

49. Pauline Julier, 'Works', [online] available at http://paulinejulier.com/works_detail/naturalis-historia (accessed 18 June 2018).

REFERENCES

Bakke, Monika. 'Art and Metabolic Force in Deep Time Environments'. *Environmental Philosophy* 14, no.1 (2017): 41–59. Available at https://www.academia.edu/34799081/Art_and_Metabolic_Force_in_Deep_Time_Environments (accessed 18 June 2018).

Basu, Paul, ed. *The Inbetweenness of Things*. London: Bloomsbury, 2017.

Bedau, Mark A., and Carol E. Cleland, eds. *The Nature of Life: Classical and Contemporary Perspectives from Philosophy and Science*. Cambridge: Cambridge University Press, 2010.

Brayer, Marie-Ange. 'La fin de la représentation?' ('The End of Representation?'). In *Imprimer le Monde* ('Printing the World'), ed. M.-A. Brayer, 84. Paris: Editions du Centre Pompidou, 2017: 73–91.

Coccia, Emanuele. *La vie des plantes*. Paris: Editions Payot & Rivages, 2016.

Demos, T. J. 'Contemporary Art and the Politics of Ecology'. *Third Text* 27, no. 1 (2013): 1–9. Available at https://www.tandfonline.com/doi/full/10.1080/09528822.2013.753187 (accessed 18 June 2018).

Dewey-Hagborg, Heather. 'Stranger Visions'. Available at http://deweyhagborg.com/projects/stranger-visions (accessed 12 June 2018).

Espace art actuel. 'Point de vue animal'. *ArtHist.net* no. 121 (15 May 2018). Available at https://arthist.net/archive/18134 (accessed 15 June 2018).

Haraway, Donna. 'Teddy Bear Patriarchy: Taxidermy in the Garden of Eden, New York City, 1908–1936'. In *Primate Visions: Gender, Race, and Nature in the World of Modern Science*. New York: Routledge, 1989.

Hayles, N. Katherine. *Unthought: The Power of the Cognitive Nonconscious*. Chicago: University of Chicago Press, 2017.

Hird, Myra. 'Digesting Difference: Metabolism and the Question of Sexual Difference'. *Configurations* 20, no. 3 (Fall, 2012): 213–37.

Howarth, Dan. 'Studio Swine's Meteorite Shoes Simulate Space Debris'. *dezeen*, (2015). Available at https://www.dezeen.com/2015/01/09/studio-swine-meteorite-shoes-aluminium-foam/ (accessed 12 June 2018).

Julier, Pauline. *Naturalis Historia*, ed. J.-P. Felley and O. Kaeser, CCS Paris; P. Julier. Paris: Centre Culturel Suisse Paris, 2018.

Julier, Pauline. 'Works'. Available at http://paulinejulier.com/works_detail/naturalis-historia (accessed 18 June 2018).

Khazam, Rahma. 'Pierre Huyghe/Philippe Parreno'. *Frieze*, (2013). Available at https://frieze.com/article/pierre-huyghe-philippe-parreno (accessed 12 June 2018).

King, Anthony, and Olafur Eliasson. 'Olafur Eliasson: Art, Science and Environmental Consciousness'. *Euroscientist* (2017). Available at https://www.euroscientist.com/artist-olafur-eliasson- artscience-environmental- consciousness/ (accessed 16 June 2018).

Kohn, Eduardo. 'A Conversation with Philippe Descola'. *Tipití: Journal of the Society for the Anthropology of Lowland South America* 7, no. 2 (2009), Article 1. Available at https://digitalcommons.trinity.edu/tipiti/vol7/iss2/1 (accessed 12 June 2018).

Latour, Bruno. 'Agency at the Time of the Anthropocene'. *New Literary History* 45 (2014): 1–18. Available at http://www.bruno-latour.fr/sites/default/files/128-FELSKI-HOLBERG-NLH-FINAL.pdf (accessed 12 June 2018).

Lyotard, Jean-François. 'A Conversation with Jean-François Lyotard'. Jean-François Lyotard interviewed by Bernard Blistène. *Flash Art* no. 121 (1985): 32–35.

Margulis, Lynn, and Dorian Sagan. *What Is Life?* Berkeley: University of California Press, 2000.

Merleau-Ponty, Maurice. 'Eye and Mind'. In *The Primacy of Perception*, trans. James M. Edie. Evanston: Northwestern University Press, 1964: 159–92.

Mieves, Christian. 'From *Nimbus Cloud* to *Cloud Canyon*', In *Wonder in Contemporary Artistic Practice*, ed. C. Mieves and I. Brown, 105–20. New York: Routledge, 2017.

Mitchell, W. J. T. 'Image'. In *Critical Terms for Media Studies*, ed. W. J. T. Mitchell and M. B. N. Hansen, 134–71. Chicago: University of Chicago Press, (2010).

Neville, Daniel. 'Classifying Mark Dion'. *Nevolution*, (2010). Available at http://nevolution. typepad.com/theories/2010/06/mark-dion.html (accessed 12 June 2018).

Pickering, Andrew. 'Neo-Sigma: Art, Agency, and Revolution'. *Leonardo Electronic Almanac* 22, no. 2 (2017): Cambridge, MA: LEA/MIT Press. Available at https://contemporaryarts. mit.edu/pub/neo-sigma/release/9 (accessed 21 June 2020).

Pickering, Andrew. 'Art, Science and Experiment'. *MaHKUscript: Journal of Fine Art Research*, 1(1), (2016): 1–6. Available at https://www.mahkuscript.com/articles/10.5334/mjfar.2/ (accessed 21 June 2020).

#postARTandSCIENCE, Wellcome Collection, 22 September 2017. Available at k/events/2017/ 8/22/postartandscience-symposium-at-the-wellcome-collection-friday-22-september-2017 (accessed 12 June 2018).

Povinelli, Elizabeth. *Geontologies: A Requiem to Late Liberalism*. Durham: Duke University Press, 2016.

Rajchman, John. 'Les Immatériaux or How to Construct the History of Exhibitions'. *Tate Papers* no. 12 (2009). Available at http://www.tate.org.uk/research/publications/tate-papers/12/ les-immateriaux-or-how-to-construct-the-history-of-exhibitions (accessed 16 June 2018).

Rapp, Regine, and de Lutz, Christian, curs. *NatureCultures*, Alfred Ehrhardt Foundation, Berlin, 2 July–4 September 2016. Available at https://www.aestiftung.de/en/exhibitions/ naturecultures-kuratiert-von-regine-rapp-christian-de-lutz/ (accessed 21 June 2020).

Serpentine Galleries. 'The Shape of a Circle in the Mind of a Fish, Part 1', (2018). Available at https://www.serpentinegalleries.org/whats-on/symposium-shape-circle-mind-fish-part-1/ (accessed 21 June 2020).

Solon, Olivia. 'Bioart: The Ethics and Aesthetics of Using Living Tissue as a Medium'. *Wired* (2011). Available at https://www.wired.com/2011/07/bioart/ (accessed 12 June 2018).

Springer, Anna-Sophie, and Etienne Turpin. 'Necroaesthetics: Denaturalising the Collection'. *L'internationale* (2016). Available at http://www.internationaleonline.org/research/pol- itics_of_life_and_death/73_necroaesthetics_denaturalising_the_collection (accessed 16 June 2018).

Stracey, Frances: 'Bio-art: The ethics behind the aesthetics', *Nature Reviews. Molecular Cell Biology* 10, no. 7 (2009): 496-500. Available at https://www.nature.com/articles/nrm2699 (accessed 21 June 2020).

Thomas-Fogiel, Isabelle. 'Isabelle Thomas-Fogiel Interviewed by Rahma Khazam'. In *Behav- ioral Objects/Behavioral Matter*, ed. S. Bianchini and E. Quinz, forthcoming.

Zeitoun, Olivier. 'Matière à penser' ('Matter for Thought'). In *Imprimer le Monde* ('Printing the World'), ed. M.-A. Brayer, 93– 110. Paris: Editions du Centre Pompidou, 2017.

Zwingenberger, Jeanette 'Les corps mutants des artistes. Bio-art'. *Rue Descartes* 64, no. 2 (2009). https://www.cairn.info/revue-rue-descartes-2009-2-page-117.htm (accessed 21 June 2020) (my translation).

5

Blind Summit/Models of Subjectivity: Surrealism, Physics and Psychoanalysis

Gavin Parkinson

Abstract

Surrealism is hardly ever discussed under the rubric of 'epistemology', yet the often-fortuitous means by which knowledge of the mind and world are formed was central to its considerations. These can be explored best through its attitude towards the object. From the mid-1920s, surrealists reflected on how found objects acted like concrete dreams. Objects were not merely decorative or aesthetic things discovered randomly, but agents of knowledge, speaking back to the finder about their own lives. This was true also of mathematical objects, first encountered by the artist Max Ernst on display not in an art museum but at the Institut Poincaré in Paris in 1934 and, more famously, photographed by Man Ray in 1934–36 then reproduced in Cahiers d'Art *in 1936, the high year in the surrealist theorization of the object. Made since the eighteenth century, mathematical models were meant to communicate one kind of knowledge to students of algebra, but their strange, ambiguous surfaces engaged surrealists from Ernst onwards very power-fully due to their metaphoric and metamorphic capacities. Meant initially to teach the potential of algebraic equations in studying map surfaces, they became the means towards fathoming analogies between natural forms by artists and poets. Given the potently sub-jective speculation that reigns over them in their surrealist appropriation, they are the means of gaining knowledge of the unconscious. With the aim of conveying not just the original use-value of mathematical models but also their extemporized, 'unofficial' one for surrealists, this chapter moves to and fro, between a descriptive and empirical mode of writing in the service of rationalist discourse, and a more improvised one typically redo-lent of surrealist poetics. Its aim is to unite two readings of the models in its content and form, to argue that knowledge can be conveyed and assimilated as much through poetic accident as bureaucratic design.*

blind summit

crowd breathed out so I thought I was okay and brought the book back up to my face again feeling not so much its weight (it didn't have a lot) than its strange surface by which I mean the texture of the binding and although I didn't know what it was about (it was titled *Metempsychotic Reflections at Mid-Life*) and was even unaware of what strange material bound it I was taken over by it and made to look out momentarily from my position crouched on the ground with my knees just brushing the slates to see from behind the eyes of what I think was one of those grinning Siberian Huskies judging instantaneously as I did from the position and the environment I observed and experienced but it didn't last long for it to be frightening or uncomfortable or even sufficiently engrossing (as not very much is anymore) to disorient me enough so as to make me forget where I was or who was around me because my attention was concentrated by the cumulative effect of being seen by others as though the stain created by what I imagined one individual was thinking about me was deepened by

In a 1935 interview, André Breton said: 'I regard the consideration of current scientific developments to be more worthwhile than that of the psychological movement, which always lags behind the former. Of all sciences, modern physics seems particularly to require our attention.'[1] For ten years from this date, surrealism afforded physical science a greater role in its development. But how could surrealism, which from its earliest days owed its existence, identity and its continuing vitality to an anti-positivist engagement with the world, take an interest in a field of theory and experiment that had traditionally based its knowledge on the most empirical modes of investigation? And how did the surrealists square their growing engagement with physics and mathematics with those already established enthusiasms for Hegelian thought, on the one hand, and psychoanalysis on the other? To answer these questions, I want to concentrate on Breton's pivotal 1936 *Cahiers d'Art* article 'Crisis of the Object', which is his most comprehensive statement on the surrealist object. The article is dominated by the author's attempts to form analogies between poetic thought on the one hand, and scientific and mathematical thought on the other. Because it also simultaneously employs the language of psychoanalysis it offers a suitable framework within which these questions can be addressed.

The main scientific authority called upon by Breton was the philosopher of science, Gaston Bachelard. As well as quoting from Bachelard's article, 'Le Surrationalisme', which had appeared around the same time in the journal *Inquisitions*, Breton draws heavily throughout his text upon the conclusions reached by Bachelard on the subjects of geometry, mathematics and physics in his 1934 book, *Le Nouvel Esprit scientifique*.[2] Of particular interest to Breton was Bachelard's that of being seen by two or more people so that I felt ineradicably dyed with the impure taint of their thoughts serving to distract me temporarily and moreover barring me from enjoying this narrow space between myself and the window I sat so close to and through which I kept looking by bringing my head up from where I was writing my middle name over and over to stare at the movement of the sea in relation to a passing *Puffinus griseus* tilting its wings one after the other so that it rolled from side to side as it was thrashed around by a fairly strong wind that wasn't wild enough to make me feel intimidated by it (even at this short distance from it) or by the worsening weather caused by the low pressure that will leave the fish and fossils residing within the underside of the sea untouched while it will have burnished nevertheless the lustreless roof of my dwelling where I destroy myself in the infinite possibility of my fellow beings neither primitive nor modern who previously were among those I ran with in the playground near the asymmetric boiler house bringing geometric perspective into the real world at the school I sadly returned

assertion that non-Euclidean geometries were an extension of, rather than a replacement for, Euclidean geometries, allowing an expanded field for thought. Bachelard's indication of the modern tendency towards the 'realisation of the rational, or [...] realisation of mathematics' was meant to describe the outward process of scientific thought during the period spanning the formulation of Einstein's Special Theory of Relativity and that of quantum mechanics.[3] This was the movement from subjective to objective, from the mathematical to the experimental, with mathematics increasingly playing the leading role. The same imposition of the will was expressed in surrealism by what Breton described as a *'desire to objectify.'*[4] For Breton, then, practicalities aside, the creation of models meant to demonstrate algebraic formulae sprang from the same impulse as that making possible the fabrication of surrealist objects. Consequently, in 'Crisis of the Object', Breton was led to assert that 'modern scientific and artistic thought present us with identical structures'.[5] At a time when it was becoming clear that surrealism had been let down by politics, it must have seemed to Breton that science was opening a new theoretical field for the movement.[6]

Breton's essay demanded a *'total revolution of the object.'*[7] How was this achieved by Man Ray's 12 photographs of mathematical models that preceded that text? Of the various kinds admired by the surrealists certain objects were of mysterious origin and left unaltered, some were made from undistinguished bric-a-brac; others were recognizable practical objects, their use-value rescinded by changes in material; still others seemed to be 'pure' creations of the imagination. Apart from being three-dimensional, these objects are difficult to connect in any conventional, formal to a few years ago to ponder what happens there between the ages of 11 and 15 but let us not assign institutionalized and contracted unhappiness to boys who probably don't feel it at the time or at least not in the broad and sweeping way that I assumed from my car where I sat scratching my knuckle with my tooth (later stung by a wasp in Sardinia) about 20 years after saying I never laugh to someone now forgotten on those very green playing fields that are greener now than ever in the summer after being mown by someone who must take so long to trim the grass up to the base of the trees in such a meticulous and pointless way given the indifference of my school friends for such systematic tidiness that I profoundly share now which must be obvious and which comes out again in contemptuous and aggressive impatience for the lesson to end and finally to get out of this too-hot room after being locked in for three hours after which I follow them down to the foot of the hundred steps which branch out indefinitely where we emerge into the cooler air outside that hideous humourless monument or humument to boredom where some of our shoe heels click

sense. In fact, certain of Alberto Giacometti's works predate the 'object craze' of the 1930s in surrealism and seem to problematize the distinctions between sculpture and object, figuration and abstraction. But for the surrealists, their shared attribute was their removal from their familiar context, or, in the case of Giacometti, their location outside of a habitual field of reference, functional or otherwise—and to the surrealists this was where their revolutionary energy resided. In turn, this led to a new potentiality, which Breton described in 'Crisis of the Object' in the language of psychoanalysis: it is the object's *latent* as opposed to its manifest content that is to be sought out and esteemed.

So, for example, the 'slipper-spoon' found and described by Breton in his book *Mad Love* (1937) underwent the same process of 'condensation' as do words in psychoanalysis where, according to Freud, 'a single word [...] takes over the representation of a whole train of thought'.[8] The freeing of an object from its familiar context can be compared to the freeing of a word from its habitual relationships in language; the material is invested with a certain malleability. This is an act that reveals the 'slippage' between the word and concept, which, as the symbolist poet Stéphane Mallarmé asserted in his 1897 proto-Saussurean essay, 'Crise de vers', is what makes poetry possible.[9] The echo of Mallarmé's title in Breton's 'crise de l'objet' suggests that Breton held a similar ambition for the object and was anxious to illustrate its location in a specifically poetic practice.

The idea of a term that has no positive value outside of the confines of the system of which it is a part and that of the arbitrary relationship between a signifier and its signified evokes Saussurian linguistics. Ferdinand de Saussure's epochal lectures of 1906–11 at the University against the smooth stone floor (covered with ephemeral chalk graffiti) like those of grown-ups making the satisfying high-pitched echoing sound that I hear again in the musicality of our footsteps as I imagine it while we walk across the old shiny flagstones (etched with wear) of Corfu Town after midnight so taken by the way that the empty street resembled a stage set all artificial and prepared for our arrival even to the most vigilant eye and so readied for an audience at that moment that I almost believed it had breathed in at some point a few seconds earlier in supernatural anticipation of our arrival under a moonlight bright enough to illuminate misleadingly criss-crossed by shadows all of the superfluous rings you wear tonight on your fingers that you refuse to place in my hand because of what I failed to say as usual at the (preordained and customary) moment as we quickly left the house late as always and rather harried in our appearance due to our typically poor organization that too often leaves me feeling out of touch with both things and events even though I have often wondered if it isn't exactly the excessive requirement to organize and systematize that excludes us

of Geneva can be seen in retrospect as heralding the arrival of a structuralist perspective in which the primacy of the subject is problematized by the necessity of its adaptation to a pre-existing language. But such a perspective was anticipated already in Hegel's treatment of the subject–object relationship a century earlier. Breton's interest in Hegel can be traced as far back as 1922 when the philosopher was mentioned in 'Leave Everything', Breton's call to his contemporaries to leave Dada; this, in spite of the lack of French commentary on and translation of Hegel's work and its obscurity in French academic circles as late as 1925.[10] The hundredth anniversary of Hegel's death in 1931 acted as a catalyst for increased interest in the philosopher, with many philosophy journals carrying new readings of his work. The joint third and fourth number of *Le Surréalisme au service de la révolution* also marked the centenary, in the same issue announcing the advent of the surrealist object through texts by Salvador Dalí and Giacometti and through the reproduction of several objects.

Hegel's systematic attempt to transcend the customary subject–object opposition serves to link surrealism, the object and modern physics. I mentioned the surrealists' emphasis on the movement from subjective to objective, where what was abstract finds material form: what Dalí called 'true realizations of solidified desires'.[11] This notion of finding a form for subjectivity in an object, or even more so, of discovering, unexpectedly, 'latent desires' in 'found objects', recalls Hegel's 'Absolute Idea', which is described as 'the eternal seeing of itself in the other, the notion that has carried itself out into objectivity, the object whose inner purposiveness is essential subjectivity'.[12] For Hegel, the 'Absolute Idea', is the highest stage so implacably from contact with the fine grain of what is called reality even if that consists simply of me raising my hands to my face or the sunflower leaning over the fence that perimeters the schoolyard that I saw over my shoulder or of a dog in the sun (or the eruption of Mont Pelée on 8 May 1902) all talk of which in sociological or phenomenological or historical or scientific or aesthetic terms I have found useless in the past because the abstract words which the tongue must enlist as a matter of course in order to bring out an opinion disintegrated in my mouth like rotten mushrooms (meaning nothing like that because that experience also stood outside of or before writing which is all metaphor) and the elusive thing hid behind the piece of thick textured paper I rubbed my soft pencil against in the hope of making something dark and miraculous come through on the white sheet in the absence of being rubbed against by that thing itself which for now reveals its presence to me only by means of its shadow cast from behind a building bearing a sign that reads for no obvious reason Suture's Medium and Stockage Supplies although what purpose it serves I am

in the self-consciousness of Spirit, and 'Spirit' is a notion derived from the philosophy of the Ego developed by Johann Gottlieb Fichte (who was also admired by the surrealists), in which the Ego's identity is not a fixed entity but a process, a perpetual 'becoming'. The Ego seeks to find and form things in the outside world to 'produce something which shall perfectly mirror and be itself', so that its transient state can be sustained.[13] It is an endeavour comparable to that undergone in Jacques Lacan's realm of the Imaginary, where the individual seeks to affirm his or her wholeness through identification with the reflected unity of a perceived *Gestalt*. It can be understood from this how far Hegelian idealism stands from what is commonly thought of as idealism.

As far as science was concerned, Hegel saw no possibility of the attainment of Truth as long as the Cartesian separation of an independent subject applying a *method* to a separate, observed object remained valid. Alexandre Kojève dealt with the relevant sections of the *Phenomenology* in his legendary seminars of 1933–39. During that period, Kojève introduced a new Hegel to a whole generation of intellectuals in France, many of whom frequented his seminar, among them Raymond Aron, Georges Bataille, Pierre Klossowski, Lacan, Maurice Merleau-Ponty and Raymond Queneau. According to the surrealist Gérard Legrand, Breton's curiosity drew him there between 1935 and 1938, though there is no documented evidence for this and it is contested by other commentators.[14] Kojève argued there that, for Hegel, '[s]cientific experience perturbs the Object because of the active interpretation of the Subject'.[15] Kojève interpreted Hegel's scientist as 'a man who lives within Nature and is unable to say and I would be unwilling anyway because there are moments when I feel altogether pricklish (defensively) at the idea of being explained even by myself to myself and feel that to stitch everything including the bits on the margin and frame into a comprehensive narrative in the way some would subsume everyday things into what is called history including the notion of everyday life itself would be against my desire a little of which tries to resist any unified architecture that will present itself to perception in the form of well-made stories with central subjects proper beginnings middles and ends and a coherence that permits us to see the end in every beginning which

under the soot-blackened limestone

only brings about differential duplication and uncertainty and while modern art and philosophy have told us repeatedly that a second perspective will contain an extra supplemental truth and so on into infinity and that the monism insisted upon by sciences and especially religions as well as histories is a futile fabrication of an infantile academic mind that

indissolubly bound to it, but is also opposed to it and wants to transform it'.[16] This was why Hegel sided with Goethe's 'poeticized science' in its open dispute with Isaac Newton's empiricism, and also probably helps explain the increasing visibility of the figure of Goethe in surrealist circles as the thirties progressed. In the same seminar, Kojève related Hegel's interpretation of science to contemporaneous developments in modern physics in which quantum mechanics had been forced to accept the formative role of the observer in the answers obtained. Bachelard's discussion of dialectics, geometry and physics and Kojève's references to quantum mechanics in this 1934–35 seminars were part of the same intellectual environment that informed 'Crisis of the Object', then, and which enabled Breton to conceive the parallel between scientific-mathematical thought and poetic thought.

If his reading of Bachelard and Hegel convinced Breton that mathematics and science need not remain alien to surrealism, a further impetus was offered by the mathematical demonstration models, discovered by Max Ernst at the Institut Poincaré in 1936. Predating abstract sculpture, some of these were purportedly made by Poincaré himself in the 1880s from wood, metal, plaster and wire to illustrate graphs and certain mathematical formulae.

Presently, I want to ask how these models achieve the 'separate identity simply through a *change of role*' demanded of the object by Breton and examine the way they are presented by Man Ray.[17] But first, I shall discuss their original meaning, that is, their manifest content, for Breton was far from indifferent to what was represented in their literal, surface register. What was described by Bachelard as the 'freeing' of seeks security in singularity and fixity through the distillation of difference to sameness and the erasure of detail in generality confirming that we are still living in the Middle Ages and history is always still a disguised theology and further verifying by its unquestioned imperial way with knowledge its determination to work against the unreason of the natural world and to fold the chaotic differences evident there into its mad rationalism without end when as has been said in the beginning was the pun and ever after even before sending one pernicious root into the hard stone floor in an undiscovered underwater city inscribed with unreadable runes and another into the thin skin of the lithosphere with the effect of slowly unstitching the pages of the book that joins them through a tension between acquiescence and rejection that once juxtaposed and multiplied 7, 447 times bursts its seams so that the desire to remain faithful to the text in fact destroys its sense altogether from within in an act of inner sabotage which is nevertheless a necessary destruction because writing must wear its limitations on its surface and sometimes it takes an external and necessary compassionate act of

rationalism through the discovery of non-Euclidean geometries around 1830 and the formulation of a 'generalized geometry' in 1870 were events in the history of thought that, for Breton, had correlates in poetry. He saw the first as the high-water mark of Romanticism and the second as corresponding with the activity of surrealism's two most important precursors: the Comte de Lautréamont (Isidore Ducasse) and Arthur Rimbaud. The inscribed lines and curved surfaces of certain of these objects demonstrate the violation of Euclid's famous fifth postulate, which reads 'through a given point can be drawn only one parallel to a given line'. It was the contravention of this law that opened the way for the new non-Euclidean geometries and, consequently, the models were seen to indicate a sentiment shared by both surrealist and scientist: the rejection of the accepted boundaries of 'common sense' in the pursuit of an expanded notion of the real. I would argue, then, that the mathematical model was the sole example of an object in surrealism that was valued for what it manifested—for its original, pedagogical purpose.

But at a second step, the surrealists could procure the models of the mathematician for their own ends. This brings me to the different ways in which Man Ray and Breton allude to the latent content of these models. Man Ray's first creative act as far as photographing them was concerned was to separate them from each other and remove them from their display cases at the Institut Poincaré. It is as isolated objects that we see them, outside of their scientific, academic context. Further disruptions are caused by the flattening effects of lighting, accentuating the Arp-like form in one case (Fig. 5.1), while elsewhere deep recesses are carved by dark shadows, serving to break up surfaces. The use of close-ups, varied angles and cropping intervene further

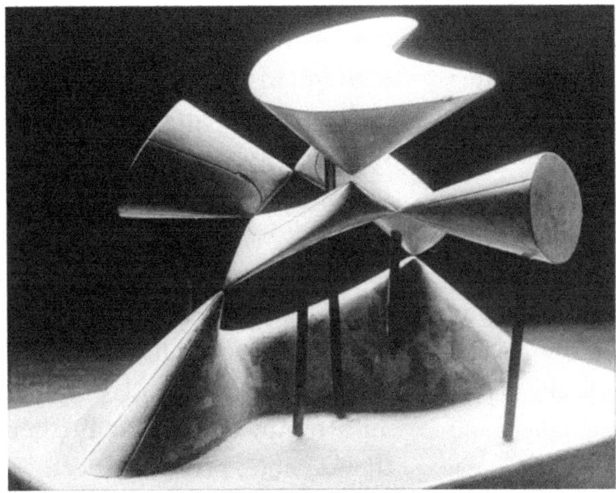

FIGURE 5.1. Man Ray, *Mathematical Object* (Surface of Kummer with sixteen double points, including eight real—extract from the mathematical object series, photograph at the Poincaré Institut, Paris), c. 1935 © Man Ray 2015 Trust/ADAGP, Paris and DACS, London. Image: Telimage, Paris.

surplusage to deliver it from its presumption towards integrity and efficiency that both seems and actually is violently excessive and intoxicative but is also a corrective reducing writing back to its two dimensions and unravelling our longstanding but futile aim of telescoping reality through our mimetic writing into three dimensions when what we really understand through experience is that we can only communicate through two (the third dimension of experience is compromised and even lost by its translation into language and indeed that signifier is itself a product of writing and plays its role in transporting us out of feeling) and we must abandon the

between viewer and object, acting, in a sense, to deny the models the 'voice' given them by science. Man Ray's knowledge and use of lighting that might seem more appropriate to fashion photography; his frequent inclusion of horizons, reminiscent of conventional landscapes; the attention he pays to texture and to the models' signs of wear; his further knowledge of the still-life genre and uses of perspective: this is the battery of effects that the painter–photographer brought to bear upon the models. The photographs were then slickly mounted and grandly presented in *Cahiers d'Art* one to a page.

The change of condition effected by Man Ray's photography creates them anew, just as Alfred Stieglitz's photograph of Marcel Duchamp's *Fountain* (1917) with its low angle, shadows and gallery setting has its own identity almost separate from Duchamp's original object, especially in the absence of that lost work. The photographic medium and its accessories were the agency through which the identities of the alluring desire to render the throb of experience in writing showing instead writing's limitation in the very act of writing itself so that our readers are brought face to face with claustrophobic walls of words with empty windows leading nowhere mimetically instead of uselessly physically representing something of light and extension to the mind's eye rather we must blacken the retinal window or at least blur its access to things and this happens due to the obstruction caused by a worm-shaped strip of fluid laid over itself once and through the discrete play of our words leading only back to themselves allowing the force of their signification to relay the hum of our bodies and to take the form of a demand that we return to that captivity in the five senses we once knew while accepting that reason has its place yet resisting its colonialism and self-justification by our defence of failure and the unavoidable Byzantine ways of the world and mind as well as those of our bodies and hands too often seated at desks in a windowless writing factory when we should be seated by an open window captive only of the generative cell clutching a pen nervously but not madly or outside placing one brick

models were transformed. In one sense they are ready-mades, as when they were displayed in the 'art' environment of the Charles Ratton gallery, which housed the 1936 Paris exhibition of surrealist objects. Duchamp's so-called indifference to the chosen object is, however, absent, for the object in surrealism is always desired, sought after. They are also 'found' objects, the significance of which is hinted at in Breton's creation of new titles alongside their descriptive ones in an attempt to suggest further depths beyond their visible, prosaic aspect: 'Ainsi parlait [...]' for instance, and 'The Rosebush Ring.' The double-naming of mathematical models in *Cahiers d'Art* only stressed, then, their dual role in surrealism, of the manifest and the latent.

Breton's naming of these objects recalls the naming of their artist-friends' canvases by the poets of the surrealist group. According to Breton, the surrealist titling procedure, which usually avoids a literal description of the subject matter of the object or painting, also entails the un-naming of the work allowing the possibility that it and its title can exist independently. The surrealists' suspicion of conventional word–image relationships was matched during those years by that of the practitioners of mathematical physics who questioned the capacity of both language and image to describe accurately the physical world. Mathematical formalism was the means by which modern physics would resist the descriptive imagery and the imprecise visuals of language. Seeing the connection, Bachelard described the symbols of mathematics as Mallarméan and spoke of physics as a 'poetic art'.

Equally, in psychoanalysis there is an intersection between the problem of language and the subject's observation of and orientation towards the object. This can be elaborated through a consideration of Freud's topography of the mind

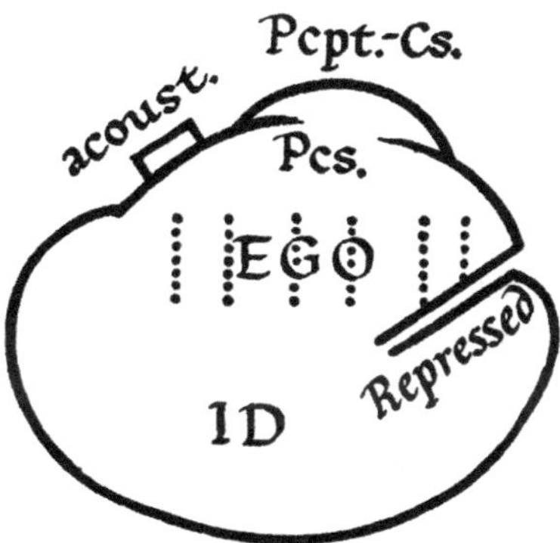

FIGURE 5.2. Sigmund Freud, speculative drawing of the mind, in 'Das Ich Und Das Es.' Published in German 24 April 1923. English translation 'The Ego and the Id,' 1927, London: Hogarth Press and Institute of Psycho-Analysis, p. 88. (Tr. Joan Riviere).

haphazardly onto another but not precariously or safely just disjointedly taking time for some minutes (let's say eight after every hour and twenty minutes for consistency) in both cases to enjoy the sight of the distant volcanoes and forests without a glance at the locomotive preyed upon by immense barometric roots before we start work again under the banyan tree as hosts to a late grey morning engaged in what is perceived by some as a crazy activity without end and which indeed for us partakes of the madness of the day (though we've never seen a schizophrenic) raised in relief in capital letters for us at the foot of a horizontal gravestone in the name of Nowell carved box-like with sharp-edged care as writing-architecture

(Fig. 5.2). In the important text 'The Unconscious' (1915), aware that a spatial rendering of the abstract agencies of unconscious, preconscious and conscious could provoke misleading anatomical interpretations, Freud described psychical topography as 'the dimension of depth in the mind'.[18] Yet when his image-model of the mind's structure appeared in *The Ego and the Id* of 1923, Freud's training in biology led him to assert that the ego can 'be regarded as a mental projection of the surface of the body'.[19] The fixed vertical posture and organic curves of Freud's model only emphasized its relationship with the human body. Freud's assertion that the lower part of the Ego joins the Id affirmed its status as an object imagined in conventional three-dimensional space and subject to the laws of gravity. Deployed again in 1932 in a lecture collected in the *New Introductory Lectures in Psychoanalysis*, it was given a more schematic rendering losing its resemblance to a cerebellum and also incorporating the superego.[20] However, when this image was reproduced in the German editions of both the *Complete Writings* and the *Complete Works* it was mistakenly turned through 45 degrees and placed on its side by the editors, too much so for us but nearly not enough to prevent it tipping over into wordplay for some to despise but let them not take offence any more than we do at their conclusions and summaries because it is those we openly plan to erase in an eternally circular speech that nods to its tail and points to its head in a gesture both deferential and expository that will prevent too much conflict between us in spite of our blatant acts of playful piracy and will perhaps even help preserve our conversations across the kitchen table where we can go over this once again face to face in the understanding that where you sit today we will be tomorrow and so on round and round in the enclosure and out again in the road at the settlement and in the office across the meadow next to the river and at the top of the hill where the playground comes into view alongside the ruined building where a child lies face down in the grass like the one seen during the earthquake that broke Bucharest in two on the night of 10–11 November 1940 and which has been only half recorded in the sense that subsequent scientific accounts and eye-witness records as well as historical representations of that disaster are available with

defeating Freud's attempt to give the image an upright anatomical address. Freud's image suggests that he was unable or unwilling to depart from a metaphorical language and imagery still tied to the immediate visual experience of physical objects. It illustrates the problem with visualizing theoretical concepts such as the mind, the atom or the fourth dimension in terms of our ordinary experience of physical spaces or objects. As revealed by quantum mechanics where a particle has to be said to be in two places at once, the prosaic description of certain phenomena does not square with the day-to-day apprehension of reality.

In fact, in the same lecture, Freud acknowledged the limitations of his illustration when he warned his audience not to think of the mind's agencies as encompassed by firm outlines but 'rather by areas of colour melting into one another as they are presented by modern artists'.[21] Here Freud's words suggest a process, but where he tried to illustrate the workings of the unconscious through its functional relationships, it was in surrealism that the unconscious was illustrated through its dynamic, in automatism. In fact, the mapping of the unconscious is made explicit in the letters exchanged in 1942 between the two young surrealists Matta and Gordon Onslow-Ford (both of whom were aware of mathematical models and introduced their morphologies into their art) where, in place of the word 'paintings' they would discuss which 'charts' they were currently working on.[22] This usage doubtless stems from Onslow-Ford's Royal Navy background and these surrealists of the late thirties seem to have seen in automatism a method, which, like early map making, consisted in a nonteleological process which itself ultimately constituted the finished product.

Lacan theorized the formation of the ego through its spatial relationships with external objects in the wake of the surrealists and the usual critical distance built in yet the eruption of human desire which it prompted and that such unsettling events subsequently cause in those who write about them has barely been discussed outside of one exception because that would demand we step outside of empiricism and positivism as well as academic rationalism when we write and concede there is no such thing as objectivity but we are all magnetically attracted to the subject of our study along more-or-less errant invisible pathways of desire and these cannot be excluded from the representation we make of things in art or writing (as modernists understood but their interpreters will not) any more than misprints and misspellings are mere accidents but are intended through an equally obscure process that we formalize and reduce with reference to an unconscious which term again has the effect of generalizing the strange yet everyday detail of events through which breathe the two mouths of fiction and poetry but which our academic philosophy and history flatten and simplify into theoretical mediocrity the better to convey them in the book and to the classroom and conference but we ask for an evasion from such

physicists. Like them, he was aware of the limitations of a language and imagery too indebted to ordinary sense perceptions. In his 1948 report, 'Aggressivity in Psychoanalysis', Lacan had asked whether developments in physics would not force a reassessment of what he described as 'the conceptual area into which we had reduced the real'.[23] Ultimately, his anxiety to reach beyond language and the formative spatial field that had determined Freud's topography led to the use of algebra, knots and ambiguous topological surfaces. His drive towards a minimal form of expression would culminate in his use of paradoxical three-dimensional objects such as the Moebius strip, where one end of a rectangle of paper is twisted and the ends joined to form a single surface. Lacan believed it could be used to express a form of temporality and multidimensionality of the unconscious. He also used Borromean rings to describe the simultaneous independence and interdependence of the three agencies of real, symbolic and imaginary. Further, the doughnut form, known to mathematicians as the 'torus' and present among Man Ray's photographs for *Cahiers d'Art*, could model Lacan's idea that death was 'a centre exterior to language', since its centre and exterior are formed by a single surface.[24]

Where Freud used a descriptive model of the mind still indebted to the vertical orientation of the perceiving subject, Lacan exploited the ambiguous orientations available in topology to achieve a silent explication of a concept, the unconscious, that knows neither ups nor downs, insides nor outsides, pasts nor futures. The torus, in fact, reconciling inside and outside in a single traversable surface, can act as a representative of that 'certain point in the mind' indicated by Breton in the *Second Manifesto of Surrealism* (1929–30) where opposites 'cease to be perceived as contradictions'.[25]

131

epistemological expediency in search of favour of what they try to suppress between their pages and in spite of the ineffaceable limitations of writing scored onto the body of writing itself and so on into the abyss we know there is the dog in the sun and the playground where a tall adult stands up straight and alone at the top of the child's slide immobile holding his breathe perhaps and looking into the far distance with one hand in his coat pocket feeling the soot between his fingertips but he is neither reflecting on nor summarizing this but just being there well beyond all philosophies of being and sociological theories and that is enough to convince that a poetics of art writing will join with poetry to communicate something of the inexplicable force of such incidents and events not through their description or interpretation and certainly not through their explanation but by a writing that in the act of recording or representing such things constantly turns on its own limitations and shortcomings at least to point to the nothing beyond nothing we hover above or to rattle noisily the flimsy narrative bridge that stretches over it in the earshot of those who

Freud's model of the mind, then, with its customary address to the viewing subject, still indebted to a teleological, Newtonian vision, contrasts with the explicit challenge made to the centrality of the subject by the paradoxical surfaces of Lacanian topology, the serendipitous practice of surrealist automatism and the abolition of habitual sense perceptions of direction and location in modern physics. It was Duchamp who described Matta as following 'the physicist in the search for new space', and I want to turn finally, now, to a single work of Duchamp, which ties together all the themes discussed so far in this chapter.[26] It means returning to the distinction made earlier between the object, its photograph and the presentation of that photograph.

It was not to be expected, perhaps, that photography, the medium that seemed the most likely to fix as separate the positions of observing subject and observed object, was able to disenfranchise the viewer by idiosyncratic reformations of the visual field. The viewer will try in vain to find his or her bearings before the close-up shot of one mathematical model, formed from thread and filling the whole of the visual field, which accompanied 'Crisis of the Object' when it was reprinted in Breton's Surrealism and Painting (1965) (Fig. 5.3). It was probably this photograph that William Rubin had in mind when he suggested mathematical models as the inspiration behind Duchamp's *Mile of Twine* (Fig. 5.4), which in spite, or, perhaps, because of its insubstantiality, initially turned the whole of the *First Papers of Surrealism* exhibition held in New York in 1942 into an object. Although the paintings could be viewed, it enacted an attack on the predominance of vision and the primacy of the subject. It was achieved through the formation of what might be called 'tactile spaces' and also by the creation of channels through which the visitors were guided and therefore kept constantly

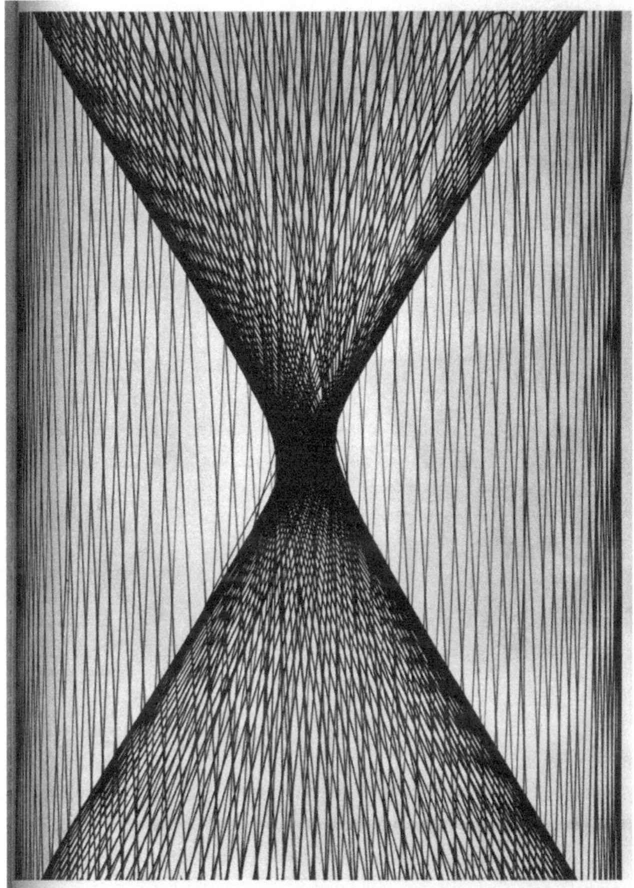

FIGURE 5.3. *Mathematical Object*: intersection of two Saint-Gilles type double-thread surfaces. Musée des Arts et Métiers, Paris. Photo: Roger-Jean Ségalat from Breton, *Surrealism and Painting*, p. 281.

will pretend that words are solid foundations but

ready to write onto the air

not I because I notice that even when I am in a disembodied state I try to speak but there is some frothy water in my mouth and that is enough to return to me my body

aware of their physicality; of their, as much as the paintings, 'being-seen'. Rosalind Krauss might also have had the photograph of *First Papers* in her mind when she described the threatening visuality theorized by Roger Caillois and Lacan as 'a mastery from without, imposed on a subject who is trapped in a cat's cradle of representation […] lost in a labyrinth'.[27]

The photograph is, then, a representation on a two-dimensional surface of a 'work' originally meant to be passed through and experienced

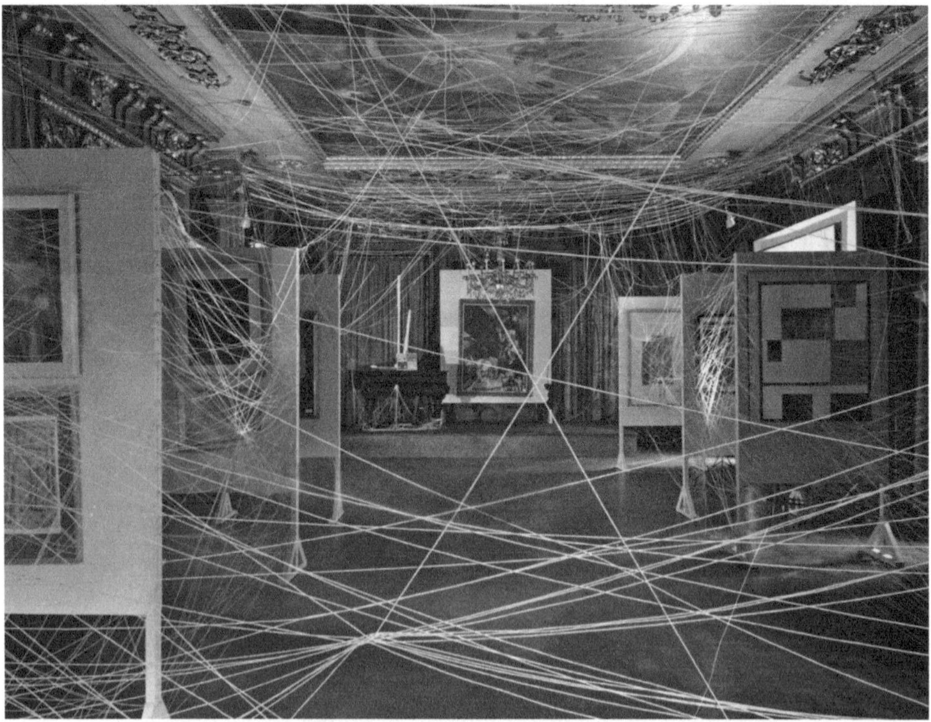

FIGURE 5.4. John D. Schiff, Installation view of *First Papers of Surrealism exhibition*, showing Marcel Duchamp's *His Twine* 1942. Gelatin silver print, 18.6 × 24.6 cm. Philadelphia Museum of Art, Philadelphia Museum of Art, Library & Archives, Gift of Jacqueline, Paul and Peter Matisse in memory of their mother Alexina Duchamp, 13-1972-9 (303). Courtesy of the Leo Baeck Institute, New York.

when with night approaching backwards under a cloudless sky I am lying on the school playing fields dry-mouthed and in this solitude and freedom I understand that this water (that permeates) revives the universal ashtray which that night and standing here today I understand to mean that this screened-off world and its contents like art can still be touched in the immeasurable swooping dive of a with reference, not to the eye, but to the body. In this chapter, I have endeavoured to maintain the disparity between the object itself and the object as photographed, and have pointed out the way that Man Ray frequently succeeded in transforming the already equivocal surfaces of mathematical models through various techniques that resist a single, indisputable viewpoint. These included image-cropping, full-frame images and tilted angles, which confound easy distinctions between interiors and exteriors and highs and lows, as in his photograph of polyhedra, also comparable to Duchamp's twine (Fig. 5.5).

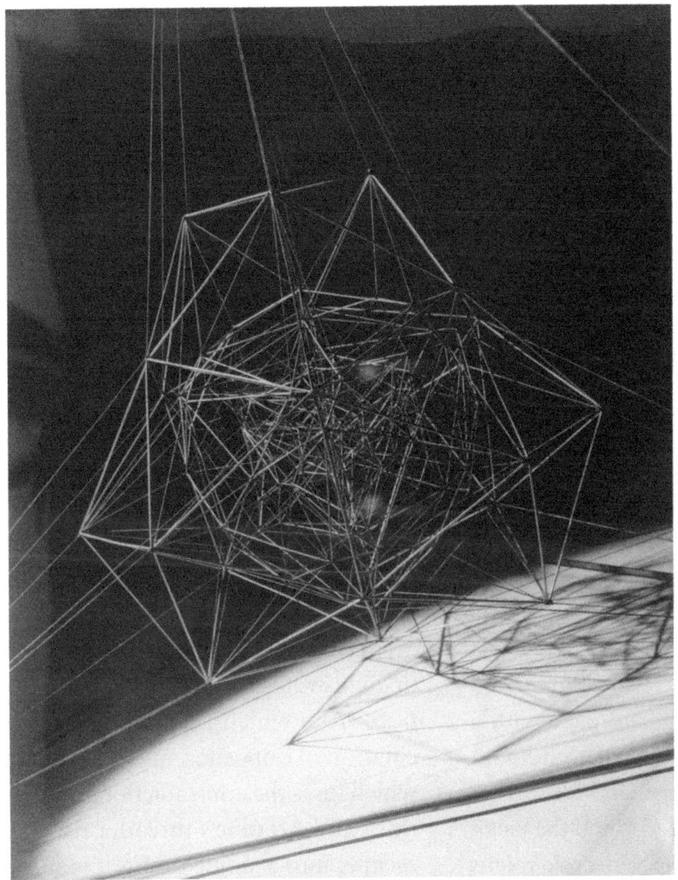

FIGURE 5.5. Man Ray, *Mathematical Object* (Polyèdres—extract from the mathematical object series, photograph at the Poincaré Institut, Paris), c. 1935 © Man Ray 2015 Trust/ADAGP, Paris and DACS, London. Image: Telimage, Paris.

writing that measures itself as both birth and entombment (generative cell again) and along these too-narrow pavements with the cars too close near the spa outside the coffee shop in my lunch hour high up in the mountains convalescing after a fever in a country that a stranger in a far-off land once mistook for an eternal

But there is a final twist, or perhaps, following my discussion of Freud's model of the mind, I should say a further rotation. For, in spite of Duchamp's position on the editorial board of the surrealists' journal *VVV*, when this photograph was reproduced there it was placed upside down on the page, mirroring the inverted orientation of image on retina. This was, presumably, an accident—one of those chance episodes from which he, like the surrealists, took such pleasure. Unlike the Man Ray photographs, however, no springtime (it isn't that) I felt that again as I scribbled on the margin of my newspaper to get my pen going and entered the slate-floored gallery a little out of breathe in this high altitude seeing the world through your eyes for an instant my dear as you asked me to in your note which makes mine fill up with tears for a second but there is work to do and what they call a weight of expectation so I step up and remove my jacket and check my watch because my friend should be here by now then I pick up the book from where I left it on the chair and look again at the left hand page with a feeling of disbelief undiminished from that I felt earlier then I come around the partition separating the two rooms and crouch down to look more clearly at the reverse of the painting which I am seeing for the first time with a great inner sense of longing accompanied by some concern that I was keeping them waiting but when I looked back

'artistic' effects have been aimed at here, and it was precisely that very literal, unfussy, journalistic non-method that combined with the unpeopled space of Duchamp's complex web arrangement to conceal the habitual up/down distinction. Duchamp's quest, as he once expressed it, to 'strain the laws of physics' is carried out here.[28] Like Yves Tanguy's flipping of his canvases through 180 degrees while they were still in progress, it serves to provoke surrealist *dépaysement* or disorientation.

Two final images from the same joint third and fourth number of *VVV* are comparable in their performance of a similar service. Breton's 1942 address to the students of Yale, 'Situation of Surrealism Between the Two Wars', which recapitulated the perennial concerns of the surrealists, was published with images by Max Ernst. Both are styled after Ernst's new 'drip' technique. The first illustrates the passage from the *Second Manifesto* from which I quoted earlier, on the reconciliation of opposites, and like Duchamp's twine, which fuses the contradictions of Daedalus's labyrinth and Ariadne's thread, prison and means of escape, into a single motif, it is suitably ambivalent in its orientation. The second, similarly reversible, mimics the 'orbiting electron' model of the atom, and accompanies Breton's prediction of a forthcoming 'spectacular discovery [...] that will arise in the realm of *physics*'.

For Breton, it was the labyrinth motif that was most urgently evoked by Duchamp's twine. At that time, during the surrealists' wartime exile in New York, the melancholy identification with the exiled Daedalus would have been pre-eminent. But, for me, Duchamp's spun architecture-object for the exhibition and its revolved photograph are the kaleidoscope which, once twisted, reveals the web of associations connecting the mathematical model, surrealist *dépaysement* and the spaces which enabled Freudian and Lacanian thought, in a vision dissolved in 'inner vision'.

NOTES

1. André Breton, 'Interview with *Indice*', in *What Is Surrealism? Selected Writings*, ed. Franklin Rosemont (London: Pluto, 1978), 144–47, 147.

2. Gaston Bachelard, 'Le Surrationalisme'. *Inquisitions* no. 1 (June 1936): 1–6. For a translation, see Gaston Bachelard, 'Surrationalism,' *Surrealism*, ed. Julian Levy (New York: Black Sun Press, 1936), 186–89.

3. Gaston Bachelard, *The New Scientific Spirit*, trans. Arthur Goldhammer (Boston: Beacon Press, 1984), 4.

4. André Breton, 'Crisis of the Object', *Surrealism and Painting*, trans. Simon Watson Taylor (London: Macdonald and Co., [1936] 1972), 275–80, 277.

5. Ibid., 276.

6. Surrealism's difficult relationship with organized politics and particularly the French Communist Party (PCF) is recorded in several places, notably: Carole Reynaud Paligot, *Parcours politique des surréalistes 1919–1969* [2001] (Paris: CNRS Éditions, 2010).

7. Breton, *Surrealism and Painting*, 280.

8. Sigmund Freud, 'The Unconscious', in *On Metapsychology: The Theory of Psychoanalysis*, trans. James Strachey (Harmondsworth: Penguin, [1915] 1991), 204.

9. Stéphane Mallarmé', 'Crise de vers', in *Divagations* (Paris: Charpentier, 1897), 235–51.

10. André Breton, 'Leave Everything' [1922], in *The Lost Steps* [1924], trans. Mark Polizzotti (Lincoln: University of Nebraska Press, 1996), 77–80, 77.

11. Salvador Dalí, 'The Rotting Donkey', in *The Collected Writings of Salvador Dalí*, ed. and trans. Haim Finkelstein (Cambridge: Cambridge University Press, 1998), 223–26, 225.

12. Hegel, *Lesser Logic*, 427; quoted from the 'Shorter Logic' by J. N. Findlay, *Hegel: A Re-Examination* (Abingdon: Routledge, [1958] 2013), 38.

13. J. N. Findlay, *The Philosophy of Hegel: An Introduction and Re-examination* (New York: Collier Books, 1958), 48.

14. 'Il est avéré que Breton [...] a fréquenté les célèbres cours de Kojève à l'Institut des Hautes Études entre 1935 et 1938,' Gérard Legrand, 'Breton et l'inauguration philosophique du surréalisme', in *Surréalisme et philosophie*, ed. Christian Deschamps (Paris: Centre Georges Pompidou, 1992), 13–19, 17.

15. Alexandre Kojève, 'The Dialectic of the Real and the Phenomenological Method in Hegel: Complete Text of the Sixth through Ninth Lectures of the Academic Year 1934–1935', *Introduction to the Reading of Hegel: Lectures on the Phenomenology of Spirit*, ed. Raymond Queneau and Allan Bloom, trans. James H. Nichols, Jr. (Ithaca: Cornell University Press, 1980), 169–259, 177.

16. Ibid., 176.

17. Breton, *Surrealism and Painting*, 280.

18. Freud, 'The Unconscious', 159–222, 176.

19. Sigmund Freud, 'The Ego and the Id' [1923], *On Metapsychology*, 339–407, 364–65 n. 2; Lucille B. Ritvo, *Darwin's Influence on Freud: A Tale of Two Sciences* (New Haven, CT: Yale University Press), 1990.

20. Sigmund Freud, *New Introductory Lectures in Psychoanalysis*, trans. James Strachey (London: Penguin, [1933] 1991), 111.

21. Ibid., 112.

22. Martica Sawin, *Surrealism in Exile and the Beginnings of the New York School* (Cambridge, MA: MIT Press, 1995), 221.

23. Lacan had asked whether developments in physics (namely, Heisenberg's Uncertainty Principle of 1927) should force a post-Freudian remodeling of subjectivity', Jacques Lacan, 'Aggressivity in Psychoanalysis', *Écrits: A Selection* [1966], trans. Alan Sheridan (London: Tavistock, [1948] 1985), 8–29, 9.

24. Jacques Lacan, 'The Function and Field of Speech and Language in Psychoanalysis' [1953], *Écrits*, 30–113, 105.

25. André Breton, 'Second Manifesto of Surrealism', in *Manifestoes of Surrealism*, trans. Richard Seaver and Helen R. Lane (Ann Arbor: University of Michigan Press, [1930] 1972), 117–94, 123.

26. Marcel Duchamp, *Salt Seller: The Essential Writings of Marcel Duchamp*, ed. Michel Sanouillet and Elmer Peterson (London: Thames and Hudson, 1975), 154.

27. Rosalind Krauss, 'Corpus Delicti', Rosalind Krauss and Jane Livingstone, *L'Amour fou: Photography and Surrealism*, (Washington, DC: The Corcoran Gallery of Art and New York and London: Abbeville Press, before '1985'), 55–112, 78.

28. Marcel Duchamp, 'I Propose to Strain the Laws of Physics,' in an interview with Francis Roberts, *Art News* 67, no. 8 (December 1968): 46–47, 62–64.

REFERENCES

Bachelard, Gaston. 'Le Surrationalisme'. *Inquisitions* no. 1 (June 1936): 1–6.

Bachelard, Gaston. *The New Scientific Spirit*, trans. Arthur Goldhammer. Boston: Beacon Press, 1984.

Breton, André. 'Crisis of the Object'. In *Surrealism and Painting*, trans. Simon Watson Taylor, 275–80. London: Macdonald and Co., [1936] 1972.

Breton, André. 'Second Manifesto of Surrealism'. In *Manifestoes of Surrealism*, trans. Richard Seaver and Helen R. Lane, 117–94. Ann Arbor: University of Michigan Press, [1930] 1972.

Breton, André. 'Interview with *Indice*'. In *What Is Surrealism? Selected Writings*, ed. Franklin Rosemont, 144–47. London: Pluto, 1978.

Breton, André. 'Leave Everything' [1922]. In *The Lost Steps* [1924], trans. Mark Polizzotti, 77–80. Lincoln: University of Nebraska Press, 1996.

Dalí, Salvador. 'The Rotting Donkey'. In *The Collected Writings of Salvador Dalí*, ed. and trans. Haim Finkelstein, 223–26. Cambridge: Cambridge University Press, 1998.

Duchamp, Marcel. 'I Propose to Strain the Laws of Physics'. In an interview with Francis Roberts, *Art News* 67, no. 8 (December 1968): 46–47, 62–64.

Duchamp, Marcel. *Salt Seller: The Essential Writings of Marcel Duchamp*, ed. Michel Sanouillet and Elmer Peterson. London: Thames and Hudson, 1975.

Findlay, J. N. *The Philosophy of Hegel: An Introduction and Re-examination*. New York: Collier Books, 1958.

Findlay, J. N. *Hegel: A Re-Examination*. Abingdon: Routledge, [1958] 2013.

Freud, Sigmund. *New Introductory Lectures in Psychoanalysis*, trans. James Strachey. London: Penguin, [1933] 1991.

Freud, Sigmund. 'The Unconscious'. In *On Metapsychology: The Theory of Psychoanalysis*, trans. James Strachey, 159–222. Harmondsworth: Penguin [1915] 1991.

Kojève, Alexandre. 'The Dialectic of the Real and the Phenomenological Method in Hegel: Complete Text of the Sixth through Ninth Lectures of the Academic Year 1934–1935'. In *Introduction to the Reading of Hegel: Lectures on the Phenomenology of Spirit*, ed. Raymond Queneau and Allan Bloom, trans. James H. Nichols, Jr., 169–259. Ithaca: Cornell University Press, 1980.

Krauss, Rosalind, and Jane Livingstone. *L'Amour fou: Photography and Surrealism*. Washington, DC: The Corcoran Gallery of Art and New York and London: Abbeville Press, before 1985.

Lacan, Jacques. 'The Function and Field of Speech and Language in Psychoanalysis'. [1953], *Écrits*, 30–113, 105.

Lacan, Jacques. 'Aggressivity in Psychoanalysis'. In *Écrits: A Selection* [1966], trans. Alan Sheridan, 8–29. London: Tavistock, [1948] 1985.

Legrand, Gérard. 'Breton et l'inauguration philosophique du surréalisme'. In *Surréalisme et philosophie*, ed. Christian Deschamps, 13–19. Paris: Centre Georges Pompidou, 1992.

Mallarmé, Stéphane. 'Crise de vers'. In *Divagations*, 235–51. Paris: Charpentier, 1897.

Paligot, Carole Reynaud. *Parcours politique des surréalistes 1919–1969*. Paris: CNRS Éditions, [2001] 2010.

Ritvo, Lucille B. *Darwin's Influence on Freud: A Tale of Two Sciences*. New Haven, CT: Yale University Press, 1990.

Sawin, Martica. *Surrealism in Exile and the Beginnings of the New York School*. Cambridge, MA: MIT Press, 1995.

6

Glimpsed Phantoms of Sensation; Or, a Psychogeographical Investigation of Various Anatomical Specimens with Reference to Christine Borland's *Cet être-là, c'est à toi de le créer!*

Edward Juler

Abstract

This chapter takes the form of a psychogeographical analysis of anatomical specimens in the context of Christine Borland's controversial 1997 photographic installation at the FRAC Languedoc-Roussillon in Montpellier. Set within the Anatomy Museum of the Faculty of Medicine at the University of Montpellier, the author retraces Borland's steps through a series of narrated object-encounters which examine how her photographs invoke the repressed, melancholic agency of the specimen. The text draws on psychogeography as an art historical strategy through which specimens and their histories (including that of Borland's own intervention) might be addressed through subjective peregrination. In the manner of Michel de Certeau, the author envisages the act of wandering among the vitrines as a critical provocation which manipulates spatial organization while simultaneously inserting discursive references and citations into the institution and its objects. The reflective, fragmentary and first-person character of the text draws on autoethnographic practices in order to foreground how questions relating to voice, affect, memory, narrative and phenomenology can enrich an understanding of both specimens and art history itself. Images and text interweave to create a peripatetic, experiential account that defamiliarizes the specimen even as it opens up new interpretations of Borland's photographs and the objects therein.

A strategy assumes a place that can be circumscribed as proper (*propre*), and thus serve as the basis for generating relations with an exterior distinct from it [...]. Political, economic and scientific rationality has been constructed on this strategic model [...]. I call a 'tactic', on the other hand, a calculus which cannot count on a 'proper' (a spatial or institutional localisation), nor thus on a borderline distinguishing the other as a visible totality. The place of a tactic belongs to the other. A tactic insinuates itself into the other's place, fragmentarily, without taking it over in its entirety, without being able to keep it at a distance.

—Michel de Certeau[1]

Being in a scientific or medical situation you just always remind yourself that you are an artist in that situation and, without meaning to sound callous, that you take what you need and you stop wherever it suits you. Often I stop at places which are irrational.

—Christine Borland[2]

The morning sun is already high as I enter the cloistered stillness of the Anatomy Museum at the University of Montpellier. Perhaps it is simply the result of finding myself amid these unfamiliar, sepulchral surroundings, but I must admit to finding something slightly unsettling in the sudden shift from the brightness of the streets outside to the stygian realm of the collections, perennially steeped as they are in the twilight needed to preserve their fragile holdings from the sunlight's rapacious glare.

Intermittently, lateral shafts of daylight penetrate the museum's gloom, shining through blinds which partially obscure high windows so as to reveal the entire length of the neoclassical edifice; its elevated ceilings and green, marble-clad Doric columns; its painted *tondi* of distinguished physicians and endless rows of glass-fronted cabinets, the cadaverous contents of which a sunbeam periodically and startlingly illuminates. Here, then, is the uninterrupted and awesome extent of Second Empire scientific ambition, running an immense gamut of disciplines from pathology and comparative anatomy to zoology, ethnology and teratology.[3]

Skeletons and écorchés of both man and beast line both sides of the central aisle; forming in their exhibitory contiguity an enigmatic taxonomy through which the correspondences between species find subtle morphological expression; whereby, for example, the fearsomely snaggle-toothed skeleton of a sea lion is arranged alongside vitrines of human remains and the sculptural mass of a hippopotamus skull (Fig. 6.1). I observe, alongside dismembered anatomies and mammalian ossuaries, the greyish, desiccated remnants of Egyptian mummies. Resinous casts of bronchial systems hang ethereally in glazed armoires near to which foetal malformations float in antediluvian, alcohol- and formaldehyde-filled tanks. In some of

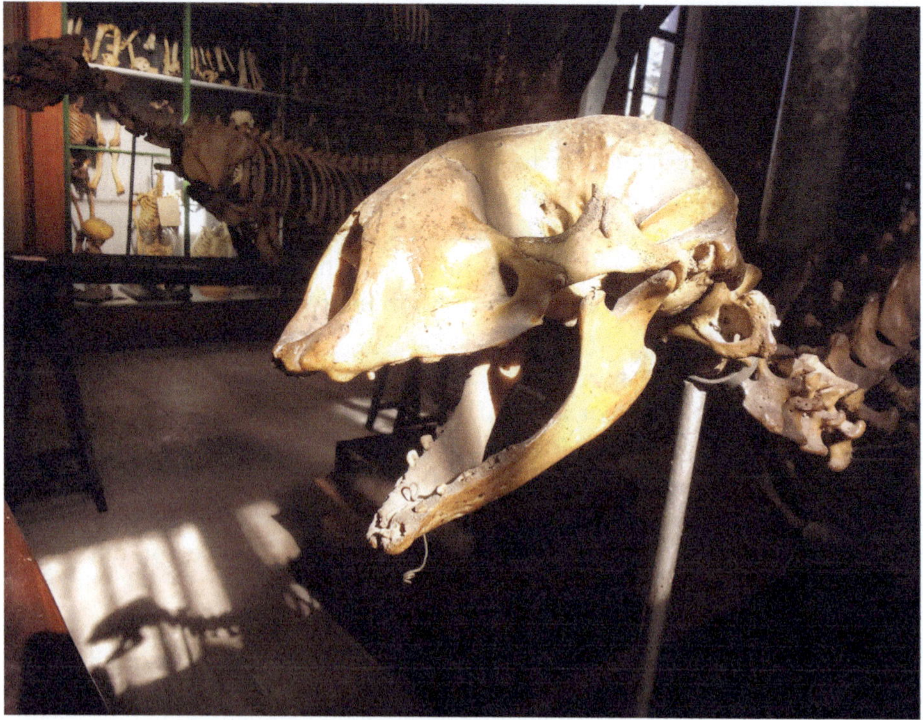

FIGURE 6.1. *...the snaggle-toothed skeleton of a sealion...*, 2017, photograph, Anatomy Museum of the Faculty of Medicine/University of Montpellier © the author.

these vessels the preserving solutions have, over the centuries, slowly evaporated, leaving behind a crystalline residue which encrusts the infant corpses in yellowish, pellucid deposits, as though they have been drawn up from corallaceous graves.

As the sun moves towards its noonday zenith, streams of light move steadily across the floor of the museum, causing the vitrines to momentarily luminesce and the objects within to emerge from their obscurity as though insisting upon their claim as progeny of the Enlightenment.

* * *

In a moment of serendipity, some days after my visit, I discover that Christine Borland had, in 1996, photographed the specimens, surreptitiously, as it were, with a spy camera carefully concealed about her person, so as to avoid a prohibition then imposed by the museum authorities on the documentation of the exhibits. This proscription extended not just to all forms of reproduction, but also to access itself which was granted only through petitioning the establishment directly. Indeed, one can imagine that such applications were readily dissuaded through such tactics as the semi-permanent sign declaring that the building was 'closed for emergency repairs' (when, as Borland sardonically notes, 'there were no repairs').[4] These policies might be seen to have been a way in which the authorities of the time discouraged public engagement with specimens which, in many cases, had been obtained in previous centuries, if not through the colonial appropriation of cadaverous material—as in the case of those mummified remains brought to Montpellier by Alire Raffeneau-Delire during the Napoleonic campaign in Egypt—then via means which at best seem now ethically questionable, such as stillborn infants taken from unwitting mothers or else bodies pilfered from graveyards by resurrectionists.[5] Even if, one might add, measures such as these were not in themselves unusual. As sites of medical education, many anatomical museums have traditionally restricted access to medical students and scholars alone or else through implementing burdensome visitation procedures designed to dampen public curiosity.[6] (When I visit the museum myself some 20 years later, few, if any, of the original prohibitions remain; permission is freely granted by the museum and I am allowed to visit unsupervised. There is but a single proviso: that the infantile monstrosities, sequestered from the rest of the collection in a dusty corner of the museum, are not to be photographed due to the sensitivities still surrounding such material.)

* * *

Presently, as my eyes grow accustomed to the gloaming, I become aware of a grisly effigy beckoning from an alcove, to my left, beneath a sizeable armoire of anatomical specimens. Attributed to 'Delmas', I assume this figure, whose dextrous facture appears convincingly flesh-like, is constructed from cured soft tissue until somewhat later when I read, in an 1820 study of medical pedagogy by John Cross, that Delmas, alongside Jean-Baptiste Laumonier, had 'raised with frightening perfection', the art of imitating in wax, specimens whose putrefaction would otherwise rob the surgeon–anatomist too quickly of his prize.[7] Prepared with an undeniable appreciation of the anatomical subtleties of subcutaneous tissue, the écorché magisterially presides over the museum's contents, one flayed arm dramatically outstretched as though to embrace the macabre entirety of its netherworld dominion, while the other hangs awkwardly by its side.[8] Propped up by a branchlike crutch which pierces its right-hand side and a slenderer, metal support which undergirds its outreaching arm, splintered and peeling, the figure recalls those Renaissance images of Saint Bartholomew in which the saint, after enduring that most appalling of punishments, regards us with an affectingly sorrowful expression, halfway between anguish and pained defiance.[9]

Yet unlike the condemned saint who, clutching a tanner's knife and with his skin wrapped around him like a grim raiment, is identifiable from a series of poses,

143

established by convention, that exposit the dreadful character of his martyrdom, the attitude of Delmas's écorché appears enigmatic either by design or, more likely, because the language of its body, through the passage of time, has slipped into obscurity and silence.[10] Thus it seems that Delmas's flayed man inhabits a mute realm within the kingdom of anatomy, where, devoid of speech, it performs to its audience—in a manner not unlike those strange, somnambulant motions one sees certain actors execute in German Expressionist cinema—the knowledge inscribed upon its body: the position of its muscles and lymphatic nodes, the yellowed filigree of arterial vessels and nerves which, like so much stretched lace, extend across the fabric of its body.

* * *

Under the pretext of making anatomical drawings, Borland was granted permission to access the collection on the condition that her activities therein would be closely supervised by a member of the museum staff. Preparing herself by tracing some illustrations from that most generic of anatomical textbooks, *Gray's Anatomy*, Borland consequently entered the museum 'with an impressive array of pencils and paper'; whereupon, under the watchful eye of her chaperone (although given the outcome of Borland's endeavour, one might ask if their vigilance was less rigorous than it might have been), she feigned sketching while, in reality, furtively taking photographs with her hidden camera. These images, obtained under duress of surveillance, are blurry and ill-focused, taken from strange, oblique angles that suggest, by means of their shaky, granular appearance, fraught, frenetic activity about the objects as much as the objects themselves.

A bristling forest of hands, fingers upstretched like so many sinewy branches, writhe silently as though they are leafless trees in a withering storm (Fig. 6.2). Or at least most appear as hands; some, truncated, deformed or rendered elsewise unintelligible by photographic blur might just as easily be brownly preserved hearts whose arterial passages extend graspingly outwards or the squirming forms of pickled homunculi. Rooted to the vitrine, they appear possessed by galvanic forces which oblige them to wave in phantomic salutation. A thick dark object obscures the far right-hand side of the image. (In all likelihood it is the cabinet door; but I cannot be completely sure: Is it some eccentric strut or long-forgotten piece of surgical equipment?) Taupe-coloured squares of parchment with indecipherable print are attached to black quadrangular bases above which forelimbs deliriously clutch and claw. The viewpoint is uncertain, oddly skewed, taken from a point that is slightly off-centre. My eye tracks the streak of light, the slantwise glimmer on glass.

Goggling out, a preserved head elsewhere besets the frame with a rictus grin (Fig. 6.3). But the photograph eludes straightforward classification; it is too out of

144

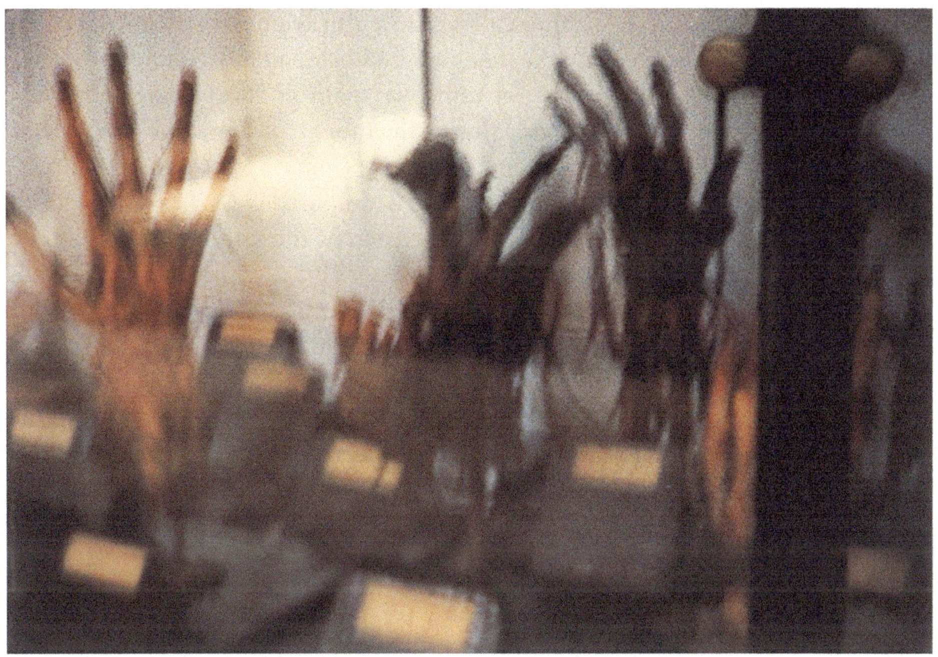

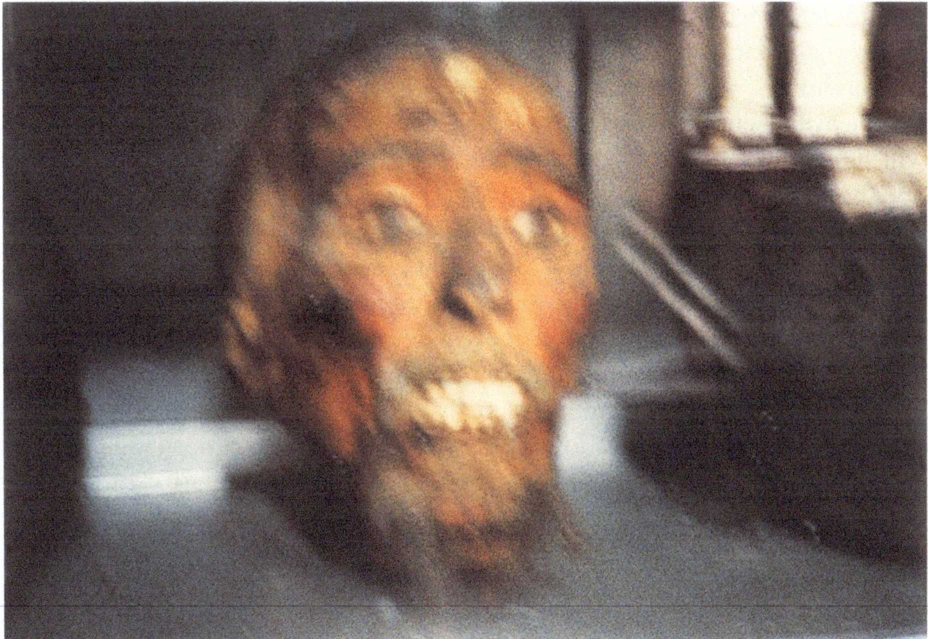

FIGURE 6.2 and 6.3. Christine Borland, *Cet être-là, c'est à toi de le créer! Vous devez la créer!*, 1997, photographs, Collection FRAC Occitanie Montpellier. © Christine Borland.

focus, too jerkily taken to be scientifically meaningful aside from the most generic of anatomical observations. Are the inflamed, reddish patches around the cheeks and eyes merely the play of light or in some way pathologically significant? The lilting shift of the camera's aperture enlivens the taught and fissured skin so as to give the mummified remains the semblance of motion; of a severed head on the cusp of speech. The eyes seem painted or made of coloured glass, like some ghastly carnival mask. Shadows and reflections dance across the vitrine. Is the window, partially shown in the upper right-hand corner, spectrally mirrored or actually present there, beside the specimen? All sense of scale melts away when faced with such visual trickery. The head is simultaneously immense and tiny; a captive of depthless space and infinite boundaries.

Everything in Borland's photographs hence appears chimerical, unfathomable and subject to an elegiac form of visual whimsy; as, one might add, does the contents of the museum itself whose classificatory indeterminacy therein seemingly undermines any sense of its original pedagogic rationale.[11] One might go so far as to propose that Borland's pictures appear to question the whole premise of objectivity as a vehicle through which an understanding of, say, normative anatomy might be inculcated through the study of museum specimens.[12] Indeed, any claim that such 'working objects' might embody those ideological values of epistemological clarity and representational truthfulness so central to the Enlightenment project is refuted by photographs that obfuscate as much as they reveal, that draw a flickering veil of light and shade over the contents of the museum.

The overall effect of this lack of focus, this disregarding of the optical rules by which photographs are usually taken (although one might surmise that the predominance of eccentric viewpoints in these photographs was a condition forcibly imposed by the clandestine nature of the activity itself), is to lend, as the curator Greg Hilty notes, the pictures a 'dreamlike, or more accurately, nightmarish, appearance' that transforms the museum into a kind of phantasmagoria whose topography is uncertain, reflected or elsewise ruptured, looping back upon itself so that the eye becomes disorientated by anatomical reiterations, unexpected erasures and convolutions of form.[13] Originally the photographs were—appropriately enough perhaps given the shadowy, insubstantial nature of the images—presented as a slide show through which documentation of Borland's tentative, meandering progress through the museum appeared as a succession of luminous plates, the superficial continuity of which masked the ruptured, fragmentary character of the journey recorded. One can certainly imagine that, on the basis of the discontinuous sequencing of the photographs, Borland's progression through the museum's thoroughfares was peripatetic, subject to unpremeditated changes of direction as she attempted to circumnavigate the entanglement of specimens so as to create new understandings of the objects that were conceptually tangential to the their original instructive purpose.

* * *

Rows of low, glazed cabinets line both sides of the central aisle. Beneath glass lids, whose ornate, trapezoidal construction resembles a hipped roof or else the fanciful lid of some baroque reliquary, I see two sets of shelves on which are arranged a series of deftly crafted models in coloured wax, each of which represent, in spite of the obscurity of their casement, mired as it is in deep shadow, a different section of the body. Peering into the vitrines, I see materialize from the shadiness, at first to my delight and then consternation, organs and even half-dissected torsos whose verisimilitude is enhanced by the lurid sheen which the waxy medium lends the fatty tissues, muscular formations and arterial vessels so that they appear freshly cut, as it were, from the flesh of a living body. Among the waxes displayed, which range from life-size models of abdominal cavities in which the viscera darkly glisten, to sagittal transections of the brain and enlarged facsimiles of the labyrinthine structures of the inner ear, it is a mucilaginous representation of a dissected head, fashioned from tinted beeswax, that most captures my attention. Set upon delicately ruffled white silk, the model ostensibly depicts the transversal section of the brain, the eye and its muscles, although its manner of representation is remarkable as much for the unsettling emotionality it elicits as for its apparent realism.

Imagine, then, a lidless, bloodshot eyeball, staring out from the ruin of its socket, above which a crosswise incision has been made so as to remove, transversely, the upper part of the head, leaving behind, in its dismal cavity, the circuitous corrugations of a portion of the brain. The pleats and furrows of this organ seem as though a line has been folded in upon itself, endlessly, so that sight itself becomes trapped in the unicursal warren of its convolutions.[14] Nevertheless, it is the contrast between the protuberant eye, set within its baleful hollow, and the marble pallor of the face, whose mute, unblemished features possess the calm serenity of a classical statue that makes Fontana's waxwork into a thing both beguiling and appalling.[15] The refinement of the face's countenance, one eye of which is closed as if in peaceful slumber, and the voluptuous crumpling of the fabric upon which it is placed, seem to emphasize in the figure a demureness, a passivity that permits the gaze to linger uncomfortably over the torn ridge of flesh that frames the dissevered eye and transected brain.[16]

* * *

147

For critics of Borland, it was the seemingly abject quality of the pathological specimens she photographed which provoked the most discussion, as they appeared to hint at the brutalities of an anatomical tradition that thought nothing of preserving and classifying childhood deformities for the purpose of scientific enlightenment or else thieving tombs so that medical pedagogy might benefit from the sad, dispossessed remnants of bodies obtained from distant colonial territories. Thus, the critic Jonathan Jones in a catalogue essay on Borland wrote:

> The specimens preserved in jars in the Montpellier Museum [...] include a face with two noses, a cabinet full of foetuses preserved in alcohol, shelves upon shelves of bones and skulls, child skeletons defined as abnormal. Little monsters. They are abandoned, forgotten, in this place far from home, in this dusty and deadly context.[17]

And, one might add, the ill-focused character of the pictures serves only to amplify this impression of incipient monstrosity by exaggerating or complicating the deformities of the specimens: the shaky image of a hydrocephalic specimen makes the head's swollen dome appear almost transparent, lacking clear physical boundaries (Fig. 6.4). So too, tiered shelves of bottled foetuses are so blurrily photographed that their bodies seem little more than fleshy globules, shapeless travesties of the disfigurements that afflicted them in life. Here it might be instructive to recall the philosopher of science Georges Canguilhem's contention that 'monstrosity is the accidental and conditional threat of incompletion in the formation of form' which overturns the 'specific consistency, [the] integrity of form' that 'gives living beings their value'.[18] Along these lines, then, one might understand Borland's distorted photographs as strengthening the prodigious attributes of the specimens. Lacking any semblance of morphological constancy or formal regularity, they reveal, better than the static objects themselves, 'the stability to which life [has] habituated us to be precarious'.[19]

Reference to teratology in the context of the photographs is especially appropriate, not simply because of how often physical deformity or foetal miscreation, as these conditions are presented by the specimens in the museum's collection, are documented but likewise because monstrosity, or rather humanity's malign ability to create fiends, both real and imaginary, formed the thematic centrepiece of Borland's exhibition of the works. To be sure, the photographs were but one part of a composite work entitled, *Cet être-là, c'est à toi de le créer! Vous devez le créer!* Appropriated from two different French versions of the final sentence of the Creature's pathetic soliloquy in Mary Shelley's *Frankenstein; or, The Modern Prometheus*; the original line reads as 'this being you must create' and represents the point in the text where the Creature issues to Victor Frankenstein,

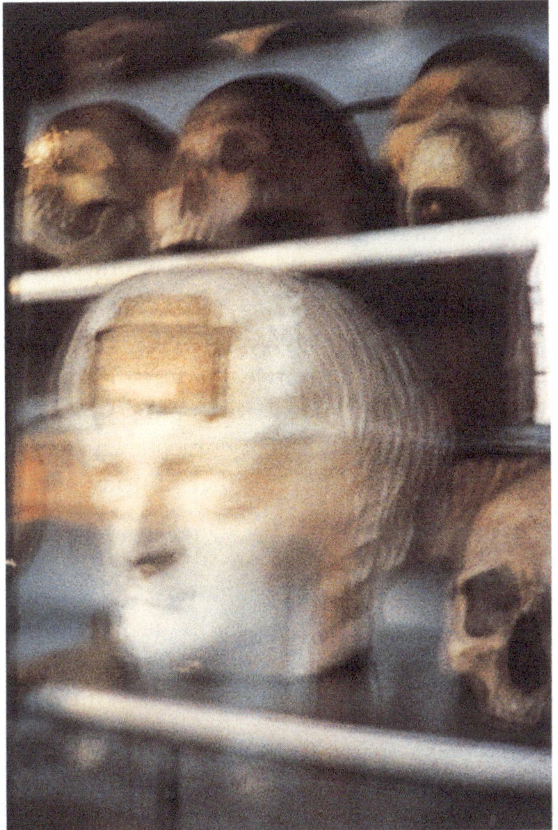

FIGURE 6.4. Christine Borland, *Cet être-là, c'est à toi de le créer! Vous devez la créer!*, 1997, photograph, Collection FRAC Occitanie Montpellier © Christine Borland.

its maker, the terrible injunction that he must create for it a companion 'of the same species, and have the same defects' to assuage the appalling solitude from which the Creature suffers and for which it unequivocally blames him.[20] This plea, delivered amid the alpine sublimity of eagle-haunted wastes and vaporous mountains, might be understood—so one reads in an introductory essay to the book by Maurice Hindle—as an act of penance to which Frankenstein is obligated for the 'presumptuous' act of creating life from the organs of purloined corpses.[21] Might then the naming of Borland's photographic series after the Creature's fateful line be seen to somehow link the grotesque assortment of specimens and the murky history of anatomical pedagogy to Frankenstein's original sin, for which some form of reparation was demanded? Certainly, for Hilty, Borland's pictures communicate the gruesome splendour of 'a slaughterhouse, with bloody severed limbs stacked high in apparently undifferentiated shelving units. Many were originally preserved by drying, rather than in formaldehyde, so that they are not even protected in jars, but exposed to the air. Frankenstein's workshop, though set up for different purposes, apparently exists'.[22] So the question limpidly hangs: are Borland's melancholy specimens the true Creatures of science's making, whose dispossession and crumbling physiognomies provide silent testimony to such cruelties as are born of objective disinterest? In this sense, one might suggest that these equivocal images, obtained under injunction yet revealing half-glimpsed teratologies, reveal the museum as anatomy's id; the 'dark, inaccessible place of [its] personality' which, as Sigmund Freud reminds us, is 'a chaos, a cauldron full of seething excitations' in which those lugubrious, wretched things that comprise unconscious biases and impulses are bottled-up and supressed.[23] Perhaps, then, the photographs prefigure a sort of 'return of the repressed' whereby those very objects which the museum quarantined from public view so as to obscure proper scrutiny of past deeds are made startlingly visible.

This rhetorical turning onto medicine the question of its culpability in fabricating the grisly abominations of the anatomy museum (and therefore also the types of atonement appropriate to mitigating its guilt) makes me inclined to think that Borland's photographic project formed part of the wider cultural engagement with anatomy evinced in the mid to late 1990s. One need but consider the controversy surrounding Gunther von Hagens's touring Körperwelten exhibitions (which hinged on the propriety of displaying real, flamboyantly posed écorchés to the general public) or else the legal efforts by indigenous groups to reclaim ancestral remains that had been obtained by museums during the colonial period to get a sense of how the final years of the millennium were riven with ethical and political debates over the possession and exhibition of anatomical material.[24] To this list we might also add exhibitions such as Deanna Petherbridge's *The Quick and the Dead* from 1997 as well as Martin Kemp's *Spectacular Bodies* (2000), both of which sought to place contemporary art and its histories within the context of anatomical display. That Borland accompanied her display with the drawings of skulls and foetuses she pre-prepared so as to feign sketching within the museum only serves to underscore the long-standing and complicated relationship between artistic practice and anatomy that such contemporary exhibitions aimed to convey and which Borland's multimedia presentation implicitly evoked. As Hilty intimates, the use of pictures traced from illustrations that were themselves originally drawn from the same types of pathological specimen as are imaged in Borland's photographs (and alongside which they were ultimately displayed) creates a strange sense of doubling, of things twinned and endlessly mirrored.[25] And I am inclined to believe that this repetition problematizes the representational function that such objects and images historically performed in medicine, not least because Borland's tracings are so densely cross-hatched and overworked that the line itself serves to obscure rather than reveal anatomical form. In this way, the drawing of specimens becomes an act of occlusion, of graphic effacement, so that the original anatomical image appears reduced to merely the slightest of pencil lines, a dark contour glimpsed within a scribbled meshwork, whose outline hesitantly intimates rather than objectively delineates.

* * *

A shelf of infant cadavers, prepared by the eighteenth-century French anatomist Honoré Fragonard, is momentarily luminesced by a sunburst so as to reveal meagre forms that are rendered ethereal by the reflections cast from the museum, the brightness of whose windows cast imperfect rectangular grids upon the children's remains, briefly obliterating their leathery physiognomies as though shimmering, geometric cavities are opening up with the passage of the day. Mirrored upon the glazed surface of the vitrine, the lines of the museum appear strangely warped owing to imperfections in the glass just as the diminutive corpses, each time I move, undergo capricious morphological changes: One moment heads and limbs balloon into extravagant grotesqueries only for these configurations to suddenly atrophy into withered arabesques barely an instant later.

Lined up in order of size, these wretched specimens were, undoubtedly, meant to collectively represent the various stages of infantile development, placed as they are amid all the zoological detritus of Second Empire anatomical instruction. Given that Fragonard originally prepared such objects for the teaching of comparative anatomy at the national veterinary school in Alfort, the morphological happenstance that occurs through, say, observing the sprightly form of a preserved foetus only to then turn and see a tiny wax model of a skinned horse, seems at first appropriate to their conception only for these comparisons to begin evoking peculiar, flamboyant couplings that, to paraphrase Canguilhem, transgress the fundamental rules of endogamy.[26] Human forms thus become more equine, while the physiognomy of the horse, upon closer scrutiny, acquires a distinctly anthropomorphic semblance. And so it is with all of the diverse specimens placed alongside these woeful children; each seems to become somehow more like the other through mere propinquity.

There is a strange vitality to these anatomical preparations which makes their dried and preserved bodies appear sensible, in spite of a mummification process which replaced blood and other vital fluids with coloured waxes and resins, and preserved membranes with varnishes that have long since darkened with age (Fig. 6.5). The rough patches of discoloured skin which cover their bodies like so much tattered parchment are agitated by the revelation of nerves and sinews which

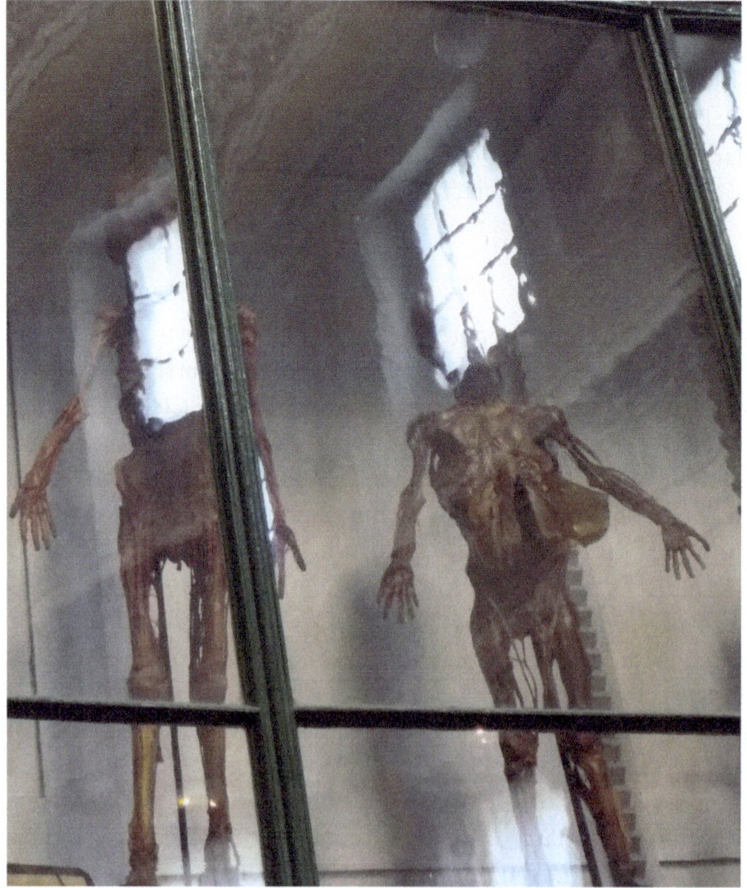

FIGURE 6.5. *...there is a strange vitality to these anatomical preparations...,* 2017, photograph, Anatomy Museum of the Faculty of Medicine/University of Montpellier. © the author.

spread like tendrils in an enervated filigree and in such a way that the cardiovascular system can be apprehended, as it were, at a single glance. These fleshy lappets of skin are miraculously held in place by some chemical marinade of Fragonard's devising so that, they too, appear oddly enlivened by vital forces. This effect is enhanced by some aberrant pullulation of muscular forces which issues a measured contraction of the facial muscles so as to suggest an ever-changing colour-wheel of pathetic emotion, ranging from the supplicatory to the choleric. (How strange it seems that these lugubrious figures, which speak of the macabre fascinations of the Baroque imaginary, the ostentation of its charnel houses and the mournful theatre of its martyrs, were created to instruct veterinary students in that most intimate yet unfamiliar of things, the human body.)

No doubt, as the historian Joan Landes has written, écorchés such as these were testament to Fragonard's own vitalist sympathies, so that the luridly interwoven tapestry of bodily vessels provided the student of physiology with dynamic evidence of the body's substantive integrity.[27] Here, perhaps, in the stringy latticework of tissue, muscles and arteries revealed by these dismembered youngsters is an illustration of what the eighteenth-century Montpellier physician, Théophile Bordeu, meant by the 'sensitivity' of an organism; a physiological susceptibility to reciprocated interaction between the various parts and organs. For in the liveliness of each figure, the way in which Fragonard made the surface of each of their bodies appear unsettled as through the action of subcutaneous energies, is there not a visible demonstration of Bordeu's notion that there is no soul or 'conscious intellectual centre' such as the brain, acting as despot or benign sovereign? Instead, the body here seemingly acts as a league of many bodily axes.[28]

Most of these children stand in silent petition, yet one holds its arm forcefully aloft, as though seeking to catch the eye of some omnipotent observer, who, moved by this beseeching spectacle, may find cause, if not to intercede, then to meditate upon those lessons of mortality seemingly imparted by these diminutive écorchés. This, at least, was presumably Fragonard's aim in producing such gruesome tableaux.[29] And certainly I find it difficult to behold these anatomized children without feeling as though they act as silent witnesses not only to the tragedy of their own arrested development, but also to the taxonomic imperatives of a science that preserved their remains as ciphers of a vital process from which they themselves were so cursorily removed.

* * *

Craig Richardson observes that Borland's documentation of the forgotten, historically maligned dead is in itself a form of remembrance through which the deceased regain some measure of selfhood after having been, for so many years, reduced to the pathological, dehumanized objects against which medical science constructed its vision of normative anatomy.[30] And, when one considers such ideas in relation to Borland's photographs of morbid specimens and the context of the Creature's homily (in which it describes the egregious lack of compassion it has been afforded by humankind) it is tempting to imagine that the act of photography repurposes the monstrous foetuses and anatomical curios of the museum, and instils within them some sense of the dignity that was denied them in their lives as the misappropriated and melancholic objects of medical pedagogy. Or, at the very least, it might be argued that Borland's photographic prints invite the spectator to compassionately reflect upon the unfortunate fate of such specimens within the museum. Nevertheless, it seems to me, rather than straightforwardly dignifying these pitiful assemblages of pathological bodies, Borland's blurry photographic still-lives purposefully interrupt the codes that underwrite the phenomenology of viewing and so destabilize the perceptual relationship between subject and object, spectator and image.

The literary theorist and historian, Peter Schwenger, has noted that 'there is a fundamental dynamic between anatomy and still life' which hinges upon how things, within phenomenology, are understood to 'constitute the sense of one's own body'.[31] Certainly, it might be argued—with due deference to the writings of Maurice Merleau-Ponty—that all objects are perceptually embodied by the mind so that 'we grasp the unity of our body only in that of the thing, and it is by taking things as our starting point that our hands, eyes and all our sense-organs appear to us as so many interchangeable instruments'.[32] And if such forms of embodiment are present, as Merleau-Ponty goes on to suggest, in the representations of things as much as in the things themselves, then still-life might be envisioned as a genre through which subjective incarnation is made manifest by personifying the phenomenological constitution of the body through the sensual world of its objects. But, in those rare, perturbing instances—such as one arguably finds in Borland's photographs—where the picture portrays corpses or their fragments, then, in the words of Alexander Nemerov, the 'secure distinctions between subject and object break down' and the corporeal imago is ruptured as the body that is reflected back to the distraught beholder appears worryingly dismembered or partial.[33] Similarly, this phenomenological self-realization as morbid part-object might be configured as a form of empathetic identification with the dead thing, so that to perceive self-embodiment in this fragmentary, dissolute manner is not simply to question 'the promise of bodily wholeness',[34] but also to recognize the damaged subjectivity of the object itself, and that the suffering inscribed upon the mutilated body of the specimen gives it subjective agency. For, as the philosopher Jean-Luc Nancy indicates, to acknowledge physical distress in any *corpus* is to elevate it to the echelon of a sensing, incarnate body, as the 'limits of suffering provide intense evidence that a body in pain, far from becoming an "object", is an absolutely exposed "subject" '.[35] Yet, in the case of photography, this sense of incipient subjectivity is decidedly uncanny; an inkling of aliveness produced by the ambiguity of the image itself. Just as it is a condition of the uncanny to elicit uncertainty over whether an object is animate or inanimate, so too photographs attest to the reality of the object in ways that subtly imply it is somehow alive: for the photograph is always a 'living image'; an index of the real even if the object itself is dead.[36] As Roland Barthes notes in *Camera Lucida*:

> If the photograph becomes horrible, it is because it certifies, so to speak, that the corpse is alive, as *corpse*: it is the living image of a dead thing. For the photograph's immobility is somehow the result of a perverse confusion between

two concepts: the Real and the Live: by attesting that the object has been real, the photograph surreptitiously induces belief that it is alive.[37]

Turned towards the question of Borland's images, their blurred, indeterminate character heightens the uncanniness of the specimens, rendering them into ephemeral, dissipated things that are felt as much as seen, products of itinerancy and motion or else glimpsed phantoms of sensation. By destabilizing the act of viewing itself, these pictures therefore cast doubt upon the very integrity of selfhood while reinfusing the saturnine, quietened part-objects with an uncanny agency which exceeds the bounds of their thinghood as specimens. Such an effect, one might conclude, does not simply intensify the viewer's consciousness of the body; but, rather, it reveals their own selfhood to be fragile and fleeting, phenomenologically constituted as much by the anatomical objects of its gaze as they are by it.

* * *

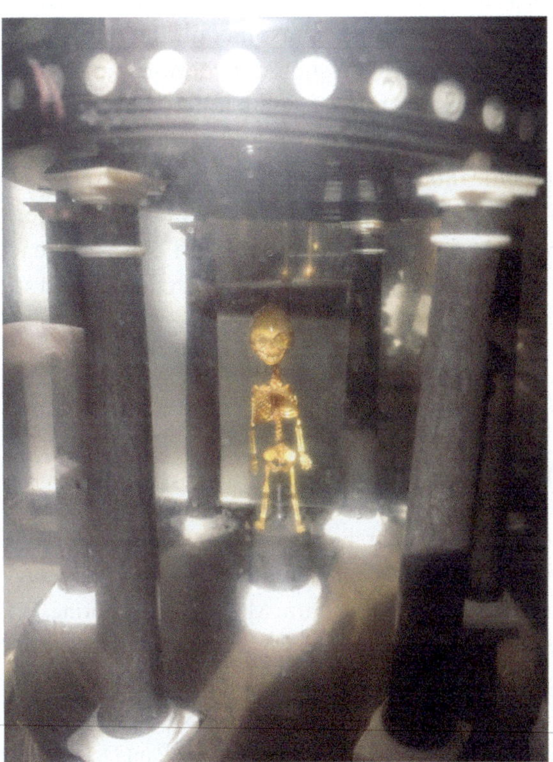

FIGURE 6.6. ...*the sunlight, by dint of small imperfections...*, 2017, photograph, Anatomy Museum of the Faculty of Medicine/University of Montpellier. © the author.

As I turn to leave, one particular exhibit catches my eye, positioned, as it is, somewhat incongruously in a vitrine otherwise occupied by jawbones and other fragmentary skeletal forms. It comprises of a bell jar, within which a tiny foetal skeleton, posed like a classical statue, holds court within a domed and colonnaded structure of black painted wood, which resembles a sort of neoclassical temple or pavilion (Fig. 6.6). The sunlight, by dint of small imperfections in the glassy medium, seems somehow to thicken and acquire substance within the vessel's chamber, rendering the mote-filled air milky yet radiant. Illumined thus the pathos of the unborn child forevermore trapped within its temple of mourning recalls those extravagant anatomical vanitas that were produced by Frederik Ruysch in the late seventeenth century, whose baroque assemblages featured embryonal skeletons, posed within Arcadian landscapes of preserved vessels and organs, weeping into handkerchiefs fashioned from body tissue. The heartrending aspect of these small, innocent bodies, whose virtue and purity were safeguarded by their unfulfilled and hence uncorrupted lives, provided them with an emotional poignancy as objects of reflection, rendering the self-pitying infants, imprisoned within their corporeal sceneries, into aesthetic foci of philosophical reflection; anatomical marvels upon which Enlightenment reason could linger in a lachrymose sense of wonderment.[38] To the modern eye such concoctions appear more maudlin than tear-jerking or morally insightful; yet, in its lonely imprisonment amidst the anatomical detritus of the collections, this foetal form appears (albeit briefly, for the mere duration of its incandescence) to cathect the epistemological priorities of the museum; of bodies bereft and sequestered; of taxonomic categories and gestational misfortune; of pathologies and prodigies. I lean closer to read the handwritten attribution on the exhibit; but it is too faded, too yellowed and stained to be legible.

NOTES

1. Michel de Certeau, *The Practice of Everyday Life* (Berkeley, LA: University of California Press, 1984), xix.

2. Christine Borland in interview with Craig Richardson, 'Interview: Living Subjects' in *Christine Borland: Preserves* (Edinburgh: Fruitmarket Gallery, 2006), 150.

3. When I returned to my hotel room that afternoon, sunk into a lassitude aggravated by the searing heat of an unseasonably warm Mediterranean Spring, I read about the history of the Montpellier collections in an essay by Hélène Palouzie in which she chronicles not only the rediscovery of the Fontana waxes after their fall into dusty obscurity but also the incorporation of the Spitzner collection whose waxworks and models were a source of particular fascination to the Surrealists and the painter Paul Delvaux especially. See: Hélène Palouzie, 'Mémoire du savoir et patrimoine : l'exemple montpelliérain', in *Du Savoir à la*

lumière : Les collections des universités montpelliéraines, ed. Alain Daguerre de Hureaux (Montpellier: DRAC Languedoc-Roussillon, 2014), 26–45.

4. Christine Borland, 'Interview: Living Subjects', in *Christine Borland: Preserves* (Edinburgh: Fruitmarket Gallery, 2006), 150.

5. The museum authorities eventually agree with Borland that these objects were 'stolen' originally. See: Ibid., 150.

6. See: Elizabeth Hallam, 'Anatomy Display: Contemporary Debates and Collections in Scotland', in *Anatomy Acts: How we come to know ourselves*, ed. A. Patrizio and D. Kemp (Edinburgh: Birlinn, 2006), 121.

7. John Cross, *Paris et Montpellier* (Paris, 1820), 162.

8. Glenn Harcourt has written elsewhere of how the cryptic postures of such écorchés made explicit reference to the statuary of ancient Greece and Rome so as to ennoble anatomical enterprise with classical virtue and elevate it above the moral ambiguity implicit in the acts of violation with which its practice was inseparably associated. Glenn Harcourt, 'Andreas Vesalius and the Anatomy of Antique Sculpture', *Representations* no. 17 (Winter 1987): 52.

9. On the iconography of Saint Bartholomew in the history of anatomy, see: Paola Pacifici, 'Chairs mortifies. Connaissance anatomique et esthétique de la souffrance dans la représentations des martyrs au XVIème et XVIIème siècle' in *Corps Sanglants, Souffrants et Macabres, XVIème – XVIIème siècle*, ed. Charlotte Bouteille-Meister and Kjerstin Aukrust (Paris: Presses Sorbonnes nouvelle, 2010), 19–26.

10. Later, I was of a mind to think that the odd, pointing gesture recalled the aesthetic tradition of Bernard Siegfried Albinus whose eighteenth-century anatomical atlas, *Tabulae sceleti et musculorum corporis humani*, depicts a striking series of dissected bodies all of whom gesticulate in a similarly obscure yet sedate manner. And, surely, as with Albinus's grimacing skeletons, such gesturing makes explicit the subtle mechanisms through which musculature and movement are bound so that each feint of the flesh-strings represents, by an instance, a particular understanding of normative anatomy, by which one might suppose that the careful positioning of a dissected limb, or the straining sinew of the neck indicates a 'truth-to-nature' of a more idealized kind. See: Lorraine Daston and Peter Gallison, *Objectivity* (New York: Zone Books, 2010), esp. 74. See also: Lyle Massey, 'Against the "Statue Anatomized": The "Art" of Eighteenth-Century Anatomy on Trial', *Art History*, (February 2017): 76.

11. For information on the *Conservatoire*'s original teaching functions, see: Hélène Palouzié, 'Mémoire du savoir et patrimonie: l'exemple montpelliérain', in *Du Savoir à la Lumière: Les collections des universités montpelliéraines* (Montpellier: DRAC, 2014), esp. 26–34.

12. On the role of specimens in the history of scientific objectivity, see: Daston and Gallison, *Objectivity*, 22, 59, 64, 74–75,111.

13. Greg Hilty, 'This Being You Must Create', *Christine Borland: Perserves* (Edinburgh: Fruitmarket Gallery, 2006), 51.

14. While the similarity between the structure of labyrinths and the brain has been often remarked upon, I point the reader towards an instructive conversation between Marina Warner and Mark Wallinger on this subject, 'Then it seemed like falling into a labyrinth [...]', in Mark Wallinger, *Labyrinth: A Journey Through London's Underground* (London: Art Books Publishing Ltd., 2014), 20–21.

15. I recall, in the soundless horror of this moment, a peculiar if affecting diary entry written by Elizabeth Vigèe Le Brun in April 1972, during a brief sojourn in the city of Florence in which time she had cause to visit Felice Fontana's celebrated ceroplastic workshop, in the Imperial Regio Museo di Fisica e Storia Naturale. At the time, Le Brun could scarcely have realized how long the memory of Fontana's lifelike models of 'the interior of the human body, all the parts of which appear so ingenious and so sublime', would troublingly linger in her mind. Guided by Fontana himself, Le Brun marvelled at the 'flesh-coloured' waxes which filled the vitrines of the atelier, and noted especially the peculiar magnificence of 'all those almost imperceptible ligaments which surround our eye, and a host of other details particularly useful to our preservation and intelligence'. The experience of witnessing these waxen and sebaceous mouldings elicited in Le Brun a sort of mystical reverie, in which she speculated upon the divine origins of human anatomy and the various theological suppositions which upheld them. 'It is', she perceived, 'impossible to consider the structure of Man's body, without being persuaded of the existence of a divinity'. Regardless of what certain 'wretched' philosophers in the Enlightenment tradition professed—and here we might suppose Le Brun was thinking of David Hume's recent, posthumously published, anti-theist tract, *Dialogues Concerning Natural Religion*—in the cabinet of M. Fontana, she concluded, 'one *must* believe and *prostrate* oneself'. Up until this point, Le Brun had seen little to cause, what she described as, 'painful sensation' yet, her awestruck comments regarding the verisimilitude of a reclining female nude, led Fontana to bid her approach more closely, whereupon he lifted, in a prestidigitatory manner, 'a type of lid' that offered to her gaze 'all of the entrails, turned as ours are'. This grisly revelation, in which, by some sleight of hand, the body's hidden interior was unexpectedly and alarmingly rendered visible, made such an overwhelming impression upon Le Brun that she felt close to finding herself ill. Indeed, for several days after this ghoulish encounter, Le Brun entered into a strangely introspective humour from which she found it virtually impossible to wrest herself; 'up to the point', so she wrote, that she could not so much look upon another person 'without mentally stripping them of their clothes and skin'. Needless to say, this gruesome compulsion to mentally flay the bodies of the living left Le Brun in a 'deplorable nervous state'; a kind of pathological reverie in which the sanguineous reality of the body continually impressed itself upon her feverish sensibility. Author's translation. Élisabeth Vigée Le Brun, *Souvenirs: 1755 – 1842*, Geneviève Haroche-Bouzinac (ed.) (Paris : Honoré Champion, 2008), 437.

16. As one of the keepers of collections, Véronique Bourgade, suggests to me later in conversation, it is perhaps the mutilated human face, whether cast directly from life or else modelled

posthumously in wax, which is the most difficult object to apprehend as it speaks of the traumatized self more eloquently than mouldings of anonymous viscera or severed limbs. Yet in the case of Fontana, it is surely not just the dreadfulness of the wounded head that terrifyingly engrosses one's attention, but rather that this horror is sublimated somehow, as Julie Kristeva might say, by the composure of the facial features and by the immaculate facture of the craft displayed. On the role classicizing aesthetics played in allowing the spectator to emotionally engage and visually dissect Fontana's waxes, I point the reader in the direction of the following text: Francesco Paolo de Ceglia, 'The Rotten, the Disembowelled Woman, the Skinned Man: Body Images from Eighteenth Century Florentine Wax Modelling', *Journal of Science Communication* 4, no. 3 (September 2005): 3–4.

17. Jonathan Jones, 'Heroes and Villains', in *Christine Borland: Progressive Disorder* (Dundee: Dundee Contemporary Arts, 2001), 53–54.

18. Georges Canguilhem, 'Monstrosity and the Monstrous', in *The Body: A Reader*, ed. M. Fraser and M. Greco (London: Routledge, 2005), 188.

19. Ibid., 188.

20. Mary Shelly, *Frankenstein, Or the Modern Prometheus* (London: Penguin, 2003), 146.

21. See: Maurice Hindle, 'Introduction' in Shelly, *Frankenstein*, xlii.

22. Hilty, 'This Being You Must Create', 51.

23. Sigmund Freud, *New Introductory Lectures on Psychoanalysis*, ed. James Strachey (London: The Hogarth Press, 1974), 73.

24. For an informative discussion of the anatomical turn in late 90s British cultural politics, see: Hallam, 'Anatomy Display', 123–24.

25. Hilty, 'This Being You Must Create', 51.

26. Canguilhem, 'Monstrosity and the Monstrous', 189.

27. Joan B. Landes, 'Wax Fibers, Wax Bodies, and Moving Figures: Artifice and Nature in 18th Century Anatomy', in *Ephemeral Bodies: Wax Sculpture and the Human Figure*, ed. R. Panzanelli (Los Angeles: Getty Publications, 2008), 51. The apparent vital energies possessing these figures may also have served medical pedagogy in Montpellier in particular ways given how a distinctive vitalist philosophy developed there which 'explicitly define[d] itself in contradistinction to both mechanistic and animistic models of life: the body is neither a warehouse, workshop, system of levers, pulleys, and clockwork, nor merely an instrument controlled by the soul': Charles T. Wolfe and Motoichi Terada, 'The Animal Economy as Object and Program in Montpellier Vitalism', *Science in Context*, 21, no. 4 (2008): 542. See also: Charles T. Wolfe, 'Models of Organic Organisation in Montpellier Vitalism', *Early Science and Medicine*, 22 (2017): 229–52.

28. Landes, 'Wax Fibers, Wax Bodies', 51.

29. Jonathon Simon, 'The Theatre of Anatomy: The Anatomical Preparations of Honoré Fragonard', *Eighteenth-Century Studies*, 36, no. 1 (2002): 72–73.

30. Christine Borland and Craig Richardson, 'Interview: Living Subjects', in *Christine Borland: Perserves* (Edinburgh: Fruitmarket Gallery, 2006), 143.

31. Peter Schwenger, *The Tears of Things: Melancholy and Physical Objects* (Minneapolis: University of Minneapolis Press, 2006), 161.

32. Maurice Merleau-Ponty, *The Phenomenology of Perception* (London: Routledge, 2002), 375.

33. Alexander Nemerov quoted in Schwenger, *The Tears of Things*, 161.

34. Ibid., 163.

35. Jean-Luc Nancy, *Corpus*, trans. Richard A. Rand (New York: Fordham University Press, 2008), 49.

36. Peter Schwenger, 'Corpsing the Image', *Critical Inquiry* 26 (Spring 2000): 396.

37. Roland Barthes, *Camera Lucida* (London: Vintage, [1980] 2000), 78–79 (original emphasis).

38. See: Julie V. Hansen, 'Resurrecting Death: Anatomical Art in the Cabinet of Dr. Frederik Ruysch', *The Art Bulletin* 78, no. 4 (December 1996): 672.

REFERENCES

Borland, Christine. *Christine Borland: Preserves*. Edinburgh: Fruitmarket Gallery, 2006.

Canguilhem, Georges. 'Monstrosity and the Monstrous'. In *The Body: A Reader*, ed. M. Fraser and M. Greco, 187–93. London: Routledge, 2005.

de Ceglia, Francesco Paolo. 'The Rotten, the Disembowelled Woman, the Skinned Man: Body Images from Eighteenth Century Florentine Wax Modelling'. *Journal of Science Communication* 4, no. 3 (September 2005): 1–7.

de Certeau, Michel. *The Practice of Everyday Life*. Berkeley, LA: University of California Press, 1984.

Cross, John. *Paris et Montpellier*. Paris: Plancher & Baillère, 1820.

Daston, Lorraine, and Peter Gallison. *Objectivity*. New York: Zone Books, 2010.

Hallam, Elizabeth. 'Anatomy Display: Contemporary Debates and Collections in Scotland'. In *Anatomy Acts: How We Come to Know Ourselves*, ed. A. Patrizio and D. Kemp, 119–35. Edinburgh: Birlinn, 2006.

Hansen, Julie V. 'Resurrecting Death: Anatomical Art in the Cabinet of Dr. Frederik Ruysch'. *The Art Bulletin* 78, no. 4 (December 1996): 663–79.

Harcourt, Glenn. 'Andreas Vesalius and the Anatomy of Antique Sculpture'. *Representations* no. 17 (Winter 1987): 28–61.

Hilty, Greg. 'This Being You Must Create', *Christine Borland: Perserves*, 48–51. Edinburgh: Fruitmarket Gallery, 2006.

Le Brun, Élisabeth Vigée. *Souvenirs: 1755–1842*, ed. Geneviève Haroche-Bouzinac. Paris: Honoré Champion, 2008.

Massey, Lyle. 'Against the "Statue Anatomized": The "Art" of Eighteenth-Century Anatomy on Trial'. *Art History* 40, no. 1 (February 2017): 68–103.

Merleau-Ponty, Maurice. *The Phenomenology of Perception*. London: Routledge, 2002.

Nancy, Jean-Luc. *Corpus*, trans. Richard A. Rand. New York: Fordham University Press, 2008.

Pacifici, Paola. 'Chairs mortifies. Connaissance anatomique et esthétique de la souffrance dans la représentations des martyrs au XVIème et XVIIème siècle'. In *Corps Sanglants, Souffrants et Macabres, XVIème—XVIIème siècle*, ed.Charlotte Bouteille-Meister and Kjerstin Aukrust, 19–26. Paris : Presses Sorbonnes nouvelle, 2010.

Palouzie, Hélène. 'Mémoire du savoir et patrimoine : l'exemple montpelliérain', in *Du Savoir à la lumière : Les collections des universités montpelliéraines*, ed. Alain Daguerre de Hureaux, 26–45. Montpellier: DRAC Languedoc-Roussillon, 2014.

Palouzie, Hélène. 'Memoire du savoir et patrimoine: l'exemple montpellierain', in *Du Savoir a la lumiere: Les collections des universités montpelliéraines*, ed. Alain Daguerre de Hureaux, 26–45. Montpellier: DRAC Languedoc- Roussillon, 2014.

Panzanelli, Roberta, ed. *Ephemeral Bodies: Wax Sculpture and the Human Figure*. Los Angeles: Getty Publications, 2008.

Patrizio, Andrew, and Dawn Kemp, eds. *Anatomy Acts: How We Come to Know Ourselves*. Edinburgh: Birlinn, 2006.

Schwenger, Peter. *The Tears of Things: Melancholy and Physical Objects*. Minneapolis: University of Minneapolis Press, 2006.

Schwenger, Peter. 'Corpsing the Image'. *Critical Inquiry* 26 (Spring 2000): 395–413.

Shelly, Mary. *Frankenstein; or the Modern Prometheus*. London: Penguin, 2003.

Simon, Jonathon. 'The Theatre of Anatomy: The Anatomical Preparations of Honoré Fragonard', *Eighteenth-Century Studies*, 36, no. 1 (2002): 72–73.

Wallinger, Mark. *Labyrinth: A Journey Through London's Underground*. London: Art Books Publishing Ltd., 2014.

Wolfe, Charles T., and Motoichi Terada. 'The Animal Economy as Object and Program in Montpellier Vitalism'. *Science in Context* 21, no. 4 (2008): 537–79.

Wolfe, Charles T. 'Models of Organic Organisation in Montpellier Vitalism'. *Early Science and Medicine* 22 (2017): 229–52.

7

… as far back as I will remember

Nadia Lichtig

Abstract:

… as far back as I will remember *is a monologue written in the form of a prosopopoeia from the point the view of the* Ziziphus zizyphus *plant, growing in the botanical garden of Montpellier in the south of France. Written in the future tense, the plant describes its direct environment in the botanical garden, its nomenclatural history, its geographic and cultural expansion as well the chemistry and benefits humans extract from its species. Progressively it also describes a future where a sixth mass extinction has taken place and where the* Ziziphus zizyphus—*or the Wild Jujube in its common denomination—becomes a "superspecies" colonizing the planet earth.*

Jardin des Plantes, Montpellier, South of France

… as far back as I will remember, I will have always been growing here, on this remote part of the earth, constantly creating the conditions of new germinations—where the living is showing itself over the ordering, blossoming in a non-sterile and daring order (Fig. 7.1).

In 1593 the soil I am expanding and flourishing on will become the botanical garden of Montpellier. The *Jardin des Plantes* will be founded by the French botanist Pierre Richer de Belleval (1555 or 1564–1632). He will create the garden on orders from Henry IV (1553–1610), the King of France from 1589 to 1610. The *Jardin des Plantes* in Montpellier will be one of the oldest botanical gardens of Europe, alongside the *Orto Botanico di Padova*, the botanical garden of Padua in Italy, which will have begun two generations earlier, in 1545. The *Jardin des Plantes* in Montpellier will encompass more than 2,500 plants and will cover nearly five hectares next to the very centre of the city. Comforted by the warm Mediterranean climate of the south of France, the garden will become an area of stunning natural beauty.

The site, with its ponds, an arboretum and landscaped areas, will be owned by the University of Montpellier, and will be used for study and research. I will be growing in the garden's Systematic School neighbouring a Judas tree (*Cercis siliquastrum*) planted by the garden's founder, a majestic Phillyrea tree (*Phillyrea latifolia*) planted in 1620, and a Ginkgo tree (*Ginkgo biloba*) that will be planted here as a tribute to the French Revolution in 1795. I will be surrounded by busts of important medical naturalists, such as Pierre Magnol (1638–1715), a French botanist born in the city of Montpellier. He will be known as one of the innovators devising the scheme of classification that all botanists adopt hereafter. He will be the first to publish the concept of plant families as it will be understood from then on as a natural classification of groups of plants that have features in common. He will become Professor of Botany at the University of Montpellier and Director of the botanical garden of Montpellier in 1697, then called the Royal Botanic Garden or *Hortus monspeliensis*, in its Latin denomination. He will also briefly hold a seat in the French Academy of Sciences, a learned society in Paris, encouraging and protecting the spirit of French scientific research, before founding the French Royal Academy of Sciences of Montpellier in 1706.

Over time, the garden's appearance will not vary excessively; only the flowers that will be planted and replanted each year will change, like a garment wrapped around a body, remaining the same below. I will have the chance to observe a range of flowers from originally different continents growing and blossoming here, including the Star of Bethlehem (*Agapanthus*), the Floss Flower (*Ageratum houstonianum*), the Flamingo Flower (*Anthurium*), the Bleeding Heart (*Dicentra*), the Snapdragon Flower (*Antirrhinum majus*), the Kaffir Lily (*Clivia miniata*), the Australian native Kangaroo Paw *(Anigozanthos manglesii)*, the Ice Plant (*Delosperma*), the nightshade plant Jaborosa *(Jaborosa integrifolia)*, the Black-Eyed Susan (*Rudbeckia*), the Desert Rose (*Dogbane*), the Wild Iris (*Dietes*), the Euphorbia *(Euphorbia L.)*, the Mexican Fireplant Pointsettia (*Cyathophor*), the Flannel Flower (*Actinotus helianthi*), the Cosmos (*Asteraceae*), the Honesty (*Lunaria*), the Cherry Pie Plant (*Heliotrope*), the Honeysuckle (*Lonicera*), the West Indian Jasmine (*Ixora*), the Baby's Breath (*Gypsophila*), the Whirling Butterflies (*Gaura*) and the Protea *(Protea cynaroides)*. The latter is one of the oldest flowers on earth, and its history, or so these scholars think, dates back 300 million years, long before grass evolved, let alone before any modern mammals began to develop.

Among all these spectacular plants, and being myself a tiny, thorny scrub, I will not attract too much attention. In fact, I will hardly be noticed. Growing here, in a removed part of the planet, in the botanical garden of Montpellier, I will remain surprised about the longevity and sustainability of my family: I know that we will be the survivors in history. At some point, my family's lineage and origin will be an object of curiosity, even a mystery. Individuals of my family will have their hour of glory and inspire portraits painted by widely renowned artists. We will appear in poems, in essays and on medallions, and we will be acclaimed in religious and medical literature. We will continue to exist, without respite. In front of everybody's eyes and yet hidden from the view of all, we will become ubiquitous. Some will call us a weed. Our omnipresence and what they think of as our banality will be our best allies. We will be botanical hitch-hikers, masters of long-distance dispersal, ready to ride along with anyone credulous enough to serve us as an agent of dispersal. Our fruits will be carried along from pond to pond, from oasis to oasis, with thousands of miles between one suitable habitat and the next. We will be the perfect example of what botanists and ecologists will mean by their term 'cosmopolitan species'. Because of our tenacity and willingness to adapt— because we are not really natives anywhere but are at home almost everywhere—I will tell you less about the past and a whole lot more about the future of our planet.

Call Me by My Name

I will be called by many different names. Due to a combination of botanical naming regulations and variations in spelling, my family will have a curious, confusing nomenclatural history. My name will be often truncated, misspelled or transformed in some way. It will be translated from Arabic or Persian writing into Greek by means of the Greek alphabet. The Arabic-Greek bilingual lexica will establish the equivalence of the terms. Transliterations of my name will result from the fact that, when Arabic texts will be rendered into Greek, the translators will not always know the exact Greek equivalent of my name and will keep the Arabic form, just reproducing it letter by letter from Arabic into the Greek alphabet.

In the Greek world, they first will speak of me as the *lôtos* or lotus. I will be mentioned in the famous *Odyssey*, which they say was written by the great Homer. They believe these words will be composed near the end of the eighth century BCE, somewhere in Ionia, the Greek coastal region of Anatolia. The oldest known extract of the *Odyssey* will be found near the remains of the Temple of Zeus, on an engraved clay plaque in Olympia, Greece. That, though, will be believed to date only from the third century CE. There, my fruits will be described as being food of the *Lotofagoi* (this is, literally the eaters of *lôtos*), and my fruits will be credited with a strange property: whoever eats my fruits will be savaged by an unruly forgetfulness. He or she will no longer want to sail home and not even give news of their adventures. The location of the *Lotofagoi* will never be clearly established: usually it will be located somewhere on the North African coast, but it will also tentatively identified in the Adriatic region, specifically Dubrovnik. Most sources will say that the island that Odysseus lands on with his soldiers will be Djerba, the largest island of North Africa. But Odysseus, the main character, will tell of what happens to three of his companions when they meet the Lotus-Eaters and partake of my fruits:

> I was driven thence by foul winds for a space of nine days upon the sea, but on the tenth day we reached the land of the Lotus-eaters, who live on a food that comes from a kind of flower. Here we landed to take in fresh water, and our crews got their mid-day meal on the shore near the ships. When they had eaten and drunk I sent two of my company to see what manner of men the people of the place might be, and they had a third man under them. They started at once, and went about among the Lotus-eaters, who did them no hurt, but gave them to eat of the lotus, which was so delicious that those who ate of it left off caring about home, and did not even want to go back and say what had happened to them, but were for staying and munching lotus with the Lotus-eaters without thinking further of their return; nevertheless, though they wept bitterly I forced them back to the ships and made them fast under the benches. Then I told the rest to go on board at once, lest any of them should taste of the lotus and leave off wanting to get home, so they took their places and smote the grey sea with their oars.[1]

Around 430 BCE, I will be seen in Herodotus's second book of *The Histories*, devoted to Africa. Herodotus will speak of me as a mythological tree that gives the Lotus fruit. The *Lotophagi* will be described as a Libyan tribe and their country as in the Libyan district bordering on the Syrtes, either of two shallow sandy gulfs on the coast of Libya, proverbially dangerous to shipping. When Odysseus will reach the country of the Lotophagoi, many of his sailors after eating the lotus will lose all wish to return home. The Lotus will be said to constitute the only food of the natives, who will also be believed to make a wine of my fruits:

> There is a cape that protects into the sea from the land of the Gindanes, and there dwell the Lotophagi, who live solely from the enjoyment of the lotus fruit. The fruit of the lotus is about as big as a mastic berry and in sweetness is like the fruit of the palm tree. The Lotophagi also make wine of this fruit.[2]

And those who will write about Herodotus will offer information about my fruits:

> Herodotus is precise in describing the lotus, because of its legendary fame in Homer as causing forgetfulness of home and family; Polybius describes it even more fully. It is a species of thorn tree, the jujube (ziziphus vulgaris) of the genus Rhamnescea, to which the English buckthorn belongs, with a fruit like a plum

in size and shape, which is eaten, especially when dried. The Egyptian lotus is quite distinct [...] A sort of wine is still made from the fruit.[3]

In Theophrastus's *Enquiry into Plants or Historia Plantarum* (Greek: Περὶ φυτῶν ἱστορία, *Peri phyton historia*), I will be listed as an Indian plant. Theophrastus (371–287 BCE) will be a Greek native of Eresós in Lesbos, the successor to Aristotle in the Peripatetic school and will be considered being the 'father of botany' for his works on plants. Theophrastus will not know my name and will describe me by comparing me to the Cornelian cherry tree. From the fourth century BCE, I will become more widely known in the Greek world, thanks to the soldiers serving Alexander the Great (356–223 BCE) and the scientists who will accompany them in their adventure to India (327–225 BCE). But the Greeks will have a word that will become my name, and it will refer to several different plants, based in part on Herodotus's assertion, and will include species of *Trifolium*, Melilot or *Trigonella*; the *Lotus corniculatus*; the fellbloom or *Medicago arborea*; the sweet persimmon fruit of the date-plum *Diospyros lotus*; a water-lily, either *Nymphaea lotus*, *Nymphaea caerulea* or *Nymphaea stellata*; the blue water-lily of the Nile, *Nymphaea caerulea*, also known as the blue lotus; the nettle-tree (*Celtis australis*) and *Zizufos*, that will be taken to be the plant meant in the Odyssey.

In Latin literature at the turn of the first century BCE/CE, I will first appear as *Ziziphus*. This name will be believed to derive from the Persian name *Zizfum* or *Zizafun*, and the very name *Zizufos* in Greek is of unknown etymology. Its Latin adaptation *Ziziphus* will not provide any clear indication on my origins: I am without origins or destination. For Pliny (23/24–79) who will write about me as well, I will be an exotic tree who has only 'recently arrived to Italy'. He will explain that I will have been introduced to Italy by Sextus Papinius, the consul during Pliny's life, and that I will have been brought from Syria in, the year of Augustus's death, in 14 CE. Pliny will tell the world I will be also called *Cappodocia*, a plant from central Asia Minor.

Twenty-one thousand months later, I will be named again. Carl Linnaeus (1707–78), a Swedish naturalist contends that I am really *Rhamnus ziziphus*, when he will write *Species Plantarum* in 1753. A little later, in 1768, Philip Miller (1691–1771), an English botanist of Scottish descent, will conclude I am sufficiently distinct from *Rhamnus* to become a new genus with a new name. He will name me *Ziziphus jujuba Mill*, using Linnaeus's species name for my genus and *jujuba* for my byname, as in the Western part of the world I will be called commonly the 'Wild Jujube'. And now I have two names, as my peers do, and just as humans have taken to do for some time. A little later the French botanist Bernard de Jussieu (1699–1777) will write about me again but spelling my genus name *Zizyphus* using a single letter different, by accident. And in 1882 the German botanist Hermann Karsten (1817–1908) will give me a name of his own—I will become the majestic *Ziziphus zizyphus (L.) H. Karst.*

In the nineteenth, twentieth and twenty-first centuries, there will be scientific quarrels about my identity and naming as scientists will constantly discover new variations of mine and will invent new bynames for my family members—epithets describing where they will have found us, whom we will make them think of or in which shades we will appear to them. The classification invented by Pierre Magnol will have been thought up before the appearance of Charles Darwin's (1809–1882) theory of evolution and will be built around the certainty of the fixity of species. Consecutively scientists will have to proceed in readjustments—a constant ballet of the naming and renaming of my kin that will draw a portrait of these scientists' time and their world. They will identify my presence all over the surface of the planet and call me *Ziziphus soporifer, Ziziphus sororia, Ziziphus spinosa, Ziziphus abysssincia, Ziziphus sinensis, Ziziphus lucidus, Ziziphus rotundifolia, Ziziphus microphylla, Ziziphus paliurus, Ziziphus amphibia, Ziziphus umbrellatus, Ziziphus insularis, Ziziphus xylopyrus, Ziziphus mucronata, Ziziphus oenophilia, Ziziphus spina Christi, Ziziphus jujuba* and *Ziziphus zizyphus*—some among many other Latin denominations that will specify my variations. *Ziziphus zizyphus* will be a name creating controversy. It will be rejected by scientists of the beginning of the twenty-first century, during the International Botanical Congress in Melbourne, Australia, in 2011. They will take the decision that *Ziziphus zizyphus* should be considered being a tautonym—a scientific name of a species in which both parts of the name have the same spelling, such as *Rattus rattus*. The then current rule for botanical nomenclature will explicitly prohibit tautonyms, and this rule will be applied retroactively. Only some years later, however, in 2019, the then appearing edition of the International Code of Nomenclature for algae, fungi and plants will stipulate that instances that repeat the genus name with a slight modification, such as *Ziziphus zizyphus*, had been contentious but will be in accord with the new Code of Nomenclature once more.

Across the other side of the world, I will be known differently. In China, they will take me and transform me into the most wondrous formulas. I will appear there as *Da Zao* (Chinese: 대讀), 'the red date', for many thousands of years, over a thousand years before Pliny. Around 200 CE, I will be mentioned as *Sheizaf* (Hebrew: שיזף השיח) and as *Rimin* (Hebrew: שיזף מצוי) in the part of the Talmud called *Mishnah*, a written collection of the Jewish oral traditions authored by Rabbi Yehudah ha-Nasi (135–217) originally from Lower Galilee. In the Christian lands, I will be known as 'the Christ's thorn', and be considered as the very tree from which Jesus's own crown of thorns will be made. In the Arab world, I will be called *Sidar, Sidr, Sing, Sidrat, Sidrah* and *Sidrat al-Muntahā* (Arabic: سِدْرَة الْمُنْتَهَى): the 'uttermost extremity or the very end of something or boundary'. My name will be synonymous with the many Arabic words for 'end'.

From Alexandria to Carthage

The memory of Djerba being a place where the *Lōtophagoi* lived will be still vivid within the twentieth century. A film will be made where the crew want to find "the otherworldly atmosphere of the Land of the Lotus-Eaters."[4] Those in China will imagine I am a native of their lands because they have used me in medicine for so very long, in fact some 2,500 years. In the Arab world, I will growing in the Jordan Valley, in Israel around Jerusalem, all along the coastal plain. My cousins will last and their longevity be a source of amazement; in Ayn Husb in Palestine, they will age gracefully and live for some 800 years.

In Africa, I will be known as a fruit tree to be found far and wide, in both the arid and semi-arid areas, whether west, east or south of Africa. In sub-Saharan Africa, I will be preserved in farmlands because of my nourishing fruit; I can act as a barrier to protect other plants and vegetation during the dry season. Their farmers will cherish me as I have strong, agile roots that can fetch water from a great depth under the earth and withstand extreme temperatures. They will name me a 'pioneer species' in preventing all of these lands becoming vast deserts. In Egypt, I will be already known when the Pharaohs live and humans will eat my fruits, their physicians will turn me into medicines and their carpenters build with me. My fruits will be made into bread by Egyptian farmers for many centuries, until the beginning of the twentieth century.

Writers will know me. One such will say this of me:

> Whether it originated in China or Syria is not clear, but it is cultivated for its fruits right across this range: in Japan, China, Afghanistan, Iran and westwards to the Mediterranean region. And so many will describe the plant as a set of thorny shrubs for which no one really remembers their place of origin. It will occur at desert oases all along the Hadhramaut region of Yemen to Damascus in Syria, across the Silk Road from Baghdad to Samarkand to Canton in China and across the Western spice route from Alexandria to Carthage and Fez. It will be found in Tucson, San Diego and Mexicali. Its fruits will have been carried by camel or horse across the deserts to be planted wherever the salty soil was wet enough to embrace it. This process will have occurred for so long that no one will discern where its natal ground is located.[5]

Life's Rich Pageant

In the Arabic world and India, their stories will centre on me. The Bedouin, Druze and Arab peoples will shape tales that I am a tree protected by benevolent spirits or dead saints. They will believe I have supernatural powers whether it is blood instead of water flowing in my 'veins', that I make a sound if I am cut, or that I am the abode of a saint's spirit. In Pakistan, in the Himalaya and Karakoram regions, they will say the power of my scent can make two teenagers fall in love. Their men will take a stem of my sweet-smelling flowers with them to court their women. I will be recorded by Muslim pilgrims generation after generation. It will be reported that pilgrims will see me in the mosque containing Muhammad's tomb in Medina and in a garden dedicated to Muhammad's daughter Fatimah. It will be said that my fruit will be sold to pilgrims, and my leaves used for washing dead bodies. By the eighth century, when the Islamic empire will spread, I will be praised in the Koran where it will say:

[10] So did Allah convey the inspiration to His Servant what He (meant) to convey.

[11] The heart in no way falsified that which he saw.

[12] Will ye then dispute with him concerning what he saw?

[13] For indeed he saw him [Gabriel] at a second descent,

[14] Near the Lote-tree beyond which none may pass:

[15] Near it is the Garden of Abode.

[16] Behold, the Lote-tree was shrouded (in mystery unspeakable!)

[17] (His) sight never swerved, nor did it go wrong!

[18] For truly did he see, of the Signs of his Lord, the Greatest![6]

This passage of the Koran will be commented by Abd al-Razzāq al-Qāshānī (Arabic: عبد الرزاق القاشاني.), a Medieval Sufi leader (d.1329) who will say of me:

> The Sidrat al-Muntahā (Arabic: سِـدْرَة الْـمُـنْـتَـهَى) [lit. Lote-Tree of the Utmost Farthest Boundary] is said to signify the greatest intermediate realm at which all knowledge and activity terminates. It is said to be the last of the named spiritual ranks without superior.[7]

And the British-Indian scholar Abdullah Yusuf Ali (1872–1953) will comment:

> [this tree] marked the bounds of heavenly knowledge as revealed to men, beyond which neither Angels nor men could pass.[8]

I will appear in the Koran as an emblem of revelation of knowledge, perseverance and nourishment; I will have the reputation of growing in the harshest environments. They will believe my roots may be bound in the soil of this world but my branches reach upward towards perfection. The Persian poet Saadi (Abū-Muhammad Muslih al-Dīn bin Abdallāh Shīrāzī; Arabic: ابومحمد مصلحالدين بن عبدالله شيرازى) will eternalize me in the famous *Bustan* (c. 1257), a book of poems written in 1257, where I will be praised in the chapter 'Isra and Mi'raj and the Lote-tree'. And in the Christian world, as jujube, my branches will be platted as a crown for Jesus to suffer; three gospels will name me and tell of how Romans twisted me to torture him:

And when they had plaited a crown of thorns, they put it upon his head.[9]

Many will see me in pictures, where I adorn his head thus. My cousins will become relics, venerated by pilgrims who believe my wood touched his head. Followers will write:

With regard to the origin and character of the thorns, both tradition and existing remains suggest that they must have come from the bush botanically known as Ziziphus spina-christi, more popularly, the jujube tree. This reaches the height of fifteen or twenty feet and is found growing in abundance by the way-side around Jerusalem [now preserved in] Capella della Spina at Pisa, as well as that at in Trier.[10]

The Europeans will have artists who will show me in their imaginings, again and again, all across the continent. The painter who will be called Lucas Cranach the Elder (1472–1553) will obsessively picture me, over and over, showing me as a crown of seven or eight branches. In the city of Venice, I will be seen in the *Scuola Grande di San Rocco*, on the ceilings, where light will radiate from within me. The Greek painter Doménikos Theotokópoulos (1541–1614), better known as 'El Greco', will show my green leaves still sticking in a crown made of three woven branches. The Flemish painter Peter Paul Rubens (1577–1640) will show me lying neglectfully in a bowl placed on the ground, bathing partly in a liquid, most likely blood. The Dutchman Rembrandt Harmenszoon van Rijn (1606–1669) will show me atop Jesus's head. And the Spaniard Diego Rodríguez de Silva y Velázquez (1599–1660) will paint me as a crown woven out of four branches, where each thorn is clear. In the monuments, museums and churches of almost every city on the planet, I will be there.

Better Living through Chemistry

I will be transformed, again and again. For some, I will be a source of afflictions. For others, I will aid them. My family will be treasured kin and despised pests, both honoured and subject to invective, bearers of medicine and food, as well as carriers of disease. They will say I have all manner of qualities that can aid humankind. That I am antibacterial. Or antifungal. That I am an antioxidant. That I can become anti-hyperglycemic. Or that I can be anti-nociceptive. Others still will believe I can be an anticonvulsant, or even an antidepressant, as though I was nature herself in her entirety in one place. There will be no limits to the experiments with my matter and my fruits.

To humans, the fragrance of my flowers will be experienced as obsessive and obnubilating (Fig. 7.2). In the high mountains of Kyrgyzstan in Central Asia, men will ornate their hats with my blooms in order to cloud the consciousness of women they want to conquer thus. The humans will boil and ferment me to assuage their anxiety. But they will find that I make them forget, and that they will forget that they have forgotten. I will offer them amnesia and they will take it, gladly or unwittingly. In traditional Chinese medicine, I will be classified within 'The Five Fruits' that 'provide support' along with the peach, plum, *Prunus mume* and apricot. I will be known for numerous benefits:

1. enhancing cellular communication;
2. combating cellular damage from free radicals;
3. easing sore throats;
4. nourishing the blood;
5. aiding in digestion;
6. supporting liver and spleen function;
7. detoxifying the body;
8. calming the mind;
9. moderating nervousness;
10. helping to overcome fatigue and weakness;
11. speeding recovery from illness;
12. inhibiting gastrointestinal infections;
13. soothing the stomach;
14. providing energy;
15. enhancing metabolism;
16. supporting cardiovascular health;
17. strengthening blood vessels;
18. providing relief from the heat;
19. boosting libido;
20. destroying parasites in the intestinal tract;
21. suppressing appetite;
22. supporting heart, lung and kidney health;
23. enhancing the immune system;
24. slowing the effects of premature aging;
25. inducing apoptosis in skin cancer cells;

26. impeding tumour growth;
27. assisting weight loss;
28. counting effects of poison;
29. remedying boils and sores;
30. relieving bronchitis;
31. reducing fevers;
32. acting as a diuretic;
33. helping in extracting energy from food;
34. alleviating allergies;
35. facilitating sleep.

Pansexuality

In time, my first name will have more than eighty second names, all of which will name spiny shrubs and small trees. And they will all live throughout in the warmer and subtropical regions of this world. Some will say my leaves will grow a pair of stipules at their base which will turn into hard thorns, with one straight and the other hooked. They will say that my zigzag branches will be very dense and that my leaf will be dentate and ovate. Time will be my friend: when I will live in a fine home, I will live a long, long life, and become great, so that some of my cousins will be 30 feet tall like the humans' houses. How our trunks will be broad and our crowns so large! Some of us will be majestic. My fruit will be eaten, and sweet to the taste, like an apple or a date. It will be yellow-brown, red or black, globular or oblong, and small. These fruits will bloom through the spring, summer and into autumn. My flowers will be small; indeed, they will be inconspicuous. They will be of both sexes at once and in a green-yellowy colour. I will secrete lots of nectar and draw forth many, many insects, and especially honey bees who will feast on it.

My flower, as I say, will be male and female. My parts will ripen alternatively, male then female then male again, to pollinate, sometimes just with the help of the wind. Two of my cousins will meet in Israel. One is *Ziziphus spina Christi*, who may be tropical or Sudanese and loves warmer, humid places, and who may have arrived in Israel from the south. And the other is *Ziziphus lotus*, more likely from the north. It is said that this one of us will 'deliberate' whether to shed leaves in winter. We will change. New variants of me will be found all the time, like *Ziziphus odysseus*, located in Mali in the year 2018. It will have densely pubescent leaves and floral buds. And many of us will never be seen by human eye and never be named, existing for some only for a tiny moment of earth's history. We will self-domesticate when we relocate. We will adapt. We will live happily in those areas that humans disturb and which fires and floods upset.

At some point, my family will have domesticated humans, who will provide another means to disperse our seeds. We will have no hostility to warmth or to dry climates. We will survive; we will prosper. When the Earth warms again, we will draw water from deep underground. In the heat we will still feed on the sun's rays greedily. We will be one of the few that can live on slopes with nothing on them.

I, *post-specimen*

I am using the term 'species' to name myself; but this will be a part of your language, not mine. This word will not appear written on any tree or animal. I will have been born 350,000,000 years ago and will have no need for this word. Life will always continue to be unstable. I will need to be versatile, to be resourceful, to be flexible. I will entangle with unexpected companions, maybe replace them and relocate. I will partner with no starting point and will remain in contact zones that are ubiquitous. I will undergo continuous change. Becoming-with or not becoming in a constant come and go will be and will always be the name of the game. Oh, I will have slept around, I readily admit it: My children will be many.

In the deepness of time, from the distance of my own birth, I will come to think of myself as a 'post-specimen', as a continuity, such as fish and human, that will appear as one vast ageing organism: a morphing, a diversification, or an impoverishment. But a survival, at least for me; but for others ...

I, *superspecies*

Cycles come and go. Some are brutal, others gentle. There will be talk of another mass extinction, a sixth, after the mass extinctions in those long-gone times that will be named the Ordovician, Devonian, Permian, Triassic and Cretaceous. Each will require some time for biotic recovery afterwards. Perhaps five to ten million years: not too long. This geological process will, in the end, always be relatively rapid. Even though recovery will not be able to begin until after the causes of the extinction will have gone.

Before my birth, the Ordovician and Devonian extinctions came and went. The first of these was a horrifying time. Four-fifths of all diversity in plants and animals—gone. The second, worse. The third as bad. How bad? Some 95 per cent of the plants and animals: all dead. In my lifetime, it has been less brutal. The fourth, the Triassic, was maybe 208 million years ago. I am not counting. The fifth, the Permian, lost the dinosaurs and others.

And now. Some will say that half of all living organisms may disappear in a century—or maybe even half a century. Just desert across much of the planet, and the heat—too much to bear. Some will survive—of course. The most versatile, or the most aggressive, will get through. The most prolific and nomadic, those of us ready to travel: we will be fine. Those who become omnipresent will be named as a superspecies. Those who can counter the extremities they will face will have some things in common. We will need to reproduce quickly; we will need to disperse widely, when given a chance; we will need to master different habitats, contrasting conditions, and take hold in strange places. We superspecies will be the generalists rather than the specialists: the opportunists, if you will. Some will say we will become plagues on the land. They will call us monopolists, exploiting the opportunity to expand when others fail. We will replace them; we will relocate. I will then have accomplished what I will have begun to dedicate myself to, some ten thousand years earlier. This is making each distinctive place on earth more like each other. Through constant change, through permanent diversification and adaptation, I will cover all parts of the earth. My roots will have penetrated every millimetre of earth; my genes will be found in every cellular organism.

Living in the Homogecene

They will think this time as one of homogeneity. It will be a time following extinctions, genocides and exterminations; if all of this diversity is gone, they will name it the Homogecene. Forests and most of my kin will have disappeared. When large quantities of my fruits ferment they will create a whole geological layer. My residues will overlay without being decomposed first, but then, due to its massive accumulation of its organic compounds and other soluble constituents, will create an entire 'biomantle'. This 'biomantle' of compost will uniformly cover the terrestrial earth. My compost will irrigate the water and the plants that will grow on it with my chemical compositions. They will accumulate and keep accumulating in the soil during this time. They will be impregnated by my mass expansion.

This era will also be known as the Amnesic, due to intense and important layering of my genetics and pharmaceutical qualities in the earth's soil. Fertile ground will be soaked by my soothing and calming medical quality. Due to the consumption of plants growing on this ground, the few highly aggressive superspecies of mammals, notably humans, rats and cats, that will have survived the latest mass extinction, will undergo an alteration of character. The extreme concentration of my agents in water and biomass, and therefore in all their food, will slowly create brain alterations. My alkaloids will actively block hormonal stress production in mammals' brains. Many of the last living organisms will have then similar qualities and traits. Amnesia and memory loss will spread throughout all vertebrates. Only plants—getting first of all nurtured by the sun, will remember; and a selection of insects, spiders, fungi, viruses and bacteria fetching their food from minerals or deep enough underground. They will become my closest companions. For those, I will be the way, the road, the matter to be overcome. But this will not be the end. It will just be a repeat point. A point within a long, violent cycle—one following which even I will have forgotten everything. As far back as I will remember …

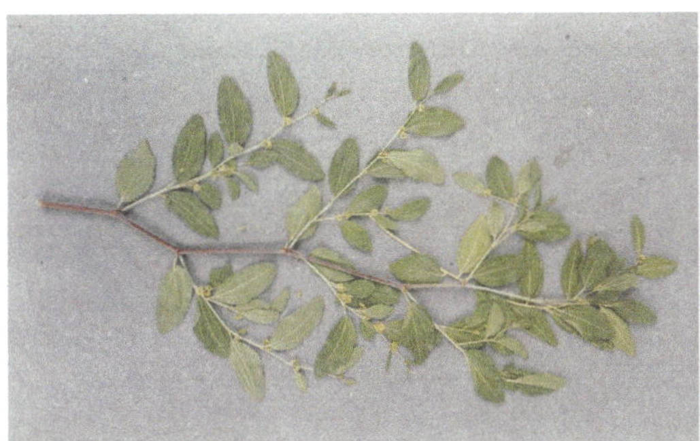 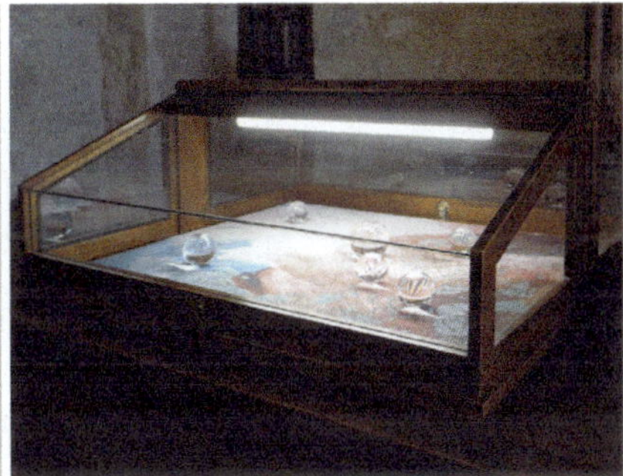

FIGURE 7.1. *Ziziphus zizyphus*, plant sample, collected on 10 July 2017, Carré de systématique, Jardin de Plantes in Montpellier, collection Caroline Loup and Nadia Lichtig N°645, Botanical Collection of the University of Montpellier, France. Courtesy of Nadia Lichtig.

FIGURE 7.2. Hand blown and hermetically sealed glass spheres containing *Ziziphus zizyphus* fragrance extract. The liquid filled glass spheres are optically distorting the surface on which they are placed, a silkscreen print on fabric. Part of the artwork *Parfum d'Oubli* (Perfume of Forgetting), in: *A Scientific Encounter: On Intersubjectivity* curated by Alistair Robinson, University of Montpellier, 2017. Courtesy of Nadia Lichtig.

Acknowledgements

I would like to thank Thierry Lavabre-Bertrand, professor at the Faculty of Medicine and director of the Jardin des Plantes of Montpellier; Caroline Ducourau, director of Scientific Culture and Historical Heritage at the University of Montpellier; Véronique Bourgade, curator of the Botanical Collections of the University of Montpellier and head of service of the Historical Patrimony of the University of Montpellier; Caroline Loup, botanist of the Botanical Collections of the University of Montpellier; Emmanuel Spicq, curator of Culture at the Jardin des Plantes of the University of Montpellier; and Régis Meuzeret, gardener at the Jardin des Plantes of Montpellier, for their cooperation and support.

I would especially like to thank Ed Juler, Alistair Robinson and Newcastle University.

The text … *as far back as I will remember* is part of a corpus of artworks across media that is questioning the construction of knowledge.

NOTES

1. Homer, *The Odyssey*, Book IX, tr. Samuel Butler (London: Longmans Green, 1898).

2. Herodotus, *The Histories, Book IV*, tr. Alfred Denis Godley (London: Heinemann, 1921–25).

3. W. W. How and J. Wells, *A Commentary on Herodotus with Introduction and Appendixes*, 2 volumes, (Oxford: Claredon Press, 1912).

4. George Lucas, director, *Star Wars*, 1977.

5. Alan Eaton Davidson, *The Oxford Companion to Food* (Oxford: Oxford University Press, 1999).

6. *The Koran*, 53:10–18. Available at https://quran.com/53/10-18 (accessed 15 March 2020).

7. Stephen Lambden, The Sidrat al-Muntaha in select Islamic Tafsir works, University of California, Merced, https://hurqalya.uc-merced.edu/node/59 (accessed 25 July 2018).

8. Ibid.

9. Mark 15:17 and John 19:2,5. Available at http://www.biblegate-way.com, King James Version, 1987, public domain (accessed 15 March 2020).

10. *Catholic Encyclopedia*, Robert Appelton Company: 1912.

REFERENCES

Catholic Encyclopedia. New York: Robert Appleton Company, 1912.

Davidson, Alan Eaton. *The Oxford Companion to Food*. Oxford: Oxford University Press, 1999.

Homer, *The Odyssey, Book IX*, trans. Samuel Butler. London: Longmans Green, 1898.

Herodotus, *The Histories, Book IV*, trans. Alfred Denis Godley. London: Heinemann, 1921–25.

Lambden, Stephen. *The Sidrat al-Muntahā in Select Islamic Tafsīr Works*, University of California, Merced. Availabke at https://hurqalya.ucmerced.edu/node/59 (accessed 25 July 2018).

Lucas, George, director. *Star Wars*. 1977.

How, W. W., and J. Wells. *A Commentary on Herodotus with Introduction and Appendixes*, 2 vol. Oxford: Clarendon Press, 1912.

8

Poetry and the Pathology Museum:
A Model of Difference

Christy Ducker

(with photographs by Phyllis Christopher)

Abstract

The Wohl Pathology Collection, Edinburgh, houses one of the largest collections of pathological anatomy in the world. Its human remains offer an index of catastrophe but also embody redemptive possibility. This chapter explores that possibility, in the encounter between historical fragments and my practice as poet and essayist.

Crucial throughout is the volatile nature of the fragment: the Wohl Collection operates as an archival space, full of objects which weigh something beyond themselves. These exhibits unsettle the orthodoxies of museum encounter and linguistic response. As Linda Nochlin suggests, any general theory of the fragment must be established on 'a model of difference'. To this end, my chapter destabilizes the conventional boundaries between critical and creative. It adopts a fragmentary form and becomes an aggregate of poetry, prose and photography. As a result, the chapter enacts my mode of encounter with the museum. Its form suggests frictions between past and present, death and life, absence and presence. This invites the reader to enter into a process of meaning-making, by opening up a negotiation of textual fragments. My writing offers an interactional experience, reflective of an encounter with the Wohl Collection itself: neither the exhibits nor any writing about them can be immured.

I suggest here that creative practice can function formatively and generate new ways of encountering the world. Key to this are 'play', the use of imagery and juxtapositions which shock the reader into seeing anew. In the museum, there is play between the living and the dead: the exhibits become entangled with our contemporary sociopolitical context. Such play is mirrored in my writing, in the entanglement of different forms and in the use of metaphor to convey the 'dual vision' of an embodied response.

The Wohl exhibits offer an immediate and uncomfortable dialogue with the past. This chapter and its poems provide a site for how that past is encountered, rather than offering an interpretation. Taking a creative critical approach, I offer new ways of modelling meaning, knowledge and social relations: my discursive momentum is regenerative; my use of metaphor reconstitutive. Neither dialectical image nor creative criticism can repair what has been lost to violence and pain. However, a creative response can defy the space that separates, by reassembling past fragments in the now. Adopting a fragmentary form itself, this chapter acknowledges that reassembly and understanding involve struggle as well as agreement.

Let's begin with an interior: its walls are high and white; sunlight pours through a glass roof; and on glass shelves, in glass containers, over 3,000 human remains are displayed. The remains are arranged in categories, ranging from Cardiothoracic to Vascular to Trauma. This is the Wohl Pathology Collection, housed within Edinburgh's Surgeons' Hall Museum. One of the largest collections of pathological anatomy in the world, it is shot through with tensions. Concentrated in this one space is much that is paradoxical: the intimate insides of the human body are exposed to public scrutiny; the light of the outside world refracts through a fragile interior; the familiar demarcations between inside and outside, past and present are destabilized. Although the museum has been curated to achieve unity, the exhibits themselves speak of sprawl. The Wohl Collection operates as an archival space, 'always at the unstable limit between public and private'.[1] Interposing my living body into the collection, I have felt the shock of proximity. Coupled with the amount of loss on display, this has produced a 'homesickness' in relation to the exhibits, a desire to reconstitute while recognizing past violence and damage done. I have expressed this in part through poetry, because of poetry's unique capacity to shuttle between 'here' and 'there', its ability to meld. Crucial throughout is the volatile nature of the fragment. In the museum, each scrap of humanity on display carries with it a charged absence. Each exhibit has intersected with historical suffering and sociopolitical forces, often visibly. Each speaks to similarities and differences in our contemporary existence. My experience in the Wohl Collection has been multipolar, and my writing about it reflects this. Neither fragments, nor an article about them, can accord with any totalizing theory. As Linda Nochlin remarked, anyone attempting to construct a general theory of the fragment would be advised to 'establish it on a model of *difference* rather than attempt to construct a unified field of discourse'.[2] Mindful of this, my chapter destabilizes the conventional boundaries between the critical and the creative: it adopts an aggregate form and is comprised of poetry, photography and prose. A fragment within this book, it is also made of fragments. Consequently, it enacts my mode of encounter with the museum, mirroring that experience of friction between part and whole, presence and absence. And in this, it explores how knowledge emerges, for 'Form is not a container for scholarly content: it is part of the scholarship'.[3]

Neither the essay form nor the pathology 'specimen' can be immured. The experience of the exhibits is interactional and I try to make sense of this through metaphor's compositing power, its ability to help us see one thing in terms of another, vault boundaries and bring the seemingly disparate into dialogue. The effects of this are regenerative, enabling new creative critical forms, and poems which are free to connect the pathology exhibit with contemporary concerns. Because the Wohl Collection is a disconcerting environment, it invariably unsettles any conventional linguistic response. And like any such environment, it suggests 'by changing space, by leaving the space of one's usual sensibilities, one enters into communication with a space that is psychically innovating'.[4] That innovation springs into expression with particular energy when our familiarity with our own body is challenged. The implications of this for language are reanimating, as Carol Rumens recognizes when she suggests 'a good poem is like a blood transfusion'.[5]

This chapter, in its poetry and prose, resists the 'dead metaphor' we use daily in our demotic speech, and the linguistic systems we may have habitualized. In this, the writing aims to generate understanding since 'new metaphors are capable of creating new understandings and, therefore, new realities'.[6] We move through the world, living and breathing language, like fish in water. Often, our relationship to our bodies can be similar: we may need to be shocked out of the familiar in order to understand and learn. The Wohl exhibits have the capacity to do this, especially when taking on a life of their own in poetry: '[t]o give an object poetic space is to give it more space than it has objectivity'.[7] Encountering the exhibits invites us to reassess our ideas of the human body, what it can be, and how it might intersect with sociopolitical forces. Inside the museum, a stock phrase such as 'war left him shattered' will be returned to us afresh as we are brought up short by the physical reality of war exhibits. From this stem expansiveness and possibility. As Joel Weinsheimer has observed, metaphor 'contains a principle of growth'.[8] And in this, there is a political dimension: highly mobile, metaphor refuses absolutism and therefore offers autonomy to the reader. The exhibits, and this writing about them, suggest we generate sense from a negotiation of fragments. On entering the museum as a twenty-first-century person, it is possible to recognize one's own body as a repository of what has grown from the fragments on display. My own body, with its scars and traces of childbearing, is a living translation of this 'archive' of human remains. It carries traces of experimental anaesthesia from nineteenth-century battlefields, of James Simpson and Queen Victoria's obstetric dabblings in chloroform, of birth blooming from death. The living and the dead are free to constellate in the space of the museum, as metaphor is free to reassemble fragments into intelligible structures:

At the Pathology Museum

You come in from the rain with your scars tucked
in your clothes, your stents, your reconstructed
bones settling on red leather benches,

as display cases stand to attention,
their feet in glass pots to guard against scuff
while you scrutinize what used to be life—
each human remain hangs in its sadness,
a silent partner to your good health.
Here, you can open a door on trachi,
open another on hundreds of eyes
or walk down the stairs that give onto gunshot
fractures. See how   `the bullet's impact`
`has forced bone into pieces`
`the shape of petals`
then see what grew next—the surgical tool
curved like a tulip to hold soft skulls,
the stems and stalks designed for delivery
of chloroform, *sweet vitriol*. See?
It's killing that birthed this calm in us
which might explain why your laughter's nervous
as you mooch through the ranks of disaster
knowing by now it's quite regular
to chat with surgeons while their hands sift
our insides. It's normal for us to drift
eighty paces from *War* to *Obstetrics*,
without suspecting a conjuror's trick.
It's almost dull to return to the street
to find the clouds broken, to loosen coats
and carry our numb old wounds so lightly.

And in this experience, we are part of a continuum. If we look at a soldier's gunshot femur from 1815, we are looking through time and space: the encounter opens up a moment of involvement that disrupts the everyday and offers the possibility of greater understanding. The musket ball, snug in its socket of bone, made me 're-cognize' my own historical conditions, my health and the pregnancies which have snuggled between my own bones. It also reminded me war won't end here, nor will the life lessons which death offers (Fig. 8.1).

This futural component to understanding recalls the dual character of the fragment, posited by Walter Benjamin: that it is an index of catastrophe but also embodies redemptive possibility in the 'spark of hope' it offers.[9] Such glimmers can occur in the encounter with historical artefacts: where history is envisaged as 'a site of contact between specific historical realities', there are more possibilities for a 'flash' of recognition when points from past and present come into fleeting alignment.[10]

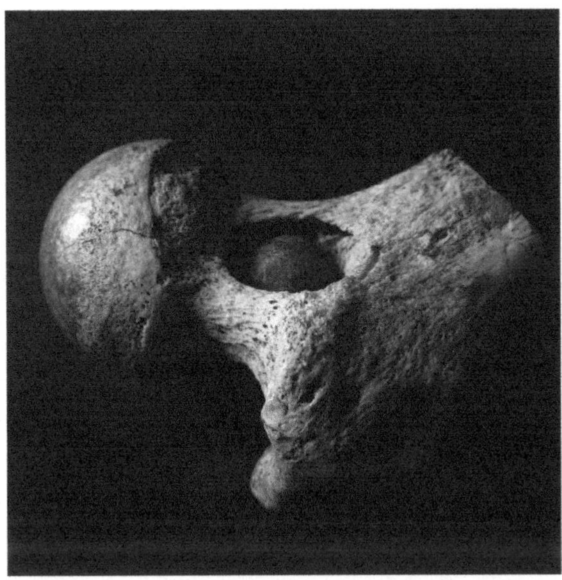

FIGURE 8.1. *Shot* © Phyllis Christopher, 2018.

A visitor to the Wohl Collection is a little like Benjamin's angel of history who 'would like to stay, awaken the dead, and make whole what has been smashed'; 'wreckage upon wreckage' accumulates about us as we look to the past while being compelled towards the future.[11] Sparks of hope endure, nonetheless: past fragments shed light on contemporary 'wreckage' and on the prospect of imagining it otherwise:

Phytobezoar

It's almost unsayable, but this gut-sized knot
of straw, cut from a girl in 1916,
is not done with. How could it be over,
her nervous chewing on stalks and hair
for want of food, when metres away
on Nicolson Street the lunchtime crowds churn
past starving men; what's given as food
are *Pizza*, *Kebab* or a neon *Fast!*
and although the gut-sized knot of straw
hangs on a wire in a glass display case,
it sticks in my craw. It's dry and familiar
as what will turn up in any system
fed for too long on approximate things.

Stems without fruit, husks without kernels,
now without then, versions of falsehood–
if swallowed often, somewhere inside us
a compact of rind and pith will form
an obstruction, a shaming, tinder.

The bezoar is a site of literal and metaphorical entanglement. Encountering it, one can see the curvature of a girl's stomach though her body is absent. That absence is particularly shocking since the girl starved to death and to nothingness. The implications of this extend into the present and scratch at us, like the straws and strands of the bezoar: historical and contemporary starvations collide and strike sparks off each other. The bezoar is incendiary. In this, it behaves like the poetic. As 'the eminent text', poetic language stands out from the demotic: it estranges

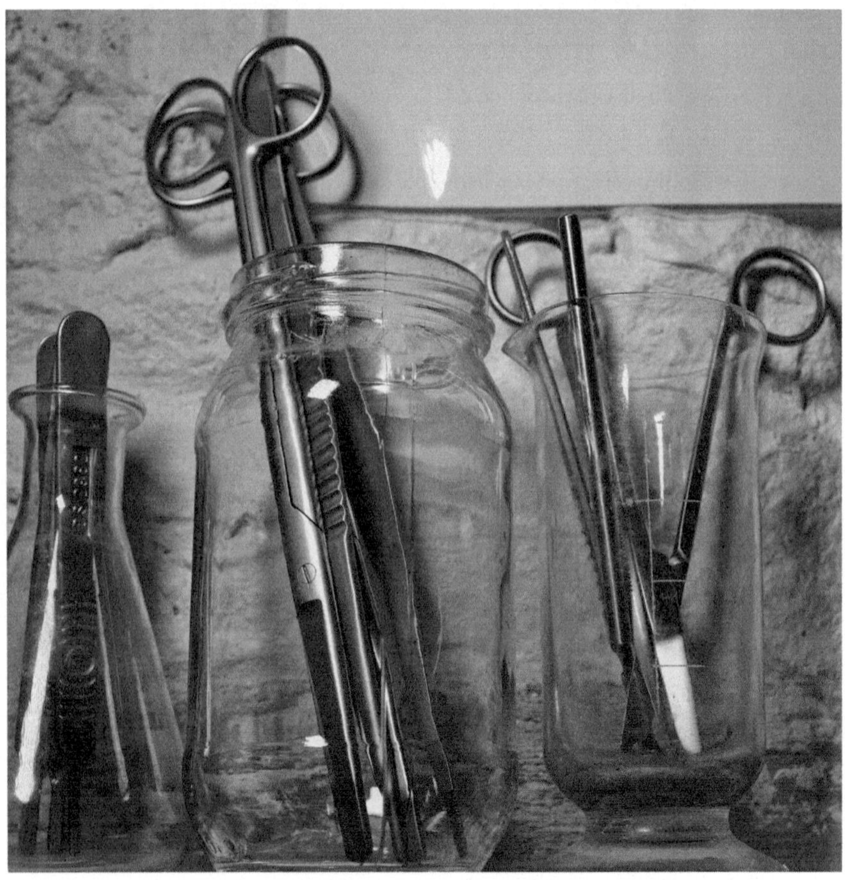

FIGURE 8.2. *Containers* © Phyllis Christopher 2018.

us to familiar words and associations; it decontextualizes then recontextualizes in ways which challenge complacency.[12] And this is where the life-affirming gleam resides with 'Phytobezoar'. By transforming the bezoar into metaphor, I make it assume generative energy and embody political intent.

'[I]t is in the opposite of capture and containment, namely discharge and leakage, that we discover the life of things.'[13] This 'leakage' is not solely ontological. The human remains are changing physically, by tiny increments, through decay and mutation. Cat Irving, the museum's Conservator of Human Remains, works tirelessly to rehabilitate and refurbish the remains' containers, their preserving fluids, their wires and anchors (Fig. 8.2). She manages daily their instability, with a keen working understanding that 'the materiality of things can disrupt and deflect human intentions. Objects can, unwittingly, carry forth their own projects'.[14] And indeed, Cat's workspace is a subversive, adaptive place where the boundaries between subject and object can shift. Unlike the early 'gentlemen collectors', Cat recognizes that objects have the capacity to 'go on', to have post-mortem social lives and literally leak. Rather than snatch the transitory from the eternal and try to contain it, Cat tries to find ways to make the transitory eternal. This is reminiscent of the fragmentist writer: using an unsettled form attempts a provisional containment; it rejects the notion that we are in control of totality.[15] Providing form that is not a confinement is life-affirming. And conservation, etymologically 'keeping together', acknowledges it is always in negotiation with the disparate. These tensions are evidenced in Cat's 'To Do' list on her noticeboard, a masterpiece of parataxis where familiarity and estrangement vie.

To Do

> *- relabel uterus shelves*
> *- Replace shelf J15*
> *- look at O2 & oversized things*

as Curator of Human Remains, she must
cut a new backplate to better display
the hairy moth of a child's lungs,
fix the brown horn of pelvis that rears
from its bath of fat in a tub in the sink—
'Fat is so hard to fix', she says—

> *- change label on H22*
> *- move conchae from B33*
> *- Testis! malformation → K4*

rehouse the hunched tubercular shoulders
in pristine glass, re-seam the case of knock-
knees with fresh white clay. She must
thread, bead, saw and file, stitch and sloosh
the view we have while time accretes
as fog in jars. She must make clear

- *'unknown shelves'*
- *ovaries!*
- *move ♀ external genitalia*

refuse to tolerate Perspex and its empty
promises. Glass is good. Deccon 90 and PKIII.
A bristle of diamond drill bits—'A man broke
in here once,' she says, 'but took nothing'.
She washes staghorn calculi, incremental stones,
must not let any human trace go down the drain.

Categorizing presents a challenge to creative practice as research: the labelling of
pathology exhibits can sometimes feel confining or one-dimensional. It can also
feel like a manifestation of rigid disciplinarity, even when we sympathize with
the museum context and appreciate its show of formal unity is pragmatic. As the
curator, conservator or creative practitioner knows, however, unity can be illusory: any exhibit will be weighing something beyond itself, beyond the walls of
the museum, and beyond the boundaries of academic disciplines. A creative critical response recognizes these other dimensions, how 'we are always more and
less than the categories that name and divide us'.[16]

Exhibit GC.13817

is a supernumerary leg, mainly
thigh and foot. Like most taboos it's intimate,
with hugged-in toes and rumpled skin

along the excision. *A simple cut
through fibro-fatty tissue* brought it
two hundred years to here, with a label—

specimen, *a part considered typical
of a group, class or whole.* But I'm looking
at the wires, how the glass reflects

my scrutiny back. This bright museum
is pulling my strings, asking me to read
the leg in inverted commas. But I can't

leave him alone, the man it came from, *cursed*
and remote his whole life. *Bogeyman*
of the Highlands stays with me past closing,

onto the bus where I read today's news
pulled out of kilter by quotes and snippets—
suicides rising among the disabled

hate crimes against the disabled rising.
He was typical only in that
there was more to him than could ever be

set aside in a glass drum and soused.

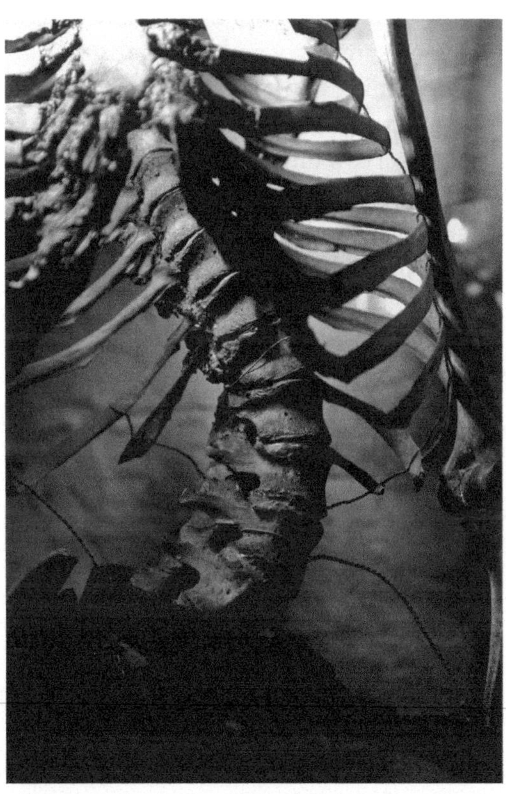

FIGURE 8.3. *Spine*, © Phyllis Christopher 2018.

If we categorize by objective label only, our experience of encounter will be distant. As George Lakoff counters, 'categories are open-ended' because we make sense of our world via context.[17] A museum label may insist 'leg' but, encountering that leg in the twenty-first century, we may find it difficult to place. We may experience traces of 'shame', 'ostracism', 'pathos' and 'hate crime'. Human remains ask us to interact with the unsaid and the absent as much as with their presence: metaphor shuttles between these different dimensions. And creative practice functions formatively here, to generate new ways of encountering the world. In this, it again attempts to redeem the fragment, by drawing it into the light of socio-political relations. The three-legged stanzas of 'Exhibit GC.13817' engage in a poetic project that aspires to find 'the image that [will] unite "whole" and "hole"'.[18]

Body Politic

Perhaps you'll hear the word *backbone*
and think of a stack or a prop
or a column supporting a roof.
Perhaps you'll think we're agreed
on symmetry and articulation,
imagining bones and words in our bodies
won't ever bend or splinter. Difficult
then, to observe a different sort of spine
wrenched in a scoliotic *S*, browning
behind museum glass. This is
what might have been prevented—
a woman left to disarticulate
out on the streets. *Of rather good face,*
they said. And though this is a backbone
it's asking too much of a body;
it's asking too much of us
that we must *show some spine*, face *difficult
times* like the TV says with no expression
of how much weight might land on us,
while talk becomes more fractious
about what *backbone* could look like
if overloaded, what shape we'll be in
under pressure, whether the roof will hold.

The exhibits in the Wohl Collection are unsettling, partly because they disrupt consensus and challenge received linguistic categories (Fig. 8.3). In Western culture, there is a persistent association of the upright, healthy body with the utopian: '[p]eople in power get to impose their metaphors'.[19] Medieval ideals of the 'body politic' endure into contemporary rhetoric about having 'backbone' and 'keeping our heads screwed on'. A scoliotic fragment can challenge this, just as the poetic can disrupt our orientation in the everyday. The remnants of a twisted spine ask us to re-evaluate our understanding of what a body can be and to make figurative language work differently to synthesize our experience. This fragment in particular opens an aperture onto what is silenced or absent in mainstream discourse, that 'loss of wholeness, a shattering of connection, a destruction or disintegration of permanent value'.[20] In the face of this, the poet seeks to reassemble, whilst recognizing the whole can never be fully restored, '[p]oetry can repair no loss, but it defies the space which separates'.[21] Negotiating the image and form to do this is to give autonomy and agency to the human remains. The form of 'Body Politic' uses the material dimensions of language, and its sensuous, corporeal qualities, to generate new meaning. This is mirrored too, in the fragmentary essay form which aims to jolt conventional discourse and historical consciousness simultaneously.

'NO TATTOOS IN THE WORKPLACE'

and little else permanent either, if
your boss has gone into business with myth
and it's *Amazon* or *Hermes*, perhaps
some other carnivorous firm. Stand back—
ask what scars this set-up might leave on you
after years of doing its packing. You
with migraines, angina, or OCD
and a string of missed appointments. As unseen
as all those hidden tattoos of mandala,
the heart, or a favourite footballer.
No-one would ever get inked-up and flaunt
a trad tattoo of the firm's *fulfilment
centre*, nor one of its vans or bleepers.
Some other era, you'd see a clipper
in full sail, etched across a man's back
more likely seen now as this relic:
the flag of his skin in a museum case
flying above the scalpels and poultice.
It's pricked out with rigging and, for courage,
sprigs of thyme leaves; for power, the image
of twin snakes, and where his shoulder bones were,

two swallows for winging past the Equator
twice by 5000 miles. At a distance
it looks like pride or maybe romance
from a time when workers might pioneer,
when commerce was still a ship you might steer.

'Language games must be accosted in each dark alley in which they are lurking.'[22] On explaining my work around the Wohl exhibits, I have sometimes been met with revulsion, confusion or suspicion about my intentions. The scale of the loss and suffering on display does not immediately suggest the museum as a place to play. These poems and this chapter are, however, engaged in a 'serious play': this is the to and fro between exhibit and visitor; it is also the negotiation I'm opening up between these words and you, the reader. 'Meaning is ultimately a dialogue.'[23] The exhibits continue to shock, and intersect with, the world of the living; they become more than they physically are. Poetic and creative critical writings behave similarly, as they unhinge language from its customary sites and suggest possibilities beyond. In creative practice, the activity of play always becomes more than itself, a 'transformation into structure'.[24] Ethics and history transform into a rhyming structure in 'NO TATTOOS IN THE WORKPLACE'. As the metaphor of the tattoo is relational, so too is each rhyme. These half-rhymes reconcile but don't quite match, in a way reflective of how past and present, unfamiliar and familiar constellate around the sailor's tattoo. Rhyme can short circuit the distances of time and space, showing us how we resonate with the political. I ask rhyme to do that here, using pattern to 'reconfigure the geometry of attention', which in turn draws us into 'conversation with what would otherwise remain silent'.[25]

'Poetry makes language care because it renders everything intimate.'[26] With the exhibits, this intimacy grows from proximity and the shock that occurs when 'what has been comes together in a flash with the now to form a constellation'.[27] I found this shock especially visceral when encountering a prisoner's heart in a jar, while feeling my own heart working in my chest (Fig. 8.4). I had heard about this exhibit in advance, in conversation with Cat Irving. Cat had spoken of it with great compassion, describing her experience of holding it in her hands, feeling the pathos of a physical connection with history. The heart had come through war to sit on a shelf: the enormity of its story boomed around it as it floated, moored by a little glass anchor. This paradox of being moored and drifting, bound and unbound, homely and alien struck me as the paradox of being a human, 'constantly more than [she] factually is'.[28] The prisoner's heart suggested a metaphor for understanding, offering the opportunity '[t]o recognize one's own in the alien, to become at home in it', and develop new understanding in the process of 'returning to [oneself] from what is other'.[29]

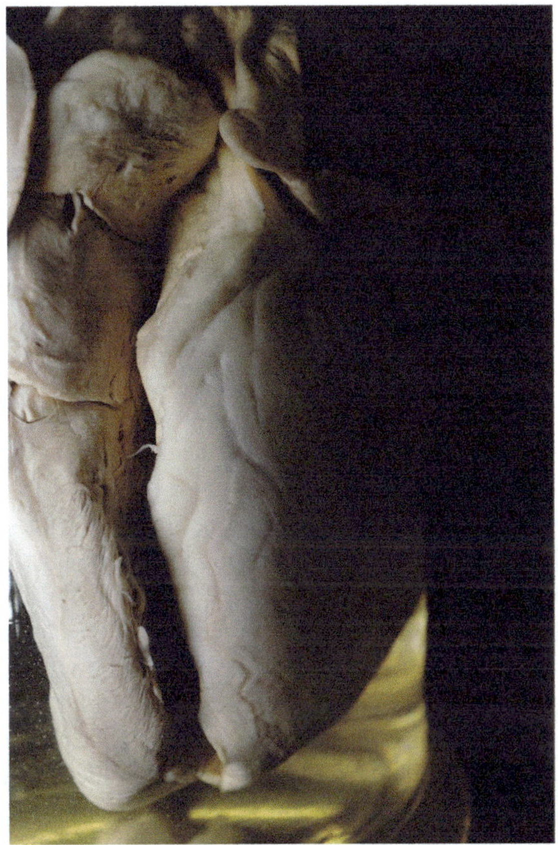

FIGURE 8.4. *Heart* © Phyllis Christopher 2018.

Muscle

Old pugilists in the half-light, the hearts
sit in their glass jars. What joy or panic
clattered through them once has stilled.
All we can see of a feud is the stab wound,
shtum in the left ventricle. Of internment,
of running from Nagasaki, just this
purple tinge and a label below: HEART,
CARCINOMA, 1950. My own heart
is a mile away. It's in your hands
in the Edinburgh spring where we'll meet
later. Beyond this museum, its shrapnel

wounds, the damaged marrow of history,
I'll join you; we'll kiss and flicker
where cold sun falls through new leaves.
We'll be the living, and staunch at it,
hearts racing to push-out-pull-in as much
love as possible. Hard to believe
ten ounces of muscle will putter out;
my heart could rest on a shelf in a jar
with no glimmer of what you made it do.
Beneath a willow, drinking giddy beers,
we're dumb to the future's blades and wars
but know the heart ends as dowdy meat,
that while we're here we'll cram it with light.

The Wohl Pathology Collection is for everyone, in the twenty-first century. No longer intended as a 'cabinet of curiosities', nor a resource for trainee surgeons, it has become a vibrant, social place that aims to foster empathy and understanding. Beyond the labels and categories, nothing in the collection can be foreclosed. The exhibits are open to being recontextualized, to shuttling wild metaphorical distances from where they began. My understanding of them has emerged from sensory encounter, from re-visiting particular fragments and leaving the museum with my view altered. The fragments remain as 'sparks' in my life and practice, springing from 'the aggregate, particulate [...] motion between past and future'.[30] Even when no longer writing about a specific exhibit, I feel my heart beating both inside and outside the vitrine. My latest poems have become more aware of their own presences and absences; each behaves more consciously as a fragment, intimating the immense. Each foregrounds some aspect of the unfashionable, the disdained, the alien.

Unfashionable Sex

is happening anyway, a touch nearer
death than youth because its lovers are
old, or ill or fat. Like other disdained things –
the slow, the lyric, the heavily
industrial – it finds its own way
to endure. Those who'd rather not look
prefer to think it dead-end and dry
but here we are, wet and baggy-arsed, in
the middle of a poem. In the middle
of our lives, we have each other spread-

> eagled against an old sheet at the edge
> of winter. We've seen it now and won't go back
> where sex might be pinking or pixel-slick.
> We're autumn, as concentrated as moss,
> committed as earthworms to gorge and surge,
> aerating whatever will mass about us.

We end as we began, with a paradoxical interior. Although 'Unfashionable Sex' takes place within walls, it also reaches beyond to consider the human life span and the commercial appropriation of lovemaking. As with the Wohl Collection, a riot of exteriority is packed into the small space of this stanza. And like my encounter with the exhibits, this wider chapter will unfold and keep unfolding in the present: '[r]ather than the sense of an ending the aspiration here is towards the possibility of an opening'.[31] A formal conclusion is somewhat arbitrary when writing a fragmentary creative critical piece. My concern has been to suggest the tensions and extensions possible, when encountering fragments. I have used metaphor and poetic language to do this, since 'language bears within itself the dialectics of open and closed [...] Through meaning it encloses, while through poetic expression, it opens up'.[32] The volatility of these exhibits sparks new semantic energies: this suggests neither the essay's component parts nor human remains can be 'neatly labelled, safely immured in vitrines and cabinets'.[33] The Wohl Collection and the fragmentary essay are both uncomfortable places. Each asks us to negotiate disjunctures and raw edges, to engage in the messy, regenerative process of meaning-making. Any redemption or renewal here can only ever be partial. Nonetheless, the multidimensionality of the pathology 'specimen' highlights the need to develop new models of writing and understanding. The poem, the fragment, the creative critical essay, like anything human, can never be fully shut up.

NOTES

1. Jacques Derrida, *Archive Fever* (Chicago: University of Chicago Press, 1998), 90.
2. Linda Nochlin, *The Body in Pieces: The Fragment as a Metaphor of Modernity* (London: Thames and Hudson, 2001), 56 (original emphasis).
3. Angelika Bammer and Ruth-Ellen Boetcher Joeres, eds., *The Future of Scholarly Writing: Critical Interventions* (New York: Palgrave Macmillan, 2015), 1.
4. Gaston Bachelard, *The Poetics of Space* (Boston: Beacon Press, 1994), 206.
5. Michael Hulse and Donald Singer, eds., *The 2018 Hippocrates Prize Anthology* (London: The Hippocrates Press, 2018), 7.

6. George Lakoff and Mark Johnson, *Metaphors We Live By* (Chicago: University of Chicago Press, 2003), 235.

7. Bachelard, *Poetics*, 202.

8. Joel Weinsheimer, *Philosophical Hermeneutics and Literary Theory* (New Haven: Yale University Press, 1991), 67.

9. Walter Benjamin, *Illuminations*, trans. Harry Zorn (London: Pimlico, 1999), 247.

10. Mandy Bloomfield, *Archaeopoetics: Word, Image, History* (Tuscaloosa: University of Alabama Press, 2016), 16.

11. Benjamin, *Illuminations*, 249.

12. Hans-Georg Gadamer, 'The Eminent Text and Its Truth', *Bulletin Mid-Western Modern Language Association* 13, no. 1 (1980): 3–23.

13. Tim Ingold, 'Bringing Things to Life: Creative Entanglements in a World of Materials'. University of Aberdeen Working Paper Series, Aberdeen, 2010, http://eprints.ncrm.ac.uk/1306/1/0510_creative_entanglements.pdf (accessed 16 May 2018).

14. Joshua Pollard, 'The Art of Decay and the Transformation of Substance', in *Substance, Memory, Display: Archaeology and Art*, ed. C. Renfrew, C. Gosden and E. DeMarrais (Cambridge: McDonald Institute for Archaeological Research, 2004), 57.

15. Brian Dillon, *Essayism* (London: Fitzcarraldo Editions, 2017), 22.

16. Geraldine Finn, *Why Althusser Killed His Wife: Essays on Discourse and Violence* (New Jersey: Humanities Press, 1996), 156.

17. Lakoff and Johnson, *Metaphors*, 122.

18. Kamau Brathwaite, 'Caliban's Guarden', *Wasafari* 8, no. 16 (1992): 4.

19. Lakoff and Johnson, *Metaphors*, 157.

20. Nochlin, *Body*, 24.

21. John Berger, 'The Hour of Poetry', in *Selected Essays*, ed. G. Dyer (London: Bloomsbury, 2001), 450.

22. Ludwig Wittgenstein, *Philosophical Investigations* (Oxford: Basil Blackwell, 1963), 167.

23. Chris Lawn, *Gadamer* (London: Continuum, 2006), 100.

24. Hans-Georg Gadamer, *Truth and Method*, trans. Joel Weinsheimer and Donald G. Marshall (London: Sheed and Ward, 1989), 110.

25. Joan Retallack, *The Poethical Wager* (Berkeley: University of California Press, 2003), 10.

26. Berger, *Selected Essays*, 451.

27. Walter Benjamin, *The Arcades Project*, trans. Howard Eiland and Kevin McLaughlin (London: Belknap Press, 1999), 462.

28. Martin Heidegger, *Being and Time*, trans. John Macquarrie and Edward Robinson (New York: Harper and Row, 1962), 185.

29. Gadamer, *Truth*, 14.

30. Dillon, *Essayism*, 136.

31. K. Hilevaara and E. Orley, eds., *The Creative Critic: Writing as/about Practice* (London and New York: Routledge, 2018), 15.
32. Bachelard, *Poetics*, 222.
33. Dillon, *Essayism*, 14.

REFERENCES

Bachelard, Gaston. *The Poetics of Space*. Boston: Beacon Press, 1994.

Bammer, A., and R. Boetcher Joeres, eds. *The Future of Scholarly Writing: Critical Interventions*. New York: Palgrave Macmillan, 2015.

Benjamin, Walter. *The Arcades Project*, trans. Howard Eiland and Kevin McLaughlin. London: Belknap Press, 1999.

Benjamin, Walter. *Illuminations*, trans. Harry Zorn. London: Pimlico, 1999.

Bloomfield, Mandy. *Archaeopoetics: Word, Image, History*. Tuscaloosa: University of Alabama Press, 2016.

Derrida, Jacques. *Archive Fever*. Chicago: University of Chicago Press, 1998.

Dillon, Brian. *Essayism*. London: Fitzcarraldo Editions, 2017.

Finn, Geraldine. *Why Althusser Killed His Wife: Essays on Discourse and Violence*. New Jersey: Humanities Press, 1996.

Gadamer, Hans-Georg. 'The Eminent Text and Its Truth'. *Bulletin Mid-Western Modern Language Association* 13, no. 1 (1980): 3–23.

Gadamer, Hans-Georg. *Truth and Method*, trans. Joel Weinsheimer and Donald G. Marshall. London: Sheed and Ward, 1989.

Heidegger, Martin. *Being and Time*, trans. John Macquarrie and Edward Robinson. New York: Harper and Row, 1962.

Hilevaara, K., and E. Orley, eds. *The Creative Critic: Writing as/about Practice*. London and New York: Routledge, 2018.

Hulse, M., and D. Singer, eds. *The 2018 Hippocrates Prize Anthology*. London: The Hippocrates Press, 2018.

Ingold, Tim. 'Bringing Things to Life: Creative Entanglements in a World of Materials'. Aberdeen: University of Aberdeen Working Paper Series, 2010. Available at http://eprints.ncrm.ac.uk/1306/1/0510_creative_entanglements.pdf (accessed 16 May 2018).

Lakoff, George, and Mark Johnson. *Metaphors We Live By*. Chicago: University of Chicago Press, 2003.

Lawn, Chris. *Gadamer*. London: Continuum, 2006.

Nochlin, Linda. *The Body in Pieces: The Fragment as a Metaphor of Modernity*. London: Thames and Hudson, 2001.

Pollard, Joshua. 'The Art of Decay and the Transformation of Substance'. In *Substance, Memory, Display: Archaeology and Art*, ed. C. Renfrew, C. Gosden, and E. DeMarrais, 47–62. Cambridge: McDonald Institute for Archaeological Research, 2004.

Retallack, Joan. *The Poethical Wager*. Berkeley: University of California Press, 2003.

Weinsheimer, Joel. *Philosophical Hermeneutics and Literary Theory*. New Haven: Yale University Press, 1991.

Wittgenstein, Ludwig. *Philosophical Investigations*. Oxford: Basil Blackwell, 1963.

9

The Scientist and the Magician

Irene Brown

Abstract

The artist Irene Brown is interested in the long history of how visual perception and illusion, and the equally long history of 'magic', intersect with orthodox histories of Western scientific 'progress'. She is also interested in how the model of the artwork as a source of illusion intertwines with these now dual histories. Her work here is an attempt to plot an alternative story in which these three ideas stand in a new relation and remain intertwined as they originally were, rather than disaggregated into disciplinary silos and deracinated forms of research. As this chapter illustrates, Brown's method is to excavate lesser-known stories about the interaction between fine art, spectacle and performance, and tease out how they might be related to the dominant story of disinterested scientific endeavour as the engine of Enlightenment, charged with an emancipatory power for all humanity. In her work, the development of scientific artefacts and specimens has been a circuitous process in which the strictly 'rational' discovery and application of scientific theories is close to myth-worship; and indeed one where mythologies acquire living logics of their own.

Science continues to be a channel for magic—the belief that for the human will, empowered by knowledge, nothing is impossible. This kind of confusion of science with magic is not an ailment of a kind that has a remedy. It goes with modern life [...] Science and occultism differ at many points, but at one they converge: they both view the world as being governed by laws.[1]

Introduction

This chapter is based on studies conducted during my time as International Research Fellow at the Bakken Museum of Electricity and Magnetism,[2] Minneapolis, USA,

"

in 2013 and subsequent studio-based investigations leading to the production of the installation *Phantasmagoria Electric* (Fig. 9.1).[3] I want to pursue the idea that the histories of the development of science and, in particular, physics concerned with electricity and magnetism, and those of the public performance of magic and the paranormal are far from comfortably separate. Even more uncomfortably, the long-standing association between art and illusion—and the idea that true art lies in the concealment of illusion corresponds closely to this latter history. In the representational tradition, the definition of artistry and artifice are a means to creating illusion (as encapsulated in the phrase *ars est celare artem*). Accordingly, the form of this chapter is one matched to its subject, just as is desired in works of art. It is presented *as if* a work of art, or else as corresponding to the principles that works of art operate upon. It is also, necessarily, presented episodically, through a series of individual vignettes that correspond to particular pregnant moments in those histories, and which should, at the risk of sounding portentous, be read allegorically rather than historically. The benefit of treating these episodes as discrete units is, perversely enough, that through that mechanism a reader then may be more readily inclined and able to envisage them reassembled, reimagined, reallocated new places in the order of things, rather than take them as Aristotelian propositions casually linked, forever, in a definite order whose logic is unassailable. The logic here is, intentionally, all too assailable, just as it was in the experiments themselves that provide my subject matter.

My reflections upon these histories are, necessarily, positioned as being those of a practising artist for whom they provide inspiration and source material, rather than those of an academic historian, for whom a set range of existing debates would provide the means of adjudication as to the truth value of the claims made. The claims made here are artistic ones, rather than scientific ones, and are necessarily intended to conjure the illusion of narrative coherence in the speculative conclusions I draw. If there is dramatic license, though, it was on the part of the 'scientists', illusionists and showmen (the gendering is apposite) whose business and whose profits lay in confounding our ordinary state of perception.

To recap briefly: my hypothesis here is that I want to pursue the idea that stories of scientific advancement, illusionism and artistic practice have in retrospect, become comfortably separated. This much is a 'known known': that the separation of disciplines over the course of the eighteenth and nineteenth centuries in Europe and North America allowed successors, including ourselves, to *imagine* the material world through several discrete frameworks. What we might call the history of the imagination, though, in which objects in the material world are no longer quite seen as specimens, and not necessarily works of art, runs differently. The chapter therefore takes a form that echoes the principles of 'pre-modern' cabinets of curiosity in which things that should (apparently) not sit together, or be

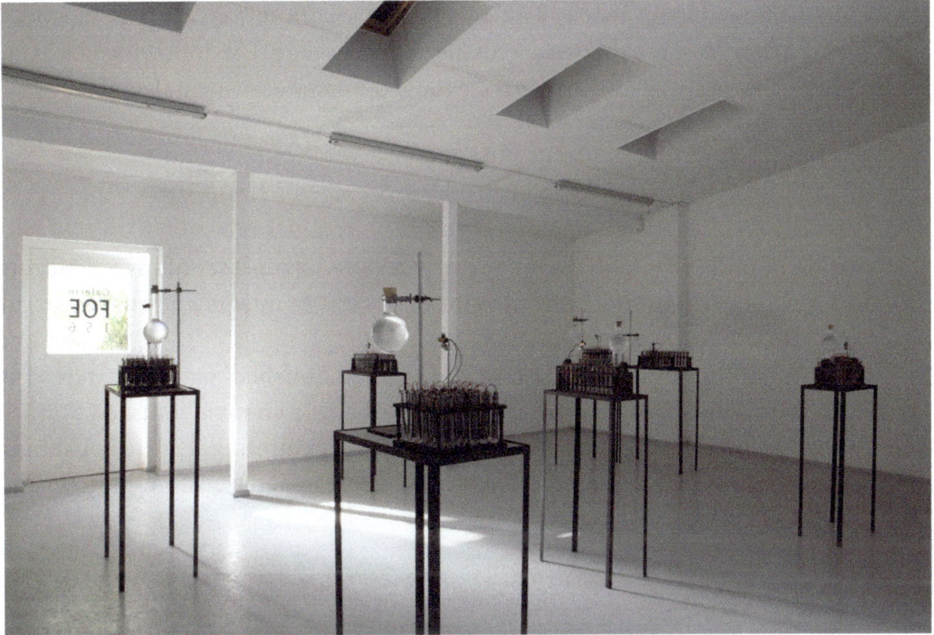

FIGURE 9.1. *Phantasmagoria Electric,* 2015, Gallery FOE 156, Munich, Germany. Photograph by Irene Brown.

seen as aligned, happily do so. Recent work by figures such as Graham Harman and Jane Bennett invites us to see material objects as if endowed with all of the vitality and the mystery of works of art. From my perspective, their work suggests that we can, therefore, see the entire history of Western scientific endeavour through a similar lens. What if, following Harman, we imagined scientific inventions and even practices—and those that were eventually disregarded or forgotten about, or 'declassified' from the terrain of science proper—as 'objects' possessed of infinite strangeness of 'things', human-made and otherwise. His work invites us, as he writes, 'to embrace the innate theatricality and deep multiplicity of every artwork'.[4] My contribution here invites us similarly to embrace the innate theatricality and deep multiplicity of 'scientific' labour—and in particular, pre-scientific attempts to render visible what is ordinarily inaccessible to our senses.

My practice as an artist proceeds from what might be articulated as a similar method—one on which rendering archival material and historical intellectual formations visible is itself an 'illusion', a form of bringing-to-life, or rather, bringing-back-to-life what has been lost to history. We know full well that 'science', 'art' and mere 'entertainment' were conceived of differently in the past. We often fail to imagine that they may be conceived of equally or more different in the near future.

The vignettes here each furnish us with an alternative conception of what 'scientific-artistic' endeavour is—I use this term with the understanding that, following Harman, we may not necessarily be able to separate these domains convincingly any longer.

A Compendium of Vignettes, or, Imagining—and Imaging—'Energy'

The starting point here is a final artwork that resulted from a set of investigations into both the physical artefacts from prior historical moments and the recorded histories that account for them.

I will begin at the end. Or at least an end point, a 'finished' work of art as seen in its exhibition conditions, insofar as any work of art can remain 'finished', rather than enacting a process through its very act of being exhibiting. Figure 9.1 shows my own installation *Phantasmagoria Electric*, consisting of ten custom-built 'magic

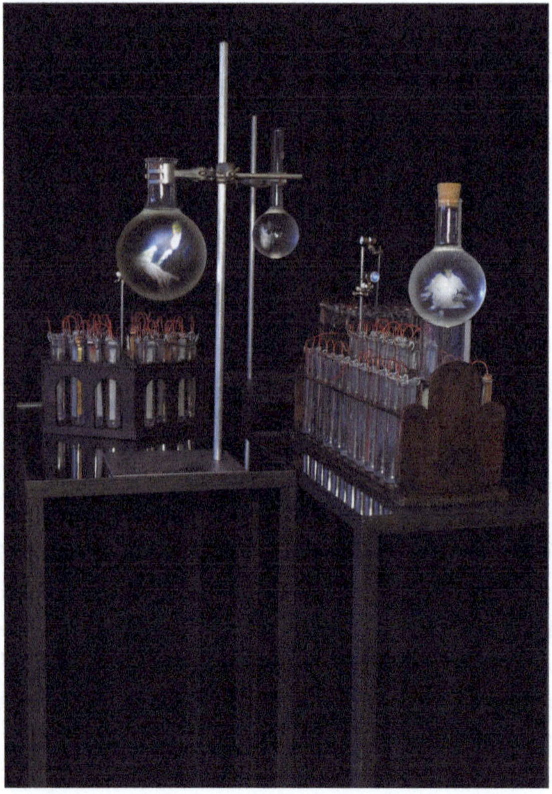

FIGURE 9.2. *Phantasmagoria Electric* (detail), 2014. Glass, wood, steel, water, copper, zinc. Photograph by Irene Brown.

lanterns' each powered by a salt-water battery, utilizing electrical technology originally developed by Alessandro Volta in 1800.[5] Each of these ten is a miniature projector, whose job is to beam a tiny image into a water-filled chemistry flask, where the glass sphere acts as a magnifying lens that distorts the image, creating the illusion that the image is floating within the liquid—or, more accurately, that the image is alive and embodied in a foetal state, suspended in amniotic fluid or in formaldehyde. It is, accordingly, possible to imagine it as either an animate being *in embryo* or a 'specimen' preserved for scientific observation (Fig. 9.2). One hypothesis is precisely, as I suggested earlier, whether the domains of 'the scientific' and 'the artistic' are mutually exclusive or must occupy expressly differentiated positions in our imagination. The form of the work is, therefore, allegorical. It is a fourth dimension, that is, temporal equivalent of the famous 'duck-rabbit' question in perceptual psychology, in which we can only see one or the other at any given time, but never both at the same time. It sets us a parallel problem: Can we register 'the scientific' at the same time as 'the artistic'? Can we avoid separating the two, at this moment in time, when we know full well that such a habit of mind was not always embedded in the European imagination?

The 'technologies' that I employ in creating works of art are now rudimentary and available to all to utilize. To employ a *strategic* anachronism, following the lead of art historians like Alexander Nagel and Giorgio Agamben, these simple contraptions were once the 'cutting-edge' of scientific endeavour. These basic forms of apparatus embodied discoveries so innovative as to appear as 'supernatural'; as sources of intense 'wonder'. My objective here is to return viewers to such a sense of pre-modern 'wonder'; to allow them to enter a state of suspension of disbelief about the illusions that artistry offers and the revelations that scientific experiments can elicit—and to, somehow, combine the two once again.

Phantasmagoria Electric echoes the shape that forms of elite and eventually more popular forms of entertainment once took in the eighteenth and nineteenth centuries. If there is an absent centre to this artwork, it is the human figure who at those times would have introduced and narrated the experiment—and made its findings vivid, dramatic—and to use Graham Harman's term—'theatrical'. There can be no denying that the dissemination of history of *disseminating* scientific discoveries and ideas is also a history of showmanship, of theatricality, of forms of persuasion that do not rely on falsifiable premises, upon logical clauses and propositions related in a causal chain and which can be tested across time and space. My wager here is simple enough. It is the post-Benjaminian proposition that we should (in Harman's terms again) 'embrace' the idea of *phantasmagoria* as a means to destabilize our current formation of knowledge. The use of intentionally antiquated technology is, I will also wager, the only likely means that we might allow any adequate and rounded alternative conceptions of the relationships between science and art to develop. Put

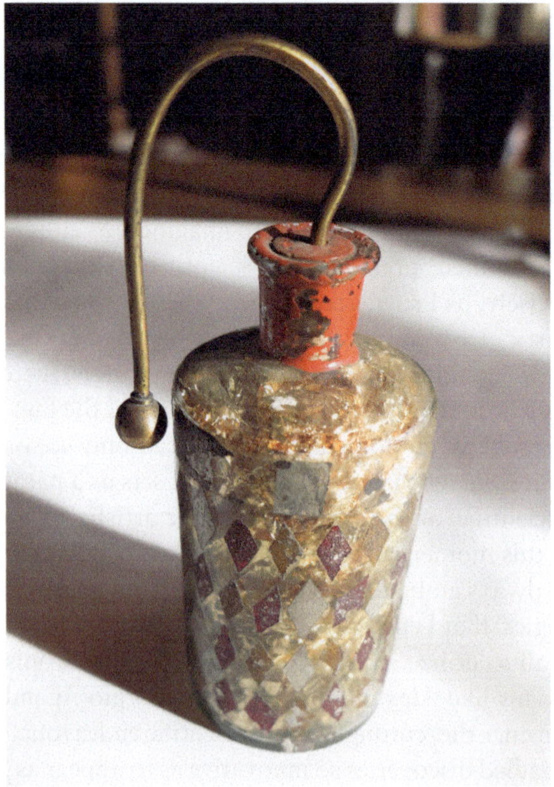

FIGURE 9.3. Layden jar, 1750–1850, France. Glass, copper, gold leaf, Bakken Museum Archives. Photograph by Irene Brown.

very briefly, Peter Osborne has persuasively argued that the history of 'modernism' in art is a history of negations and of laying claim to imagined futures.[6] Modernism's value lies in its claim to futurity. Only after the twentieth century has passed, have the pleasures—indeed, the ethical necessities—of strategic anachronism begun to be explored in art practice and art history alike. 'Time' in art is no longer strictly a 'political' matter in Osborne's terms, but a creative one, as historians like Christine Ross have correctly identified.[7] My own work follows Ross's argument that creative construction of alternative temporalities is the defining characteristic of contemporary art in the last decade. My means of conjuring such imagined temporalities into being is precisely through returning us to what north-western Europeans often take the imagined origin-point of modernity itself: the ability to generate and harness electricity. (There are, of course, manifold other turning points and starting points laid claim to, relating to colonial conquest and to the exploitation of fossil fuels independently of their use to generate electrical power.)

A counter-temporality can readily be imagined if we take the premises of this work seriously. One purpose of *Phantasmagoria Electric* is to imagine a world in which the means of producing electricity could be—or even have been—individualized, with each household generating its own electrical needs rather than being reliant upon a centralized system of production, itself (in the UK at least) both privately owned and run for profit and run in a thoroughly unsustainable way that remains reliant upon fossil fuels. If *Phantasmagoria Electric* is or can be read as an allegory, one reading is indeed that the past may well resemble the future in an inverted mirror image. It proposes a world in which the creation of electricity is undertaken on a small scale and upon an 'amateur' basis, in which the existing division of labour has been thoroughly overtaken. The political implications of such a world in which each individual household unit or individual held control over the means of energy production can be imagined rather than given exposition here. The artist's job is still to show, not tell. In the near future, each of us may be responsible for the miracle of light, of a sustainable energy. The form which my works take—of taking 'ordinary' experiments and allowing them to take Benjaminian forms as magical apparitions—exemplifies the need to see modernity not as a teleological and endless form of progress towards hyper-consumption, but as an evolutionary blip, a temporary aberration, and one where the party is all but over.

I have dwelt upon this work because it condenses an alternative history of scientific endeavour, magic and artistry within itself. It does so by containing ten images that here provide me with a set of vignettes to explore and expand upon and which provide a collective set of episodes that may be reunited into a new story. The images span the earliest electrical experiments through to the Victorian and Edwardian commitments to mesmerism to spiritualism. The ten images comprise a series, a linear sequence of its own that has not been created to date.

Deus ex machina: From the Magic Lantern to the Layden Jar

The images begin in Paris, at the end of the eighteenth century—in this at least, I do, intentionally follow the dominant precedents in constructing scientific histories. One of the most celebrated inventions from this time is Étienne-Gaspard Robert's *Phantasmagoria,* a device for conjuring apparitions using a magic lantern. Somewhat less well known, however, is his *Salon de Physique* where 'serious' scientific endeavour was as gilded with theatrical artifice as modern-day party politics seemingly is. As I suggested earlier, what I want to engage with here is how our predecessors (and, by implication, how we) have attempted to figure the *idea* of electricity. After all, electricity is all too easy to imagine as a form of energy that is godlike in its form—as form-less, infinite, all-powerful, deadly, able to move mountains and mobilize all kinds of matter into states of animation. And it can, with greater difficulty, be imagined as an animate life form of its own—yet as one that is invisible, inaudible, and indeed inaccessible to all of the senses, except to touch. And for those foolhardy enough to touch it, an Icarus-like fall can be the only outcome: electricity's sublime power can only stun or kill us if we come too close to its awesome, destructive power. It is, therefore, unsurprising that there is an extensive body of scientific, literary and religious or spiritualist writing that has attempted to give figures to electricity and reveal imaginative visions of what it is and can be and can do. And documentation of how, in European lecture halls, scientists acted as showmen and in the séance room, the magician was the rational sceptic.

The research that contributes towards this chapter, and which led to the creation of *Phantasmagoria Electric*, was begun on a residency at the Bakken Museum, which has an exceptional collection of historical, and highly delicate Layden jars, decorated with gold leaf (Fig. 9.3). These devices were used to store electricity and do indeed allow us to imagine it as simultaneously invisible and yet thoroughly material. The Layden jar (is itself a kind of 'duck-rabbit' device, in other words: something that allows us to see electricity as either/or material—immaterial, compounding the effect that I am aspiring towards in my works.

The Bakken Museum's archive contains varied apparatus and texts from early experiments in electrochemistry that provided a focal point for my investigations. Through my own experiments, I created a salt-water battery sufficiently powerful to light a single LED bright enough to project an image. As well as creating my own electricity, by forming a small copper cylinder with a lens at one end and a tiny 6 mm slide slotted in the centre, I was able to create a rudimentary projector. Like the early scientists, I had both created electricity and a cinematic illusion of animate life.

What follows is an outline of the ten vignettes that compose the magic lantern show in *Phantasmagoria Electric* as an alternative history of what I will call the intellectual materials of its own making: the ideas, assumptions and pathways that preceded it and which it is logically dependent upon for its own existence. As mentioned, the sequence of vignettes is intended to bring phenomena back into alignments and conjunctures that were once taken for granted, but which the process of disaggregation that underpins almost all scientific methods have dissolved. Together, the ten vignettes tell the story of how the search to discover scientific explanations for *all* invisible phenomena gave credence to practices now called pseudo-science. What we might call the fallibility of 'the scientific method', in the face of deliberate deception is one area of interest to me here. The persistence of a collective need for 'wonder' in the face of an apparent de-enchantment of the universe is a second. What we might call the conceptual strength as much as the popular power of 'magic' is a third concern.

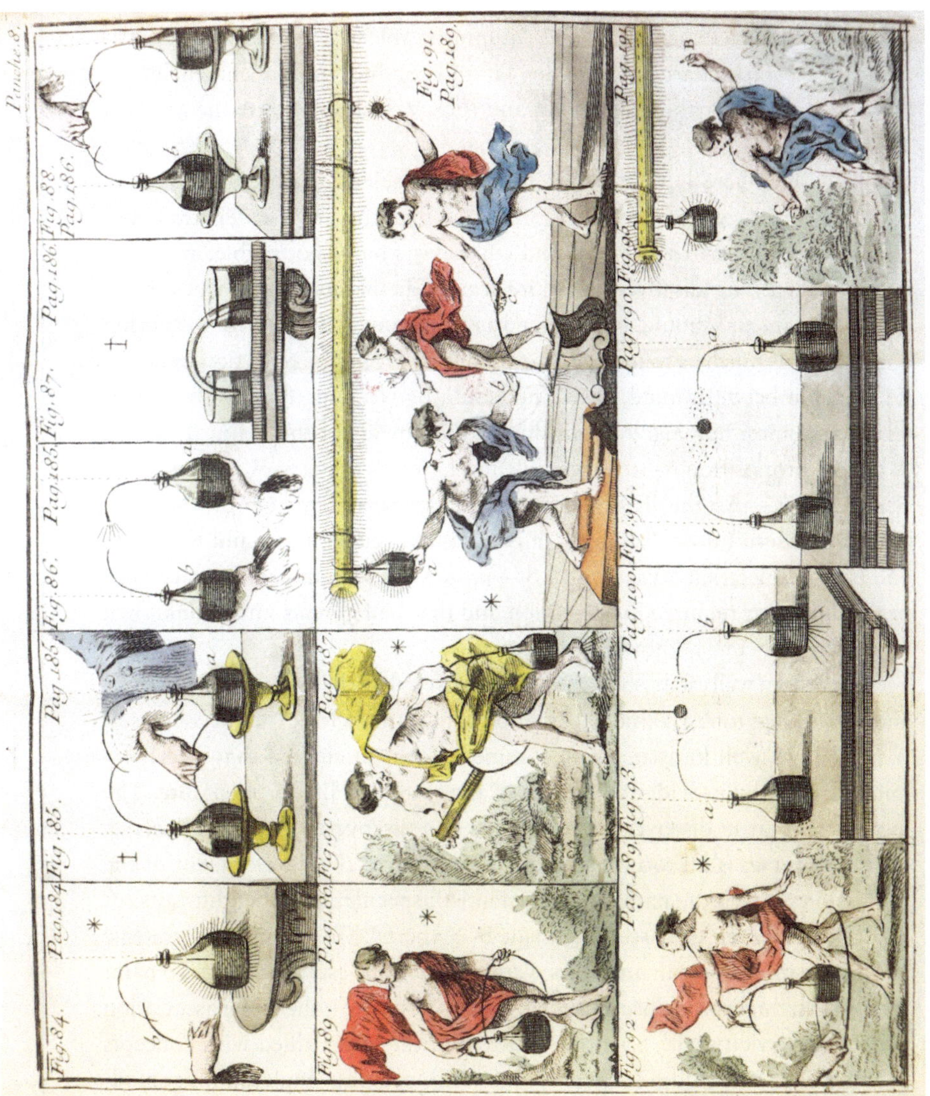

FIGURE 9.4. A fold-out page from Charles Rabiqueau's 'Le Spectacle du feu élémentaire ou Cours d'électricité expérimentale' (1753). Bakken Museum Library. Photograph by Irene Brown.

#1: A First Experiment—Imagining Electricity

Vignette 1. A detail from Charles Rabiqueau's *'Le Spectacle du feu élémentaire ou Cours d'électricité expérimentale'* (1753) (Fig. 9.4). The illustrations describe electrical experiments and equipment able to generate static electricity, store a static charge in a Leyden jar and conduct experiments including lighting a candle, making bells ring and (Fig. 9.6, slide 1) raise the fur on a squirrel's tail.[8]

The wager here is that electricity was *the* scientific obsession of later eighteenth-century Europe: that it prompted the most intense debates about the nature of the material world, and what exists but is not visible, and what does not exist. The 'discovery' or more accurately the study and harnessing of electricity can, and should, be imagined as a fundamental challenge to existing ontologies, as much as to medical knowledge. It prompted reflection upon the relationship between mind, body and 'soul'; between matter and the immaterial; and upon humans' relationship to the powers of the 'natural' world. A related proposition is—following Bruno Latour's thesis in *We Have Never Been Modern*—that the division between the natural and the cultural instigated in early-modern Europe is hardly unrelated to discussions around electricity and energy. Electricity was a form of—indeed the pre-eminent form of 'natural magic' that required investigation and that had gone from an 'unknown unknown' to being a 'known unknown'.

As has been well established, the attempts to explain the existence of electricity and its workings took a considerable period of time to reach the current consensus.

As is also well known, many commentators anticipated that electricity might eventually provide the answer to the source of life, or its nature. The hypothesis that in discovering it, humans had discovered the hidden secrets of the universe, is all too understandable. Prior to the development of the profession or even the naming of a 'scientist', speculations of enthusiasts sat alongside and even surpassed any made by 'experts'.[9] To use another strategic anachronism, gentleman amateurs were the scientific establishment. To paint with an extremely broad brush indeed, my concern here is the initial association between electricity with scientific endeavour, the latter allied with concepts of some form of world-historical or universal 'progress' underpinning 'modernity'. My hunch is that artworks, like other forms of historical and literary speculation, can start to unpick such associations and trains of thinking; and that these forms of speculation echo the unsuccessful forms of 'science' that have been discredited or forgotten:

The prevailing understanding of the enlightenment is one in which there was only scientific and rational thinking, but there was also a significant number of people contributing to the enlightenment who were absorbed in dubious scholarly pursuits like alchemy, mythology, astrology and secret societies.[10]

This observation forms the backbone of this chapter: what are now science's 'others' were once the things that constituted it at its very core—and that can, again following Latour, provide us with the tools to liberate ourselves from a modernity that threatens to exhaust the material basis it rests upon, and destroy many thousands of species in the process.

The first vignette here reintroduces a world in which anyone of means could demonstrate the creation and the applications of electricity, as an example for the present day. It also proposes that then, as now, the interpretation and meaning of the phenomenon was contestable—indeed, was up for grabs. This speculation provides a connective tissue through the vignettes that follow. As I have suggested, my work also partakes of the forms of experiment that are no longer active or practised: as the canonical histories of science outline, electrical experiments became a popular parlour game. It is well recorded that electrical experiments were 'the most pleasing and surprising appearances for the entertainment of one's friends'.[11]

Of course, alongside these forms of lucrative showmanship, the idea that therapeutic effects could be exercised through electricity gained traction; those styling themselves as 'natural philosophers' perceived a link between electricity, bodily ailments and psychological states. And my own work continues that proposition by introducing new states of affect precisely by reintroducing pre-scientific concepts, as the following vignette outlines.

Vignette II. A Detail from Edward Nairne's 'The Description and Use of Nairne's Patent Electrical Machine: With the Addition of Some Philosophical Experiments and Medical Observations' (1783). Nairne's electrotherapeutic instruments are seen applied to a (disembodied) female patient's arm (Fig. 9.6, slide 2). Nairne promoted his device as having applications in both medicine and physics.

My work *Phantasmagoria Electric* is intended to re-embody scientific knowledge through practice—on the empirical grounds that my own ignorance of basic electrical principles and production is nearly complete; and that this echoes the experience of my entire circle of acquaintances. The division of labour that the disciplinary organization of knowledge has created has its costs, as well as benefits. It argues for a new form of 'amateurism'—a rhizomatic form of knowledge production, let us say, (or one across a 'hive mind', to mix my metaphors) where valid contributions to the production of new knowledge can come from multiple sources.

It is also intended, of necessity, as a kind of a cautionary tale: a window onto cost incurred by the innocent in modernity. It is a window onto the history of the medical applications of electrical 'therapies' in which shock treatments were applied to many thousands of individuals across time and space. The affect associated with 'wonder' that I want to conjure is one of non-knowledge, echoing medical professionals' lack of knowledge of the changes wrought on the body when receiving an electrical charge. The artistic imperative is to provide a 'shock to the system' of knowledge production.

Vignette III. Luigi Galvani's 'Aloysii Galvani [...] De Viribus Electricitatis in Motu Musculari Commentarius', (1791). The book describes Galvani's electrical experiments that later became known as 'Galvanism', where dissected frogs and a dead dog are 'animated' through a static charge (Fig. 9.5).

Falsification is generally more useful than verification, if only because it is easy to find evidence in support of established views, whereas when we falsify a theory we learn something new.[12]

The form of *Phantasmagoria Electric* gives animate life to the body of images it encompasses; and hypothesises that it is not an accident that we talk of a 'body' of images, or of ideas. It takes Galvani's ideas and misappropriates them—strategically misemploys them for artistic purposes. The intent is, I hope, to reorder the chain of association that his work began. Galvani's work prompted debates about the brain (and the body) generated an electrical 'fluid'; containing (an image of) Galvani's work inside fluid itself provides a poetic image—an

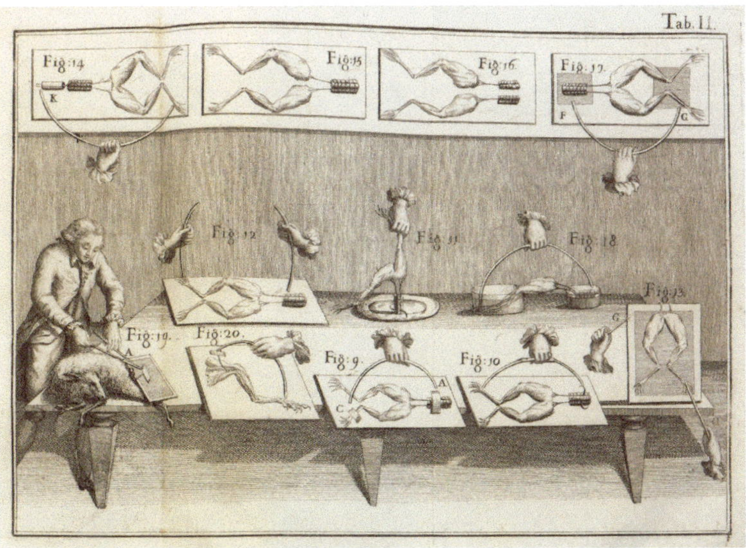

FIGURE 9.5. Luigi Galvani's *Aloysii Galvani [...] De Viribus Electricitatis in Motu Musculari Commentarius, 1791.* Bakken Museum Library. Photograph by Irene Brown.

objective correlative, let us call it in the terms of poetry itself—for this idea. Galvani's animation of frogs' legs 'demonstrated', wrongly, that electricity was the animating force of all animal life (Volta later proved his experiment to rest on the electric current generated between the two metals applied). The idea that we *are* electricity, in some form, proved difficult to dislodge or deny; it is an understandable intuition. Even into the nineteenth century, figures like John Abernethy were promoting the idea of life 'itself' as being a fluid equivalent to electricity. My work tempts those encountering it into entertaining the idea again, as another cautionary tale, a false turn taken.

Vignette IV. A Detail from 'Principes du magnétisme', c.1786. This anonymous French manuscript includes discussion of the theory and principles of animal magnetism (Fig. 9.6, slide 4).

In the entire history of electricity's applications, the positing of a relationship between electricity and magnetism is one of the undeniably most important.

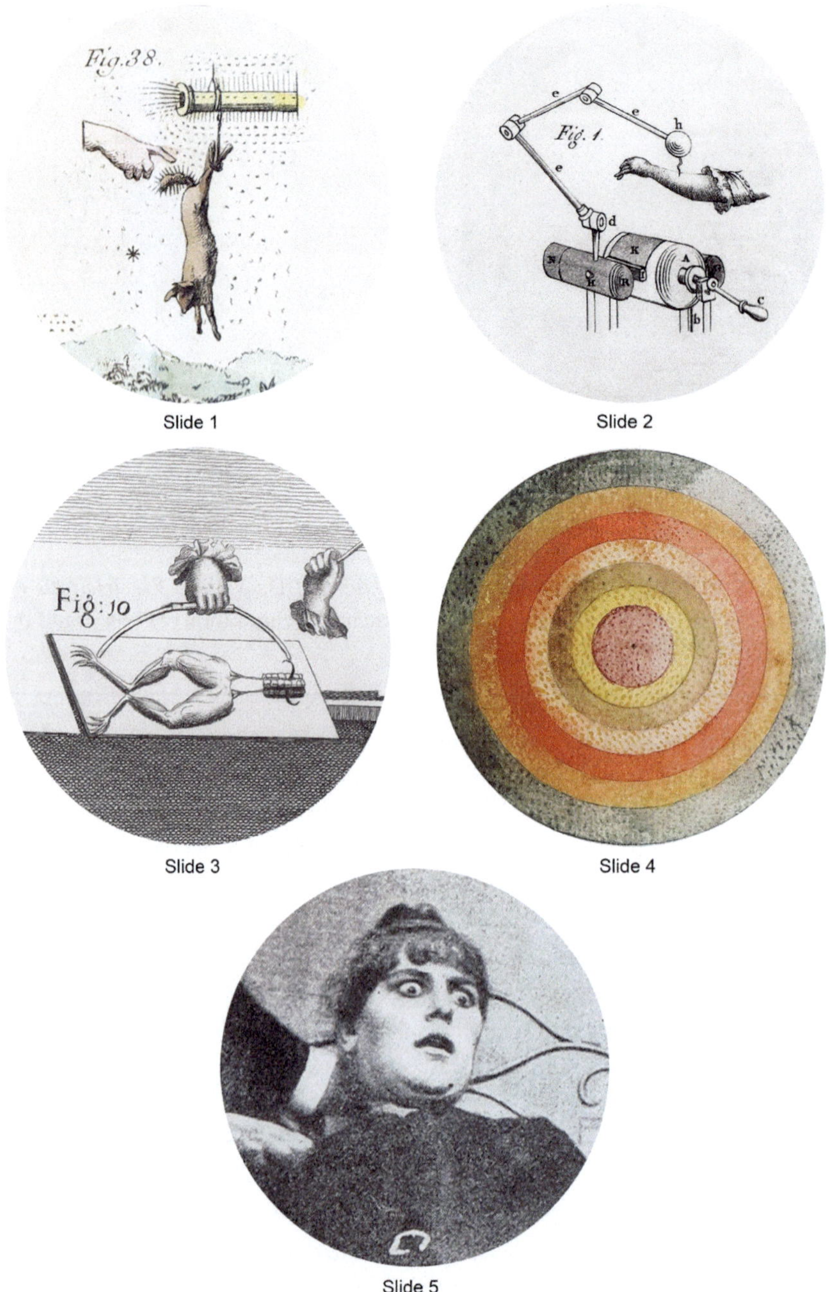

FIGURE 9.6. Images for slides 1–5, from Bakken Museum Library.
Slide 1: Detail from Charles Rabiqueau's 'Le Spectacle du feu élémentaire ou Cours d'électricité expérimentale' (1753). Photograph by Irene Brown.

William Gilbert, acknowledged as the 'father' of electrical studies, authored *De Magnete Magneti cisque Corporibus et de Magno Magnete Teure Physiologia* (1600). Gilbert proposed the idea that Earth itself was a kind of magnet to explain why compass needles point north. I draw attention to Gilbert's findings because they are the unlikely intellectual materials that are the basis of mesmerism, which is the fourth vignette of the *Phantasmagoria Electric*. The fluids that it is made from intentionally echo the appearance of art-historical representations of sublime, infinite seas, and to a lesser extent, moonscapes. Franz Anton Mesmer (1734–1815) hypothesized that the human nervous system was made up of 'magnetic fluid': an invisible substance similar to electricity, but affected by planetary motion just like the ebb and flow of the ocean tides.[13] We ourselves are mere liquid, in this vision, held in dynamic equilibrium and given motion by a 'current'. The coincidence between these figures—of flow, motion and transfer of energy—is no coincidence at all, of course. The attention implicitly drawn to it in the work is one intended to alert us to the limits of our language and to the fragility and *fallibility* of the figures by which we imagine the world's workings. Mesmer's methods 'treated' haemorrhoids, vomiting, paralysis, blindness and all kinds of convulsive and hysterical disorders.[14] His work features in the piece not least because his techniques included curative baths in magnetized water, mesmeric massage and his 'banquet'. This was a large wooden tub filled with magnetized water that Mesmer claimed acted like a huge Layden jar, charged with his own personal animal magnetism 'stored up and concentrated, like electric fluid'.[15] Pierre Bourdieu has helpfully called 'art' the domain of 'the charismatic ideology': the place where objects are invested with quasi-magical or spiritual powers to intercede on our behalf.[16] The wager played out here in my work is that there is an uncanny alignment between Mesmer's analysis of bodies' (spiritual) power and potency, and Bourdieu's description of what works of art are, at least under the current form of capitalist individualism. In the latter's words, the 'charismatic ideology of "creation" [...] directs the gaze towards [...] the magic power of transubstantiation with which the "creator" is endowed'.[17] The homology implied between artistic creativity and pseudo-scientific powers is not, of course, a complete one; but it suggests that all domains of knowledge are a matter of faith and of suspending disbelief, by their very nature. Any successful artwork is testimony to the power of the imagination to persuade, and even to deceive—or at least to generate a successful illusion. To expand the hypothesis a little: the successful work of art generates an *illusion of coherence* rather than merely a perceptual illusion: it provides an explanation for the world, or at the least some *model* of its order, and this allows us to hold faith in it, in our encounter with it. It exerts a kind of magnetic pull upon our imagination, just as Mesmer's patients willingly subjugated themselves to the 'magnetizer' who manipulated them by just a look or simple sign.[18] A successful work of art instigates an alternative form of consciousness at best—for as fellow artist Hans Haacke writes, 'art [...] belong[s[to what has aptly been called the "consciousness industry"'.[19] Mesmer's role, and my role alike, are to realign consciousness. The glories— and the dangers—of this thinking have been seen more clearly by Haacke than anyone else. And as he has extrapolated,

> the artist's business requires his [sic] involvement in practically everything. He works in reference, not to a section of the world, but to the whole world [...] the artist's business is how to [...] manipulate the findings of perceptual psychology [...] Theoretically there are no limits to his involvement.[20]

This beautiful, horrifying image—in which art is akin to advertising, propaganda and scientific experiment rolled into one—is one I subscribe to wholeheartedly, and which this entire chapter is an attempting to account for. Mesmer's work, in this thesis, is repositioned somewhat counterintuitively as a branch of perceptual psychology that preceded the manipulation of consumers through advertising and voters through propaganda.

Vignette V. Ernest Abraham Hart Smith's 'Hypnotism, Mesmerism and the New Witchcraft' (1896): Chapters on 'Hypnotism and Humbug', 'Animal Magnetism and Hysteria', 'Mesmerism and the New Witchcraft', 'Gropings after the Supernatural' and 'The Eternal Gullible'(Fig. 9.6, slide 5).

Mesmer's work is, also, a precursor of beliefs in the 'occult' and the 'paranormal' that are routinely seen as pseudo-science. The door that was opened by his work and that of peers was that connecting electricity as a potential portals or connections to the 'other' world of the afterlife. The flourishing of such beliefs into the twentieth century has been under investigation by artists across Europe and North America since around the millennium: many believe that the investigation of the 'darker' side of modernity has been one of the dominant motifs in contemporary art since as a whole across the last two decades. Survey exhibitions on both sides of the Atlantic testify to this. The history of the imagination has, I want to suggest, taken a 'turn' towards re-examining the repressed or even frankly ridiculous sides of modernity and of modernism in the visual arts. My work echoes the cultural theorist and latterly artist Mieke Bal's warrant to construct a 'preposterous history' through positively anachronistic means, or rather positive forms of anachronism.[21] Accordingly, as outlined earlier, some investigation of the existing histories in play is a necessity in order to relate how my own recasting of them has been achieved.

This chapter in my work examines authorities' support of such notions and the cultural authority that they lent to what are now deemed ideas outside the mainstream or worthy of official approval. In France, an 1826 report commissioned by the Académie Royale de Médecine in Paris was supportive of the idea of 'animal magnetism', although reclassified Mesmer's magnetic fluid as a 'non-specific fluid' still able to be directed by willpower. A second report of 1831 also validated the realities of animal magnetism and somnambulistic paranormal phenomena, advising that used correctly, they were real medical tools. A third commission of 1835 produced a report that flatly contradicted the earlier ones entirely: the lack of consensus between the class of 'experts' about the nature and capabilities, of electrical and electromagnetic treatments was clear. Other commentators of that period imagined that magnetism would eventually 'render the mystical scientific, rather than science mystical'.[22] The connection I am drawing here is between the spirit world and magnetic somnambulism, as endorsed by, for example, the Swedenborgian Stockholm Exegetic and Philanthropic Society. The idea at play was that 'magnetizing' allowed the body and soul to separate, activating an 'inner sight' to render the invisible spirit world present. The idea this rested upon was that the fundamental forces not only guiding matter, but guiding our souls and minds, were magnetic.

Vignette VI. Chauncy Hare Townshend's 'Facts in Mesmerism, with Reasons for a Dispassionate Inquiry into it' (1840) (Fig. 9.7, slide 6).

The development of *public* as opposed to professional scientific debate has, I contest, developed episodically, in response to particular flashpoints where publicity draw attention to issues of pointed contestation. One such episode is the alarming case of the Fox Sisters, who in 1848, came to represent spiritualism in America. The sisters became the first celebrity 'mediums' whose self-induced somnambulism or hypnotic state—with no need for a controlling, Svengali-like mesmerizer, captivated audiences. This idea spread across social groups, becoming a form of entertainment. One early Victorian British spectator wrote that 'table moving' is all the rage [...] Every evening party must of course have its experiments'.[23] The Fox Sisters are a part of my work, as they have long represented the return of 'experiments' as forms of public entertainment. The development of a scientific body of language, or its misdirection and contestation, are important here, as my work is concerned precisely with how we figure, and imagine, the interplay of mind and body—or soul. The image of the Fox Sisters that I have selected and cropped positions them precisely as 'floating' into an expanded sea of consciousness—a limitless space that had not been conquered previously, but which willpower, and science, could open up. The image is, of course, as tantalizing as it is misleading—but has its own power *as an image*. And it reminds us that the power to 'conjure' objects into being—here, deceased others—is a form of artistry that artists have not had a monopoly over.

Vignette VII. The Davenport Brothers Public Cabinet Séance at the Queens Concert Rooms, Hanover Square, London in 1865 (Fig. 9.7, slide 7).

> The standard line of scientific naturalists—Thomas Huxley in the nineteenth century, Richard Dawkins in the twenty-first—is that science subverts belief in God [...] [but f]ar from destroying faith, science is impossible without it.[24]

My contestation here is that 'mediumship' in its public reception is the signature development of the mid-nineteenth century, including the misappropriation of 'scientific' ideas about electricity (here imagined first as a physical 'fluid' within the body, then as a kind of universal theatre of operations which individual consciousness could travel across). 'Electricity', in other words, became a kind of peculiar catch-all term: an open signifier which almost any phenomenon could be attached to, and which all forms of magical wish fulfilment could be realized through. 'Electricity' can be understood as the meta-sign under which *Phantasmagoria Electric* stands and allows me to connect together multiple other signs and stories with relative impunity—as the term is already connected to every other.

The seventh story brought into play in the work is that of the American brothers Ira and William Davenport, who operated on the threshold between magic and mediumship, and who presented ghostly manifestations on theatre stages. Their signature act was to invite spectators to tie them fast into a cabinet filed with musical instruments, and once the doors were closed, music would emanate and ghostly hands appear through the cabinet windows. Their use of phosphorescent paint in their theatre séances convinced many that they had accrued such an electrical charge that they could make objects fly of their own accord, creating their own living paintings. The painterly image I have employed accordingly speaks of them as artists *manqués* with good reason. It positions their actions and my own as again in alignment, as part of an unintentional shared project.

Vignette VIII. Double-exposure Spirit Photograph by Eugène Thiébault, 1863, of Henri Robin.[25] (Fig. 9.7, slide 8).

> For some of its practitioners psychical research—a new science, as they liked to think of it—was in fact a type of magical thinking [...] The psychical researchers turned to science looking for [even] more than immortality.[26]

The development of spiritualism and the possibility of accessing previously undetectable aspects of the world through innate, but usually latent 'super-powers' is an ongoing idea that has been repeatedly exploited. The discovery of electromagnetic (radio) waves and X-rays can be seen to have reinforced such ideas; and given licence to those who wanted to prove the scientific basis of psychic and other phenomena.[27] They raised the question of precisely how many 'invisible' worlds within our own there actually are, waiting to be revealed by science.

The eighth image in my compilation is from the group of eminent English Victorians called the Society for Psychical Research (henceforth SPR). The group included eminent scientists and philosophers committed to strictly scientific enquiry, and had the collective wealth to conduct extensive international research.[28] The sheer quantity of experiments undertaken and strict adherence to methods of logical deduction and even (what we now call) falsifiability are undeniable.

The SPR's establishment membership simply could not agree upon the roles that electricity, and invisible forces played in the physical, or spiritual worlds. But *pictorial* representation proved an answer: photography itself could be imagined as an impartial, mechanical, reliable, objective scientific tool. The camera was the ultimate witness, free of prejudice, credible in its account, diligent in its watch. Photographic images, occupied a different ontological state to words—to verbal claims made by participants. They acted as a guarantee, as they continue to do in legal cases today.

It became obvious to the SPR that the camera could capture phenomena that were not necessarily evident to the naked eye: the magic of 'freezing' a slice of time from its endless flow allowed scientific investigation to be objectified, made permanent, and findings circulated through reproduction. And here, of course, the photographs of the SPR themselves act as evidence of their own time: they are as date-stamped, ideologically speaking, as any artefact could ever be. And they are more akin to art objects in their artistry, their pictorial rhetoric, and their ability to conjure and cajole than to any scientific artefact or specimen. But a specimen they remain, in court, and in scientific enquiry. Is it possible to see a photograph as an illusion and as an indexical representation at the same time? Or is this, too, a duck-rabbit problem of another kind?

Vignette IX. Stanley De Brath's 'The Physical Phenomena of Spiritualism', London Spiritualist Alliance Publications, 1930: 'the making of a thumb-print by a Materialized Hand on dental wax softened by hot water' (Fig. 9.7, slide 9).

> There is a persisting need to believe that the order that is supposed to exist in the human mind reflects one that exists [independently of it] in the world. A contrary view seems more plausible the order pleasing any view of things is to the human mind, the less likely it is to reflect reality.[29]

As I have suggested, the apparatus of both the pictorial and performing arts alike were called upon to verify and not just to dramatize, scientific endeavours. In the thought process that generated my work, elaborated upon here, this is just as true. In the ninth vignette, I have alighted upon a photograph of the medium Mina 'Margery' Crandon (1888–1941), who popularized the idea that 'ectoplasm' was produced when spirits were called forth to enter this world from their own. The idea of 'ectoplasm' first appeared during experiments in the 1880s.

Accounts of how such matter 'transported' across dimensions related only vaguely to ideas of electrical transference, but can be seen as sitting in parallel to them.

The invention of the figure of 'ectoplasm' is a triumph of the imagination: the naming of an imagined substance in defiance of all known laws of physics. It was usually figured as a luminous, light-emitting substance— therefore somehow 'charged' with energy, implicitly aligning the electrical with the spiritual, as if the two were one and the same. 'Ectoplasm' was visible only under low lighting, conveniently, and therefore able to be documented with infrared film, again capturing a frequency of light, or a type of energy, ordinarily beyond the naked eye.[30] My purpose here is to render visible historical accounts of how 'the invisible' has been presented; the job of such accounts is in effect that proposed by Jean-Francois Lyotard as the role of modernist artworks tout court as 'presenting the unpresentable'.[31] What is notable here is how even Lyotard's imagery seems directly indebted to the vocabulary developed around the image and idea of electricity. The dominant images of the role of art, and those of electricity, have come into strange alignment, with or without my own contribution or attempt to achieve that.

Vignette X. Harry Kellar: 1894: 'the Levitation of Princess Karnac'.[32] *(Fig. 9.7, slide 10).*

The final vignette in my work makes visible the magician Harry Kellar's popular illusion of 'the Levitation of Princess Karnac'. In his act, a woman floating in the centre of a brightly lighted stage, is seemingly held in place by the electrical rays emanating from Kellar's hands. Such episodes in the history of magic and illusion remain intriguing precisely because from the earliest days of spiritualism, it was magicians who openly challenged mediums as frauds.[33] Kellar was one of the first to openly acknowledge that he was practising a mere trick and an illusion, rather than a 'wonder'. He presented his act not as feats of psychic mystery but as ingeniously crafted trickery. Similarly, the climax of Houdini's final tour in 1925–26 was an extraordinary spirit exposure, demonstrating on a fully lighted stage how mediums duped their customers. And so, the vaunted self-reflexivity of artworks is a mere pale imitation of the manoeuvres practised on stage, rather earlier. We have come full circle.

Reflecting upon the Presence of Magic in Artwork, and Artistry of Magic and Science: Some Inconclusive Conclusions

The decline of psychical research has not gone with a loss of interest in the paranormal. Research has continued [to this day] [...] though the results have been inconclusive.[34]

My understanding of the 'experiments' mentioned is, in part, that they must indeed be deemed inconclusive, were misguided, or otherwise blatant forms of misdirection or disinformation. They are all the better for this as forms of inspiration. Failure is always more interesting than unmitigated success. Deception, and self-deception, always prove more potent weapons than the self being open to its own propensity for being deceived. I have set out a chain of events here which, I hope, offers windows onto other possible ways in which we might yet configure knowledge; other ways in which we might figure and understand the most fundamental aspects of our material universe; and other ways in which art might yet be a vital part of the body politic, in representing the unrepresentable, rather than merely a form of parlour game for the wealthy as it so often is reduced to, today.

My work embodies early Enlightenment approaches to the investigation of electricity and magnetism that were, despite their 'unscientific' methods by present-day

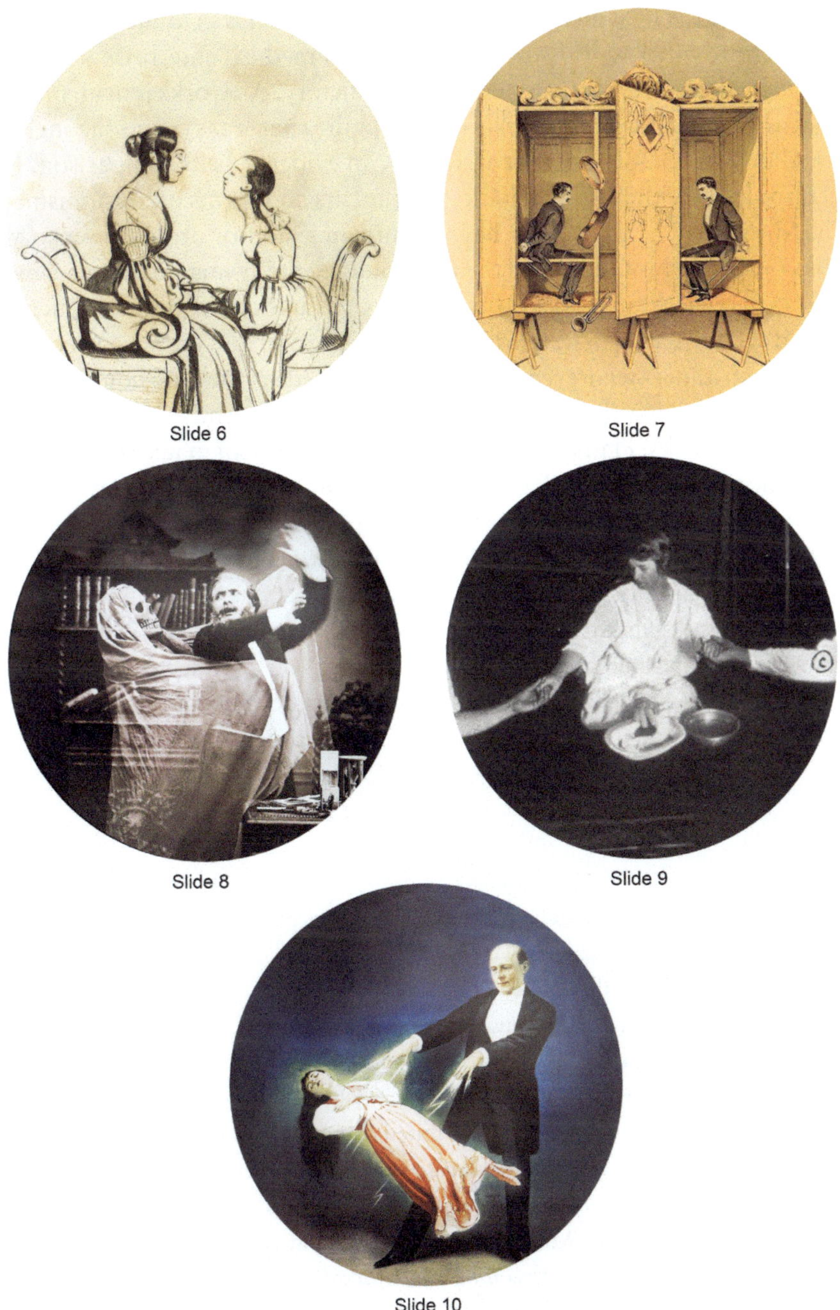

FIGURE 9.7. Images used for slides 6–10.
Slide 6: Rear book plate from Chauncy Hare Townshend's 'Facts in Mesmerism, with Reasons for a Dispassionate Inquiry into it' (1840). Photograph by Irene Brown.

standards, a means by which a philosophical revolution was founded—and hence by which entire other worlds of imaginative and medical enterprise were begun. Their legacy, therefore, is complex and contradictory. Artworks remain one of the few means by which we might test or reconfigure that legacy; and the ingenuity, guile and love of complexity that artworks can evidence bear comparison. I have wanted to show, with both the finest experiments and forms of illusionism.

The 'discovery' of worlds far beyond human vision or ordinary sensory perception could only be understood through fundamentally imaginative endeavours.

And so magicians, in this story, come out well, at least at one level. Their sheer artistry, if we can call it that, in the creation of illusion and the suspension of disbelief, is a constant—whatever inventions or new ideas they are competing with. Magicians are sharing the secrets of their trade with scientists in order to study how the brain works: Hans Haacke was right.[35] The use of magic tricks in experiments in the science of vision has divulged that our consciousness is aware of only a fraction of the information that enters our eyes.[36] My own work exploits this. It echoes the claim made by philosopher Paul Carus a century ago, that:

> While magic as superstition and fraud is doomed, magic as an art will not die. Science will take hold of it and permeate it with its own spirit, changing it into scientific magic, which is destitute of all mysticism, occultism and superstition, and comes to us as a witty play for our recreation and diversion.[37]

NOTES

1. John Gray, *The Immortalization Commission: Science and the Strange Quest to Cheat Death* (London: Allen Lane, 2011), 205, 219.

2. A Smithsonian affiliate, the Bakken Museum and Library collections include approximately 11,000 books, journals, and manuscripts and 2,500 artefacts from the eighteenth century to the present day. The subject of the collections is the history of electricity and magnetism with a focus on their roles in the life sciences and medicine.

3. *Phantasmagoria Electric* was first exhibited as part of the conference *Twice Upon a Time: Magic, Alchemy and the Transubstantiation of the Senses*, 2014, at the Centre for Fine Art Research, School of Art, Birmingham Institute of Art & Design, UK, and subsequently at Gallery Foe 156, Munich, Germany, 2015 and a condensed version was included in the exhibition *A Scientific Encounter: On Interobjectivity*, at Montpellier University's l'École de Médecine, Montpellier, 2017.

4. Graham Harman, *Art and Objects* (Cambridge: Polity Press, 2019), advance information [online] available at https://www.amazon.co.uk/Art-Objects-Graham-Harman/dp/1509512683 (accessed 19 July 2019).

5. Each battery is made from 36 glass test tubes filled with salt water, each containing a strip of copper and a strip of zinc wired together in series.

6. Peter Osborne, *The Politics of Time* (London: Verso, 1994).

7. Christine Ross, *The Past Is the Present; It's the Future Too: The Temporal Turn in Contemporary Art* (London: Bloomsbury, 2012).

8. As is well known, a Layden jar is an early form of capacitor consisting of a glass jar with layers of metal foil on the outside and inside surfaces and a metal terminal projecting vertically through the jar lid to make contact with the inner foil.

9. The word 'scientist' was not coined until 1833; prior to this the term 'natural philosopher' was commonly used.

10. Humanities at Stanford, *Dark Side of the Enlightenment*, 2009, [online] available at www.shc.stanford.edu/news/research/dark-side-enlightenment (accessed 25 July 2018).

11. Joseph Priestley, *The History and Present State of Electricity: With Original Experiments* (London: Printed for J. Dodsley, 1767), x.

12. Gray, *The Immortalization Commission*, 225.

13. Christopher Turner, *Mesmeromania, or the Tale of the Tub* (Cabinet Magazine, issue 21 2006, 'Electricity'), [online] available at www.cabinetmagazine.org/issues/21/turner.php (accessed 15 July 2018).

14. Adam Crabtree, *From Mesmer to Freud: Magnetic Sleep and the Roots of Psychological Healing* (Cambridge, MA: Yale University Press, 1993), 7.

15. Turner, *Mesmeromania*, n.p.

16. Pierre Bourdieu, *The Rules of Art: Genesis and Structure of the Literary Field*, trans. Susan Emanuel (Stanford: Stanford University Press, 1996), 167.

17. Ibid., 167.

18. Turner, *Mesmeromania*, n.p.

19. Hans Haacke, 'Museums, Managers of Consciousness', *Art in America*, no. 72 (February 1984): 9–17.

20. Hans Haacke, *Arts/Canada* 26, (1969): 75; and *Art international*, no. 13 (1969): 56; cited in: *Art Inquiry: Recherches Sur Les Arts*, no. 1–4 (1999): 116.

21. Mieke Bal, *Quoting Caravaggio: Contemporary Art, Preposterous History* (Chicago: Chicago University Press, 1999).

22. Crabtree, *From Mesmer to Freud*, 193.

23. Ibid., 237.

24. Gray, *The Immortalization Commission*, 221–22.

25. Magazine Poly, 'Art- Poltergeist', [online] available at www.poly.fr/poltergeist/ (accessed 20 July 2018).

26. Gray, *The Immortalization Commission*, 221, 205.

27. Marina Warner, *Phantasmagoria* (Oxford: Oxford University Press, 2006), 227.

28. Ibid., 227.

29. Gray, *The Immortalization Commission*, 221–22.

30. Raymond Buckland, *The Spirit Book: The Encyclopaedia of Clairvoyance, Channeling and Spirit Communication* (Canton, MI: Visible Ink Press, 2005), 119.

31. Jean-Francois Lyotard, 'Presenting the Unpresentable': The Sublime', first published in *Artforum* (April 1982), [online] available at https://www.artforum.com/print/198204/presenting-the-unpresentable-the-sublime-35606 (accessed 18 July 2019).

32. Keller Magic poster image [online] available at www.commons.wikimedia.org/wiki/File:Flickr_-_%E2%80%A6trialsanderrors_-_Kellar,_Levitation,_magician_poster,_ca._1894.jpg (accessed 20 July 2018).

33. Annette Hill, *Paranormal Media: Audiences, Spirits and Magic in Popular Culture* (Abingdon: Routledge, 2010), 133.

34. Gray, *The Immortalization Commission*, 206–7.

35. CBC News, *The Science of Magic* (2018), [online] available at www.cbc.ca/natureofthings/features/what-magic-has-taught-us-about-how-the-brain-works (accessed 10 August 2018).

36. University of British Columbia, *Age-old Magic Tricks Can Provide Clues For Modern Science* (Science Daily, 2008), [online] available at www.sciencedaily.com/releases/2008/07/080722192354.htm (accessed 13 August 2018).

37. Ridgely Evans, *The Old and the New Magic* (Chicago: Open Court Publishing Company, 1906), 18.

REFERENCES

Bal, Mieke. *Quoting Caravaggio: Contemporary Art, Preposterous History*. Chicago: Chicago University Press, 1999.

Bourdieu, Pierre. *The Rules of Art: Genesis and Structure of the Literary Field*, trans. Susan Emanuel. Stanford: Stanford University Press, 1996.

Buckland, Raymond. *The Spirit Book: The Encyclopaedia of Clairvoyance, Channeling and Spirit Communication*. Canton, MI: Visible Ink Press, 2005.

CBC News, *The Science of Magic*, (2018). Available at www.cbc.ca/natureofthings/features/what-magic-has-taught-us-about-how-the-brain-works (accessed 10 August 2018).

Crabtree, Adam. *From Mesmer to Freud: Magnetic Sleep and the Roots of Psychological Healing*. Cambridge, MA: Yale University Press, 1993.

Evans, Ridgely. *The Old and the New Magic*. Chicago: Open Court, 1906.

Gray, John. *The Immortalization Commission: Science and the Strange Quest to Cheat Death*. London: Allen Lane, 2011.

Haacke, Hans. 'Museums, Managers of Consciousness'. *Art in America*, no. 72 (February 1984): 9–17.

Harman, Graham. *Art and Objects*. Cambridge: Polity Press, 2019.

Hill, Annette. *Paranormal Media: Audiences, Spirits and Magic in Popular Culture*. Abingdon: Routledge, 2010.

Humanities at Stanford. *Dark Side of the Enlightenment.* 2009. Available at http://www.shc.stanford.edu/news/research/dark-side-enlightenment (accessed 25 July 2018).

Lyotard, Jean-Francois. '"Presenting the Unpresentable": The Sublime', first published in *Artforum*, April 1982. Available at https://www.artforum.com/print/198204/presenting-the-unpresentable-the-sublime-35606 (accessed 18 July 2019).

Osborne, Peter. *The Politics of Time.* London: Verso, 1994.

Poly (Magazine), 'Art- Poltergeist'. Available at http://www.poly.fr/poltergeist/ (accessed 20 July 2018).

Priestley, Joseph. *The History and Present State of Electricity: With Original Experiments.* London: Printed for J. Dodsley, 1767.

Ross, Christine. *The Past Is the Present; It's the Future Too: The Temporal Turn in Contemporary Art.* London: Bloomsbury, 2012.

Turner, Christopher. *Mesmeromania, or the Tale of the Tub* (*Cabinet Magazine*, issue 21, 2006, 'Electricity'). Available at http://www.cabinetmagazine.org/issues/21/turner.php (accessed 15 July 2018).

University of British Columbia, *Age-old Magic Tricks Can Provide Clues for Modern Science* (*Science Daily*, 2008). Available at http://www.sciencedaily.com/releases/2008/07/080722192354.htm (accessed 13 August 2018).

Warner, Marina. *Phantasmagoria.* Oxford: Oxford University Press, 2006.

10

Choosing, Unpicking and Connecting: On Drawing Museum Objects

Richard Talbot

Abstract

Richard Talbot's chapter offers a practice-led reflection on the thinking and creative processes involved when he visually responds to research collections and scientific objects in particular. Given that research collections, especially within universities, often range across numerous disciplines and are largely not mediated for public consumption, this creates situations where the artist seems able to make 'free' and anachronistic associations across the collections and between specimens. Talbot's chapter focuses on the creation of one specific drawing, Point, Line, Plane, Solid, *which took the form of a still-life depicting various scientific objects, in a manner reminiscent of the elaborate tableaux found in perspective treatises, such as Francois Niceron's seventeenth-century treatise on linear perspective.1 The artwork explicitly shows the mechanisms and expressions of linear perspective—projections, light paths, reflections and shadows, and the complex matrix ('a bundle') of lines used to construct (and connect) the visual phenomena and objects that are depicted. As this chapter will demonstrate, the content and form of the drawing became, inadvertently and serendipitously, an embodiment of the act of choosing, of making visual and mental connections between the objects, and the processes of depiction.*

Since the late 1970s, my practice has been oriented around drawing, although I initially began my life as an artist making sculpture. My drawing practice, however, is highly 'sculptural' in its emphases, and concerned with objects, rather than being determined by affiliation with particular genres, whether portraiture, landscape or figurative composition. My commitment to drawing comes from the fact that it provides me with a high degree of freedom and latitude as an artist: we might say that it is a medium or way of working that can encompass the world within it, rather than being defined by the parameters of the material world, as sculpture necessarily is. It can allow for the creation of imagined objects that, nevertheless, might also exist outside of the picture plane. With drawings I can make them (forms, lines, etc.) 'perform' how I want them—I can make objects float in space if I want to and, importantly, the scale of what is shown becomes indeterminate. This shift away from actual material and specific scale also has its roots in a desire, perhaps misplaced, for some kind of idealism and sense of pure form. This also relates to what we might call four-dimensional objects, that is, objects existing in time as well and along X, Y, Z axes of width, depth and length. In the same way that a point moved through space produces a line, this notion of a four-dimensional entity is the speculative and imaginative area of what is produced when a solid moves through space. Likewise, in the same way as a shadow is a two-dimensional projection from a three-dimensional object, the question arises as to whether a solid three-dimension object is a shadow of a four-dimensional entity.[2] As an approach to, or, an imaginative tool for thinking about objects in collections and museums, the reference to fundamental dimensions, as well as time, seems remarkably apposite

Choosing

Museum collections have long held a peculiar fascination for me, as an artist. Since I began my career, I have always had a particular set of preferences about different kinds of museums, and about how museums display their holdings. In particular, I have always enjoyed visiting museums whose permanent collections leave as much to the imagination as possible and present the visitor with as little text as possible about particular objects, allowing each individual to begin to form their own impression of what something is and was, and why it was first brought into being, and why it is here in front of them now. Textbooks can impart information better than any other medium; where museums have a distinct advantage as a medium is that they can spark curiosity and inquisitiveness and allow the imagination to grapple with objects. The fewer explicit directions that museums provide the better, up to a point, for an artist. When excessively directed, our imagination can in effect only run along particular pre-existing pathways: one of the very purposes of museums is to invite people to think in ways other than in straight lines. In almost every other aspect of life, instrumental reason guides people towards clearly defined objectives, mostly shaped by self-interest. Museums are one of the very few spaces where we can really experience 'things'—not in a plainly 'disinterested' way, as it used to be called, but in a way where our own imaginative faculties have to work hard in order to find a way around an object or a way 'into' it. Museums offer so much precisely because objects are themselves inexhaustible in so many regards.

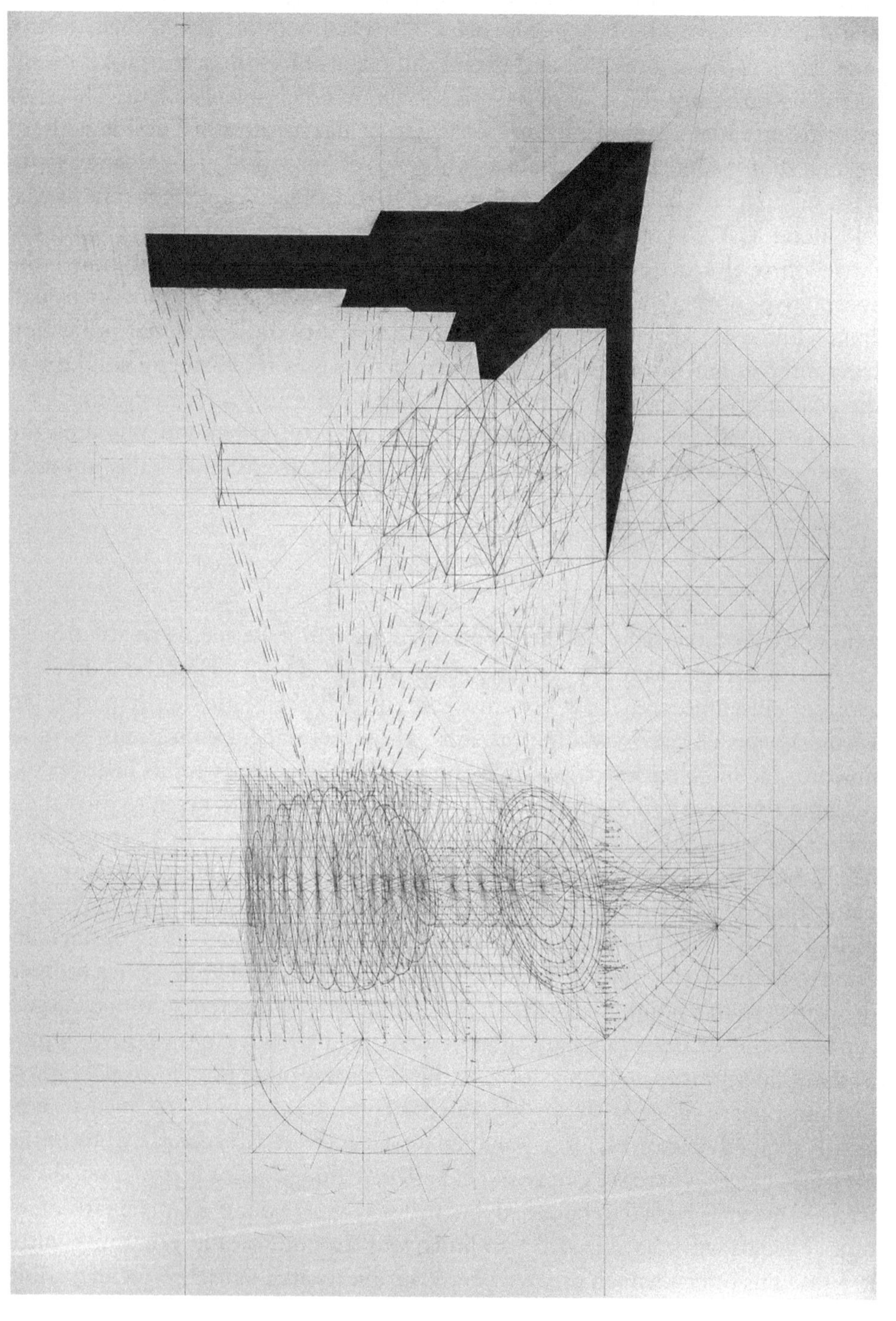

FIGURE 10.1. Richard Talbot: *Point, Line, Plane, Solid* (2017). Pencil on paper.

That approach is, no doubt, a result of being an artist rather than a scientist; the cliché that retains some force is that for the latter the goal is always the finding of answers and solutions to problems, whereas for artists, the focus is in generating questions, and the actual process of the search itself is the objective. My fascination with the lives of objects also comes from the starting point of having a fundamental interest in the forms rather than the functions of objects: in what they are in themselves, or for themselves (rather than what they can do for us). In the main, what they can do is well established and already known, or better known by other professions than artists. Creating artworks provides one means of thinking about material objects, which as a method often consists of finding or creating connections between them. All objects, as things in the material world among others, have particular forms and shapes—often defined by their functions, admittedly, but not always. To paraphrase Denise Scott Brown and Robert Venturi, there are contradictions and complexities in almost every type of object, whether organic or human-made; and whether animal, mineral or vegetable. Probably the only type of object in which form and function are the same, inseparable and able to be read from one another are crystals. Everything else, including ourselves, include or allow for complexities. As an artist, my analysis of objects is not strictly morphological; therefore, though I do not want to burden it with the label 'relational': but through their forms, things can and do begin to relate to others. Viewing things only through their functions condemns the analyst to only see that object of investigation in relation to their own prior categories; imaginative leaps are implicitly prohibited. Moreover, few objects are in reality mono-functional. A functionalist analytical frame risks not only prescribing what relationships objects can or should have, but what state of being they can occupy. Art is, perhaps, the single academic realm in which other forms of logic can begin to apply, and other forms of relation be brought to the imagination.

Unpicking

In 2017 I was invited to create a work as part of an exhibition entitled, *A Scientific Encounter: On Inter-objectivity*, which examined how we see the world through scientific objects and how these objects may be seen to act on us as viewers. At that moment the methods by which we might start to understand objects, and collections of objects amassed over centuries whose relationships are often prosaic or by definition delimited, were paramount in my mind. The invitation to create a new work allowed for a spirit of enquiry in relation to the collections at Montpellier, and I was allowed free access to objects from across the university's vast archives, libraries and reserve collections. The risk inherent in that offer, as

I suspect every other artist would say, is that an artwork can itself appear under-whelming in comparison to a museum and its extravagant contents. The question of what an artist can do, in the face of millions of objects accumulated over centuries, pressed upon me, as it did with the other participants. What any one artist can do may look meek or insubstantial, at least in relation to the curiosity that millions of assembled objects can pique. Accordingly, when I came to making this new work, I determined that my approach should be to enter into a spirit of what might be called free association between artefacts across two and three dimensions. Or rather, that I should examine objects both real and imagined, that are tools and that are represented, and draw together things that had not cohabited or intermingled to date, and which range across collections of scientific apparatus and published treatises. In particular, the treatises upon perspectival drawing that the library owns, which date back to the Renaissance, are some of the finest preserved copies in the world. But they live separate lives to examples of the equipment often depicted in them, being confined to the library, and only exhibited on special occasions because of their fragility or to limit their exposure to natural light. There is an anecdote that I have not been able to verify that exemplifies what my approach attempts to achieve. When the Museum of Modern Art in New York set to work to accession an early work by the conceptual artist Joseph Kosuth's from the late 1960s, the museum and the artwork failed signally to have a meeting of minds. The work famously juxtaposed a real chair with a photograph of a chair, and a dictionary definition of the concept 'chair' printed as text. The three objects were, at their point of accession, originally destined to be separated and sent to three separate departments—sculpture, print and photograph—where the different bodies of expertise about them lay. Museums, in other words, can contain a world of knowledge through their objects, or else exemplify how 'knowledge', shaped by institutional logics, separates rather than connects. The will to disaggregate that lies at the heart of what we, very loosely, might called the orthodox scientific project, is not the only method of knowledge production. Interestingly, in Joseph Kosuth's work 'Un'Osservazione Grammaticale. Modus Operandi' (1986–96), the work 'is alluding to the possibility of art to be both a mental experience and a modus operandi. It is understood as a model of intellectual reflection that critically redefines the sphere of our thoughts'.[3] Similarly, the making of a work from a scientific collection is both an intellectual and practical pursuit; a process of choosing, unpicking and connecting.

The creation of a work to be seen in a museum—and a museum associated with scientific endeavour at that—drew me back to my formative experience of working with museums, at the Horniman Museum in London in the late 1970s, when still a student. I still vividly recall the encounter with that museum some 40 years later, and it informed my approach to working with the university's collections.

The Horniman then exemplified many of the tendencies I have just outlined, and it fostered a particular attitude—a commitment to speculative enquiry about the very nature of objects—that defines my work to this day. On entering a museum, I prefer not to go out of my way to glean information about particular objects, but prefer the serendipity and sense of discovery they engender. The Horniman, of all the museums in England, seemed to me to be special in its commitment to making connections between things that were not ordinarily connected, either in academic or everyday life. The approach that I had adopted when working in the Horniman seemed equally appropriate when being introduced to other diverse collections. Selecting an object or objects to present alongside my own work, which was the second half of the brief, proved relatively painless (Fig. 10.2). Montpellier's collections include a wealth of artefacts that relate directly to my interests in the histories of drawing, of the invention and uses of perspective, and in the relationship between scientific endeavour and the artistic imagination.

I want to dwell upon the experience that I remember the Horniman Museum as allowing for a moment. In its previous incarnation at least, it seems almost to be a

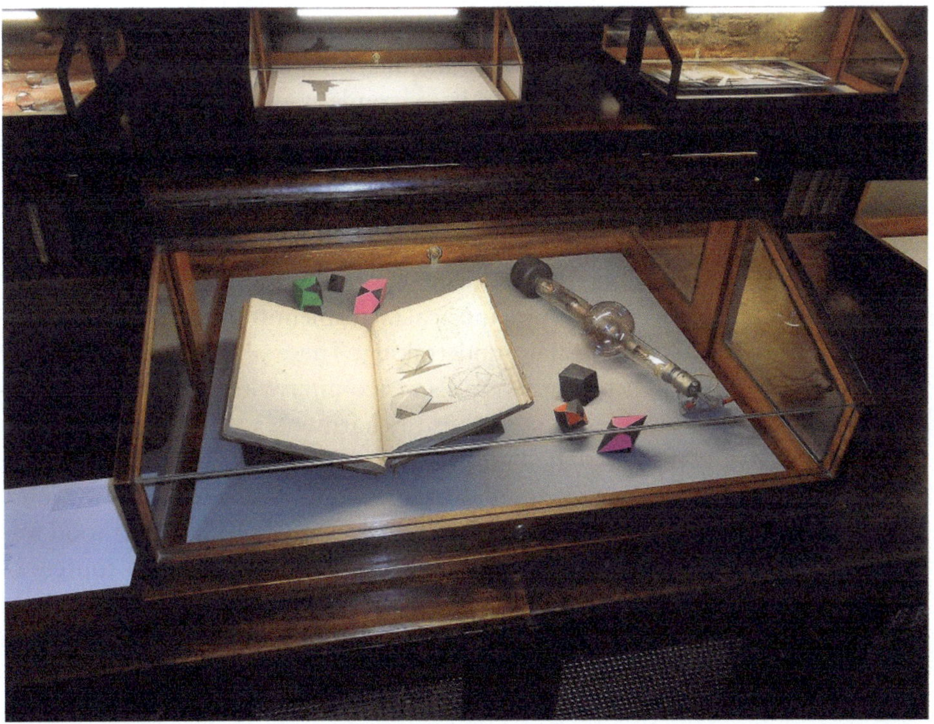

FIGURE 10.2. Cabinet containing chosen objects from museum collections, with finished drawing in background. Université de Montpellier, Faculté de Médecine, Montpellier 2017.

museum that an artist might have designed or curated in its range of interests, in its diversity, its commitment to finding inspiration in anything and everything, from anywhere in the world. Some 40 years ago it also provided me with an example of how an artist starts to think 'with' a microcosmic 'world of things', rather than merely 'about' it. The distinction is, I think, important. A generation ago, its approach was to present objects with the absolute minimum of information, animating them in part through a particular rhetoric of display but mainly through the sheer unexpectedness of what one might find the museum contains an extraordinarily eclectic mix of things. Of course, we now recognize that when objects are entirely shorn of an anthropological context, a museum could be described as presenting 'the world as sculpture'[4] and thus reducing it to 'pure' form. But in the Horniman Museum, two things were notable. First, 'functional' objects were presented alongside artworks (put another way, utilitarian objects were adjacent to ones with more symbolic functions). Second, objects that were culturally familiar, and those that were culturally distant for the majority of the audience were placed together. Figures like Michael Baxandall have long argued that such juxtapositions between different cultures in exhibitions and museums are essential to stretch our imaginative empathy, and to keep prompting visitors to pose questions to objects.[5] At its best such an approach encourages a spirit of extended curiosity: we do not find 'answers' about objects, as though definitive answers about objects could exist, but are asked to keep probing, to keep wondering.

In Montpellier, there was one three-dimensional object that affected me in particular, and in part it struck me with such force precisely because it recalled an object from the Horniman, albeit one with a different function. The object was a glass X-ray tube that recalled a 'glass harmonica' in the Horniman: a series of concentric glass dishes or bowls that are on a central spindle that spins to create different sounds and tones. Making a musical instrument from glass, of all materials, seemed to be an extraordinary undertaking. These object encounters were intensely memorable: that I should recall an encounter with an object four decades later seemed utterly improbable, but the harmonica was imprinted in my memory, and vividly recalled. The shapes of both objects were, on first encounter, mesmerizing. Both caught my attention in part as they could be related to my interests in perspective and scale. In the 1970s, my understanding of objecthood was of course naïve and rudimentary; but my experience of museums as sources of inspiration was founded in such discoveries and in the intuitive sense that I could connect disparate things together. I began to see the project as an opportunity to complete a kind of 'unfinished business' around a particular drawing known as the 'Chalice', about which I had previously undertaken a very detailed study four decades earlier.[6] This sentiment was reinforced through finding in the library a classic work of seventeenth-century perspectival theory by Jean François Niceron. This discovery chimed with my particular fascination for these text books, which set out to demonstrate the principles and axioms of geometry, of optics, and of their applications to the theory and practice of depiction using linear perspective. The reality for me is that the drawings in these books are undoubtedly more exciting than their intended pedagogical purpose.

Connecting

I began *Point, Line, Plane, Solid* by planning to create a drawing based on the X-ray tube in the university's collection of scientific apparatus. As well as recalling other object encounters, the form of the X-ray tube also initially reminded me of the shape delineated in one of the most famous drawings of the early Renaissance. The attribution of this drawing (Fig. 10.3), is still disputed but is most commonly attributed to Paulo Uccello or Piero della Francesca and dated around 1450. It is a 'wireframe' drawing of a chalice made in perspectival linear construction, and is actually physically as well as conceptually extraordinary: it is barely 'drawn' at all in the orthodox sense. It is also small, but exerts an unusual power. When we now see it in reproduction, we usually only see it through a photograph made in the early twentieth century, which was taken under a raking light. Any ordinary photograph would show an almost blank sheet of paper, with incisions that are scarcely visible rather than bold graphite marks. The sheet of paper itself essentially looks blank to the naked eye. The photograph is able to reveal the construction lines of the drawing that are actually scored into the paper. There are scholars who argue that this is a merely a preparatory drawing because there are pinpricks in it which are elsewhere used to plot outlines from onto a finished composition or painting. My own view is that they must have been using a compass and a pair of dividers. Those pinpricks are from the sheer precision needed to make this extraordinary drawing. The drawing is much cleverer than that. At the outset of making *Point, Line, Plane, Solid*, I was interested in setting this up a similar pictorial scenario. To create the Renaissance drawing, light was essential in two senses to draw the object. There is light in the system of the perspective used and the fact that the artist must have seen it under raking light to make it. For the exhibition itself, I chose a trio of objects to display alongside my own work. One of these was a collection of crystals that are Platonic solids—that is, ideal forms. These, of course, are central both to scientific endeavour at every level and across physics, chemistry and biology, and to the origin story of modern art that runs through Cézanne and analytical cubism.

I imagined making *Point, Line, Plane, Solid* as a form of unfinished business because I had for so long imagined making a drawing constructed in a similar way

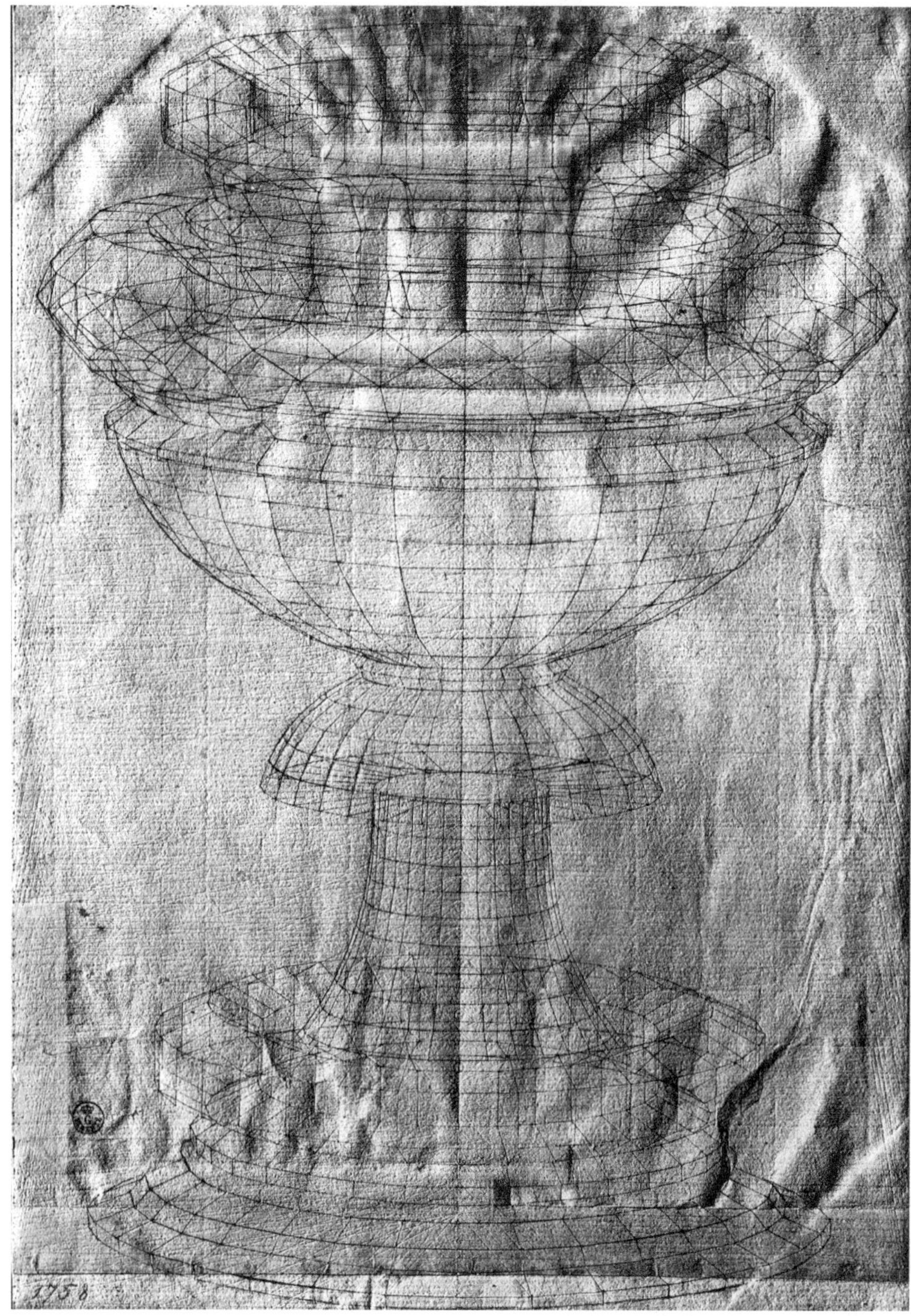

FIGURE 10.3. *Perspective Study of a Chalice*, 1430–40? Attributed to Paolo Uccello, (1397–1475). Gabinetto dei Disegni e Stampe, Uffizi, Florence, Italy, Alinari/Bridgeman Images.

to Uccello or Piero's but never undertaken it. So this seemed like an opportune moment to begin that adventure: to put myself to the test. When I first tried it, it proved almost impossible to recreate such a technique some six centuries after it was first pioneered. I could well imagine, at least in theory, how this drawing had been made; how one could reverse-engineer it, as it were. I had envisaged the entire scenario needed to create it, which would most importantly have required the right lighting conditions, including a strong directional light, such that the artist was probably sat by a window. Indeed I recognized that they would only be able to make a drawing that way for a few hours at each sitting, as the light changed over the course of the day. In the end, I went back to pencil construction rather than only dividers, but still hoped to follow Uccello or Piero in my degree of precision. In particular, I committed to dividing the tube into 32 separate segments, which exponentially increased the technicalities of building a 'wireframe' that could accuracy describe it in perspective. Dividing the object into 4 or 8 sections is relatively straightforward; the level of accuracy needed when it reaches 32 sections is simply much more taxing, more exacting (Fig. 10.4). Making a drawing like this is almost a feat of attentiveness and concentration. In such a drawing the viewer is free to roam across the entire 'frame' of the object, rather than being concentrated upon a particular passage or two. The spread of attention across the page requires of the artist that every mark, every pressure exerted upon the paper needs to be even. You need to avoid muddying the drawing; that is the first criterion. That can only be achieved by sustaining a perfectly light touch throughout: consistency of touch is crucial.

Such drawings are at one level architectural as much as sculptural, or can be described as such. It is a work of construction. In the actual process of making, I have to respond to the contingencies generated by the process of construction. This almost invariably results in things that are extraneous or accidental being generated and incorporated into the finished work. This is, of course, the case with architectural design and building. No building ever matches a drawn design, as though there was no materials involved, and no labour, no happenstance, no process of discovery or adaptation in the making itself.

In the instance of *Point, Line, Plane, Solid* the emphasis that ended up being laid upon the central column of the imagined object caused other complications to come into play. Nevertheless, 'my' column remains still very similar to that of the glass object itself, in the end. But the other two elements in the drawing were generated by it, and came about also as other kinds of unfinished business from other, earlier works and ideas. In particular, the work became a way to continue my preoccupation with shadows in relation to perspectival construction. My understanding of shadows also relates to notions of Plato's cave: that is, of never being able to fully know the nature of objects or artefacts, of them always

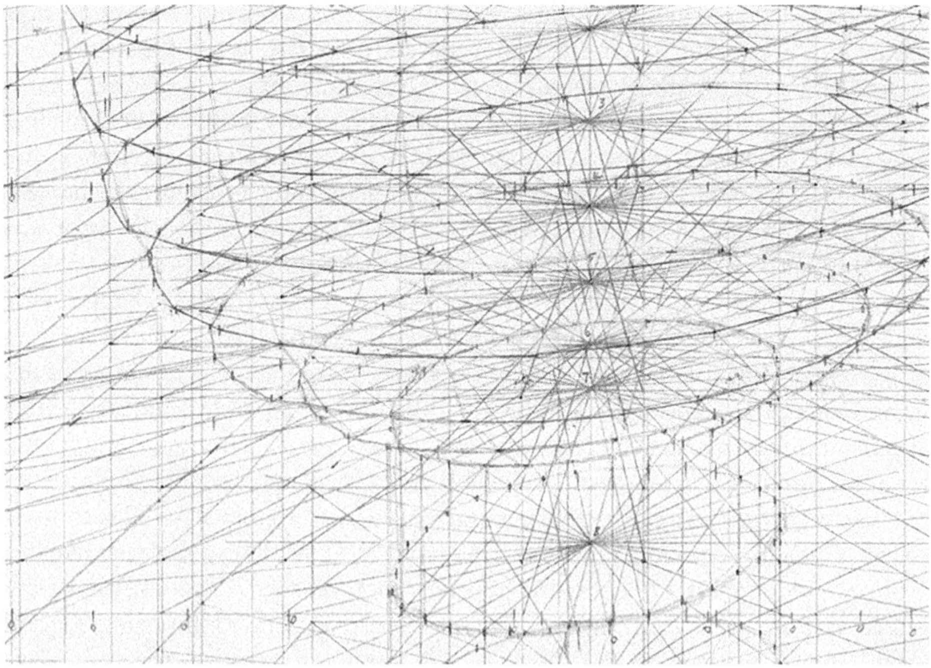

FIGURE 10.4. Detail from *Point, Line, Plane, Solid* (2017).

being partially occluded, unknown, or unknowable. One might say that, following Graham Harman's work in particular, those ideas have come back into focus in new ways.

The title of the drawing, *Point, Line, Plane, Solid,* is important of course: it alludes to ideas about how things can be known mathematically by studying how they move through space, rather than being known as merely static Platonic objects. One implication contained within the drawing is that one 'object' might be the shadow of another; a shadow is not ordinarily considered an 'object' in and of itself, but from a scientific point of view that is exactly what it is. The shadow sits on the right of the sheet, in an ambiguous relation to the tube, but with the most likely probability being that it is the tube's shadow cast from left to right, such that the light source must be from the left. My preoccupation with shadows also arises from the idea that they are seen as a kind of 'projection' of one object, instead of an object in and of itself. The idea of objects 'projecting' into the world is crucial to the idea of perspective. So I wanted to suggest a link between the different projections—perspective really is fundamentally a projection. One the one hand there are the 'projections' that X-rays make (X-rays 'send out' rays that see 'through' solid objects in space); and the 'projection' of the tube through its shadow. I want there to be something of a circular connection between the iconography, the process of production of the drawing itself, and ideas of mathematics about four-dimensional objects in space, such that they all touch one another or are interconnected. This, I hope, should be a subtle relation rather than a didactic one, but still present (Fig. 10.5).

Creating *Point, Line, Plane, Solid* also allowed me to think about what we might call the 'reversibility' of perspective, in the history of perspectival drawings. The orthodox description of such drawings is that the world inside the picture plane is 'projected' outwards from the picture into 'our' world towards the viewer, as though the perspectival lines would surround you and meet your gaze. In this descriptive model, the starting point is the picture, and the viewer is a kind of recipient of its information, where they become enveloped into the geometry of the artwork, into the internal system it creates. It is a model where the artwork 'projects' out into the world and into your eye. This is counter-intuitive, though.

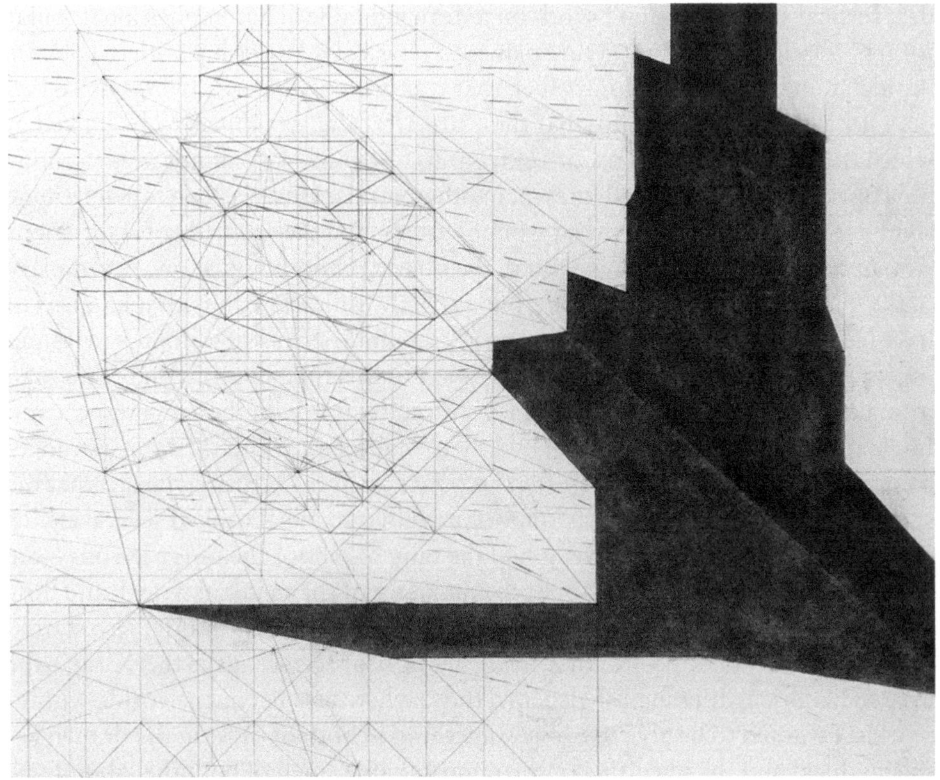

FIGURE 10.5. Detail from *Point, Line, Plane, Solid* (2017).

I have a sense that reversing that equation allows for a more productive form of description.

It was once thought that light emerged in lines 'out' of your eye towards an object to know it and to retrieve information. 'Modern' science has established that light waves hit our eye from without, of course. The two conceptions of how light and vision works—intro-mission and extro-mission—both have their merits and truths. The latter is perhaps more intuitively and psychologically enticing and satisfying: the idea of an object being drawn into us, becoming appropriated by us visually, pulled into our eyes. The way we talk about visual experience is through metaphors such as that we 'attach our gaze' to objects, or that objects 'catch our eye' and 'catch our attention'. I am making drawings with an awareness of these ambiguities—these tensions between the scientific explanation and the lived—experience, as a backdrop.

Relatedly, when visiting the collections at Montpellier I was graphically reminded that museums expect or demand particular types of specifically visual attention; but also that people subvert that or swerve around that demand upon them, and bring their own, unexpected types of attention. I ordinarily work on a flat, vertical surface—I don't work on a drawing table. That implies a particular form of relationship to the picture plane—a physical relationship with the objects 'inside' it. In the cases in Montpellier, that was not possible—drawings presented on a horizontal surface imply that these are artefacts, are things to be looked at which do not look back at us, or confront us as equals. We cannot predetermine how our objects are seen and known, in other words. However, we can determine some aspects of the framing of our work as artists, and the spectrum of associations we can bring into play. For one thing, the object I choose was at once exemplary of the 'progress' of modern science, but a strictly utilitarian thing that happens to have its own strangeness and own beauty, presented here as a Duchampian 'found object'. I have, I suspect, paid more attention to this tube than anyone other than its maker has (or even more). I wanted both to treat it with the same respect and fascination as Piero or Uccello treated their chalice; and with the same estrangement and slyness as Duchamp treated his *objets trouvés*. Actually, the fact that the starting point was glass was very important in that to me; it evoked several chains of associations. In my own case, it had the tang of school chemistry lessons—the point where we start to learn about the make-up of the material world, and how all of the things we encounter in it are actually made and built. And it also started to speak about its opposite, that is, alchemical processes, as it the X-ray tube evoked historical drawings of alchemy, those where we encounter worlds-within-worlds. I wanted to be able to evoke something of both of those in the drawing—the mythical and the scientific, or the unmistakable smell of both the laboratory, and something of the witching hour when all is possible, and imagination rules.

Nevertheless, I don't want my drawing to be seen as a mere fantasy. The precision of the technique and the solidity of the object should indicate that it is a 'real' structure. It is, in art historical parlance, a 'figure'; what is intentionally left more ambiguous is the 'ground' upon which it is set. Much is left to the imagination there. If we can deduce anything, it is that the space within the picture is not only a shallow, but also a tactile space, and not a deep perspectival space as a landscape would have. There is, for example, no horizon line: there is a figure not quite without a ground, but the ground is left for the viewer to shape or interpret for themselves, and be guided by the shape of the shadow. Only the shadow suggests any end to the space: it marks an otherwise invisible enclosing wall that terminates the space rather than leaves it infinite or illimitable. This, then, is the space of a still-life painting, in effect. I wanted the process of making the drawing to be like building a sculpture within a shallow space. I have long been fascinated by Spanish seventeenth-century still-lives, where objects are intensely illuminated, and constructed with exquisite care within a small, shallow, box-like illusionistic space, which if made explicit might almost be theatrical, but to be successful needs to be almost clinical in the precision of its construction.

Although the construction of the tube and shadow are indeed meticulous, as with all drawings, contingencies are involved, and the actual production process determines what one ends up creating. I had initially imagined the shadow of the vessel as falling flat across a horizontal plane; that seemed the most natural thing to do. In the end, the sheet of paper I was working on was simply not large enough to contain the whole shadow cast by the object in the way I had initially imagined it. The size of the sheet was predetermined by its intended display conditions inside a vitrine, so another solution had to be found to incorporate it within the sheet as a single entity. I was forced to 'invent' an imagined, unseen wall for it to fall against. That also seemed to be a solution of how I could both offer a sense of a very particular space—almost mimicking or paying tribute or homage to the framing box found in Juan Sanchez Cotan's paintings (Fig. 10.6). Norman Bryson describes, in terms which have resonance for my practice, Cotan's methodical images as emphasizing the visual above the tactile:

> That bodily or tactile space is profoundly unvisual: the things we find there are things we reach for—a knife, a plate, a bit of food—instinctively and almost without looking. It is this space, the true home of blurred and hazy vision that Cotan's rigours aim to abolish.[7]

Cotan's use of a 'shallow space' as opposed to a 'deep space' holds significance for me, as in the relations struck between visual and haptic, thinness and depth are embedded notions of scientific truth and objectivity (as well as their opposites)

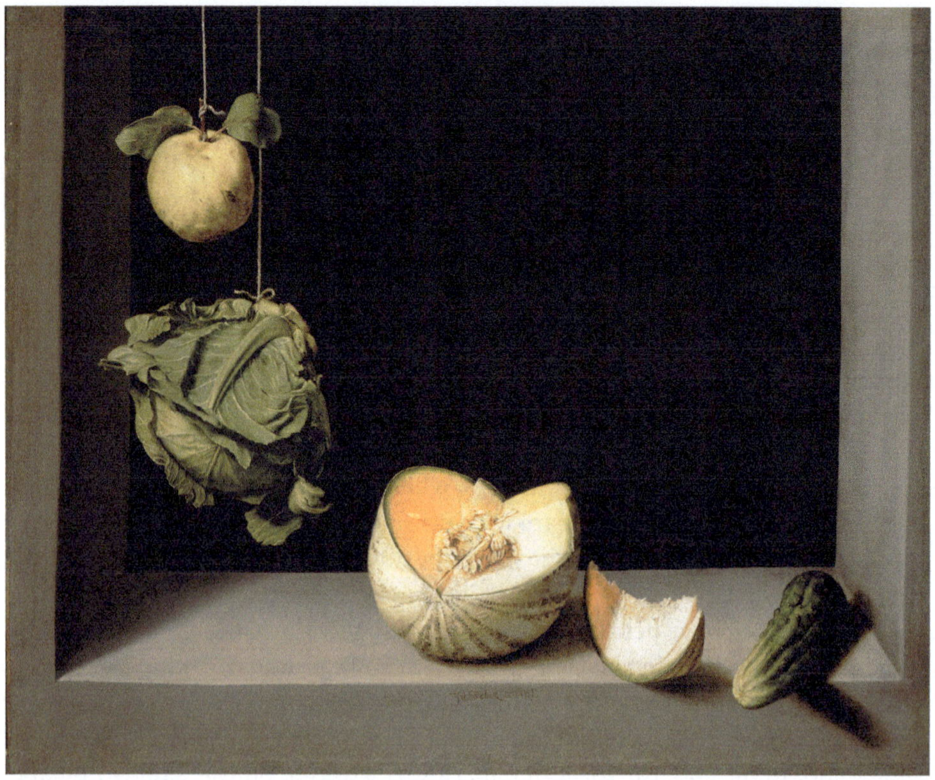

FIGURE 10.6. Juan Sanchez Cotan: *Still Life with Quince, Cabbage, Melon, and Cucumber.* c. 1602. San Diego Museum of Art. Gift of Anne R. and Amy Putnam Bridgeman Images.

which can be interrogated in an artwork through optical devices and equivalents such as orthographic projection (plans and elevations), illusion, occlusion, shade and shadow.

What you can do with perspective as an artist is, in some ways limited, but what we might call the paraphernalia—the apparatus around perspective—is amazing. The drawings generated in order to explore the consequences of perspective as a system, and a kind a logic, are fascinating to me. In particular, some of the eighteenth-century perspectival treatises illustrate the play of light and shadow in quite extraordinary ways—they are quite clearly constructions of a very special complexity. I am still astounded by their visual clarity and clarity of purpose. There might be seen to be some legacies of the interest in geometry and systems in twentieth-century art—that is, across geometric abstraction, systems art and in constructivism. Originally having studied astronomy and physics at university, as a young artist I had some interest in these areas—partly from having discursive conversations with Peter Lowe,[8] who had been a student of the leading constructivist Kenneth Martin. While drawn to it in some ways—particularly the unfolding of an internal logic within a painting or relief, I also couldn't accept that geometry itself could hold meaning other than in a symbolic way. As a student, I was exposed to, and was drawn to and very inquisitive about quite wide-ranging practices, including Arte Povera and Fluxus. At that time, I also began looking at medieval art as much as modern art, where forms of spatial play seemed more adventurous and much richer immediately prior to the invention and codification of single-point perspective, in part because overt illusion was not the central objective. This attitude around art practice, and what it draws on, perhaps personifies my 'anachronistic' approach and a sense of being part of a continuum of art making and enquiry.[9] My aim, in other words, is to make use of materials— conceptual materials, ideas, techniques, processes—that are slightly overlooked in contemporary practice, but which are nevertheless thoroughly contemporary concerns. Those materials, hopefully, allow me to generate other questions that are not being posed elsewhere; to create other lines of enquiry which have not yet been exhausted or where they are few present-day parallels. I see my practice as existing in a liminal area, as it were, and as referring to things that could exist, but which float in an 'in-between space', both literally and figuratively. The illusionistic space in which objects exists is an in-between one, defined but almost opaque. And the position which my practice occupies is at a tangent to, or between those that might expect or predict of my medium or mode of working. I see my methods as at one level related to Duchamp's, again perhaps in unexpected ways, as one of unpicking things. And at another it is centred upon making novel connections, upon alternative forms of pattern formation, at a conceptual level. Put another way, in creating works like *Point, Line, Plane, Solid,* I create a system, or logic, to generate it, but am also characteristically anarchic within that logic even while keeping within the inner truth of that logic. When the logic as here relates to the idea and practice of perspective, it must necessarily be a self-contained logic: perspective is an invented system with its own procedures, own protocols and limitations. And yet, the process of creation involved in making any artwork can allow that work in its final shape to connect to experiences of various kinds, which stand quite outside of that logic. Those twinned methods, of system-building and of anarchy within a system; and of unpicking and reconnecting, are what excite me as an artist.

NOTES

1. La Perspective curieuse, ou magie artificiele des effets merveilleux de l'optique, par la vision directe, la catoptrique, par la reflexion des miroires plats, cylindriques & coniques, la

dioptrique, par la refraction des crystaux [...]. par le P. F. Jean-François Niceron. Nicéron, Jean François (1613–1646); Billaine, Pierre (15..-1639); 1638.

2. This is an area well-trodden—first by nineteenth-century mathematicians and the likes of Charles Howard Hinton, and later E. A. Abbott's Flatland. Its impact on twentieth-century art is discussed in Dalrymple-Henderson's The Fourth Dimension and Non-Euclidean geometry in Modern Art, Princeton University Press (1983). Rene Daumal's *Mount Analogue: A Novel of Symbolically Authentic Non-Euclidean Adventures in Mountain Climbing*, also grapples with the imaginative possibilities.

3. Joseph Kosuth, 'Un'Osservazione Grammaticale. Modus Operandi' (Naples: Madre Museum, 1986–96).

4. James Hall, *The World as Sculpture* (London: Chatto and Windus, 1999).

5. Michael Baxandall, *Painting and Experience in Fifteenth-Century Italy: A Primer in the Social History of Pictorial Style* (Oxford: Oxford University Press, 1988).

6. Richard Talbot, 'Design and Perspective Construction: Why is the Chalice the Shape It Is?', in *Nexus VI: Architecture and Mathematics,* ed. Sylvie Duvernoy and Orietta Pedemonte (Turin: Kim Williams Books, 2006), 121–34.

7. Norman Bryson, *Looking at the Overlooked* (London: Reaktion Books, 1995).

8. https://www.tate.org.uk/art/artists/peter-lowe-1530 (accessed 4 May 2020).

9. Alexander Nagel, *Medieval Modern: Art Out of Time* (London: Thames and Hudson, 2012).

REFERENCES

Baxandall, Michael. *Painting and Experience in Fifteenth-Century Italy: A Primer in the Social History of Pictorial Style.* Oxford: Oxford University Press, 1988.

Bryson, Norman. *Looking at the Overlooked.* London: Reaktion Books, 1995.

Hall, J. *The World as Sculpture.* London: Chatto and Windus, 1999.

Kosuth, Joseph. '"Un"osservazione Grammaticale: Modus Operandi'. Naples: Madre Museum, 1986–96.

Nagel, Alexander. *Medieval Modern: Art Out of Time.* London: Thames and Hudson, 2012.

Richard Talbot, "Design and perspective construction: Why is the Chalice the shape it is?". In *Nexus VI: Architecture and Mathematics,* eds. Sylvie Duvernoy and Orietta Pedemonte, 121–34. Turin: Kim Williams Books, 2006.

11

Post-Specimens and Present Ancestors: Passing Fables & Comparative Readings at The Wildgoose Memorial Library—An Artist's Response to the 'Unique Status' of Post-Colonial Human Remains in Museums

Jane Wildgoose

Abstract

In 2007 the remains of an adult male Tasmanian, with many skeletal elements present, which had for many years been referred to as the specimen PA HR 590, was returned to Tasmania from the Natural History Museum in London (NHM) together with osteological fragments from 16 other individuals, most of which consisted of teeth and crania.[1] This chapter describes my first encounter with the skeleton known as PA HR 590, in documentation at the NHM concerning a claim from the Tasmanian Aboriginal Centre (TAC) for its repatriation, when I was commissioned as resident artist/consultant, to write a report on the human remains collection at the museum. It reveals how the skeleton was first acquired from a grave on Flinders Island during British colonial settlement in the 1870s, and reflects on the impact that learning about this context from the submission accompanying the TAC's claim for repatriation would have on my practice as an artist. It also presents an account of how I subsequently developed a new archive of my own collection, The Wildgoose Memorial Library (WML), as a means of presenting evidence of the historical circumstances in which human remains were procured for museums from countries under British rule during the colonial era. In conclusion, it reflects on public response to the WML archive, and the new artwork I devised to accompany it: which commemorates the lives of ancestors whose remains were acquired in great numbers, in order to provide data for theories of the so-called races of mankind in metropolitan museums during the late nineteenth and early twentieth centuries.

Human remains have a unique status within museum collections. They have the potential to make a contribution to the public good, through research, teaching and, in appropriate cases, display. In many instances, they also have a personal, cultural, symbolic, spiritual or religious significance to individuals and, or, groups. This places a special responsibility on those museums that hold them.[2]

In 2006, I was commissioned as resident artist/consultant to write a report on the human remains collection at the Natural History Museum (NHM) in London. As an artist with a track record for engaging with the history of collecting and the representation and display of the dead, especially in a medical context, I was no stranger to the discussion about the dead and their dismemberment. But despite my previous experience I would find myself little prepared for what I would learn during the course of my research for the report. This chapter offers an account of the profound impression that my research into the human remains collection at the NHM would have on me. It discusses how the evidence I encountered at the museum would lead me to reflect deeply on my perception of the foundations of knowledge concerning the human body on which some of our most respected museums are established, and concludes with an account of how I would go on to develop my practice as an artist as a means of communicating the discoveries I made to the public.

Some Background Information about My Practice as an Artist

During the 1990s I contributed to public debate about the arrest and imprisonment of the artist Anthony-Noel Kelly, who took anatomical specimens from the Royal College of Surgeons of England, which he cast in plaster and gilded. I published a number of articles in the press contextualizing Kelly's practice (and his misdemeanour) within the wider historical context of the routine objectification of the dead by artists and anatomists working with human remains.[3] In collaboration with the medical historian Ruth Richardson,[4] I subsequently co-convened a multidisciplinary conference considering access to, and display of, the dead human body in light of the public scandal surrounding the retention, without parental consent, of the organs of children who died at Bristol Royal Infirmary and Liverpool's Alder Hey Hospital.[5]

At that time, I had for some years been developing my own collection of objects, photographs, documents and books dedicated to mortality and remembrance, which would become known as The Wildgoose Memorial

Library (WML).[6] Deliberately naming the collection a library (rather than a museum), I was interested in combining historical research with a close 'reading' of the narratives and associations that may become attached to remains of all kinds. Inspired by Lewis Hyde's analysis of the trickster-artist's capacity to 'move between the living and the dead'—and taking my lead from Marcel Proust's observation that '[t]he past is hidden somewhere outside the realm, beyond the reach of intellect, in some material object (in the sensation which that material object will give us)'[7]—my collecting policy for the library focused on 'the capacity of an object to resonate with the viewer's imagination through its appeal to the senses, and to evoke memories and emotional associations'.[8]

Developing the work of the library for presentation in the public domain for the first time in 2003, I co-devised a BBC Radio programme about a wisp of Horatio Nelson's hair bought on eBay, reflecting on the stories it might tell and the responsibilities of possessing it.[9] From 2005 to 2006 I used the WML collection as a studio setting in which to photograph and interview people talking about items of personal significance to them: exploring the deep connections that become established with objects and the ways in which they may be associated with relationships with others (both living and dead), and with perceptions of personal and cultural identity and continuity.[10]

It was as a result of this combination of specialist aspects of my research and practice that I was commissioned by the NHM's Curator of Contemporary Art, Bergit Arends and Head of Special Projects and Innovation, Bob Bloomfield to spend three weeks developing a report on the human remains collection at the museum. My research for the report coincided with—but was otherwise independent from—the work of the Human Remains Advisory Panel that advised the museum's trustees about a claim made by the Tasmanian Aboriginal Centre (TAC) for the return to their home country of the remains of 17 Tasmanian people in the museum's collection.[11]

Some Context for the TAC's Claim for Repatriation of Human Remains from the NHM's Collection

When I was commissioned to write the report on the human remains collection at the NHM, the TAC had been campaigning for 'return of all ancestral remains from all museums and institutions worldwide' for over 20 years and from the NHM in London 'consistently since 1985'.[12] In their Submission to the Museum concerning their claim for repatriation, the TAC welcomed the 'opportunity to recommend [...] appropriate ways to implement the intention' of a joint press statement made by the UK Prime Minister Tony Blair and the Australian Prime Minister John Howard in July 2000, to '*"endorse the repatriation of indigenous human remains wherever possible (and appropriate) from both public and private collections"* of British Museums'.[13]

The prime ministers' joint public statement had emerged against a background of wider developments internationally during the latter part of the twentieth century, in response to claims from Aboriginal and Indigenous peoples from around the world for the return of their ancestors' remains from museums. These efforts had been met with varying degrees of dispute and resistance from the museum sector,[14] but there was a 'significant' development in 1989,[15] when the World Archaeological Congress adopted the Vermillion Accord on Human Remains and recognized 'that the concerns of various ethnic groups, as well as those of science are legitimate and to be respected'.[16] In 1990 the Native American Graves Protection and Repatriation Act (NAGPRA) was introduced in the United States and in 2000 a special Repatriation Unit was established in the National Museum of Australia.[17] In 2001 the International Council of Museums published a revised Code of Professional Ethics, which included guidance concerning both human remains and 'material of sacred significance'.[18]

As a result of the prime ministers' joint statement, the UK Government set up a Working Group on Human Remains, which invited and received submissions from a range of interested parties within and beyond the UK. A scoping survey was undertaken in order to determine the number and distribution of human remains in collections and when the working group reported in 2003, it found there were 'at least 61,000 human remains' housed in museums in England, with 'collections of over 500 items [...] held by 25 institutions'.[19]

Some idea of the overall scope and significance of the NHM's collection at that time may be gauged from information on the museum's website today, where the published number of human remains in its collection is largely consistent with that at the time of the Working Party's Report. According to the NHM's website, the museum's 'human comparative collection is one of the largest collections of human remains in the UK, comprising around 25,000 individuals and representing a worldwide distribution of the human population'. Of those, 'around half of the remains originate from archaeological excavations in the British Isles' while the other half (i.e. the remains of some 10,000 individuals) were obtained 'from over 50 countries, covering all of the inhabited continents'.[20]

My brief for the report for the NHM invited investigation into the content and care of human remains in the museum's collection and their public display, together with a consideration of attitudes to and perceptions of death in Western culture, all of which I intended to view through the 'lens' of my role as Keeper of the WML. From the outset I was informed that, as an artist, I would not be eligible to view any part of the human remains collection as access is restricted to accredited scientists working on approved research projects. With my capacity for *viewing* the collection withheld, I found myself *listening* very attentively to the information that was revealed during my research. As a result, I began thinking about exploring methods for presenting archival evidence in ways that would allow it to 'speak' for itself, as it would speak so vitally to me when I first encountered it.

What I discovered during the research at the NHM would at first leave me puzzled, then shocked and profoundly angered. As a result of my response to my discoveries in the archives, my practice as an artist—and my outlook on the history of collecting—would be substantially changed. What began as intellectual and artistic curiosity would turn, virtually overnight, into an awakening political purpose: to engage the public with an aspect of collecting for museums in the past, and the foundations of knowledge on which they are built, which continue to cast a very long shadow in the present.

At the Natural History Museum, London, 21 November 2006

On the morning of 21 November 2006, I sat in the library at the NHM in London, checking through a database printout: listing the museum's collection of 450 human remains from Australia and the Torres Strait Islands. I was searching for documentation, concerning the bones of 17 people from Tasmania who were the subject of a claim for return to their home country from the TAC.

By midday I had located all 17 of the individuals, whose surviving bones had been classified by the museum as PA HR 590, 'an adult male [...] with many skeletal elements present' and PA HR 332, 334, 335, 337, 338, 340–345, 412, 593, 594, 598 and 604: 'the majority' of which consisted of 'teeth and crania'.[21]

I was puzzled to learn that the majority of the remains consisted of no more than skulls, jaws and teeth, and I went to lunch pondering what the reason for this might be.

When I returned I found that a folder, with the museum's logo printed on the front cover, had been left for me on the desk where I had been working. The folder contained a press release concerning an announcement made the previous week that the museum's trustees had 'decided to transfer the remains of 17 Aboriginal people to the Australian Government which has designated the TAC to be the receivers of the Tasmanian remains'.[22] The folder also contained numerous other documents: principal among which were copies of the museum's report to its board of trustees on NHM Human Remains from Tasmania and the TAC's Submission to the Trustees of the NHM for the Repatriation of Tasmanian Aboriginal Human Remains.[23]

The museum's report explained that the majority of the remains had been transferred to the NHM's collection from other museums: six of them, classified as PA

HR 332, 334, 335, 337, 338 and 412 had been presented to the NHM from the collections at the University of Oxford during the 1940s; another six, classified as PA HR 341–345 and 604, had been transferred from the Royal College of Surgeons of England in 1955 and 1968; one individual, classified as PA HR 597, was transferred from the Wellcome Collection to the NHM in 1982, while another from the same source, originally designated as being from Tasmania had been reclassified as being 'Japanese/Mongolian in origin'.[24]

The bones of the remaining four people had all been received directly into the museum's collection during the late nineteenth century—that is, shortly after the British Museum's natural history collections transferred, during 1881 to 1883, from Bloomsbury to South Kensington: where they would be known as the British Museum–Natural History or BM (NH) until 1963, before being 'officially renamed the Natural History Museum' in 1992.[25] Of the four individuals acquired directly by the British Museum–Natural History in the late nineteenth century, the one classified as PA HR 590—the 'adult male [...] with many skeletal elements present'—had been 'purchased by the BM (NH) in 1898 for £195' from the Anthropological Society of London, which had originally 'obtained [it] from Morton Allport curator of the Hobart Museum in 1873'. The skull of 'an adult Tasmanian of unknown sex', classified as PAHR 340 had been presented to the 'British Museum of Natural History original collection' by Mr. W. Savile Kent; another, classified as PA HR 593 had been 'donated by Mr. G. C. Trench, [in] 1894 [...] when he was fifteen years old'; the fourth individual, 'represented by a single tooth found with the previous skull [PA HR 593]' was classified as PA HR 594.[26]

Summarizing the circumstances in which the Tasmanian human remains in the NHM collection were originally acquired, the museum's report explained that they were predominantly obtained,

> through donations from visitors or European residents of Tasmania and Australia. Few of these remains are associated with documentary evidence providing details of how they were obtained. Documentation from the donating museum is not always complete and a more extensive search of the NHM archives (possibly including re-reading all of the correspondence between the donating individual and the Museum) would be necessary to determine whether such evidence exists.[27]

The museum provided supplementary documentation in the form of extracts from George Augustus Robinson's (1791–1866) Journal of 1838–39 (published by Plomley during the 1960s to 1980s) concerning post mortem dissections carried out on two of the individuals and the presentation of their skulls to a man named

Captain Monarchie and to Lady Franklin (1791–1875), the wife of John Franklin who was lieutenant governor of Tasmania from 1837 to 1843.

The museum's report also offered recommendations concerning the value to science of the collection, as well as information about past and current research and publications relating to the Tasmanian human remains. Arguing that 'the NHMs [sic] collection of historical Tasmanian [human] remains' was at the time 'one of the largest and most well-provenanced collection [sic] in existence,' the report proposed that 'failure to maintain scholarly access to these remains would reduce the ability to know aspects of their common human heritage to the detriment of both Tasmanians and the wider community'.[28]

An Artist's Response (i)

Instructive as this information was, I remained puzzled as to why the collection of Tasmanian human remains consisted predominantly of skulls and teeth.

Turning to the submission from the TAC, I would find a much more detailed account drawn from evidence in Robinson's journals: concerning the historical context in which human remains from Tasmania entered the NHM collection in the nineteenth century and the collections of the University of Oxford, the Royal College of Surgeons of England and the Wellcome Collection, from which they were transferred to the NHM during the twentieth century.

Reading the two accounts concerning the Tasmanian human remains collection at the NHM in close succession would highlight questions of interpretation: about notions of 'truth' concerning the historical record, the natural world and the human body, and wider concepts of 'common human heritage'.[29]

What I would learn that day would lead me to reflect deeply on the foundations of knowledge that historically underpin some of our most respected institutions, on the role they play in holding collections in trust for the nation, and as cultural ambassadors in a national and an international context in the postcolonial world.

What I would learn from the TAC's Submission would leave me profoundly shaken and angry.

It would also bring me close to vomiting up my lunch.

The TAC's 'Submission to the Trustees of the Natural History Museum for the Repatriation of Tasmanian Aboriginal Human Remains'

According to the TAC's Submission, 'all' of the Tasmanian human remains in the NHM collection that were the subject of their claim for repatriation, in 2006, 'were acquired during the period of British imperial expansion and the subsequent invasions of the countries of native peoples'.

Furthermore,

> Not a single one of these remains was taken from Aboriginal people with the consent of Aboriginal people. In fact, most remains were gathered by grave robbing or through the outright slaughter of our people in the illicit trade [in human remains] of the period.[30]

In addition, the TAC's Submission stated that 'the collections of remains of our people held in the UK are tainted with illegality and the worst forms of abuse of the right to life'.

In support of this allegation the TAC presented detailed evidence concerning the procurement of Tasmanian Aboriginal human remains: which included information from Robinson's journals. Their account is reproduced here at length (rather than in summary) so that readers may experience it in the same form in which I first encountered it:

> Tasmania is an island to the south of Australia. Currently it has a population of less than half a million, of whom roughly 5000 are Aborigines. When the British landed in Tasmania in 1803 an estimated 4000 Aborigines were living there.
>
> From 1803 all Tasmania became a killing field. In 1829 the colonial government contracted George Augustus Robinson to round up the remaining Aborigines to free up the land for white settlers and farmers. On his travels he noted '*There is not a boat harbour along the whole line of coast but what numbers of the unfortunate natives have been shot; their bones are strewed on the ground*'.[31]
>
> Robinson imprisoned the surviving few hundred Aborigines in camps, first at Wybalenna on Flinders Island and finally at Oyster Cove, in the south of mainland Tasmania. By 1860 only 15 of the imprisoned tribal people were left alive, and all were dead by 1876.
>
> About a dozen Aboriginal women escaped the camps. Most of these had been captured to work for British sealers living in tiny enclaves in the Furneaux island group off the north east tip of Tasmania. There they established a cohesive and self-sufficient family based community from whom most of today's Aboriginal population descend. Two other Aboriginal women, one of them the sole survivor of Oyster Cove, married European men on the Tasmanian mainland; their families complete our community. No Aboriginal men survived the onslaught of British invasion and colonization.

> [...] Furthermore, as the people died in the camps, Robinson, who had been given the title 'Protector of the Aborigines', cut up their bodies to distribute among his friends, military officers and representatives of the Crown.
>
> [...] The graveyards of Wybalenna and Oyster Cove were repeatedly ransacked to supply the flourishing trade in Aboriginal body parts well into the early decades of the twentieth century. [...] Most of the Tasmanian human remains in British museums can be traced directly either to George Augustus Robinson's own collection, or the graveyards of Oyster Cove and Wybalenna.

The TAC's submission also noted that,

> All these events have been extensively documented, including accounts by the grave robbers themselves. [...] In all cases, Tasmanian materials were acquired either by coercing vulnerable and oppressed people, or by theft and looting of the dead, these behaviours deemed justified by the overriding 'right' of conquest.[32]

Some Other Perspectives on the History of Tasmania in the Nineteenth Century

Writing more recently about the history of British settlement in Tasmania during the nineteenth century, the historian Rebe Taylor argues that 'since the 1960s' the events just cited have 'become international shorthand for all colonial guilt' and 'the yardstick [for white Australians] of "our" brutal past, the worst of what "we" did': providing a significant narrative for those 'seeking to break the "silence" over Australia's frontier past'.[33]

Yet in the UK that silence had remained absolute for me, right up until I encountered the TAC's Submission to the Trustees of the NHM in the museum's library in November 2006.

As I read the evidence from Robinson's journals with growing horror, and as my feeling of nausea mounted, I was reminded of learning geography at secondary school during the 1970s: surrounded by maps of the world on which the British empire was coloured in pink.

I reflected that I had been taught *nothing* about this aspect of British colonial history at school. I also reflected that, as an adult with a keen interest in the history of collecting, I had remained largely ignorant about the history of the genocide that occurred in Tasmania and the osteological collecting that accompanied it—despite having read reports in the press (and elsewhere) about the repatriation of human remains from museums in recent years, including from the Hunterian Museum of the Royal College of Surgeons of England, The Manchester Museum and the University of Edinburgh.[34]

I was not alone.

Although the British historian Tom Lawson would publish a comprehensive investigation, in 2014, of the British government's role in the genocide in Tasmania during the nineteenth century, the journalist and biographer Peter Stanford was arguing in 2013—in the explicit context of 'London's Natural History Museum's […] [agreement] to send back 17 sets of remains of indigenous Tasmanians' in 2006—that:

> In clearing the land for the settlers to farm in, for example, Australia, pioneers unearthed whole Aboriginal burial sites, later shipping off the skeletons they had found, some of them thousands or tens of thousands of years old, to museums in Britain without a by-your-leave to the Aboriginals whose ancestors they were.[35]

Stanford makes no mention of the violent extermination of Aboriginal peoples that accompanied settlement in Australia and the Torres Strait Islands, or the ways in which the remains of the recently dead were ransacked for the benefit of museums from the communities whose homelands were occupied by force. Instead, he muses briefly on 'the difficult ethical questions' that may be raised today concerning the display of human remains in museums but dismisses the issue with the observation that (in full), 'curiously, in an age where we are reluctant to look our own death in the eye, we manage to get worked up about the rights of individuals who have been dead for thousands of years'.[36]

An Artist's Response (ii)

My anger at my own ignorance of our shared cultural heritage—that is, of the circumstances of an intertwined history, in which ancestral remains from the colonies entered museums in the UK in the past and continue to maintain a complex and divisive legacy in collections that are kept in trust for the nation today—would mobilize the development of my report into the human remains collection at the NHM into a new frame of reference.

Following up on the suggestion in the museum's report about 'possibly […] re-reading all of the correspondence between the donating individual and the Museum', I made a request to the NHM's archives to view documentation relating to the remains of the four Tasmanian people that entered the British Museum–Natural History's collection directly during the late nineteenth century.[37] Following up on this, I was given access to a collection of letters dating from the early decades of the twentieth century: the contents of which opened my eyes further to the circumstances in which human remains historically entered the museum's collection, 'from over 50 countries, covering all of the inhabited continents'.[38]

Some Correspondence Concerning Human Remains in the NHM Collection

The correspondence I gained access to in the NHM's archives dated from 1910 to 1934 and included letters from around the world, as well as from within the UK.[39] In 1910, for instance, Major R[alph] C[ecil] Batley wrote from Dorchester in England offering to donate human remains to the museum: 'Sir, I have very much at my disposal, since my wife declines to have them any longer in the house, 2 skulls, and a few bones.' Explaining that, 'I was, in 1893, in the advance guard of the Force which (with Dr. Jameson) took Matabeleland, and I happened a few days after the occupation of Bulawayo to go out on patrol [...] through the "Execution Place" of King Lo Bengulo [sic]' where 'I picked up, and eventually brought home, a specimen of each,' Batley added, 'these specimens, under compulsion, are very much at your service, if you care to have them.'

The director of the Ethnographical Department of the Museum, the ornithologist and comparative anatomist W[illiam] P[lane] Pycraft (1868–1942)—who was 'Assistant Keeper, Osteological Collections, British Museum,' a Fellow of the Linnean Society, and a Fellow of the English Eugenics Society (1924, 1937) of which he was a member of Council from 1925 to 1935[40]—wrote in reply to Batley on British Museum–Natural History letterhead: 'We shall very gladly avail ourselves of your kind offer. Such specimens are always *most* acceptable'.

In 1923 Captain K[eith] Caldwell wrote to Pycraft from the Game Warden's office in Nairobi, apparently in answer to a direct request:

> Many thanks for your letter—I shall be delighted to do all I can to help you—
> Re skulls I have now and again come across them [...] but the happy Bantu has
> a most violent obsession about anything in the way of human remains and it
> will be a problem to make a porter add it to his load however I will have a try.

Caldwell's indifference to prevailing local attitudes (and people) extended to taking photographs—which he had also apparently been requested to do:

> Re photographs—I know exactly what you want and will try to get them—in
> fact it will add a considerable interest to my safari—men are easy—women [...]

are harder [...] I am going right down the Tana River [...] next month and will try to get the Pukomo and Wa Boni for you—they are very little known tribe and very shy. As long as I am in this job I have unrivaled opportunities [...] with every tribe in the Colony—the wilder the tribe the more our duty to know them.

Three months later, Caldwell wrote again, saying,

I fear I have done little photography lately but have one or two pictures [...] I was on safari in the Massai country [...] and found 3 skulls on the plain which I hasten to send you [...] the photograph is of the Boran [...] they are like hawks and very hard to get touch with—I got the photo by stealth and any attempts to get them to strip for the purpose would have been quite hopeless.

In a letter to Pycraft written in 1926 Herman Lundborg, first director of the Swedish State Institute for Racial Biology in Uppsala, brought requests for photographs into clearer focus while also revealing anxiety about his institution being connected with supplying them:

Herewith I am sending to the British Museum of Natural History under your name the majority of the promised photographs. They are men and six women [sic], three photographs of every individual. In about two weeks you will get some more photographs. If you publish any of the photographs, I beg you not to name, where you have got them from*. If you are in need of their anthropological measurements, we can send you copies of them. I shall be very glad to receive in exchange the photographs of Asiatic types /unclad/ you spoke of.

* i.e. I beg you not to name our institution.

The selection of extracts from correspondence in the NHM's archives just cited would be included in the report, entitled *Possession: Nine-Tenths of the Law?* that I produced for the museum.[41] Although there was insufficient time to follow up with further research to accompany the documentary evidence, as part of the investigation into the history of the display of human remains at the museum that I was briefed to produce, I was able to provide some context for the way in which human remains were displayed in the public galleries at the British Museum–Natural History in the early decades of the twentieth century.

According to a gallery guide published by the British Museum–Natural History in 1931, human remains were exhibited at the museum with a particular focus on the skull, as the following excerpt describing the Upper Mammal Gallery explains:

Table case IV, at the west end of the Gallery, illustrates some of the more important differences between man and the apes, the different types of human skulls and methods of measuring and estimating brain capacity.

'The human skull', the guide adds,

differs from that of the other mammals in the great relative size of the brain-case, and the reduction of the bones of the face; this is related to the high development of the brain, the disuse of the jaw and teeth as weapons, and the perfection of binocular vision. The races of mankind with prominent jaws and small brain-cases are consequently regarded as being of a lower type than those in which the jaws are more reduced in size and the brain-case is larger.

Accordingly,

All the different existing races of mankind are commonly treated as belonging to a single species and [...] three main groups are here recognized. These groups, best defined by the character of the hair, are typified by (1) the Caucasian, or white races of Europe; (2) the Mongolian or yellow races of Asia; and (3) the Negro, or black races of Africa.

Cases 1 and 2 illustrate the zoological characters of the white races. The Polynesians, Maoris, and Australians are also included in this section. The Mongol or yellow and red races occupy cases 3 and 4. [...] With the exception of the last case containing the American monkeys, the remainder of the cases on the south side are devoted to the negro or black races: here are found not only the typical African negroes, but also the negritos of the Andaman Islands, the Melanesian inhabitants of Eastern Polynesia and Papua, and the Tasmanians.[42]

An Artist's Response (iii)

In response to all that I learnt at the NHM, I would go on to read widely and discover the work of scholars who have been researching the history of Tasmanian and Australian human remains in museums for many years, including the Australian historians Helen MacDonald and Paul Turnbull, and the British archaeologist and historian Cressida Fforde. I soon learnt that Fforde had analysed and contextualized the early-twentieth-century displays in the Upper Mammal Gallery at the British Museum-Natural History in work published in 2002—four years before the NHM produced its *Report on NHM Human Remains from Tasmania* concerning the claim for repatriation from the TAC.[43] I also learnt from Fforde's work that, 'by the late nineteenth century the human remains of Aboriginal people were housed in most, if not all the major collecting institutions throughout Europe, as well as numerous local museums and university departments', and that 'the larger institutions aimed' to accumulate 'representative collections of all the human "races" in order to describe and quantify humankind'—so that, 'by the end of the [...] century most contained the remains of peoples from all around the world.'[44]

From Fforde's and Turnbull's work, I gained detailed insight into the development of the comparative anatomical and physical anthropological theories that underpinned those collections.[45] Turnbull's work also informed me about the extraordinary lengths to which collectors in the colonies would go, to supply Australian human remains to museum collections.[46] I became acquainted through Fforde's and Turnbull's work with 'the infamous affair of the post-mortem mutilation of William Lanne, [who was] allegedly the last man of the Tasmanian race': Lanne became

> the focus of scientific rivalry in 1869 between the Hobart surgeon William Crowther (1817–1885), who sought to procure the skeleton for the Royal College of Surgeons of England in London, and leading members of the Royal Society of Tasmania.[47]

From MacDonald I learnt about this incident in forensic detail. Through her work I began to comprehend the central role played by the Hunterian Museum of the Royal College of Surgeons of England and the British Museum-Natural History in 'a chain of events': that began with the theft of Lanney's[48] skull from a dissecting room at the General Hospital in Hobart Town shortly after he died, and had 'not ended yet' when the TAC made their claim to the NHM in 2006.[49]

An Artist's Response (iv): Passing Fables & Comparative Readings at The Wildgoose Memorial Library

Following the completion of the report for the NHM, I continued to develop my role as Keeper of the WML: combining historical research with a willingness to engage with the emotional charge that may be connected with remains of all kinds and exploring means for presenting archival evidence so that it might 'speak' for itself. Using these methods, I turned my attention to investigating the historical circumstances that have led to a 'unique status' being ascribed to human remains in museums today.

My new research was framed by a response to the Department for Culture, Media and Sport's acknowledgement, in their *Guidance for the Care of Human*

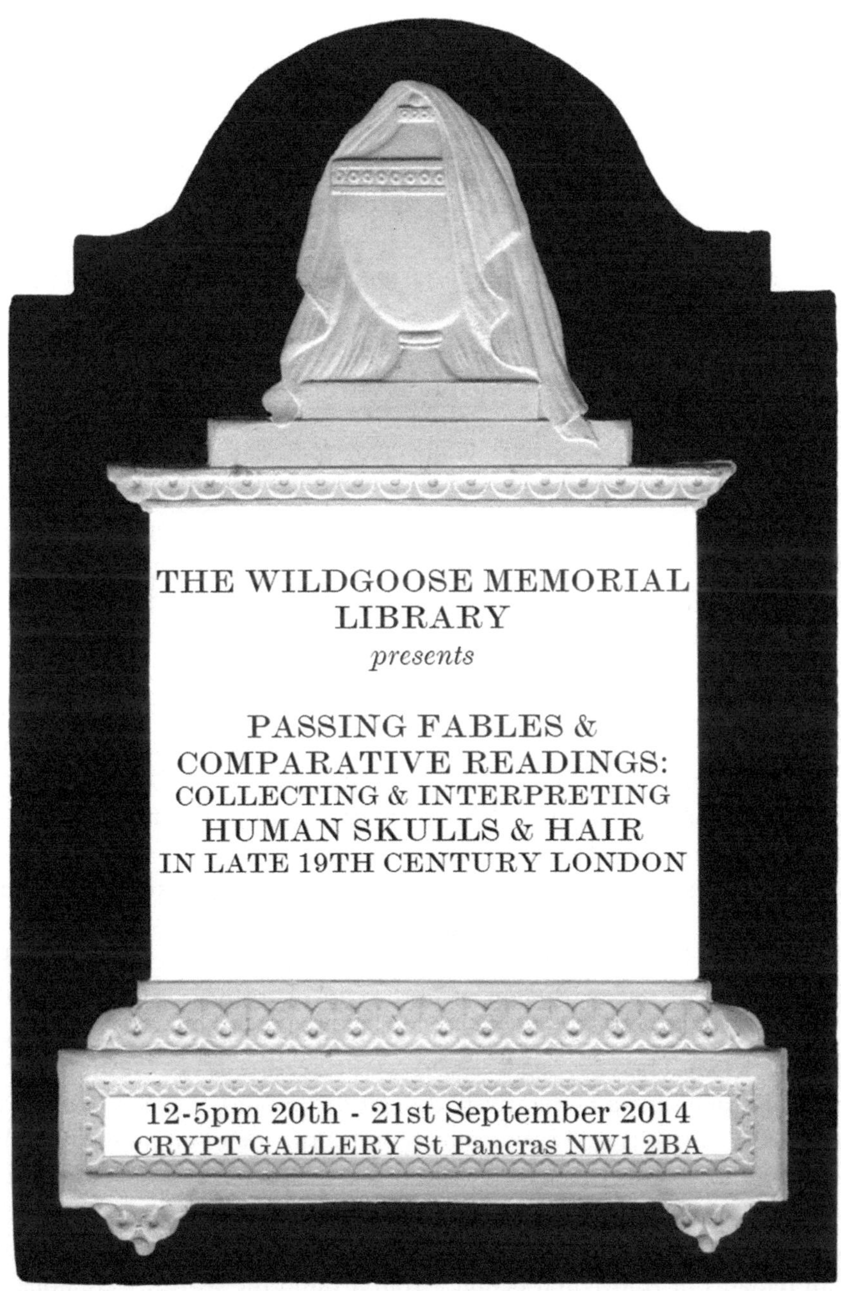

FIGURE 11.1. Jane Wildgoose, publicity for *Passing Fables & Comparative Readings*, 2014. © Jane Wildgoose.

Remains in Museums, that, while human remains may be of value as objects for research, 'in many instances, they also have a personal, cultural, symbolic, spiritual or religious significance to individuals and, or, groups'.[50] My investigations would develop into a comparative study, entitled *Passing Fables & Comparative Readings at The Wildgoose Memorial Library* (Fig. 11.1), in which the objectification of human skulls collected from the colonies for metropolitan museums, during the late nineteenth century, would be contrasted with the popular use of human hair as a commemorative material in mourning jewellery in wider British society at that time.

At the beginning of my research I was introduced to Helen MacDonald when she was visiting London and she generously advised me on where to search in the Archives of the Royal College of Surgeons. Through Helen's help, I was able to access an extensive collection of previously unpublished correspondence from a wide network of men posted in the colonies who either personally took, or requisitioned others to take human skulls for museums: removing them largely without consent—as their correspondence explicitly and repeatedly reveals—from graves both new and old; from the recently deceased in hospitals and from execution grounds and battlefields.

Central to my enquiry was a question posed by Elizabeth Edwards and Matt Mead, who highlight 'the "invisibility" and "disavowal" of the colonial past in the historical narrative developed by museums, and the anxieties that cluster around such narratives in a postcolonial and multicultural society'.

Edwards and Mead ask, 'Which histories are told [by museums] and how, and which histories are not told and why'?[51]

With this question in mind, I would develop my findings into a new 'archive' of the WML. At the heart of the archive is a work in progress: a commemorative wreath entitled *Lost but Not Forgotten*, made from donated human hair, which is inspired by the work of nineteenth-century northern European amateur hair workers, who made wreaths from hair to commemorate the lives of loved ones[52] (Fig. 11.2). The *Lost but Not Forgotten* wreath has a convex mirror at its centre and is literally and figuratively designed to promote reflection. Each hair flower in the wreath (Fig. 11.3) commemorates the life of an individual whose skull, according to the evidence of my research, was taken without consent from the colonies for the purposes of the development of theories of racial 'science' at a metropolitan museum during the late nineteenth century: at a time when 'the human remains of Aboriginal people [from around the world] were housed in most, if not all the major collecting institutions throughout Europe, as well as numerous local museums and university departments,' with the aim of producing 'representative collections of all the human "races" in order to describe and quantify humankind'.[53]

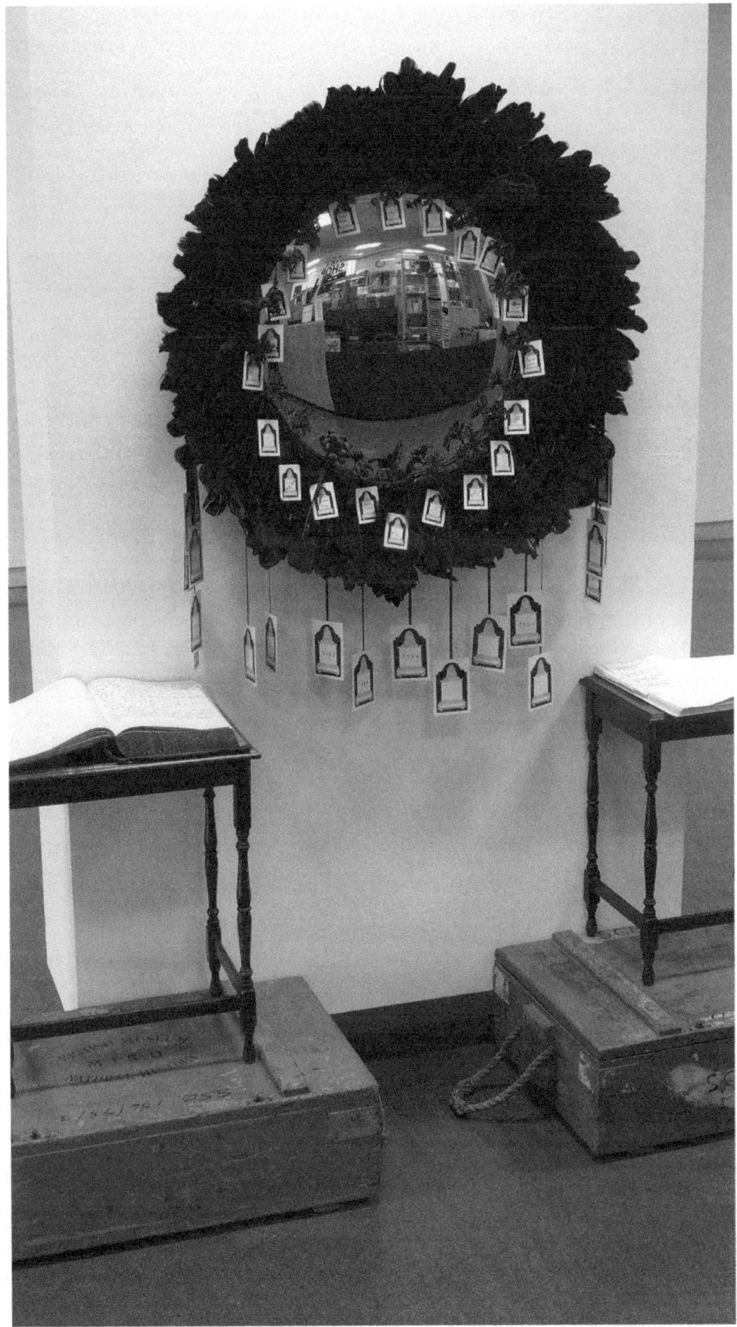

FIGURE 11.2. Jane Wildgoose, *Lost but Not Forgotten* wreath, installation view, 2015. Human hair, Victorian mourning pins, printed card, ribbon, black turkey feathers on convex mirror in wooden frame. 32″ × 49″. Platform Gallery, Kingston University London. © Jane Wildgoose.

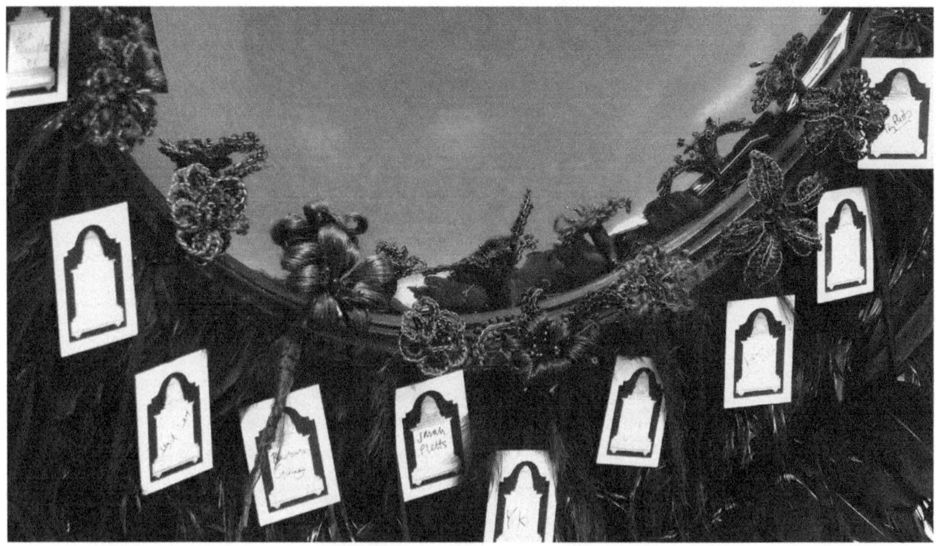

FIGURE 11.3. Jane Wildgoose, *Lost but Not Forgotten* wreath, detail, 2015. Human hair, Victorian mourning pins, printed card, ribbon, black turkey feathers on convex mirror in wooden frame. 32″ × 49″. Platform Gallery, Kingston University London. © Jane Wildgoose.

Accompanying the wreath in the *Lost but Not Forgotten* Archive are the transcriptions I have made from hundreds of previously unpublished letters from the men in the colonies, who ransacked the places of the dead in order to provide specimens for physical anthropological and comparative anatomy collections in London during the nineteenth century (Fig. 11.4). The archive also includes copies of published catalogues and gallery guides (purchased second-hand) that accompanied the collections of human skulls, containing information about the ideology on which the collections were based (Fig. 11.5). Included among these primary sources are editions of the catalogue of human osteology contained in the Hunterian Museum of the Royal College of Surgeons of England, which include descriptions of the college's extensive collection of human skulls (as well as other bones and whole skeletons) prior to the damage the college sustained during enemy bombing in World War II[54] and the subsequent removal of several thousand specimens to the NHM from the late 1940s to the late 1960s.

The 1879 and 1907 editions of the catalogues of the collections at the Royal College of Surgeons contain revealing information about the provenance of many of the human osteological remains in its Hunterian Museum. This evidence confirms and further informs the account of the ways in which human remains were obtained from Tasmania for museums, submitted to the NHM by the TAC in 2006. According to the 1907 edition of the catalogue, for instance,

256

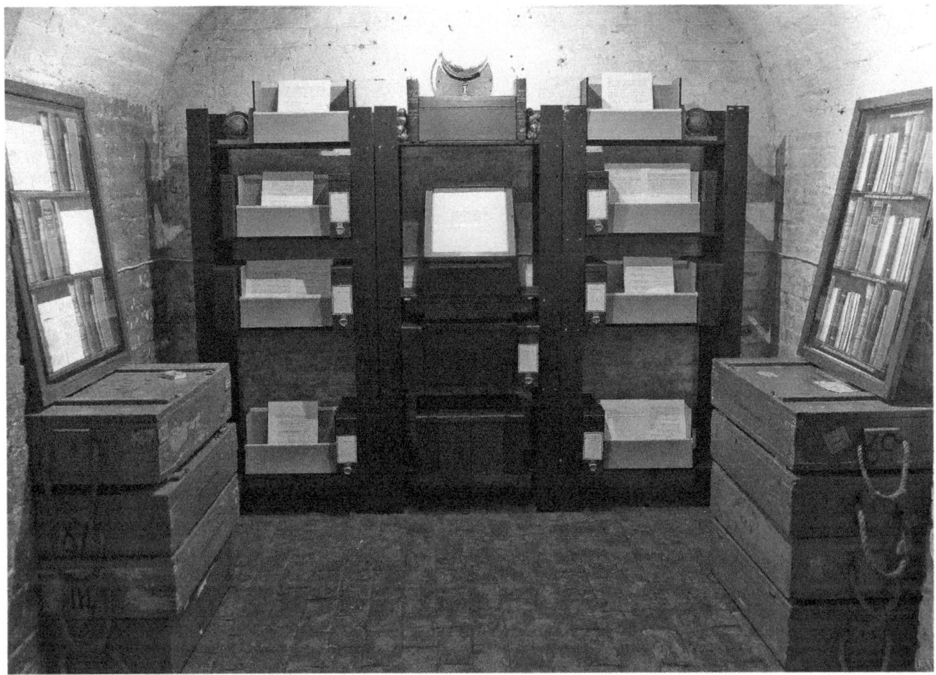

FIGURE 11.4. Jane Wildgoose, *Lost but Not Forgotten* Archive, installation view, 2014. Crypt Gallery St Pancras. © Jane Wildgoose.

an 'articulated skeleton of an adult male native of Tasmania' (later destroyed by wartime bombing in 1941), presented by Morton Allport to the College in 1872, was '[o]btained from a grave on Flinders Island, where the remnant of the aboriginal population, when removed from Tasmania, was located between 1832 and 1847, and where nearly two hundred of them died'. 'The skull of a Tasmanian: ♀' presented to the College by an officer of the Royal Navy in 1854 was removed by the donor with the help of accomplices in 1842, from 1 of approximately 12 graves on Bruni Island near 'the ruin of the house where the few unfortunate natives who survived had been confined previous to their intended transportation to Banks's Island'.

The donor and his accomplices disturbed several graves before finding the skull that was presented to the collection. Having 'dug six feet down' in one and 'to our disappointment found ashes of a burning', they excavated 'another grave and found it had been [previously] disturbed'. Finally,

> on opening a third [...] a layer of *Eucalyptus*-bark stopped the spade, and on being opened disclosed the body of a young female in a perfect state of

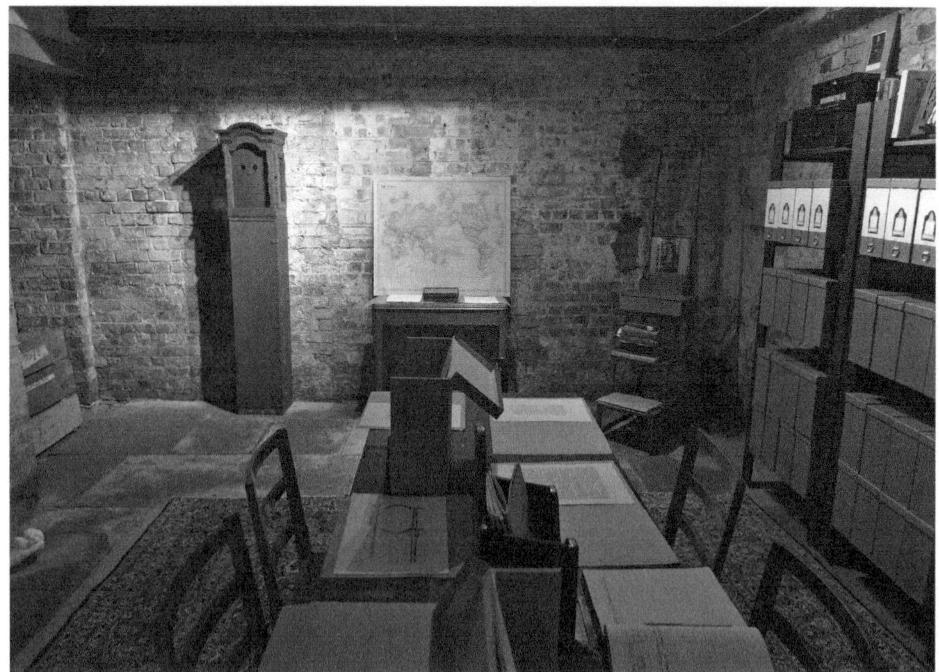

FIGURE 11.5. Jane Wildgoose, *Lost but Not Forgotten* Archive and Reading Room, installation view, 2014. Crypt Gallery St Pancras. © Jane Wildgoose.

> preservation. The water began to flow into the grave; but we soon obtained and carried off the head, which accompanies this note.[55]

The guides to the galleries of the British Museum–Natural History included in the *Lost but Not Forgotten* Archive offer vivid insight into the foundations of 'knowledge' on which collections of human skulls in metropolitan museums were built (Fig. 11.6). A guide to the galleries at the British Museum–Natural History published in 1921, for instance, explains that

> Australians and Tasmanians have [...] a comparatively small brain-cavity, thick skull-bones, receding forehead, overhanging brows, flat nasal-bones, long, low eye-sockets, very broad and low nasal-opening, forwardly projecting jaws but receding chin, and large teeth. In each of these respects they strongly contrast with Europeans'.[56]

As Fforde observes, 'displays such as this informed the public that Aboriginal inferiority was a biological fact, a "truth" demonstrated by science'. She adds that,

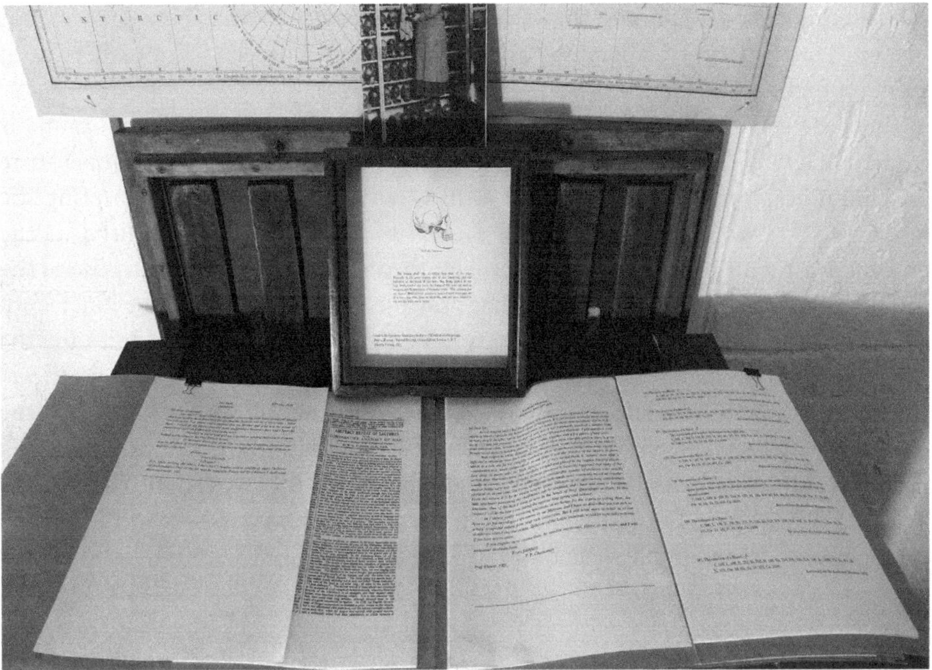

FIGURE 11.6. Jane Wildgoose, *Lost but Not Forgotten* Archive, installation view, 2018. Lumen Crypt Gallery, St John on Bethnal Green. © Jane Wildgoose.

> the collecting and study of human remains was firmly situated within power relations that already existed between the West and its colonized peoples. [...] Imperialism and colonialism were not simply techniques of accumulation and acquisition executed on a grand scale but wide-ranging political processes.[57]

With this point of Fforde's in mind, my ongoing research examines primary sources that reveal how the craniometric ideologies developed in metropolitan museums fed into and exacerbated the unequal power relations existing between the colonizer and the colonized, with reference to the published work of collectors whose correspondence and catalogues are included in the *Lost but Not Forgotten* Archive.

Mindful of Edwards and Mead's question about 'which histories are told [by museums] and how, and which histories are not told and why,' I continue to develop the *Lost but Not Forgotten* Archive and present it in public exhibitions, in conference and seminar papers and in publications.[58] Drawing on my understanding of Proust's conception of the past being held within the sensation that a material object will give us, and Hyde's trickster-artist's capacity 'to move between the living and the dead', wherever possible I present the archive site-specifically in contemporary art galleries that double as nineteenth-century burial places: for instance, at the Crypt Gallery St Pancras (2014) and Lumen Crypt Gallery at St John on Bethnal Green (2018).

In these settings, the question of contested human remains in museums is framed in a way that would be impossible in a white cube gallery, a temperature and humidity-controlled museum or a university seminar room. Prompting the audience to respond thoughtfully to 'facing up to one's own mortality [...] the end game after all'[59]—and reminding them, through the fabric and purpose of the buildings, of traditions of mourning that prevailed in the UK during the nineteenth century at the same time that graves were being violated in the colonies for the purpose of supplying human remains to museum collections—one visitor reflects that, 'I was able to participate in your research process by walking through the work presented in a physical way'; another observes that '[the exhibition] breaks a modern taboo: death here is not only present but physically woven into the living'. Another asks, 'were I not entering these dreamlike chambers—could I find the psychic space to encompass the moral dilemma?'[60]

Conclusion

It is over a decade since I sat reading the TAC's Submission to the Trustees of the NHM in the library at the museum. I look back with embarrassment now, at my level of ignorance concerning the worldwide procurement of human skulls for museums during British colonial rule, when I accepted the museum's commission to report on its human remains collection in 2006. Out of that ignorance the seeds of the *Lost but Not Forgotten* Archive were sown: when I wondered why 'the majority' of the Tasmanian human remains that were the subject of the TAC's claim for repatriation consisted mainly of 'teeth and crania' and responded with shock, revulsion and anger to evidence in the Centre's Submission concerning the circumstances in which they were acquired. The *Lost but Not Forgotten* Archive would take root as part of the steep historical learning curve that attended the discoveries I made while researching into correspondence concerning the human remains collection at the museum. Now, about 14 years later, the archive has extended to contain published and previously unpublished evidence regarding the interlinked histories of racial 'science' and both medical and natural history collecting in London, from the period of colonial expansion during the nineteenth century to the eve of World War II in the twentieth, and shedding a harsh light on the foundations of knowledge on which some of our most cherished institutions stand.

While much of the evidence contained in the *Lost but Not Forgotten* archive has not previously been published, the study of the overall history to which it points is not new. The interconnections between the histories of racial science and museums have been investigated and debated by academics and members of the museum sector, nationally and internationally—and eloquently raised in claims for repatriation made by representatives of Indigenous peoples worldwide—for many years. Nonetheless this aspect of the history of museums and the taxonomic ideologies that historically underpin the collecting institutions that hold them, remain virtually unknown among members of the British museum-going public today.

A defining aspect of the development and presentation of the *Lost but Not Forgotten* Archive is the maintenance of my independent voice as an artist: unencumbered by the issues of institutional reputation, strategic aims, funding streams, sponsors' agendas and calculations about visitor numbers that accompany working within (and for) a museum. As such, this response to the 'unique status' of postcolonial human remains in museums is designed to extend the frame of reference for considering the ongoing legacies of colonial collecting while offering a space for reflection for the public: for whom the national collections are kept in trust.

Acknowledgements

My doctoral research was supported by a full-time PhD Studentship from Kingston University London; I am most grateful to my supervisors Duncan Grewcock and Charles Rice for welcoming and supporting my practice-based research in the School of Art & Design History at Kingston and for their always constructive criticism; to Helen MacDonald for pointing me in the right direction in the archives at the beginning of my research, and Ruth Richardson for introducing me to her, and for their combined encouragement and support. I would like to thank Annie Reynolds and the Tasmanian Aboriginal Centre for permission to reproduce sections of the TAC's *Submission to the Trustees of the Natural History Museum for the Repatriation of Tasmanian Aboriginal Human Remains*. My thanks also go to staff in the archives and library at the NHM and the Royal College of Surgeons of England and at the British Library for their help; Hannah Young for inviting me to speak about the *Lost but Not Forgotten* Archive at the *Troubling Objects: Interrogating collecting and collections* symposium at the Victoria and Albert Museum and Melanie King at Lumen Crypt Gallery St. John on Bethnal Green for giving me the opportunity to exhibit the Archive while I was writing this chapter during 2018; also Kiera Lindsey for her thoughtful comments on an early draft and for introducing me to the work of Rebe Taylor; Tamara Capellaro and James Metcalf for their insightful reading of early drafts, as well as the editors and the anonymous reviewer who have provided valuable feedback; John and Barbara

Furlong for their generous practical support; all the people who have donated hair to the *Lost but Not Forgotten* wreath and Cyana Madsen for her assistance with documenting the archive.

NOTES

1. Report on NHM Human Remains from Tasmania, Board of Trustees TP06/54ii, Human Remains Advisory Panel 06 10HRAP4b: 9, 2.

2. Department for Culture, Media and Sport, *Guidance for the Care of Human Remains in Museums* (2005): 7.

3. Jane Wildgoose, 'Grave-robbing, Crucifixion, Dissection: How Far Should We Go in the Name of Art?' *New Statesman*, 15 August 1997, 41–43; 'An Acceptable Body of Work?' *Daily Telegraph*: Arts & Books, 9 May 1998, A7; 'Zones of Morbidity', in *Psycho*, ed. Danny Moynihan, (London: Anne Faggionato, 2000), n.p.

4. Author of the key work bringing to light evidence of the medical profession's historical collusion in grave-robbing for the supply of human cadavers to anatomical schools, and the introduction of the 1832 Anatomy Act. See Ruth Richardson, *Death, Dissection and the Destitute* (London: Routledge & Kegan Paul, 1987).

5. Jane Wildgoose, 'The Business of the Flesh', *Guardian*, 31 October 2002, [online] available at http://www.guardian.co.uk/society/2002/oct/31/1 (accessed 4 May 2020); BBC News, 'Organ scandal background', [online] available at http://news.co.uk/2/hi/1136723.stm (accessed 4 May 2020).

6. Jane Wildgoose, 'About the Library', The Wildgoose Memorial Library (WML), http://www.janewildgoose.co.uk/jane_wildgoose.html (accessed 26 July 2018).

7. Lewis Hyde, *Trickster Makes This World: Mischief, Myth, and Art* (New York: North Point Press, 1999), 6; Marcel Proust, *Remembrance of Things Past*, vol. 1, trans. C. K. Scott Moncrieff and Terence Kilmartin (London: Penguin, [1913] 1983) 47–48.

8. Jane Wildgoose, *Promiscuous Assemblage, Friendship, & the Order of Things. An Installation by Jane Wildgoose in Celebration of the Friendship between Mrs. Mary Delany & the Duchess Dowager of Portland* (New Haven: Yale Center for British Art, 2009), 11.

9. Gregory Whitehead, Neil McCarthy and Jane Wildgoose, 'On One Lost Hair', BBC Radio 4, 10 May 2004; see: Gregory Whitehead, 'On One Lost Hair', *Cabinet* 16/The Sea (Winter 2004–2005): 83–85.

10. *The Wildgoose Memorial Library Portrait Project*, supported by a NESTA (National Endowment for Science, Technology and the Arts) Dream Time Fellowship from 2005 to 2006.

11. The TAC is 'a non-profit community based organization […] providing legal, health, educational, culture and welfare services to Aborigines throughout Tasmania'. Michael Mansell, *Tasmanian Aboriginal Centre Submission to the Trustees of the Natural History Museum for the Repatriation of Tasmanian Aboriginal Human Remains*, Board of Trustees TP06. 54i, Human Remains Advisory Panel 0610HRAP4a (London: NHM, 2006a): 2.

12. Ibid., 3.

13. Ibid., 2 (original emphasis).

14. See for instance: Michael Pickering and Phil Gordon, 'Repatriation: The End of the Beginning', in *Understanding Museums: Australian Museums and Museology*, ed. Des Griffin and Leon Paroissien, National Museum of Australia, 2011, [online] available at https://nma.gov.au/research/understanding-museums/MPickering_PGordon_2011.html; for insight into the debate in the United States see Clayton Dumont Jr., 'Dead Family or Archaeological Collections?: On the Significance of Native Dead', *Race, Gender & Class* 9, no. 2 (2002): 8–31; concerning debate in the UK see Pete Brown, 'Us and Them: Who Benefits from Experimental Exhibition Making?', *Museum Management and Curatorship* 26, no. 2 (May 2011): 129–48; Tiffany Jenkins, '"Who Are We to Decide?" Internal Challenges to Cultural Authority in the Contestation over Human Remains in British Museums', *Cultural Sociology* 6, no. 4 (July 2012): 455–70, [online] available at http://cus.sagepub.com/content/early/2012/05/15/1749975512445432 (accessed 21 July 2018), and Tiffany Jenkins, *Contesting Human Remains in Museum Collections: The Crisis of Cultural Authority* (New York: Routledge, 2014).

15. Department for Culture, Media and Sport (DCMS), *The Report of the Working Group on Human Remains* (London: DCMS, 2003), 176: 58, National Archives, archived on 13 January 2010, 'dcms, department for culture media and sport', 'Working Group on Human Remains Report' http://webarchive.nationalarchives.gov.uk/20100113212249 and http://www.culture.gov.uk/reference_library/publications/4553.aspx (accessed 21 July 2018).

16. 'World Archeological Congress Code of Ethics', 'The Vermillion Accord on Human Remains', World Archaeological Congress (WAC), http://worldarch.org/code-of-ethics/ (accessed 24 July 2018).

17. 'NAGPRA Law and Regulations Home', National Park Service, U.S. Department of the Interior (NPS), http://www.nps.gov/nagpra/MANDATES/INDEX.HTM (accessed 24 July 2018); Australian Government Department of the Environment (AGDoE), 'Repatriation of Indigenous Property', http://www.deh.gov.au/soe/2006/emerging/repatriation/index.html (accessed 24 July 2018).

18. DCMS *Report*, 179–81: 59. Liz Bell notes that at this time museums in England 'managed to stay on the sidelines of the repatriation debate, failing in numerous instances to address satisfactorily the concerns of Indigenous groups'; she adds that, 'several English institutions [...] earned themselves something of a poor reputation due to the negative stance they [...] [took] towards repatriation'. Liz Bell in Paul Turnbull and Michael Pickering, ed., *The Long Way Home: The Meaning and Values of Repatriation* (Oxford: Berghahn Books, 2010), 29.

19. DCMS *Report*, 13.

20. 'Human Comparative Collection', Natural History Museum, http://www.nhm.ac.uk/our-science/collections/palaeontology-collections/human-comparative-collection.html (accessed 25 August 2018).

21. *Report on NHM Human Remains from Tasmania*, Board of Trustees TP06/54ii, Human Remains Advisory Panel 0610HRAP4b (London: NHM, 2006), 9, 2.

22. 'Press Release Friday 17 November 2006: Human Remains to be Returned from Natural History Museum's Collection' (London: NHM, 2006).

23. NHM, *Report on NHM Human Remains*; Mansell, *Tasmanian Aboriginal Centre Submission*.

24. NHM, *Report on NHM Human Remains*, 2.

25. 'Evolution of the Museum', in *Art and Architecture*, Natural History Museum, [online] available at https://www.nhm.ac.uk/about-us/history-and-architecture.html (accessed 20 July 2018).

26. NHM, *Report on NHM Human Remains*, 7, 9–10.

27. Ibid., 2.

28. Ibid., 1.

29. Ibid., 1.

30. Mansell, *Tasmanian Aboriginal Centre Submission*, 3.

31. Plomley 1966, 405. Original emphasis.

32. Mansell, *Tasmanian Aboriginal Centre Submission*, 4–6.

33. Rebe Taylor, 'The National Confessional', *Meanjin Quarterly* 71, no. 3 (2012): n.p., [online] available at https://meanjin.com.au/essays/the-national-confessional/ (accessed 4 May 2020).

34. See for instance Ewen MacAskill, 'Britain Pressed to Return Aboriginal Bones', *Guardian*, 5 July 2000, [online] available at https://www.theguardian.com/uk/2000/jul/05/ ewenmacaskill (accessed 4 May 2020); Terri Judd, 'Manchester Museum Returns Aboriginal Remains to Australia', *Independent*, 30 July 2003, [online] available at https://www. independent.co.uk/news/uk/this-britain/manchester-museum-returns-aboriginal-remains-to-australia-98210.html (accessed 4 May 2020); 'Losing Your Marbles: Bodies Are More Valuable Than Buildings', Leader, *The Times*, 30 July 2003; Tristram Besterman, 'Returning the Ancestors', (Manchester: Manchester University, 2004), [online] available at http:// documents.manchester.ac.uk/display.aspx?DocID=32595 (accessed 14 September 2018); Caroline Lewis, 'National Museums Given Powers to Return Human Remains', *Culture24*, 6 October 2005, [online] available at http://www.culture24.org.uk/places-to-go/north-west/ manchester/art30860 (accessed 4 May 2020).

35. Peter Stanford, *How to Read a Graveyard: Journeys in the Company of the Dead* (London: Bloomsbury, 2013), 34; also see Tom Lawson, *The Last Man: A British Genocide in Tasmania* (London: I. B. Tauris, 2014).

36. Stanford, *How to Read a Graveyard*, 35.

37. NHM *Report*, 2.

38. NHM, 'Human Comparative Collection'.

39. W. P. Pycraft, 'Correspondence and Papers on Anthropology 1912–1934: Notes and Correspondence Relating to Registered Specimens ff 123–124', Natural History Museum.

40. 'Eugenics Society Members A-Z 2012', SCRIBD, [online] available at https://www.scribd.com/doc/97123506/Eugenics-Society-Members-A-Z-2012 (accessed 24 August 2018).

41. The title of the report referred to the following assessment of the old adage 'possession is nine-tenths of the law': '"possession", n. (1) any article, object, asset or property which one owns, occupies, holds or has under control. (2) the act of owning, occupying or having under control an article, object, asset or property. "Constructive possession" involves property which is not immediately held, but which one has the right to hold and the means to get (such as a key to a storeroom or safe deposit box).

    "Criminal possession" is the holding of property which it is illegal to possess such as controlled narcotics, *stolen goods* or liquor by a juvenile. The old adage "possession is nine-tenths of the law" is *a rule of force* and not of law, since *ownership requires the right to possess* as well as actual or constructive possession.' (emphasis added) in 'Search Legal Terms and Definitions: possession', https://dictionary.law.com/Default.aspx?selected=1555, Law.com website (accessed 19 July 2019). Jane Wildgoose, 'Possession: Nine-Tenths of the Law?' (Unpublished report for Natural History Museum London) (London: The Wildgoose Memorial Library, 2006).

42. Charles Carmichael Arthur Monro and John Ramsbottom, *Illustrated Guide to the Exhibition Galleries* (London: Published by Order of the Trustees, British Museum [Natural History] London S.W.7, 1931), 158–59.

43. Cressida Fforde in Cressida Fforde, Jane Hubert and Paul Turnbull, ed., *The Dead and Their Possessions: Repatriation in Principle, Policy and Practice* (London: Routledge, 2002), 31–32.

44. Fforde, Hubert and Turnbull, *The Dead and Their Possessions*, 26.

45. See Cressida Fforde, *Collecting the Dead: Archaeology and the Reburial Issue* (London: Duckworth, 2004), 7–42; Paul Turnbull, 'British Anthropological Thought in Colonial Practice: The Appropriation of Indigenous Australian Bodies, 1860–1880', in *Foreign Bodies: Oceania and the Science of Race 17*, ed. Bronwen Douglas and Chris Ballard (Canberra: ANU E Press, 2008), 205–28; Paul Turnbull, 'British Anatomists, Phrenologists and the Construction of the Aboriginal Race, c. 1790–1830', *History Compass 5*, no. 1 (January 2007): 26–50. https://doi.org/10.1111/j.1478-0542.2006.00367.x.

46. Paul Turnbull, 'Theft in the Name of Science'. *Griffith Review* 21: Hidden Queensland (2008): n.p., [online] available at https://griffithreview.com/edition-21-hidden-queensland/theft-in-the-name-of-science (accessed 10 September 2018); Paul Turnbull, 'How Australian Ancestral Remains Were Originally Procured', in 'Scientific Theft of Remains in Colonial Australia'. *Australian Indigenous Law Review* 11 no. 1 (2007): n.p., [online] available at http://www.austlii.edu.au/au/journals/AILRev/2007/7.html (accessed 10 September 2018).

47. Turnbull, 'Scientific Theft of Remains'; Fforde, *Collecting the Dead*, 44–48.

48. Fforde and Turnbull both refer to William Lanne, but MacDonald refers to William Lanney; it is clear from the details of their respective accounts that they discuss the same person and the same incident concerning the post-mortem treatment of his body. I am

grateful to Annie Reynolds, Repatriation Officer at the Tasmanian Aboriginal Centre, for letting me know that the 'skull of William Lanne (Lanney)' was 'repatriated to Tasmania by the TAC from Edinburgh in 1991'; also for drawing my attention to the fact that 'the hair of Aboriginal people carries another story of brutality, appropriation and racist ideology' (email to author, 12 August 2019). For discussion of the latter issue see Emma Tarlo, *Entanglement: The Secret Lives of Hair* (London: Oneworld, 2016), 267–69, 271, 280–81.

49. Helen MacDonald, 'The Bone Collectors', *New Literatures Review* 42 (October 2004): 46; Helen MacDonald, *Human Remains: Dissection and its Histories* (New Haven: Yale University Press, 2005), 111–17, 129–50.

50. Department for Culture, Media and Sport, *Guidance for the Care of Human Remains in Museums* (DCMS) (London: DCMS, 2005), National Archives, archived on 12 May 2010, 'dcms, department for culture, media and sport', 'Guidance for the Care of Human Remains in Museums', 7, [online] available at http://webarchive.nationalarchives.gov.uk/+/http://www.culture.gov.uk/reference_library/publications/3720.aspx (accessed 21 July 2018).

51. Elizabeth Edwards and Matt Mead, 'Absent Histories and Absent Images: Photographs, Museums and the Colonial Past'. *Museum & Society* 11, no. 1 (2013): 19.

52. See Jane Wildgoose, 'Collecting and Interpreting Human Skulls and Hair in Late Nineteenth-Century London: *Passing Fables & Comparative Readings at The Wildgoose Memorial Library*. An artist's response to the *DCMS Guidance for the Care of Human Remains in Museums* (2005)' (PhD diss., Kingston University London, 2015); Jane Wildgoose, 'Ways of Making with Human Hair and Knowing How to "Listen" to the Dead', *West 86th* 23, no. 1 (Spring–Summer 2016): 79–101.

53. Fforde, Hubert and Turnbull, *The Dead and their Possessions*, 26.

54. Sam Alberti, *Hunterian Museum at the Royal College of Surgeons Guidebook* (London: Royal College of Surgeons, 2011), 30.

55. William Henry Flower, *Catalogue of the Specimens Illustrating the Osteology and Dentition of Vertebrated Animals, Recent and Extinct, Contained in the Museum of the Royal College of Surgeons of England, Part 1, Man.* 2nd ed. (London: Taylor and Francis, 1907), 337, 341.

56. Richard Lydekker, *Guide to the Specimens Illustrating the Races of Mankind (Anthropology) Exhibited in the Department of Zoology, British Museum (Natural History), Cromwell Road, London, S. W. 7* (London: Printed by Order of the Trustees of the British Museum, 1921), 10–11.

57. Fforde, Hubert and Turnbull, *The Dead and Their Possessions*, 29, 32.

58. Edwards and Mead, 'Absent Histories', 19. Jane Wildgoose, 'Presenting "Lost But Not Forgotten" at the Crypt Gallery St. Pancras: Negotiating and Constructing Active Critical Conversation Concerning Contested Human Remains in Museums', in *In This Place Cumulus Association Biannual International Conference Proceedings*, ed. D. Higgins and J. Pinches (Nottingham: Nottingham Trent University, 2016), [online]

available at http://www.cumulusnottingham2016.org/about/ (accessed 4 May 2020); Wildgoose, 'Ways of Making with Human Hair'; Jane Wildgoose, 'Collecting Human Skulls and Hair: In Pursuit of Wonder in Death's Chambers', in *Wonder in Contemporary Artistic Practice*, ed. Christian Mieves and Irene Brown (Abingdon: Routledge, 2017).

59. Mary Hooper, email to author, 9 October 2014.

60. Roberto Sanchez-Camus, email to author, 20 September 2014; Kay Syrad, letter to author, 13 October 2014; Sara van Riemsdjik, email to author, 20 October 2014.

REFERENCES

Alberti, Sam. *Hunterian Museum at the Royal College of Surgeons Guidebook*. London: Royal College of Surgeons, 2011.

Australian Government Department of the Environment (AGDoE). 'Repatriation of Indigenous Property'. Available at http://www.deh.gov.au/soe/2006/emerging/repatriation/index.html (accessed 24 July 2018).

BBC News. 'Organ Scandal Background'. Available at http://news.bbc.co.uk/2/hi/1136723.stm (accessed 26 August 2018).

Besterman, Tristram. 'Returning the Ancestors'. Manchester: Manchester University, 2004. Available at http://documents.manchester.ac.uk/display.aspx?DocID=32595 (accessed 14 September 2018).

Brown, Pete. 'Us and Them: Who Benefits from Experimental Exhibition Making?'. *Museum Management and Curatorship* 26, no. 2 (May 2011): 129–48.

Department for Culture, Media and Sport (DCMS). *The Report of the Working Group on Human Remains*. London: DCMS, 2003. National Archives. Archived on 13 January 2010. 'dcms, department for culture media and sport'; 'Working Group on Human Remains Report'. Available at http://webarchive.nationalarchives.gov.uk/20100113212249/; http://www.culture.gov.uk/reference_library/publications/4553.aspx (accessed 21 July 2018).

Department for Culture, Media and Sport (DCMS). *Guidance for the Care of Human Remains in Museums*. London: DCMS, 2005. National Archives. Archived on 12 May 2010. 'dcms, department for culture, media and sport'; 'Guidance for the Care of Human Remains in Museums'. http://webarchive.nationalarchives.gov.uk/+/http://www.culture.gov.uk/reference_library/publications/3720.aspx (accessed 21 July 2018).

Dumont Jr., Clayton. 'Dead Family or Archaeological Collections?: On the Significance of Native Dead'. *Race, Gender & Class* 9, no. 2 (2002): 8–31.

Edwards, Elizabeth, and Matt Mead. 'Absent Histories and Absent Images: Photographs, Museums and the Colonial Past'. *Museum & Society* 11, no. 1 (2013): 19–38.

Fforde, Cressida. *Collecting the Dead: Archaeology and the Reburial Issue*. London: Duckworth, 2004.

Fforde, Cressida, Jane Hubert and Paul Turnbull, eds. *The Dead and Their Possessions: Repatriation in Principle, Policy and Practice*. London: Routledge, 2002.

Flower, William Henry. *Catalogue of the Specimens Illustrating the Osteology and Dentition of Vertebrated Animals, Recent and Extinct, Contained in the Museum of the Royal College of Surgeons of England, Part 1, Man.* 2nd ed. London: Taylor and Francis, 1907.

Hyde, Lewis. *Trickster Makes This World: Mischief, Myth, and Art.* New York: North Point Press, 1999.

Jenkins, Tiffany. '"Who Are We to Decide?" Internal Challenges to Cultural Authority in the Contestation over Human Remains in British Museums'. *Cultural Sociology* 6, no. 4 (July 2012): 455–70. Published online 12 July. Available at http://cus.sagepub.com/content/early/2012/05/15/1749975512445432 (accessed 21 July 2018).

Jenkins, Tiffany. *Contesting Human Remains in Museum Collections: The Crisis of Cultural Authority.* New York: Routledge, 2014.

Judd, Terri. 'Manchester Museum Returns Aboriginal Remains to Australia'. *Independent* 30 July 2003. Available at https://www.independent.co.uk/news/uk/this-britain/manchester-museum-returns-aboriginal-remains-to-australia-98210.html (accessed 14 September 2018).

Law.com website. 'Search Legal Terms and Definitions: Possession'. Available at https://dictionary.law.com/Default.aspx?selected=1555 (accessed 19 July 2019).

Lawson, Tom. *The Last Man: A British Genocide in Tasmania.* London: I. B. Tauris, 2014.

Lewis, Caroline. 'National Museums Given Powers to Return Human Remains'. 6 October 2005. *Culture24.* Available at http://www.culture24.org.uk/places-to-go/north-west/manchester/art30860 (accessed 14 September 2018).

Lydekker, Richard. *Guide to the Specimens Illustrating the Races of Mankind (Anthropology) Exhibited in the Department of Zoology, British Museum (Natural History) Cromwell Road, London S. W. 7.* London: Printed by Order of the Trustees of the British Museum, 1921.

MacAskill, Ewen. 'Britain Pressed to Return Aboriginal Bones'. *Guardian,* 5 July 2000. Available at https://www.theguardian.com/uk/2000/jul/05/ewenmacaskill (accessed 14 September 2018).

Mansell, Michael. *Tasmanian Aboriginal Centre Submission to the Trustees of the Natural History Museum for the Repatriation of Tasmanian Aboriginal Human Remains,* Board of Trustees TP06/54i, Human Remains Advisory Panel 0610HRAP4a. London: NHM, 2006.

Monro, C. C. A., and J. Ramsbottom. *Illustrated Guide to the Exhibition Galleries.* London: Published by Order of the Trustees of the British Museum (Natural History), 1931.

National Park Service, U.S. Department of the Interior (NPS). 'NAGPRA Law and Regulations Home'. Available at http://www.nps.gov/nagpra/MANDATES/INDEX.HTM (accessed 24 July 2018).

Natural History Museum. *Report on NHM Human Remains from Tasmania.* Board of Trustees TP06/54ii, Human Remains Advisory Panel 0610HRAP4b. London: NHM, 2006.

Natural History Museum. 'Press Release Friday 17 November 2006: Human Remains to be Returned from Natural History Museum's Collection'. London: NHM, 2006.

Natural History Museum. 'Human Comparative Collection'. Available at http://www.nhm. ac.uk/our-science/collections/palaeontology-collections/human-comparative-collection.html (accessed 25 August 2018).

Plomley, N. J. B. (ed). *Friendly Mission: The Tasmanian Journals and Papers of George Augustus Robinson, 1829–1834*, Tasmanian Historical Research Association. Launceston: Queen Victoria Museum and Art Gallery, 1966.

Proust, Marcel. *Remembrance of Things Past*, vol. 1, trans. C. K. Scott Moncrieff and Terence Kilmartin. London: Penguin, 1983 [1913].

Pycraft, W. P. 'Correspondence and Papers on Anthropology'. London: Natural History Museum (NHM), 1912– 1934.

Richardson, Ruth. *Death, Dissection and the Destitute*. London: Routledge & Kegan Paul, 1987.

SCRIBD. 'Eugenics Society Members A-Z 2012'. Available at https://www.scribd.com/doc/ 97123506/Eugenics-Society-Members-A-Z-2012 (accessed 24 August 2018).

Stanford, Peter. *How to Read a Graveyard: Journeys in the Company of the Dead*. London: Bloomsbury, 2013.

Tarlo, Emma. *Entanglement: The Secret Lives of Hair*. London: Oneworld, 2016.

Taylor, Rebe. 'The National Confessional'. *Meanjin Quarterly* 71, no. 3 (2012). Available at https://meanjin.com.au/essays/the-national-confessional/ (accessed 17 July 2018).

The Times. 'Losing Your Marbles: Bodies Are More Valuable Than Buildings'. Leader. 30 July 2003.

The Wildgoose Memorial Library (WML). Available at http://www.janewildgoose.co.uk (accessed 26 July 2018).

Turnbull, Paul. 'Scientific Theft of Remains in Colonial Australia'. *Australian Indigenous Law Review* 11, no. 1 (2007): 92–104. Available at http://www.austlii.edu.au/au/journals/ AILRev/2007/7.html (accessed 10 September 2018).

Turnbull, Paul. 'British Anatomists, Phrenologists and the Construction of the Aboriginal Race, c. 1790–1830'. *History Compass* 5, no. 1 (January 2007): 26–50. Available at https://doi. org/10.1111/j.1478-0542.2006.00367.x (accessed 19 July 2018).

Turnbull, Paul. 'British Anthropological Thought in Colonial Practice: The Appropriation of Indigenous Australian Bodies, 1860–1880'. In in *Foreign Bodies: Race in Oceania*, ed. Douglas Bronwen and Chris Ballard. Canberra: ANU E Press, 2008.

Turnbull, Paul. 'Theft in the name of science'. *Griffith Review* 21 (2008). Hidden Queensland. Available at https://griffithreview.com/articles/theft-in-the-name-of-science/ (accessed 13 September 2018).

Turnbull, Paul, and Michael Pickering, ed. *The Long Way Home: The Meaning and Values of Repatriation*. Oxford: Berghahn Books, 2010.

Whitehead, Gregory, Neil McCarthy and Jane Wildgoose. *On One Lost Hair*, BBC Radio 4, 10 May 2004.

Whitehead, Gregory, 'On One Lost Hair'. *Cabinet* 16/The Sea (Winter 2004–2005): 83–85.

Wildgoose, Jane. 'Grave-robbing, Crucifixion, Dissection: How Far Should We Go in the Name of Art?'. *New Statesman*, 15 August 1997, 41–43.

Wildgoose, Jane. 'An Acceptable Body of Work?'. *Daily Telegraph*: Arts & Books, 9 May 1998, A7.

Wildgoose, Jane. 'Zones of Morbidity'. In *Psycho*, ed. Danny Moynihan. London: Anne Faggionato, 2000, n.pag.

Wildgoose, Jane. 'The Business of the Flesh'. *Guardian*, 31 October 2002. Available at http://www.guardian.co.uk/society/2002/oct/31/1 (accessed 26 July 2018).

Wildgoose, Jane. 'About the Library'. The Wildgoose Memorial Library (WML). Available at http://www.janewildgoose.co.uk/jane_wildgoose.html (accessed 26 July 2018).

Wildgoose, Jane.'Possession: Nine-Tenths of the Law?' (Unpublished report for Natural History Museum London). London: The Wildgoose Memorial Library, 2006.

Wildgoose, Jane. *Promiscuous Assemblage, Friendship, & the Order of Things. An Installation by Jane Wildgoose in Celebration of the Friendship between Mrs. Mary Delany & the Duchess Dowager of Portland*. New Haven: Yale Center for British Art, 2009.

Wildgoose, Jane. 'Collecting and Interpreting Human Skulls and Hair in Late Nineteenth-Century London: *Passing Fables & Comparative Readings at The Wildgoose Memorial Library*; An artist's response to the *DCMS Guidance for the Care of Human Remains in Museums* (2005)'. PhD diss., Kingston University London, 2015.

Wildgoose, Jane. 'Presenting "Lost but Not Forgotten" at the Crypt Gallery St. Pancras: Negotiating and Constructing Active Critical Conversation Concerning Contested Human Remains in Museums'. In *This Place Cumulus Association Biannual International Conference Proceedings*, ed. D. Higgins and J. Pinches, 40–47. Nottingham: Nottingham Trent University, 2016. Available at http://www.cumulusnottingham2016.org/about/ (accessed 7 May 2020).

Wildgoose, Jane. 'Ways of Making with Human Hair and Knowing How to "Listen" to the Dead'. *West 86th* 23, no. 1 (Spring–Summer 2016): 79–101.

Wildgoose, Jane. 'Collecting Human Skulls and Hair: In Pursuit of Wonder in Death's Chambers'. In *Wonder in Contemporary Artistic Practice*, ed. Christian Mieves and Irene Brown, 211–29. Abingdon: Routledge, 2017.

World Archaeological Congress (WAC). 'World Archeological Congress Code of Ethics'; 'The Vermillion Accord on Human Remains'. Available at http://worldarch.org/code-of-ethics/ (accessed 24 July 2018).

12

Moving beyond the Specimen: From Drawing Objects to Drawing Processes

Gemma Anderson

Abstract

This chapter focuses on drawing as a way of knowing that requires engagement with scientific collections and specimens. As an artist, I have been working with museum specimens since 2006, mainly studying the resemblance between animal, mineral and vegetable species through the collections of the Natural History Museum, Kew Gardens and University College London. This work has been based on the hypothesis that a group of underlying morphological characteristics (forms and symmetries) are shared by animal, mineral and vegetable species. In the space of the page, the physical distance between museum specimens, normally housed in different parts of the museum, is confounded and allows for 'extra-scientific' comparisons revealing general patterns and processes at different scales and in different orders of being. Despite my lack of formal scientific training, I have embedded my artistic practice within the conventions of scientific institutions and collections. This practice has generated unconventional questions and has resulted in an unconventional body of knowledge. During this process, it has been important to observe the practice of scientists at the museum in order to realize what is shared between these scientific practices and my own method, for example; observation, trained judgement and abstraction. This practice allowed the rare opportunity to offer 'artistic visualization as critique'. Although this work is nested in the emerging field of 'drawing research', it is distinctive in its proposal of observational and conceptual drawing practice as a way of knowing form and formative process, as inspired by Goethe's morphology.

A flower with four petals bought in the stream of morning rush hour commuters exiting South Kensington tube station enters the NHM protected by my hands. As organized through countless emails, this morning there will be specimens from the zoology, mineralogy and plant collections together on a desk specified for me to draw from. The specimens are not how I imagined, their fourfoldness is not so obvious as in my imagination. I handle them, rotate them to 'find' the fourfold in perspectives not offered in the display cases. I freeze the specimen there, in my hand, resting on a prop; sometimes a pen, a specimen box or a book and I draw. As I draw, I see the morphology, and it suggests to me relations to the other fourfold specimens that can only be found in this way, in this menagerie, on this day. The dragon-wing suggests the leaf, the spread of the wings suggests the crossing lines of the cubic mineral and so the drawing continues as a chain of resemblances, towards a landscape of resemblances, organised by morphologies silent suggestions and populated by the play of similarity. In the drawing, the real merges with the imagination as it dances in and out of many bodies (relates to the drawings of William Bartram but different). Animal, mineral and vegetable weave themselves into a cavern of likeness, a temporal home for their unseen relations.

This chapter aims to illuminate how my artistic practice moved from working with museum specimens to a practice that is decidedly 'post-specimen' (Fig. 12. 1). This involved a shift from the observational drawing of specimens as 'objects' to drawing biological processes as a form of simulation where there is no 'object' at all; resulting in a move away from the specimen itself as an object of study. This change in my practice has involved conceptual leaps and the creation of new artistic methods.

Changing Environment: Changing Practice

Let's begin by taking a quantum leap back to 2005. After studying for a BA in Fine Art at Falmouth College of Art (FCA) I arrived in London to begin an MA at the Royal College of Art (RCA). In Falmouth there was an abundance of morphology to draw from in nature (especially plants) and I would find things to sketch while walking in the 'field'.[1] It was Aristotle who said 'it is form [...] which furnishes the foundation of all biology [...]. Anyone who has ever collected animals and plants knows how the eye is caught by the formal regularity of an organised being'.[2] Perhaps Aristotle's understanding of regularity in organic form could be thought of as kind of morphology, and, as an artist who responds to this sense of natural form, I am a kind of morphologist. For me morphology is like the entrance to the maze. Forms, symmetries, lines, angles and textures invite observation and investigation on an endless path where 'all forms are alike and none is like another, so that their chorus points the way to a hidden law'.[3]

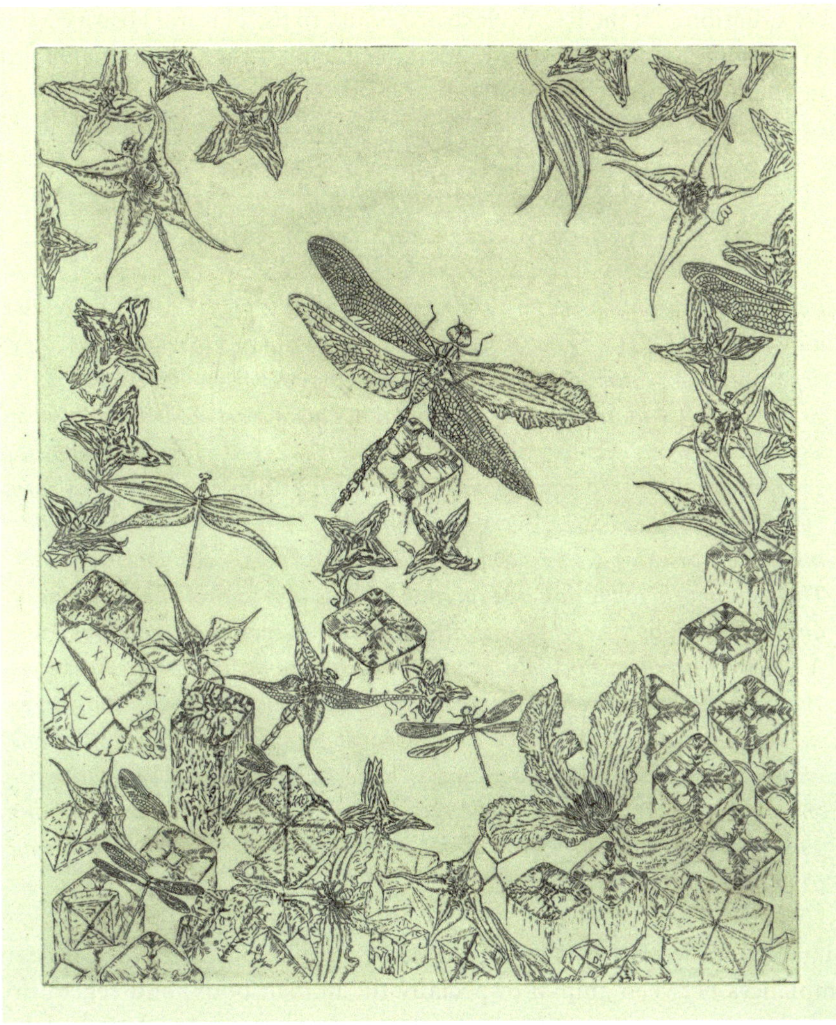

FIGURE 12.1. Gemma Anderson, 'Fourfold symmetry', Isomorphology series (Drawn from The Natural History Museum collections), 2012, copper etching. © Gemma Anderson.

On arriving in London, I was overwhelmed by the urban environment and worried about how I would 'find' my subjects. As the RCA is beside Hyde Park, I went for a walk to see how my previous method would work.[4] I tried to find a quiet spot to draw. It was difficult to find somewhere without other people and hard to access some plants due to the fences. Planes flew overhead and cars hummed in the distance, disturbing any momentary sense of peacefulness. I realized that the way I worked would have to change according to the distracting nature of the new situation. Yet the RCA's close proximity to the Natural History Museum (NHM) seemingly offered a solution to this dilemma for within this institution was an abundance of natural forms.

Morphological Interest Leads to the Natural History Museum and Its Collections

I meet the palaeontologist for the first time beside the giant sloth in an exhibition hall of the NHM which is next to the staff entrance to the Palaeontology department. We open the door. The palaeontology department is hard to navigate; it has lifts, doors and staircases that don't quite meet up. It's best to have a guide. The main chamber of the department is full to the brim with objects. There are beautiful old wooden museum cases and drawers as well as modern metal cupboards and cases. Everywhere objects are piled on top of one another. Inside these cases are drawers crammed with fossils, corals, echinoids and flints. This is the world of the museum specimen. These objects provoke questions of time and place, of their relation to other specimens, species and environments. As the palaeontologist introduced me to the collections, I asked her questions about the specimens; their relations, times, places, deformations and idiosyncrasies. It was a rare opportunity to ask a scientist questions about the collections on a one-to-one basis and I later came to understand this as an important epistemological feature of the 'collections visit'. Questions led to further questions and I found myself learning about palaeontology via the activity of 'drawing from the collections'.

My interest at the time was in comparative morphology; by which I mean the resemblances between animal (especially the human body) and vegetal forms. This had been a fascination for me since my school days when I made drawings of the veins of leaves and of humans interchanging. For me these relationships are poetic reminders that humans are inherently connected to other species. As a relational practice comparative morphology has been a way for me to connect to non-human life forms and to draw connections between unrelated species. The aim of this kind of study can be summarized by Johann Wolfgang von Goethe who claimed that with morphological knowledge

> it will be possible to go on forever inventing plants [or other species] and know that their existence is logical; that is to say, if they do not actually exist, they could, for they possess an inner necessity and truth.[5]

274

I see morphological drawing as a means through which to invent forms that 'could be' and for me this is the idea that drives my practice. In Falmouth, I had been combining life drawing in the studio with drawings of plants/vegetable material from 'the field'. When I first visited the NHM, I realized that there was a wealth of 'morphology' inside its walls that could be drawn. But I did not want to just stand in the halls and draw from the vitrines, amongst the bustle of the other visitors. I wanted to draw specimens in a similar way to how I had drawn in Cornwall, at close range, with the ability to hold, to rotate and to scrutinize each form individually (Fig. 12. 2).

The NHM is a research institution that holds around 80 million specimens. It is a building with two lives; one open to the public, and one 'behind the scenes' full of specimens and scientists. 'Behind the scenes' was where I wanted to be, but it was not obvious how to get there. I wrote to many scientists at the museum, introduced myself and my work and asked if I could visit the collections to pursue my interest in morphological drawing. I sent images of my work. After a while, I got a reply from a palaeontologist. She was interested in art and prepared to help me access the collections. So, we started there. Although at first this connection to palaeontology was merely fortuitous, later I can see how thinking about the 'history of the organism' may have influenced my work. The scientific imagination of the palaeontologist that reconstructs the historical development of species through the fossil record is similar to the act of drawing the developmental process of an organism; both require research and understanding through direct observation but also imagination and speculation. In order to test my intuitions of the shared morphological characteristics of animal, mineral and vegetable species, I chose to observe directly from specimens in the museum, and vital to this exploration was the handling of each specimen, which activated a toing and froing between the optic and the haptic. Handling and sensing the specimen evoked ideas about representing form and texture through line and mark-making.

Drawing in the palaeontology department thus gave me a sense of what was possible. The experience of aligning my ideas about the specimens with the reality of meeting them in person helped manage my expectations and guide my imagination towards possible tasks. The potential for creative interactions with the collections, through and beyond drawing, was palpable and so began a long 'extra-scientific' collaboration between an artist and a number of scientists within the museum. I chose to draw 'problematic flint', so-called because it is 'unclassifiable', problematic because it resembles human figures, animal heads and limbs; altogether representing a lively subculture of pseudoscientific observations made by the keen observer who donated these specimens of flint to the

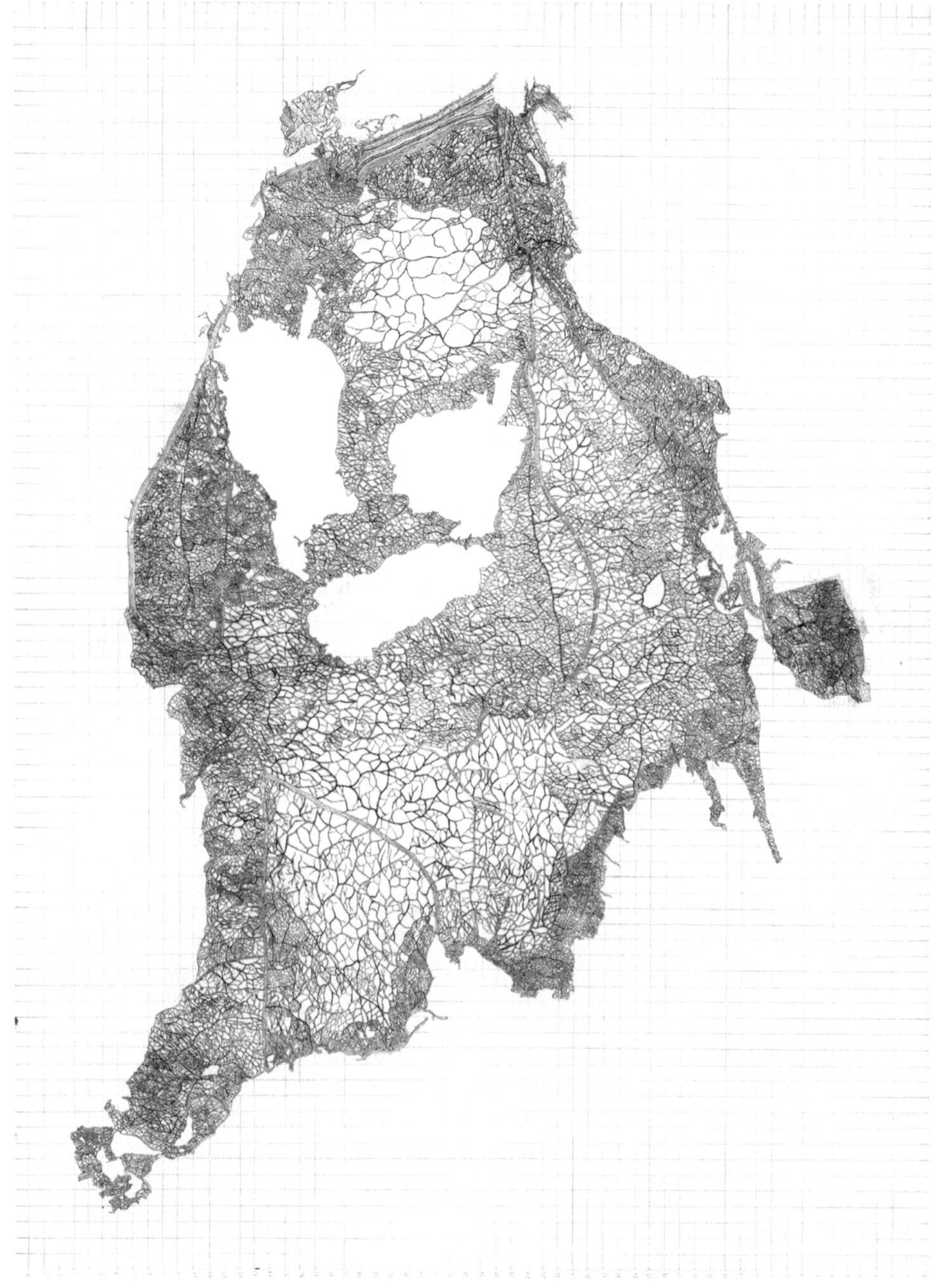

FIGURE 12.2. Gemma Anderson, 'Gunnera Leaf', 2004, copper etching, 100 × 80 cm. © Gemma Anderson.

museum. With many examples of 'problematic flint' to draw, I asked for a quiet space with natural light. The palaeontologist set me up in the 'visitor room'—situated just off the main collections room with large windows and a scientific lab bench (Fig. 12.3).

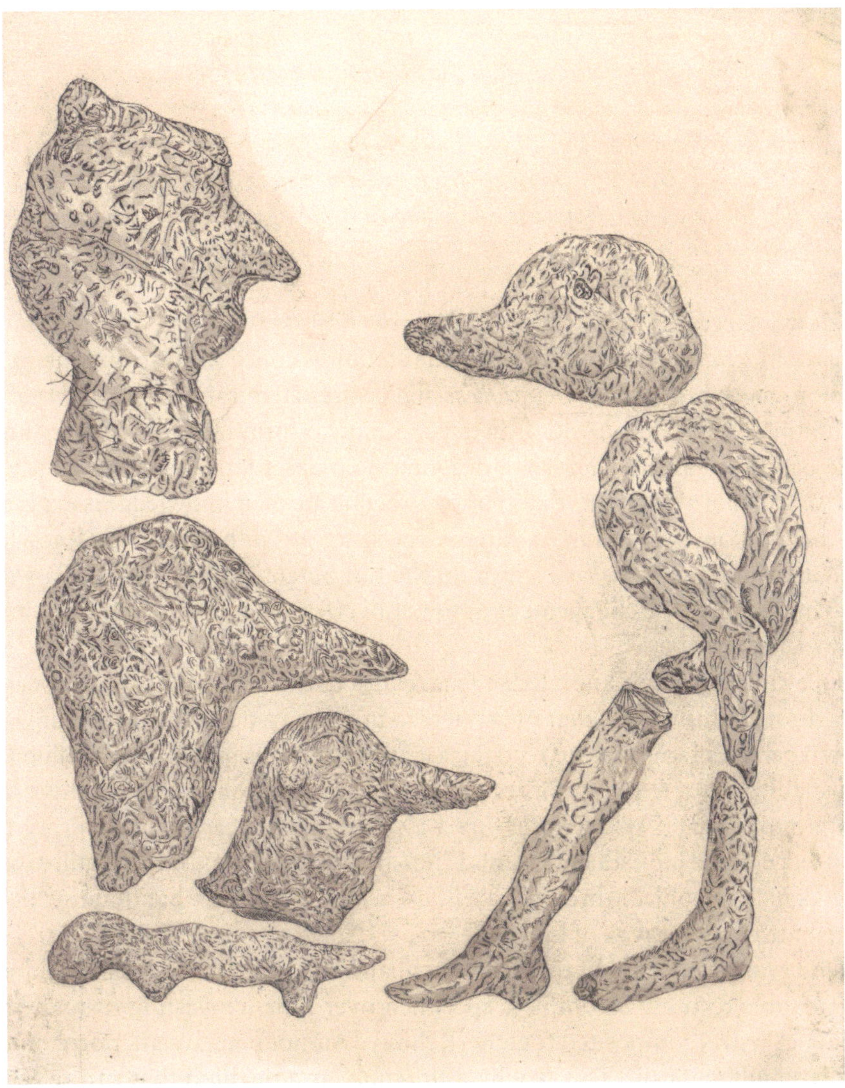

FIGURE 12.3. Gemma Anderson, 'Problematic flint (Drawn from The Natural History Museum palaeontology collection)', 2012. Copper etching and Japanese inks. © Gemma Anderson.

On Drawing

Observational drawing involves hand-eye coordination, analysis, delineation, abstraction, improvisation, collage and deep concentration. This is enhanced through handling the specimen, which allows for the rotation of the object and the selection of a perspective to draw from. Perception of the object is a process of transition from experience to judgement, insight to application. Concentrated observation within the act of drawing creates new perceptual knowledge, activating the process of comparison and selection of salient features. Each form observed joins a 'bank' of knowledge in the observer's mind and each new drawing experience triggers a different formal memory 'stored' in this 'bank'. New drawings add value to drawings previously made, and vice versa.

The drawing process involves feedback: as dynamic sensory transference from the optic to the kinaesthetic to the haptic that requires concentration and interactive decision-making. The drawing process aligns internal duration with external representation. Observation and drawing combine to form tacit and sensory knowledge of the specimen. Therefore drawing, like observation, is its own teacher. Michael Polanyi also tells us that the key to acquiring tacit knowledge is experience and that without some form of shared experience it is difficult for this knowledge to be disseminated.[6] The realization of the full potential of drawing as a way of knowing requires the engagement of the drawer, or what Polanyi refers to as 'the knowing subject'.

An example of tacit knowledge that relates to delineating morphological features through drawing, is that of facial recognition given by Michael Polanyi, 'We know a person's face, and can recognize it among a thousand, indeed a million. Yet we usually cannot tell how we recognize a face we know, so most of this cannot be put into words'.[7] When observing a face, or in this case a museum specimen, knowledge of the individual features is not always conscious, but it is still possible to recognize the object through recall, association or direct handling, which all contribute to a tacit way of knowing.[8]

Observation consists of the zooming in and zooming out of details. Although it is possible to draw a complete specimen over time (consisting of many morphological parts composited together), the eye cannot perceive all morphological details simultaneously. This is why a drawing, as a medium that can select and represent salient features of morphological characteristics and the whole simultaneously, holds a unique epistemological value. Therefore, any single drawing represents multiple and continuous observational acts of focusing in and out, which form a drawn image over time. The drawing then offers a view of an object that is otherwise impossible without the time endured in the patient act of drawing, and allows us to observe and compare details simultaneously.

Drawing from life is always an experiment because the individual nature of the specimen can be very unpredictable. The individual variations of specimens bring challenges and surprises to the work, and also to any process of classification. What occurs is an improvised response motivated by ideas and observations, which are reified through engaging with the real. One morphological character can be compared to another and through drawing body parts can merge, transplant and exchange as form takes precedence over scale. In this improvisation, morphology suggests art, and the lengthy and patient observations are rewarded through a joyful and creative experiment in drawing, each with its own individual modifications. Goethe insisted that this combination of insight and judgement required the observer to detect 'the idea in the observation'.[9] Building on this idea of 'the idea in the observation', Lorraine Daston and Peter Galison consider that the qualifications necessary to see like a naturalist include synthesis, adding that 'to see like a naturalist required more than just sharp senses: a capacious memory, the ability to analyse and synthesize impressions, as well as the patience and talent to extract the typical from the storehouse of natural particulars'.[10]

Drawing brings a deep sense of embodiment and connection to our experience of the world, providing a space to hold and to unfold complexity. There are continuous changes: pausing to observe, choosing direction, changing tempo, transitioning between focused and wider attention, inside and outside the line, of selecting what to take forward and what to let go. The handling of museum specimens thus allows for an intimate gaze and connection to the object. The ability to rotate and to choose a perspective from which to draw is crucial in order to find the angle that reveals the morphology clearly and makes it comparable to the morphology of others. The draftsman/draftswoman must select the salient information from the subject.

Drawing from the Museum Specimens

As there are many possible answers to the question 'what are the forms and symmetries of this animal, plant or mineral?', it is the consequence of choosing one perspective to draw from the automatic exclusion of a thousand others. With any given specimen there are many possibilities for observing forms and symmetries, depending on focus. First comes observation of forms that are more obvious, for instance branching forms, and then of more subtle or complex forms, like the spiral arrangement of the inner flower. The chosen perspective opens up new possibilities for abstraction, for example: a cross section of the

stem can be viewed as a multi-sided prism or rocks abstracted to isosceles tri-
angles, each individual a variation on a theme.

I infiltrated the museum. I drew in every department, from every collection, from slides, to herbarium sheets to 'wet specimens' to classical taxidermy. I met all the different kinds of scientists in the museum. I witnessed something about their differing practices and I joined them for fieldwork to learn more about the process of collecting specimens. Starting this work in the palaeontology department made me more aware of the specimen as a historical being. As I worked in other departments, I viewed the narrative around each specimen as to some extent discovered and to some extent imagined. I learnt about the museum's relationship with contemporary artists[11] and about Centre for Arts and Humanities Research, the library, the imaging department, the staff canteen, and so on.

I brought a prepared copper plate to the museum (Fig. 12.4). This intrigued the palaeontologist and others as many scientists are familiar with etchings as scientific images but not the process of their creation. A standard approach to etching is to make a drawing on paper and then to transfer this drawing onto the copper plate. But I drew directly on to the copper plate from life. This surprised the scientists at

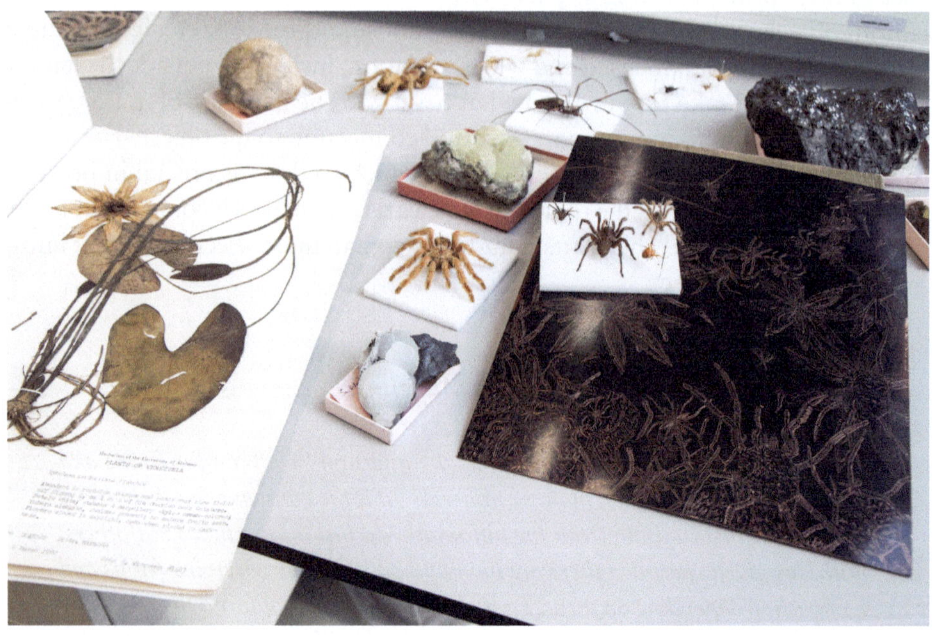

FIGURE 12.4. Gemma Anderson, 'View of designated bench space for Isomorphology study in the Sackler Lab, Darwin Centre, The Natural History Museum', 2013. Photograph. © Gemma Anderson.

the museum and highlighted to me why I liked this way of working: First, a mistake is recorded and must become part of the work; this demands improvisation and creativity in a process of 'fixing' the image and ensures that the drawing will develop 'organically' rather than replicate a preformed image. Second, copper is a valuable material; there is just one attempt at the work, no rubbing out, no starting again. This risky way of working, that is so amenable to trial and error, is an aspect of science that is frequently downplayed and is maybe what so fascinated the scientists as observers of my practice. Perhaps this intervention within the museum challenged the very idea of 'objectivity' in science through making transparent the slightly messy and uncertain process of knowledge production. Certainly, the decisions I made when drawing from the museum specimen were different from the decisions scientists generally make when drawing, although the approach has many shared characteristics.[12]

Through this process, I began to notice morphological relationships between specimens: animal, mineral and vegetable. I saw that morphological relationships existed despite specimens being classified in different sections of the museum and I drew these 'extra-scientific' relationships.[13] As I had drawn the relationship between the human (animal) and the plant in Cornwall, I could now draw the relationship between the human (animal), plant (vegetable) and mineral. The limitation I had first felt on arriving into London's urban environment compared to Cornwall's 'field' had inverted. I realized that in drawing specimens in the 'field' I was somewhat limited to the 'surface of things', to the external, optically visible morphology. As I was also limited by the weather and the difficulty in finding a space to draw, I would often collect what I could carry and draw in the studio. Perhaps the most limiting factor of drawing in the field was that I could only draw what was local, in the museum however, I could draw morphology from around the world. While the NHM permitted morphological drawing with global reach, the vastness of the collections could make decisions of what to draw overwhelming.

Through questioning scientists and my own research in this way I was able to move beyond the visible to realm of theoretical morphology. In drawing I was uncovering relationships that had not been 'made visible' before and I was thinking about what this could mean in relation to the Linnaean system of scientific classification which is the foundation for the order of things at the NHM.[14] I was organizing and relating the specimens in the act of drawing and I was seeing for myself a new way to make order and classify objects of the museum: animal, mineral and vegetable.

Annotating Morphology

Drawing the natural world as a chain of resemblances, merging object bodies into one another and creating a newly classified order all require artistic improvisation. Through improvisation the morphology of different bodies can be freed from the artist's agency and suggest art within the parameters of the drawing space. Improvising through drawing is a kind of 'sampling' or re-mixing of natural form—recombining like a strand of DNA creating a new order for the parts. This improvisation runs throughout the creation of each Isomorphology etching, which is drawn directly onto the copper plate. This immediate way of drawing, in which each line is a permanent, non-erasable commitment is surprising, challenging and uncomfortable. The drawing is often driven by solving the initial feeling of 'this is not working', which needs to be overcome, and requires improvisation to continue. The drawing process can be compared to building: each drawing, which selects morphological features from a specimen, either attaches to a drawing made earlier or generates a new drawing site for building on the plate. This process does not follow a linear order but unfolds in response to the drawing as it arises.

Drawing morphological characteristics (of forms and symmetry) approximates to the notation of an *isomorphic* alphabet: a character set of form, but without the syntax of language.[15] This process is somewhat like comparative morphology, but with different questions and motivations. I coined the term 'Isomorphology' as 'the study of the shared forms and symmetries of animal, mineral and vegetable species through drawing'.[16]

I compiled a list of specimens held within the NHM collections that related to the form species of Isomorphology that I had generated through developing a two-dimensional *bauplan* or visual 'body plan' for each species. Of particular importance to me were the images in *Evolution without Selection*[17] that pertained to Isomorphology's form species, for example: hexagonal patterns in body forma-tion of mineral, animal (vertebrate and invertebrate), plant and fivefold symmetry, ramified patterns in the body formation of molecules, protozoa vertebrate and invertebrate bodies and leaf patterns (bilateral symmetry) in animal, mineral and vegetable species.

These lists, which collected many more species' names than could be drawn, operated as a flexible way to navigate the morphology of animal, mineral and vegetable specimens within the collections. This morphological triangulation pro-cess aimed to select specimens based on the criteria of resemblance to the form species of Isomorphology. The next stage utilized these inventories to 'screen' hundreds of specimens with curators in the zoology, mineralogy and botany col-lections at the NHM.[18] My intention was to systematically bring together spe-cimens of the museum's collections into one physical space where I could draw their morphological resemblances together into one image, allowing one form to become another. Thus, the drawings 'accumulated' organically, but at each stage there was a conscious selection and deformation of form. This purposeful coming together of specimens normally separated might be seen as a kind of spatio-temporal menagerie, a temporary disruption of the order of the museum's collections and a drawing that would forever be a celebration of morphological kinship rather than difference. In this way, Isomorphology functions as a critique of the Linnaean system of classification and a reminder that there can be many other ways of classifying and many ways of knowing. For instance, the notion of 'radial symmetry' achieves this critique of classification by highlighting radial forms in starfish, minerals and plant forms. Upon looking at the image, the viewer must ask, what is animal, what is mineral and what is vegetable, and the answer will not be clear because the morphological resemblances have been drawn out of each body, abstracted into linear relations that show similarity rather than difference (Fig. 12.5 and Fig. 12.6).

Isomorphology

Isomorphology symbols are two-dimensional symbols that have been abstracted from the observation of three-dimensional specimens. In observations in the field and of museum specimens, this dynamic is reversed and the two-dimensional symbols are projected on to three-dimensional objects: plant, mineral or animal. The process of applying an abstraction to the reality of the observed specimen depends on the motivation and training of the individual observer. Observing in the field is both an act of interpretation and of translation, and so it requires a conceptual flexibility of working between the two-dimensional and three-dimensional forms. The observer's mind, which the project inclines towards symmetry, completes the imperfections of the reality of a specimen by projecting the abstract onto the observed to complete the picture.

The philosopher of biology John Dupré argues that as there are many properties upon which classification can be based there can be no universal system of taxonomy. He notes that 'there are countless legitimate, objectively grounded ways of classifying objects in the world. And these may often cross-classify one another in indefinitely complex ways.'[19] The shared forms and symmetries of Isomorphology can therefore be viewed through the lens of Dupré's 'species' concept as 'a class of objects defined by a common possession of some theoretically important property'.[20]

Isomorphology proposes visual 'form species' that set priority on form and symmetry. These two properties turn standard classification on its head to show that there are alternative ways to classify natural life across kingdoms. As

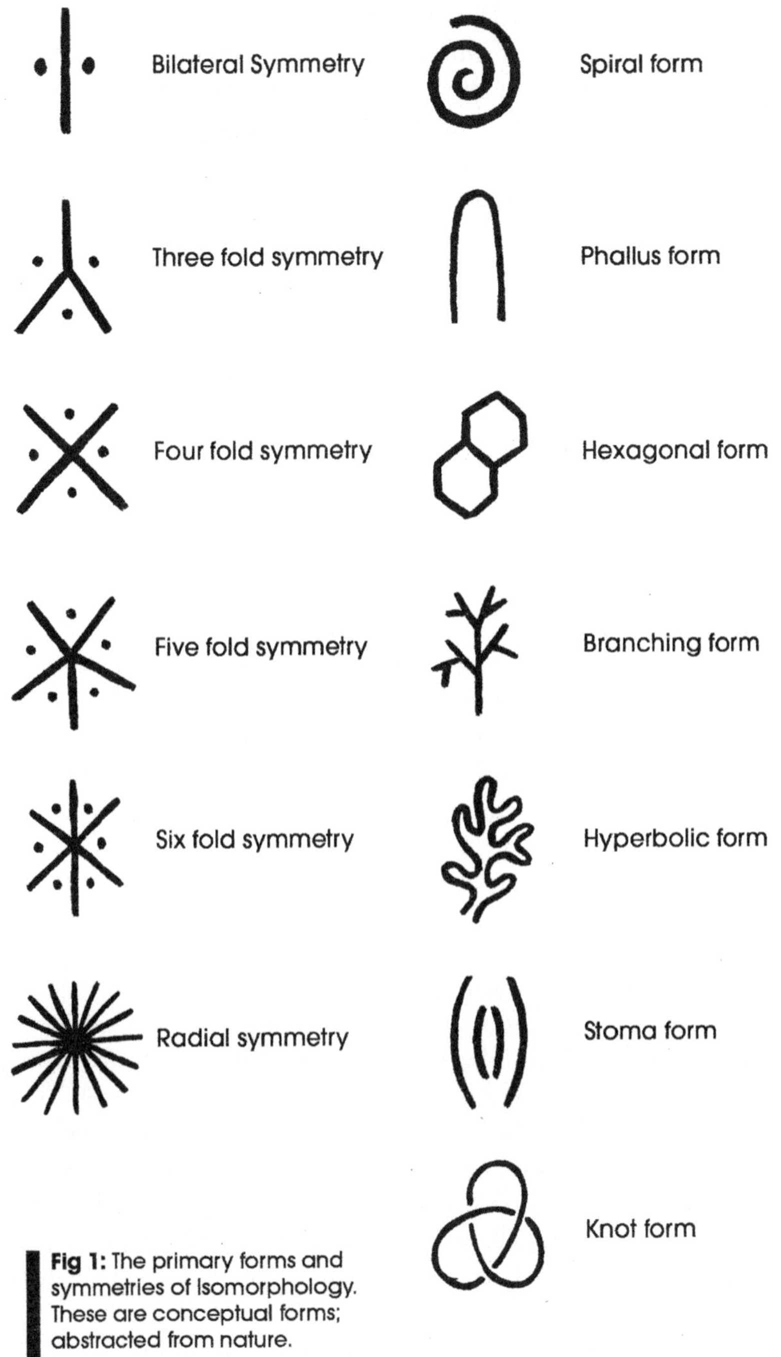

FIGURE 12.5. Gemma Anderson, 'Visual list of forms and symmetries of Isomorphology (a page from *Isomorphology*)', 2013. © Gemma Anderson.

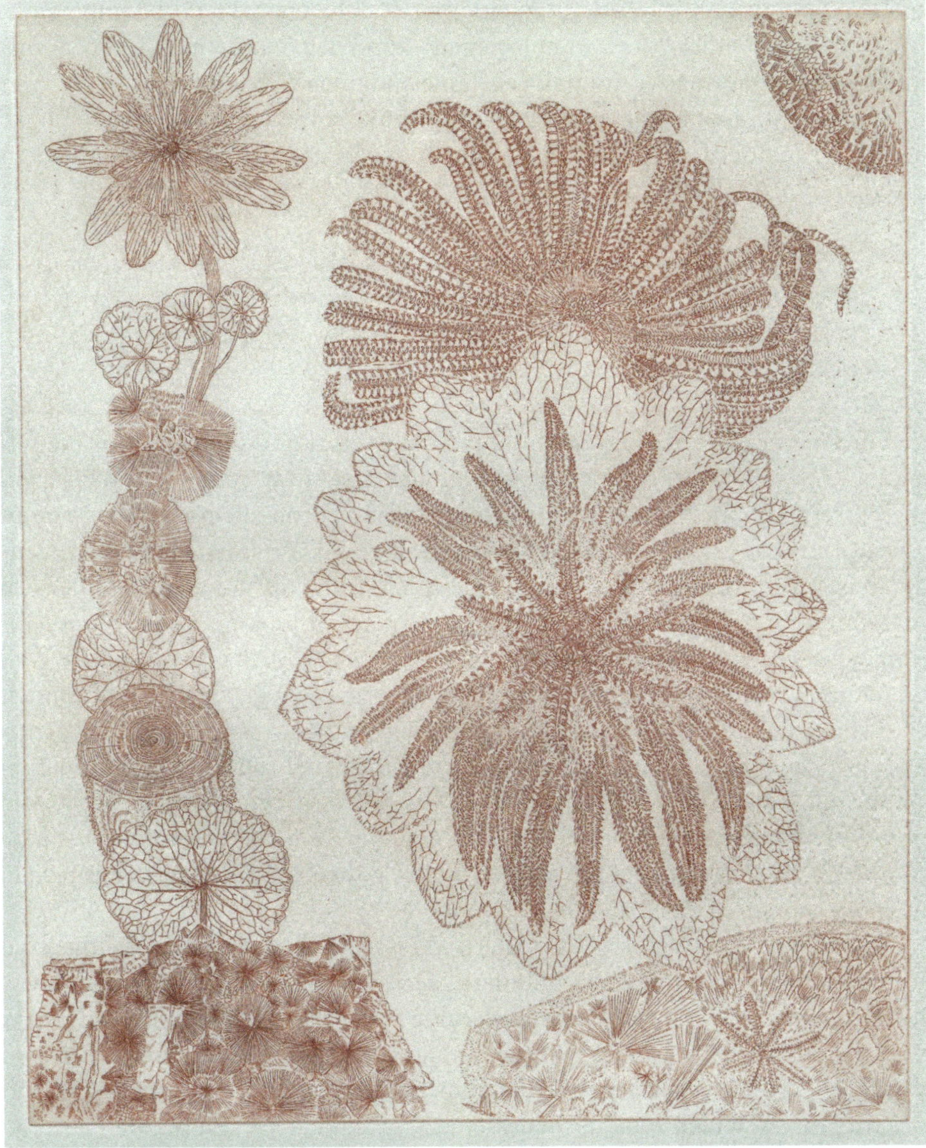

FIGURE 12.6. Gemma Anderson, 'Radial Symmetry', Isomorphology series, 2014. Copper etching. © Gemma Anderson.

such, Isomorphology is in line with Dupré's pluralistic view. Yet, in as much as Isomorphology rejects Linnaean classification it nonetheless appropriates those qualities from its taxonomy (and its place within the museum system) which, although imperfect, serve to organize nature. To do otherwise would result in such taxonomic confusion that any attempt at coherency would be impossible. Isomorphology is therefore a complementary approach to ordering specimens that intends to blur normative animal, vegetable and mineral boundaries.

Consideration of Isomorphology and Dupré's 'process philosophy of biology' necessitates a discussion of Goethe's original concept of morphology. Goethe characterized morphology as a means

> to understand living formations as such, to grasp their externally visible, tangible parts in relation to one another, to take these parts as indications of what lies within and thus to acquire a degree of mastery over the whole through intuition.[21]

For Goethe, morphology was the most universal and important of the sciences.[22] He believed the morphologist should first study completed forms and then investigate the forces that give rise to them. Through close observation of physical structures and processes, he felt that it was possible to achieve conscious awareness of morphological genesis of which all forms are merely a physical manifestation.[23] Goethe described how 'every act of looking leads to observation, observation to reflection, reflection to combination, in every attentive look on nature we already theorize'.[24] Applying a Goethean logic to draftsmanship, it could be said that concentrated observation within the act of drawing itself generates new perceptual knowledge about the specimen. Morphological information can be observed in detail, thus activating the process of comparison; each form observed stimulates a new understanding and joins a 'bank' of knowledge in the observer's mind. Each new drawing experience then triggers a different formal memory 'stored' in this 'bank'.

Goethe's morphology was characterized by striving to reach beyond the fixed form (Gestalt) to the dynamic (Bildung): 'That which is formed, is straightaway formed again, and if we would to some degree arrive at a living intuition of Nature, we must on our part remain forever mobile and plastic, according to her own example'.[25] He saw static form as a momentary phase, an instance, of this formative process, which could be considered apart and in itself only by an abstraction (or when static through death as in the museum object). Rather than reduce phenomena to either structure or process, Goethe wanted to allow both into the study of morphology.

As I drew from the collections, I found my questions changing from questions of *form* to questions of *formation*, towards a view that aligned with Goethe's morphology and his use of the term 'genetic' not as the term is understood today—as the science of genes—but rather as seeking the origin or *genesis* of phenomena. He explained:

If I look at the created object, inquire into its creation, and follow this process back as far as I can, I will find a series of steps. Since these are not actually seen together before me, I must visualize them in my memory so that they form a certain ideal whole. At first I will tend to think in terms of steps, but nature leaves no gaps, and thus in the end, I will have to see this progression of uninterrupted activity as a whole. I can do so by dissolving the particular without destroying the impression itself.[26]

Specimens were selected based on their visible relation to the Isomorphology form species and then classified in the lab space before drawing, during which some were de-selected. Then there was a further selection/classification process when choosing what to draw, which parts to draw. The presence of each specimen was motivated by an enquiry into form and symmetry, which determined organization whilst allowing for chance operations to occur. But I had a problem: How to make visible something that I could not directly observe? How to draw an imaginary specimen? I found myself in a conundrum that has been experienced by many other artists and succinctly outlined by Wassily Kandinsky:

[A] terrifying abyss of all kinds of questions, a wealth of responsibilities stretched before me. And most important of all: what is to replace the missing object? The danger of ornament revealed itself clearly to me; the dead semblance of stylised forms I found merely repugnant [...] it took a very long time before I arrived at the correct answer to the question: what is to replace the object? I sometimes look back at the past and despair at how long this solution took me.[27]

What was to replace the absent specimen, the morphological missing link? The questions I asked the scientists at the NHM had to change. Instead of asking to see specimens that displayed certain forms and symmetries I asked questions about growth and development, genesis and I found myself reading in the field of developmental and theoretical morphology in relation to creative computing and generative art. I reflected on how imagining absent forms is particularly acute for palaeontology and archaeo-anthropology where the missing link is continuously present. At the same time, I began collaborating with Dupré on work less to do with classification than with process ontology, an approach that addresses the biology's hoary question of 'whether the living world should be thought of as a hierarchy of objects, or rather as composed of processes, and thus as essentially dynamic'.[28] As a result of this co-operation, my work became no longer interested in the specimen as merely *object*, but in the specimen as the by-product of a *process* both developmental and *curatorial*. This view challenged the conventional understanding of the museum 'object' as fixed and clearly demarcated by seeing the 'object' itself as process. I needed to change the way I worked again, and I was grasping in the dark. Out of this period of reflection came the idea of 'Isomorphogenesis': a drawing practice or 'experiment' that explores the potentialities of representing morphology as a dynamic and formative process. Isomorphogenesis strongly builds on Isomorphology as it progresses from the empirical study of the morphology of static specimens towards a conceptual study of morphology as dynamic.

Isomorphogenesis

Analogies emerge through the act of drawing, allowing resemblance to be discovered rather than invented. Observational drawing allows for the comparison of what is already known and what is observed, and for extending this comparison until what is known, what is drawn and what is observed are consistent.

Isomorphogenesis brought together my experience of working with scientific practitioners in that it united the observational and the abstract—experiment and theory—through drawing. In Isomorphogenesis I applied theory from other domains—selecting key ideas based on my experience and knowledge—in parallel with the development of practice. Through the lens of Isomorphogenesis, this harvesting of information enabled the adaptation of key ideas from other domains to feed my own practice. As such, Isomorphogenesis sampled aspects from the work of others and employed theory in the service of practice.

Just as the Isomorphology study developed a typology of form, Dupré and I recognized the potential for the Isomorphogenesis method to create a typology of process, along with methods for representing this. This would involve identifying heterogeneous biological processes through similar methods used to identify heterogeneous forms in Isomorphology. Isomorphogenesis reveals a series of drawing actions that explore the nature of primitive and developed form, as assemblages created through process. The first Isomorphogenesis series developed form in a more or less 'vertical descent' manner but future iterations could be developed to evolve form through network-based models. Isomorphogenesis offers drawing 'actions' that re-enact movements of biological processes, and begins to classify these 'actions' into primary and secondary categories by organizing them into two categories during the drawing process itself. Isomorphogenesis therefore suggests a classification of processual movements or 'actions' that emerges through a drawing process rather than a traditionally scientific process.

This practice developed through a series of experiments that relate to the artist Bruce Gernand's observations of his own practice-based research: 'Although one can make plans and project ideas in advance, there are also aleatoric structures, random occurrences: mutations begin to drive actions which are a lot less deterministic than we think'.[29] Gernand's practice, especially his *Coded Chimera* (2011), has been deeply influenced by D'Arcy Wentworth Thompson's magnum opus, *On Growth and Form* (1917) which developed an understanding of morphology from the perspective of the action of physical forces on organic matter. In *Coded Chimera*, Gernand took Thompson's theory of transformations as a starting point and used animal scans and computer software to blend and morph different animal specimens together to suggest hybrid, *in-between* species. In so doing, Gernand's cross-breeds emphasized Thompson's notion of an organism as a 'diagram of the forces that have acted upon it';[30] they became 'chimeras' of process rather than stasis. As Gernard states:

> As the work progressed, I became less interested in the deformations of the composite of a cat and a crocodile, the expression of the disjunction of reptilian and mammalian anatomy. Rather than looking at the chimera in a literal, prosaic way, I responded more to the renderings which expressed a fluidity, a transforming from one condition to another, a sense of becoming one another. Although the specimens I paired had, very generally, similar body plans, trying to 'integrate' their respective meshes revealed considerable stresses. So, the sense of fluidity has to be qualified: the meshes also judder, shake and break apart, being the products of dynamic and turbulent reactions.[31]

D'Arcy Wentworth Thompson is a useful figure to consider in relation to the agency of Isomorphogenesis as his curation of the University of Dundee's zoological collections was concurrent with the development of his theory of transformations. Thompson's thesis—which drew directly upon his work with museum specimens—asserted that natural form was the product of growth and that this, stated simply, was conditioned by protoplasm responding to internal energies and external forces to produce unique conformations.[32] As demonstrated in the case of Gernand, Thompson's work has had a great influence on a number of artists, such as Naum Gabo and Henry Moore, who have engaged with morphology and the representation of the dynamic nature of form.[33]

Isomorphogenesis has therefore evolved from the struggle to find a method that accommodates, and indeed capitalizes on, the uncertainty that characterizes the creative process. As a drawing process, it does not claim to directly contribute to the science of evolutionary biology; but Isomorphogenesis does offer a method for representing, exploring and theorizing the processual nature of biological phenomena, which subsequently offers insight into biological development and has the potential to inform the ontological shift towards conceiving or theorizing form *as* process.

Isomorphogenesis builds on the aesthetics of development, especially those of visually sequencing development, but contributes by drawing development as a connected series rather than as a series of instances as in standard biological textbooks. The idea of representing development as a visual series has influenced the creation of my drawing methods. However, a developmental series is conventionally represented as a series of isolated instances (or slices of time) of form change when, in reality, transformation does not occur in isolated stages but in a continuum. The intention of Isomorphogenesis is to create drawn developmental sequences that show the development of form as a continuous process. Drawing is chosen to represent the development of biological form through an intrinsically connected image: A 'moving present'. In Isomorphogenesis, morphological change can be understood as a series of drawn 'movements', each defining a stage of development. And if Isomorphogenesis offered a means through which to understand the forms and symmetries shared among specimens, then Isomorphogenesis allows a move *beyond* the object into the hypothetical, the *post*-specimen (Fig. 12.7 and Fig. 12.8).

Conclusion

This chapter aimed at illuminating how my artistic practice moved from working with museum specimens to a practice that is 'post-specimen'. This involved a shift from observational drawing of specimens as 'objects' to drawing biological processes as a form of simulation where there is no 'object' at all.

Perhaps Isomorphology could be used to redesign the modern museum itself. Isomorphology focuses observational skills and in doing so has the potential to radicalize classification, to inspire a new fascination with the morphological resemblances across kingdoms that might suggest new approaches to old understandings, in that contemporary museums may productively look back to older ordering systems and in so doing transform the classificatory and epistemological rationale of the museum itself. Indeed, Isomorphogenesis can transform our awareness of museum taxonomy as it helps to see form and formative process in a kind of noun/verb, object/process relationship, to see specimens and the living world not as objects, fixed, like parts in a machine, but as processes, interconnected and intersected, in an ecological relationship with us. Isomorphogenesis can also help to 're-animate' the specimen in the imagination, to imagine the history of the organism as a palaeontologist could, and to dynamically realize this vision through drawing. These practices, if implemented could transform the way we relate to museum specimens, towards a non-human centric relational connection, towards understanding ourselves as processes, connected to all others. This way

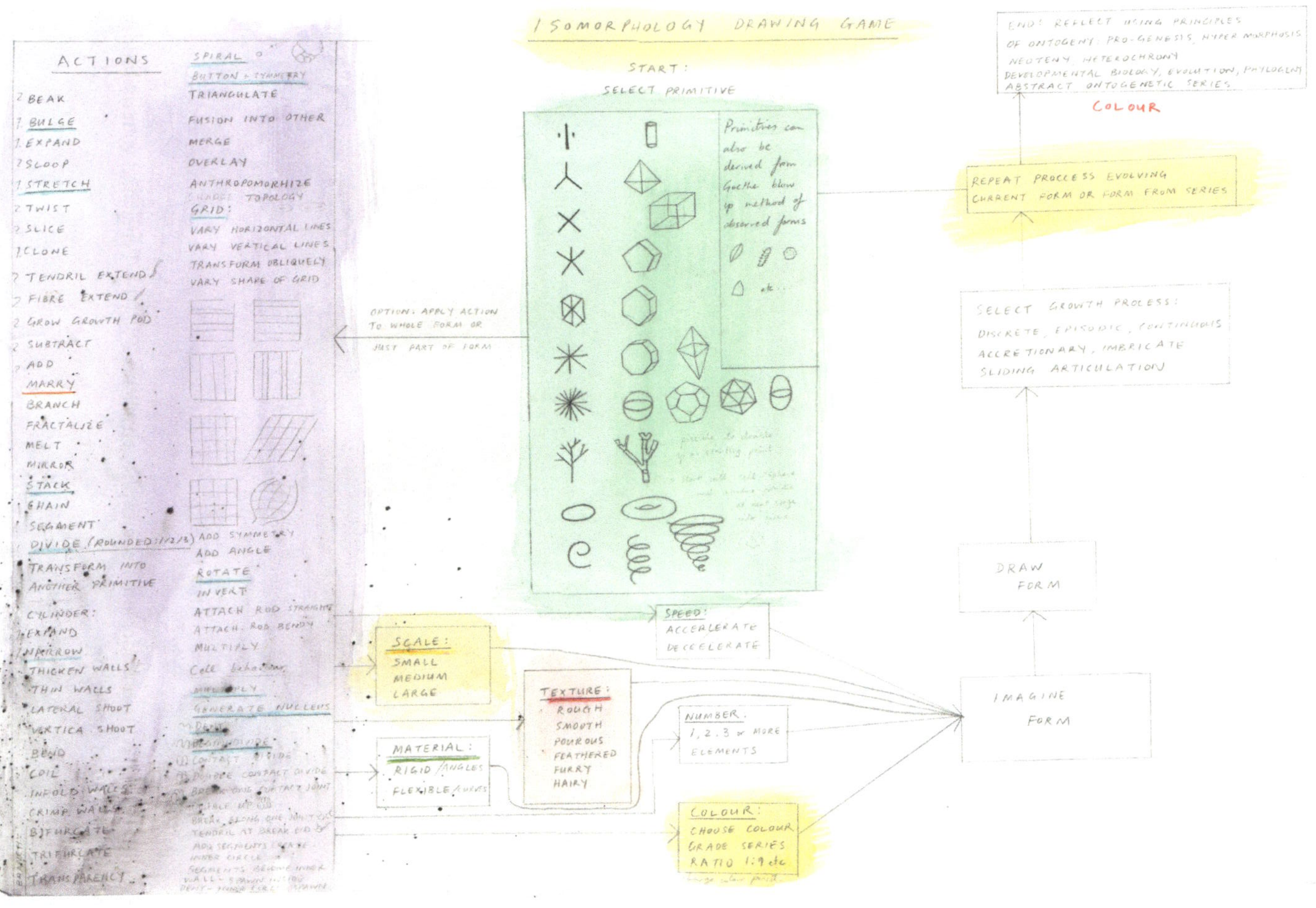

FIGURE 12.7. Gemma Anderson, 'Isomorphogenesis flow system', 2014. Pencil and watercolour on paper. © Gemma Anderson.

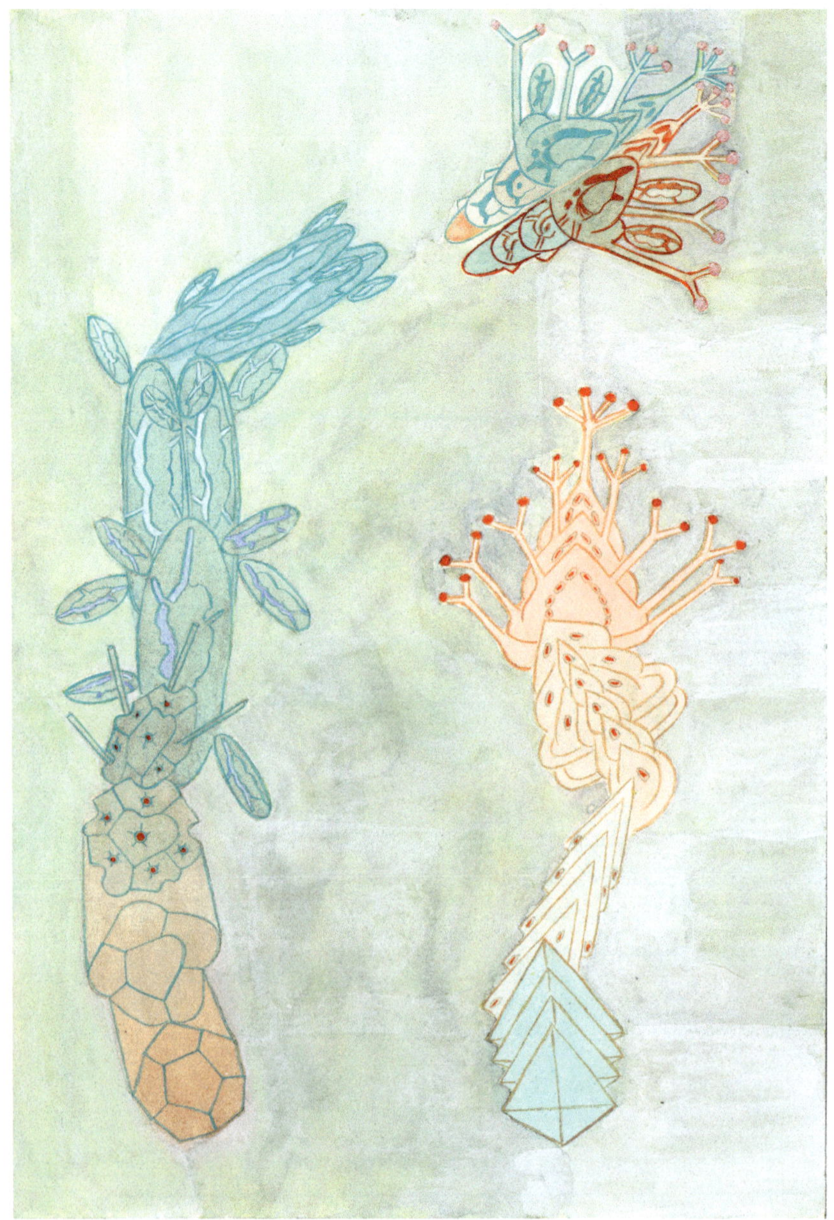

FIGURE 12.8. Gemma Anderson, 'Isomorphogenesis no.2', 2014. Pencil and watercolour on paper. © Gemma Anderson.

of perceiving specimens could provide a much-needed critique of current object centred curatorial rationales[34]. Beyond this, lets imagine that both Isomorphology and Isomorphogenesis can help reveal the multi-dimensional nature of taxonomy and also radically reconfigure systems of knowledge from object to process ontologies. I imagine a museum where the object is always presented as a 'time-slice', where drawings of formation surround the object, where stories of transformation inspire us to look again at the object, and imagine it, *as* process, back and forth and side to side in the space of our own imagination.

NOTES

1. The term 'morphology' was coined by Goethe in 1792. Steigerwald defines Goethe's morphology simply as 'the theory of form [Gestalt], formation [Bildung] and transformation [Umbildung] of organic bodies'. Joan Steigerwald, 'Goethe's Morphology: Urphänomene and Aesthetic Appraisal', *Journal of the History of Biology* 35, no. 2 (2002): 295.

2. Gerry Webster and Brian Goodwin, *Form and Transformation: Generative and Relational Principles in Biology* (Cambridge: Cambridge University Press, 1996), 6.

3. Johann Wolfgang von Goethe quoted in Webster and Goodwin, *Form and Transformation*, vi.

4. Mainly involving solitary walking in nature and prolonged periods of drawing in isolated and quiet places.

5. Johann Wolfgang von Goethe, *Italian Journey* (London: Penguin, 1962), 310–11.

6. Michael Polanyi summarizes the idea of tacit knowledge in his work *The Tacit Dimension* with the assertion that 'we can know more than we can tell' See: Michael Polanyi, *The Tacit Dimension* (London: Routledge & Kegan Paul, 1967), 4.

   By this he implies that there is knowledge that cannot be adequately articulated by verbal means, and suggests that all knowledge is rooted in some kind of tacit knowledge. Polanyi tells us that tacit knowledge can be acquired without language and this is part of the reason why it can be difficult to share and to describe.

7. Polanyi, *The Tacit Dimension*, 4.

8. Another way that I have come to understand the tacit nature of drawing as a way of knowing has been through comparing drawing with walking. Rather than considering walking as an artistic medium, I see walking as a practice that helps direct thought—often as a linear movement; a function comparable to drawing. Walking has enabled me to think about drawing as a parallel activity one dimension up: walking is drawing in three dimensions. The linear movement, forming through space, is sometimes punctuated by observations and restful reflections that weave in and out of focus. Walking is a dynamic way of experiencing the movement, rhythm and tempo of the body as it creates invisible lines within a landscape. As such, the trace of a walk can be compared to the trace of a drawing; a body scaling the landscape as the hand and drawing tool scale the page, or, as

Klee famously put it 'taking a line for a walk'. And in the museum perambulation is central to experiencing objects, mainly through walking around the vitrines and passageways to grasp the nature of the objects themselves.

9. Johann Wolfgang von Goethe quoted in Lorraine Daston and Peter Galison, *Objectivity* (New York: Zone Books, 2010), 233.

10. Ibid., 58.

11. For example, Mark Dion's commission at the Natural History Museum in 2007 'Systema Metropolis'.

12. Gemma Anderson, 'Endangered: A Study of Morphological Drawing in Zoological Taxonomy', *Leonardo*, 47, no. 3 (2014): 232–40.

13. Here my practice is attempting something at odds with mainstream science. I am following older models of knowing (such as the 'doctrine of signatures' an analogic approach of the Renaissance) while also relating to a D'Arcy Thompsons idea that forms are related as the geometric product of the same shaping physical forces.

14. The particular form of biological classification (taxonomy) set up by Carl Linnaeus, as set forth in his *Systema Naturae* (1735) and subsequent works. In the taxonomy of Linnaeus there are three kingdoms, divided into *classes*, and they, in turn, into *orders*, *genera* (singular: *genus*), and *species* (singular: *species*), with an additional rank lower than species.

15. 'The idea of an invariant in the form of a common structural plan or static 'schema' is a comparative methodological principle for finding our way through the multiplicity of forms'. Tournefort quoted in Webster and Goodwin, *Form and Transformation*, 15.

16. Gemma Anderson, *Isomorphology: An Introduction* (London: Super-Collider, 2013), 2.

17. Antonio Lima-de-Faria, Antonio. *Evolution without Selection: Form and Function by Autoevolution* (Amsterdam: Elsevier, 1988).

18. As this work demanded the observation of specimens, it required a process of attaining permission to observe and to draw, which I coordinated on each occasion. Access to many specimens, especially valuable minerals in the NHM collections, was limited and the Isomorphology artworks offered an alternative mode of display and means of making these collections visible.

19. John Dupré, *The Disorder of Things: Metaphysical Foundations of the Disunity of Science* (Cambridge: Harvard University Press, 1993), 18.

20. Ibid., 22.

21. Steigerwald, 'Goethe's Morphology: Urphänomene and Aesthetic Appraisal', 314.

22. Johann Wolfgang von Goethe quoted in Jeremy Naydler, ed., *Goethe on Science: A Selection of Goethe's Writings* (Edinburgh: Floris Books, 1996), 48.

23. Ibid., 49.

24. Johann Wolfgang von Goethe quoted in David Seamon, *Goethe's Way of Science: A Phenomenology of Nature* (New York: SUNY Press, 1998), 57.

25. Goethe, *Italian Journey*, 91.

26. Goethe quoted Naydler (ed.), *Goethe on Science*.

27. Kandinsky quoted in Kenneth Lyndsay and Peter Vergo, eds. *Kandinsky: Complete Writings on Art* (London: Faber & Faber, 1982), 1:370.

28. Eric Bapteste and John Dupré, 'Towards a Processual Microbial Ontology', *Biology & Philosophy* 28, no. 2 (2013): 379. See also the European Research Council-funded project 'A process ontology for contemporary biology', led by Professor John Dupré at the University of Exeter.

29. Bruce Gernard, *Coded Chimera* (London: Crucible Network, 2010), 5.

30. 'D'Arcy Thompson Zoology Museum Art Collection: Bruce Gernand', University of Dundee, [online] available at https://www.dundee.ac.uk/museum/collections/zoology/renew/gernand/ (accessed 11 October 2018).

31. Bruce Gernand, 'Mediated Animals, Little Monsters', in *Coded Chimera* (2011), quote published on artist's website, 'Bruce Gernand', [online] available at http://www.brucegernand.com/texts7.php (accessed 11 October 2018).

32. See: D'Arcy Wentworth Thompson, *On Growth and Form* (Cambridge: Cambridge University Press, 1942).

33. See: David Thistlewood, *A Continuing Process* (London: Graphics Press, 1981), 14.

34. Through the Arts and Humanities Research Council grant application 'Representing Biology as Process' we are currently working towards this drawing-centred object to process shift, specifically in the field of cell biology and molecular biology at the University of Exeter, 2017–20.

REFERENCES

Anderson, Gemma. *Isomorphology: An Introduction*. London: Super-Collider, 2013.

Anderson, Gemma. *Isomorphology*. London: EB & Flow Gallery, 2014.

Anderson, Gemma. 'Endangered: A Study of Morphological Drawing in Zoological Taxonomy'. *Leonardo* 47, no. 3 (2014): 232–40.

Bapteste, Eric, and John Dupré. 'Towards a Processual Microbial Ontology'. *Biology & Philosophy* 28, no. 2 (2013): 379–404.

D'Arcy Thompson Zoology Museum Art Collection. ' Bruce Gernand', University of Dundee. Available at https://www.dundee.ac.uk/museum/collections/zoology/renew/gernand/ (accessed 11 October 2018).

Daston, Lorraine, and Peter Galison. *Objectivity*. 2nd ed. New York: Zone Books, 2010.

Dupré, John. *The Disorder of Things: Metaphysical Foundations of the Disunity of Science*. Cambridge: Harvard University Press, 1993.

Gernard, Bruce. *Coded Chimera*. London: Crucible Network, 2010.

Goethe, Johann Wolfgang von. *Italian Journey*. London: Penguin, 1962.

Lima-de-Faria, Antonio. *Evolution without Selection: Form and Function by Autoevolution*. Amsterdam: Elsevier, 1988.

Linnaeus, Carl, M. S. J. Engel-Ledeboer and H. Engel. *Systema naturae, 1735*. Nieuwkoop: Hes & De Graaf, 2003.

Lyndsay, Kenneth, and Peter Vergo, eds. *Kandinsky: Complete Writings on Art*. London: Faber & Faber, 1982.

Naydler, Jeremy, ed. *Goethe on Science: A Selection of Goethe's Writings*. Edinburgh: Floris Books, 1996.

Nicholson, Daniel. J., and John Dupré. *Everything Flows: Towards a Processual Philosophy of Biology*. Oxford: Oxford University Press, 2018.

Polanyi, Michael. *The Tacit Dimension*. London: Routledge & Kegan Paul, 1967.

Seamon, David. *Goethe's Way of Science: A Phenomenology of Nature*. New York: SUNY Press, 1998.

Steigerwald, Joan. 'Goethe's Morphology: Urphänomene and Aesthetic Appraisal'. *Journal of the History of Biology* 35, no. 2 (2002): 291–328.

Thistlewood, David. *A Continuing Process*. London: Graphics Press, 1981.

Thompson, D'Arcy Wentworth. *On Growth and Form*. 2nd ed. Cambridge: Cambridge University Press, 1942.

Webster, Gerry, and Brian Goodwin. *Form and Transformation: Generative and Relational Principles in Biology*. Cambridge: Cambridge University Press, 1996.

13

Desiccation, Suspension, Extraction:
The Inhuman Art of Christine Borland

Andrew Patrizio

Abstract

Scottish artist Christine Borland (1965–) has reached international attention for her impressive sculptural work across collections, ethics and research processes. This chapter will consider her botanical works in parallel to her more familiar anatomical works, in mutual interaction and interdependence. By doing so, various post-human literatures will be invoked (a currently burgeoning network of scholarly and creative writing) to widen our appreciation of the particular speculations that Borland offers around the botanical as central to modern experience. A number of artworks offer starting points. In early works Apples with Holes *(1991) and* The Velocity of Drops *(1993) apples and water melons stand in as human body parts, as recipients of unlocated violence. In* Spirit Collection: Hippocrates *(1999) plane tree leaves act metonymically for the spread of medical knowledge. Later plant works include* Black, White and Shades of Grey *(2006). She fuses botany and the human particularly through the idea of the herbarium and other botanical storage sites, for example,* Conservatory *(2004) a piece largely constituted by engraved and fragmented porcelain skeleton,* Ecbolic Garden *(2001),* To be Set and Sown in the Garden *(2002),* The History of Plants, According to Women, Children and Students *(2002) and* Medicine Cabinet (Desiccated) *(2006). All draw on traditional strategies of display. Other-than-human animals featured in* Girl Grasping Eel *(1997),* Bison-Bison *(1997) and* Bullet Proof Breath *(2001) the latter of which was partially made from spider silk. Patrizio will use motifs of desiccation, suspension and extraction in the interstices of the cellular, botanical, geological and anatomical.*

> Nature is what you may do [...] Nature is the tyrannous circumstance, the fixed skull, the sheathed snake, the ponderous rock-like jaw; necessitated activity, violent direction.[1]

Introduction

Look at Christine Borland's *Medicine Cabinet (Desiccated)* from 2006—ten framed plants, each with a shared property. But before considering how Borland has populated her cabinet, consider the names, the words that make up these plants. Savour their sounds. *Forking Larkspur (Consolide ajacis)* and *Black Spleenwort (Asplenium adiantum-nigrum)*. These worts and spurs are forking and black and they speak of spleens and larks. Nature here seems shadowy, dark and distorted, lively in its forest malice. There are no more spurs among her ten plants, but *Birthwort (Aristolochia clematitis)* and *Dropwort (Filipendula vulgaris)* keep the sense of managing exoticism alive. There are feral tastes here too—*Wild Parsnip (Pastinaca sativa)*, *Winter Savoury (Satureja montana)*, *Juniper (Savin Juniper) (Juniperus Sabina)* and *Hogs Fennel (Dog's Fennel) (Peucedanum officinale)*. The folkish directness of the English term extends differently into the incantatory Latin binomials with their oblique hints of ancient worlds. The ninth plant in her collection, *Pot Marigold (Calendula officinalis)* is the most benign and most domesticated among this wilder company. But what is this company exactly, and what is the property they all share? Borland found them listed in a book by Leonard Fuchs called *Significant Notes of the History of Plants* (1542). The word 'ecbolic' means capable of causing a birth to be aborted, and ecbolic plants would be long known to women as a means of releasing themselves from unwanted births. Borland's plants in *Medicine Cabinet (Desiccated)* are framed, dried and pressed with their medicinal powers presumably now as desiccated and lost as the life within them. They are only now a pale echo of what they do, an illustration of the form not the medicine itself, but once we know what the plants might have done to women's bodies before modern medicine developed sharper tools, we know why Borland makes a work out of them. They speak of indigenous knowledge, of bio-power, female strategies of preservation, lost human lives and of the porous border between the corporeal bodies of humans and the botanical materialities that intimately intersect with and are ingested by them. The desiccated specimens in this particular medicine cabinet have afterlives of profound interest to the artist.

We have mentioned nine plants and will return to the tenth, *Pennyroyal (Mentha pulegium)* in due course.

Medicine Cabinet (Desiccated) is a work about inexact lines of demarcation between plants and humans, an idea that has origins for which the *Birthwort*

(Aristolochia clematitis) holds a clue. It was Aristotle who mused that 'Nature proceeds little by little from things lifeless to animal life in such a way that it is impossible to determine the exact line of demarcation, nor on which side thereof an intermediate form should lie.'[2] Taken literally, Aristotle evokes a world in which intermediate forms find it not just difficult but impossible to find a fixed and settled place. This hovering indeterminacy is a marker for many artists working in recent decades, of which Borland is a noted internationally recognized example. Yet, to follow the logic to the kind of extreme position that Aristotle speak of, means venturing beyond her obvious and sustained interest in the human body and to take more seriously the plant and animal life that feature persistently in her work and yet have never quite been given the weight—and a sense of their disruptive role—that they deserve. They sit like a spectral presence in numerous works by Borland, sometimes pointing directly to the materially shared realities of humans in their wider ecology; at other times speaking more of analogies, resemblances and mirroring patterns which can be perceived between animal, vegetable and human (false) categories in post-Enlightenment culture. The implicit idea here is that Borland's work does not just question humanist readings but goes a long way to radically destabilizing the human schema, certainly far beyond where more complacent form of liberal humanism would seem to move us.[3] For some artists, this might seem grounds for playful postmodernist moves but there is little in Borland's work, or her statements about her work, that have any such tone of arch indifference. Whether it be in relation to the human or other points of reference in her work, the aim is particularity and the enemy is generalization: 'It doesn't always make sense to generalise *the human subjects*, most of the time I feel they deserve an individual focus.'[4] A necessary implication of her work is to widen vividly what the term 'attachment' might mean. She does this, in part, through spending time with other-than-human objects, life forms and materials and in doing so suggests ancient and global sympathies far beyond the context of 1990s neo-conceptual abjection in art, the context to which she is most usually tied. Her work resonates with the sentiments expressed by Philippe Descola in *Beyond Nature and Culture: Forms of Attachment* where he notes that in so many global cultures

> humans and nonhumans are not conceived as developing in incommunicable worlds or arriving to quite separate principles. The environment is not regarded objectively as an autonomous sphere. Plants and animals, rivers and rocks, meteors and seasons do not exist all together in an ontological niche defined by the absence of human beings.[5]

It is clear from interviews she has given, that from her earliest experiences growing up in rural Ayrshire, southwest of Glasgow, nature was enfolded into playful learning and the narratives that attached to the plants and animals she found. As she has noted, 'Although there was certainly a pragmatic prioritising of the usefulness of plants and animals; folk-lore, story telling and myth were really bound up in those relationship too'.[6]

Many writers on Borland's subsequent formal education note the seminal impact that the Environmental Art course at Glasgow School of Art had on her, and others, in the 1980s when she trained there. They also cite one of its guiding principles (taken from a manifesto by the Artist Placement Group [APG]) that 'the context is half the work'.[7] The context here is always assumed to be a spatial property rather than where I want to extend it—to the biosphere. The human body is not fully human, in the sense that it is increasingly recognized that human life is symbiotically co-dependent on many other life forms, such as thousands of bacteria and microbes hosted in our mouths and guts, and that far outnumber human cells, not to mention the flows of smaller animals, food and liquid that pass continuously through and over us.[8] So indeed, we must rework the APG phrase to acknowledge that the external context is half the human. We must extrapolate from this an ecology of practice that can be found in Borland's work that is profoundly environmental and provocatively post-humanist. I use the term 'post-humanist' here to capture a broad front of theoretical enquiry that has, over recent decades, pushed against identarian models as the primary organizing principle in politics and society. Taking a more inclusive view on other-than-human somatic life, and on how materiality and energy need to be more seriously regarded as political and active, a growing literature pursues a radical programme of taking down human-centred world views.[9] Distinctions between humans, animals and plants, and between the conventionally regarded 'living' and 'non-living' domains, are falling away or being problematized under such a view. I believe that artists from the latter half of the twentieth century onwards have increasingly responded enthusiastically, if diversely, to the underlying propositions behind post-humanist theory.

Borland then belongs to a wider movement in creative and cultural endeavour in the sense of offering, through consideration of her work, ways of going beyond liberal humanism and the distortions of anthropocentric perspectives on our planet (a planet which of course is no more ours than it belongs to the animals, plants and microscopic life forms that also populate it). Borland's work wakes us from 'the dream of human exceptionalism' (as Donna Haraway puts it).[10]

The philosopher Mary Midgley in the final chapter of *Evolution as a Religion*, entitled 'The Vulnerable World and Its Claims on Us',[11] creates an ambitious list of those agents, bodies and groups that for some powerful groups normally fall outside of a conventional 'non-contractual' moral duty. These are endangered, through neglect and exploitation, by those in charge. In the sector marked human she includes in her list the dead, posterity, children, the senile, the temporarily and permanently insane, defectives (including 'human vegetables') and human embryos. She includes also sentient and non-sentient animals followed by 'inanimates' such as plants, works of art and structured objects including crystals, rivers and rocks. In what she calls a comprehensive category she includes human groups such as families, and villages, cities and the species and wider multispecies groups such as ecosystems, forests, countries and ultimately the biosphere. In her final category—miscellaneous—sit arts, sciences and oneself. I think this helps position the human in relation to the other-than-human in Borland, who I suggest is a most subtle challenger of anthropocentricity in art. Indeed, I would say that this claim rests on considering various by-products of her approach rather than explicit artistic intentions. If her work is not entirely 'anthrop-de-centric'[12] then it is at least, to coin a phrase, anthopo-con-centric, in the way that it cultivates a wide ecology of respect extending out far beyond the human. She exemplifies the kind of attentiveness that Gillian Beer ascribes to Darwin, in particular his talent at weaving persuasive narratives:

> Only by giving up the will to dominate the material world and to relate it to our own needs, conditions, and sensibilities will it be possible for us to find a language that gives proper attention to the nature of things.[13]

Here is a list of Borland's materials and objects, noted by Fiona Bradley: 'diamonds, birds, guns, apples, watermelons, leaves, plants and trees'.[14] Here is another, by Ian Hunt: 'smashed melon pulp, fat, molecular machines, darned blankets, broken crockery, spent bullets, sawdust, money, gems, cotton wool and the stone of melancholy'.[15] To Bradley and Hunt's catalogues of things that feature in Borland's work we could add spiders' silk, sphagnum moss and bison bones on top of the more conventional artistic media—clay, plaster, marble, steel, wood, plastic, glass and projection screens—that she also uses. The extreme diversity contains its own message—that any material essentialism based on the human alone is untenable and inadequate. So widely distributed and so materially porous are these constituent elements in her art, we can only conclude that the animal, vegetable and the mineral lie at humanity's centre not its periphery—not below it, but deeply mixed into its ontological and epistemological structures. In her work they are discovered, turned over, the subject of dialogues with others, they are repurposed, reinscribed, recovered, represented and decontextualized. They—including minerals, bones, plants, cotton wool and mosses—reappear in works now many decades apart. And in turn they underscore the profoundly post-human sensibility that has propelled so much of Borland's art since its start.

In Isabelle Stengers's essay 'Comparison as a Matter of Concern', the phrase 'ecology of practices' is used. It is, for Stengers, a way of thinking through how practice can be a moment simultaneously of divergence and destruction. It is the linking of these two terms that makes me think of Borland, additionally as Stengers uses 'ecology' as what she calls a 'transversal category, to help define relational heterogeneity [...]',[16] Borland herself has an 'ecology of practices' that traverse the human, animal, vegetable and geologic while she, of course, sits at a juncture of other ecologies of practice (human and otherwise). In this way she can be understood within art historical terms as aligned to relational aesthetics, environmental art and the abject. Yet it should become clear that the implications of her art lie further within post-humanism, post-Young British Artist (YBA) and the post-specimen.

As an ecological practitioner (following Stengers), Borland surely accords with the kind of sensibilities that Donna Haraway promotes in her writing on animals, the human and the boundaries of the biosphere. Haraway is similarly steeped in transversality and the co-mingling of identities and practices. In bio-theory, she parallels Borland's visual art practices using an expanded notion of 'the figure' to make the point. As Haraway writes:

> Figures are not representations or didactic illustrations, but rather material-semiotic nodes or knots in which diverse bodies and meanings mutually shape one another. For me, figures have always been where the biological and literary or artistic come together with all of the forces of lived reality.[17]

Borland's is a figurative art (in Haraway's sense) of the 'force of lived reality' within which resides not only her own body and those of other humans who she knows as well as those she does not know. The figures also include the bison, the gene, the sphagnum moss and the thread of spiders' silk. She does this with the dexterity of what I would characterize as an 'amniotic minimalist' whose carefully grotesque figurations disassemble histories and flatten difference. I have grouped the works to be discussed under three thematic headings that speak of processes, perhaps the kinds you would find in the medical laboratory, the archive and museum, or the artist's studio—I refer to the desiccated (or destroyed), the suspended and the extracted.

There was a certain coherence in Borland's early experiences of museum displays to her later formal training and emerging interests in ideas of the specimen, collections and taxonomy.

> As a child I was often able to spend a lot of time contemplating the wonderful natural history collection of a local museum (The Dick Institute, Kilmarnock) where the insects, rocks, minerals and plants that I played with were pinned, labelled and ordered. The love of museums and familiarity with collections has

been consistently important to me. I have a comfortable relationship with the mysterious, even magical potential of the plant and animal kingdom, as well as a fascination with both the aesthetic and scientific significance of classification systems, which are often linear; starting with the stuff of the earth and ending with the human.[18]

Borland trained at a time when identity politics was firmly established in the UK arts curriculum and the practices, more widely, of politically engaged artists across the world. Her own training in Glasgow and Belfast would have forced the live issues of 'identity' hard on her. Borland's own approach to identity has been oblique in most respects, without a strong and unilateral approach to the politics of identity. Rather, her 'poetics' rather than 'politics' of identity engages strategically with these themes in a way that reorients attention towards ideological and contextual narratives behind identity formation. So many of her major pieces, such as *From Life* (1994), *The Dead Teach the Living* (1997) and *HeLa (Hot)* (1999) show human identity as situational and highly vulnerable. This obsession with the constructed contours of identity was almost second nature to artists who, like Borland, emerged in the 1980s and 1990s. So, in this chapter, I want to respond with an equally oblique take on Borland's own obliquities. The anthropocentric focus of many of Borland's projects do a couple of things. First, they are often about receiving *lost*, *suppressed* or *violently exploited* human identities. Second, they are fringed with 'other-than-human' identities, and it is these that I think are worth being considered more attentively than has heretofore been attempted. In such a picture, identity transforms into a wide spreading, rhizomatic concept that encircles but is not fully contained by the term 'human'. My instinct is that Borland has been working these particular fringes more actively and provocatively than has been realized.

Clearly themes of care and obligation lie close to the surface of numerous works by Borland. The deontological premise of this, though, is assumed to be the care of humans and the obligations we have to human bodies, whether warm (living) or cold (lifeless), near to us or distant historically or in space. But the ecologies of care impel us to the view that 'obligations' stretch well beyond the human alone, and to truly care for human subjectivities means caring for the wider world in which they are embedded. To be neglectful, let alone violent, towards the ecosphere within which humans are set is to be neglectful to humans too. I am aware that this an anthropocentric argument, that takes as its starting point the idea that cultivating ecological care is for ultimately human benefit. So this cannot be enough—either for the moral argument or as the way to appreciate Borland's wider contribution. To be interested in care and obligation, properly constituted, is to flatten the assumed hierarchies and promote an extensive plateau of deontological attention that supports the flourishing of animal, plant and geological life.

The Desiccated

A number of the botanical and organic specimens used in Borland's work are objects of violence—both perpetrated by the artist herself and the wider social forces that surround them. I have grouped them loosely under the term 'desiccated', though even the drying out involved in these works manifests itself in different ways. Objects become dried through neglect, in the sense of being left without water over the duration of an installation. Other objects are purposely dried in order to preserve them in some form, for display, like pressed plants. It might be additionally observed that desiccation is a form of extraction, the removal of water, thus resonates with my third thematic grouping here—objects that have had something pulled out of them. Associations continue as we stay with these sets of processes, in the sense that extraction and the removal of water is the opposite of the absorption of liquid. Unsurprising then, that a number of Borland's works also involve meditations on the absorptive capacities of forms and materials, as we will see.

An early example of a work comprising objects that fall along the desiccated-destroyed axis is *Shot Apples* (1991). The piece was made from 12 apples punctured with holes the size of 45 mm bullets (though manually carved out by the artist rather than by a pistol). In their seemingly shot state, they lie scattered on the floor, as if tumbled from a cart or market stall. Their number and displacement have all kinds of associations—in this case from the biblical, the folkloric and horticultural. Yet we are left in doubt as to whether these holes, blackened around their edges, are made by guns, worms or the human hand. Of course they have artistic precedents and comparisons (from shocking ballistic works by Chris Burden or Matt Collishaw to the critical seeding-planting-composting processes that are central to installations by Dieter Roth, Joan Hills, Hans Haacke or Anya Gallaccio). Their interest lies more in Borland's signature blend of formal singularity disturbed by unnerving violence and the vestiges of recent transgression, to which we are given only minimal clues.

This work pre-empted a series begun in 1993, with later iterations, called *The Velocity of Drops* (Fig. 13.1). Two ill-fitting modes or situations are aligned—the materiality of edible fruit and the violently forensic photograph. The basic form of the work is a small group of melons broken and lying strewn in settings as disparate as tenement stairwells (1993), bar rooms and underpasses (1995), stately homes and snowy pavements (2003) and hospital wards and operating theatres (2003, 2006). They are both temporary installations, at first glance, though take a final form as photographic series. All lie resplendently broken, with juices flowing as evidence of past violence or accident.

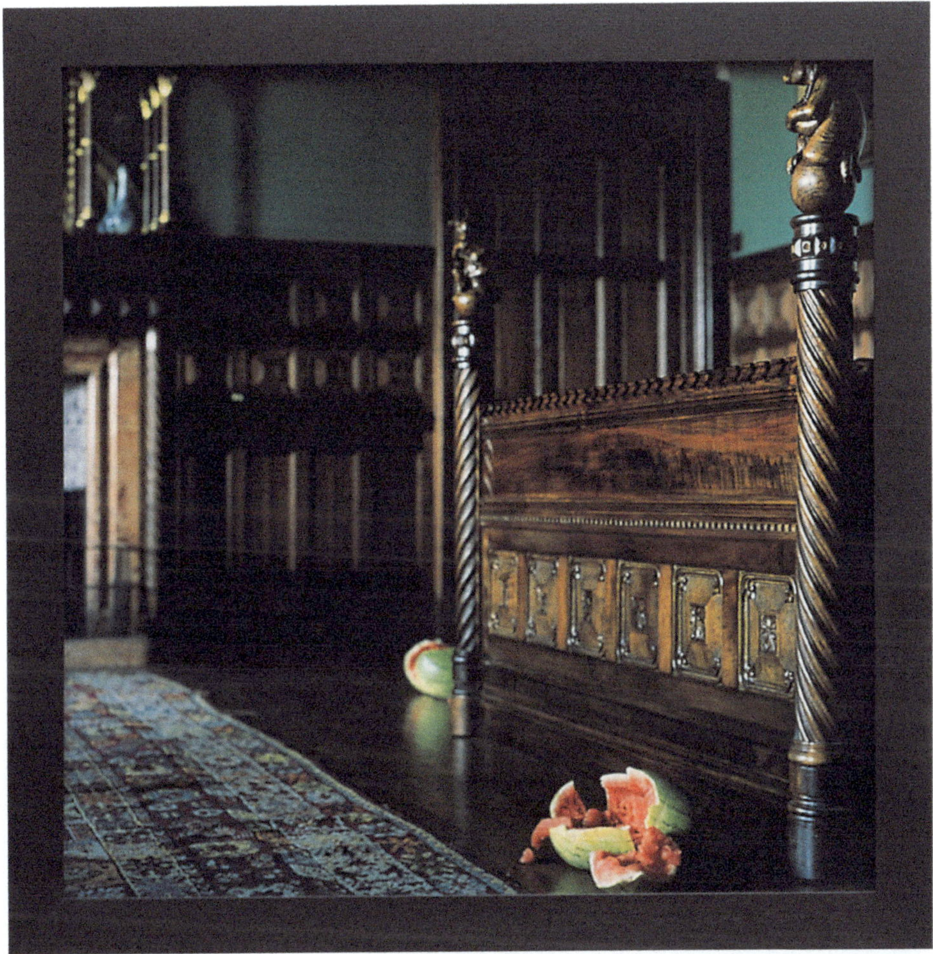

FIGURE 13.1. Christine Borland, from *Velocity of Drops: An Hospital* (2003), photograph, 67.5 × 67.5 cm. © the artist and Patricia Fleming Projects, Glasgow, 2003.

Velocity of Drops broadly equates water melons with human heads (the parallels are clear though, anatomically speaking, not fully accurate), derived from the genre of crime fiction in particular, and the works are slightly comical and uncanny, yet impregnated with dread. In each of the series, Borland present us with photographic evidence of a faux-crime re-enacted through the melons' destruction but these works speak, as so many of Borland's works do, more of an 'afterwards'—a post-period—in which only slowly cooling off evidence of past hot violence or action remains visible.[19]

The formal motif of evidential and multiple objects laid out is a long-standing one in Borland's work, mainly in the form of objects on trestle tables—*Small Objects That Save Lives* (1991–), *Black Museum* (1994) are early examples with no particular animal or vegetable association that fit our purpose here. However, one work, *Bison-Bison* (1997) (Fig. 13.2) uses precisely this arrangement for animal remains. In this installation, a long white table on which are arranged a line of bison vertebrae is flanked by two smaller tables that have bison rib-bones set on them. The vertebrae bones have had their mineral compounds extracted (a technique that anticipates my third section here on extraction) leaving them dried out and chalky. The rib-bones have been treated differently (using recipe instructions found in a 1930s edition of *Gray's Anatomy*) after immersion in weak mineral acid until they become flexible, they have been twisted and bent

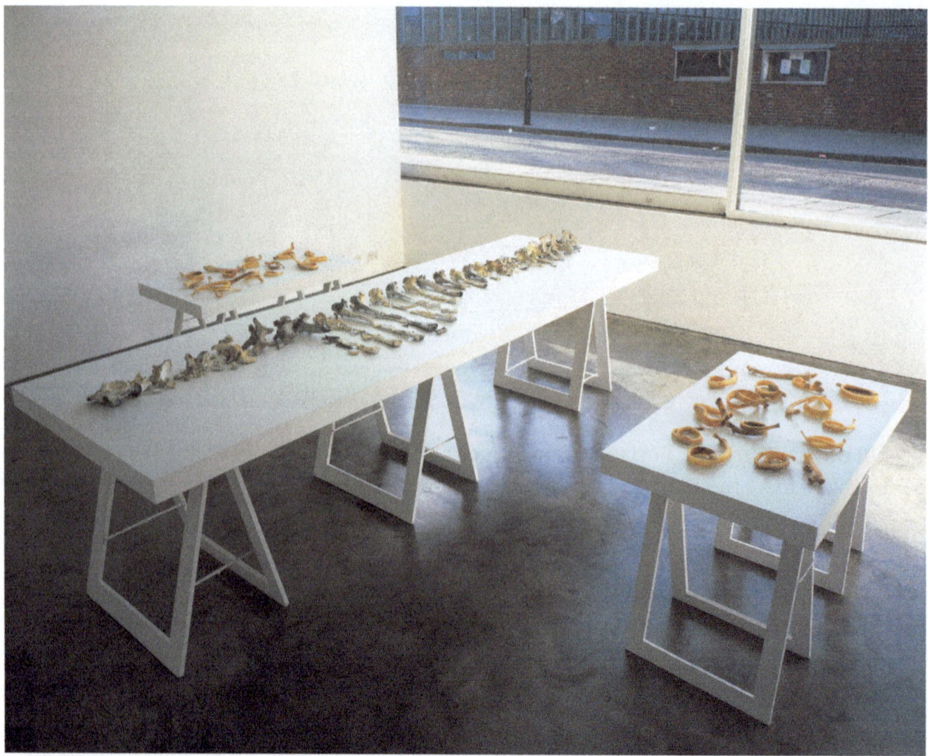

FIGURE 13.2. Christine Borland, *Bison-Bison* (1997), three trestle tables, bison vertebrae, mineral compounds extracted, bison ribs, organic compounds extracted. Dimensions variable. Installation: Lisson Gallery, London. © the artist and Patricia Fleming Projects, Glasgow, 1997.

over into various shapes so they populate the table surface like a set of dancing calligraphic gestures.

In their counterposed states of desiccation and contortion they seem to say something about human-enacted violence and invasive processes that might stand more generally for an exploitative attitude towards animals. (After all, the bison itself as a species speaks already of mass colonial exploitation and devastation as settlers moved towards industrial slaughter of the large North American herds in the previous two centuries.) So Borland's fascination with the dark forces of technological manipulation on the natural, under human hands, lies forcefully at the heart of this work. It is blended, however, with another of her interests in 'the specimen' or taxonomic display that follows the implied logic of orderly arrangement. The way the length of vertebrae lies down the long table looks like a workshop set-up in a natural history museum or pathology laboratory. The twisted rib-bones look more ethnographic and tribal, as if gathered from an archaeological dig. Then 'relational heterogeneity' that I cited from Stengers at the start of this chapter is clearly demonstrated here in the paired manipulations of bison bones as Borland deliberately mixes modes of the animal, the human and the specimens and exhibits of what the latter make out of the former. She has spoken of using a deliberate minimalist presentational mode as an artistic reimagining of scientific strategies of reduction, particularly in the face of information overload.[20] Yet under the grid of minimalist rationalism, the coiled violence of human intervention moves like a ghost.

The Suspended

It is striking how many of the works featuring plants and animals that Borland has made over the years involve lifting objects into space. Their hanging or suspension happens both by thread and in solutions—the effect is to preserve and hold up for inspection the objects of her focus. A very early, and previously unpublished exploratory work, called *Hung Birds* (1989), is discussed in passing by Charles Esche in the catalogue for *From Life* (1994) (Fig. 13.3). There he describes a piece which placed

> study specimens of different bird species back among the trees of the surrounding park, hanging upside down from the branches like a brace of game birds just after slaughter. From having fake lives in museum dioramas, the corpses were again integrated with their living environment and most honest in their expression of death. The transmutation was a simple change of site but in its use of unchanged found materials, its involvement of a non-art institution, its lack of

over didacticism and its honesty in presentation, *Hung Birds* prefigures many
of the artist's later concerns.[21]

To this reading, we can add that non-human subjects appear as an early concern
too, this time made to perform a 'zombie rewilding' of public space. The strategy
of hanging most prominently appears around a decade later with a major piece,
Spirit Collection: Hippocrates (1999). The specimens in this work constitute plane
leaves taken from a descendent of the tree in Kos under which Hippocrates was
said to have taught the first Western medical students. Each leaf has been stripped
of its colour so that, in its amniotic minimalism, we are confronted with something
that seems illustration-like in its formal linearity and light-drenched exposure. The
glass vials that hold each single leaf hanging from a height seem to partly echo
the absent tree from ancient history, as well as the ubiquitous figure of the medical museum preserving jar, but it also has something of the startling honesty that
Esche saw in *Hung Birds*. Pair this insight with the 'plant philosopher' Michael
Marder, whose writings are an appeal to take plant life seriously as a metaphysical approach, a widening of our ethical parameters. He writes:

> The mystery of life is not buried in the deep recesses of the seed or of the earth,
> for it resides in the very figure of the surface, of that which is given to sight and
> turned toward light, the figure of being-exposed, the leaf.[22]

This passage complicates what might seem to be a positivist approval of empiricism
and the observable (sight and light) but Marder is pointing rather to what he calls
an 'anti-metaphysics' and non-dualism that resists orthodox notions of science
and positivist progress: 'vegetation accomplishes a living reversal of metaphysical values and points toward the collapse of hierarchical dualisms'.[23] He offers,
then, both a way of understanding the often commented upon light-saturated yet
darkly themed faux-objectivity of Borland's presentational choices—and the classificatory systems that, the artist says, simply do not work for her[24]—and adds
something too about how to read her work *vegetally*.

It is commonly appreciated just how often Borland returns to themes of loss and
suppression of identity in many of her works. But less appreciated is how she uses
the vegetal or arboreal to extend this work beyond the human alone. The reference to Hippocrates' tree in Kos returns with *Support Work (Hippocrates 1:075)*,
(2006) which in effect keeps alive a tree distant both temporally and geographic-
ally from its first instantiation in Edinburgh. In a practical sense it is a replica of
a real steel scaffolding whose looping extensions were constructed beneath and
around the ancient plane tree in Greece. Historically speaking we cannot be sure
the tree as identified is the original or indeed the only tree under which Hippocrates

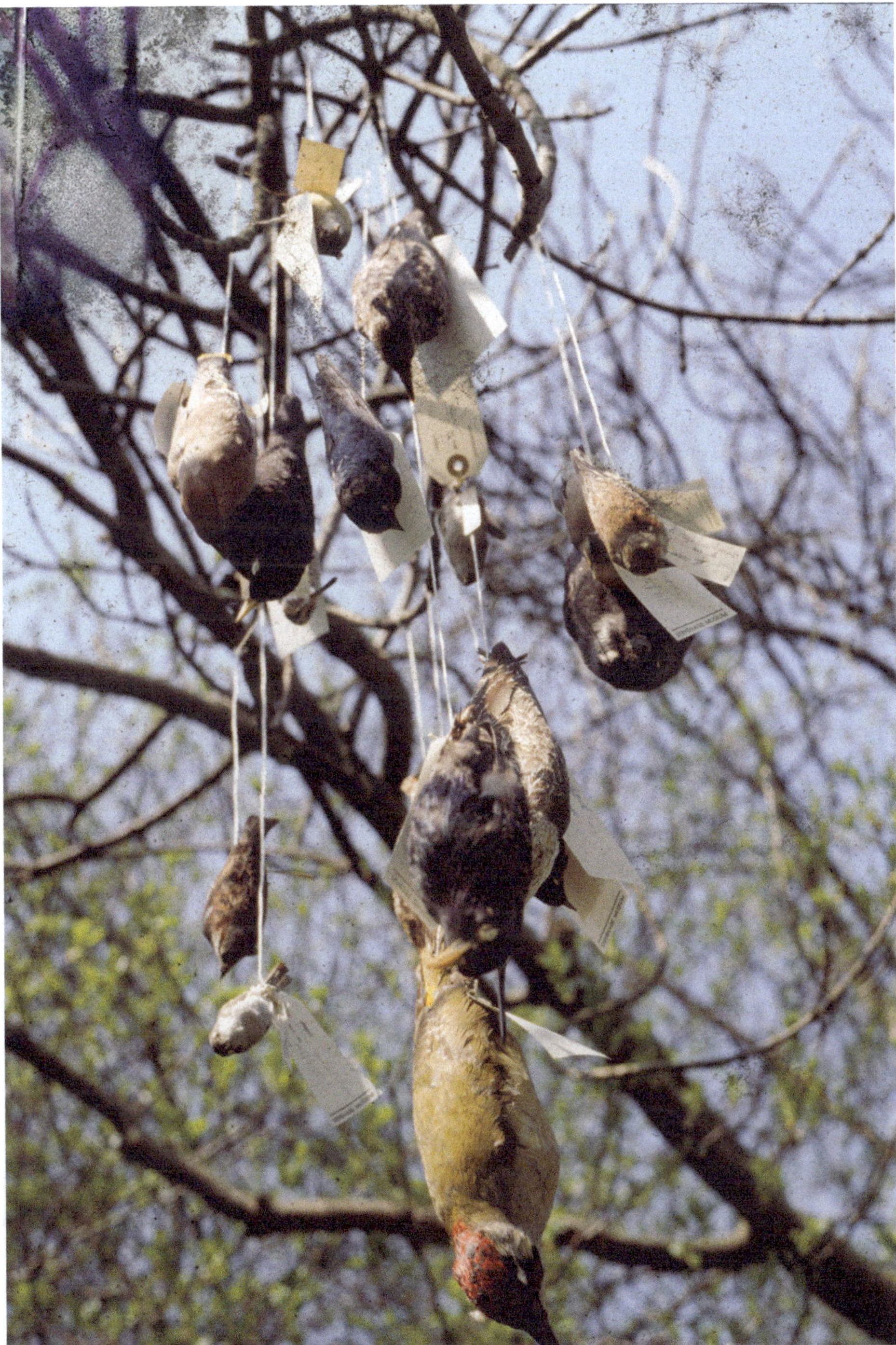

FIGURE 13.3. Christine Borland, *Hung Birds* (detail), 1989, taxidermed museum specimens from Stevenage Museum. © the artist and Patricia Fleming Projects, Glasgow, 1989.

taught. Rather, the idea of the Greek authorities building such a structure lies in a belief in the power of original sites and honouring as long as possible what was cultivated under that tree, on that spot. The tree's geriatric infirmity invites assistance in the form of steel scaffolding so its fragile branches can rest in place. Take away the scaffolding and, as with the tourists in Kos, you are virtually back in ancient times alongside the first medics. Add the tree when you are standing in front of Borland's replica scaffolding and you have Kos and medical teaching in your mind and all that goes with it.

Borland's artistic process involves what we might think of as a form of concretism, in the sense of an early meaning of the word 'concrete', namely, 'to grow together'[25]. Borland's suggestive process in predicated upon the entwining of at least two concepts and allowing them to grow together, grafted to become a hybrid form of quasi-mental object which resonates in entirely fresh ways. The scaffold and the plane tree in *Support Work (Hippocrates 1:075)* in a sense have already become a concretion—a growing together of tree and metal—to form a hybrid monument to ancient medicine. In building the scaffold alone she concretizes not only the supportive structure but the tree too, as a figure of the imagination.

These concretely fused forms are everywhere in Borland's work. *Preserves* (2006) is a deceptively simple piece—30 jars of unlabelled apple jelly set along five wooden shelves, 6 to a shelf. What is preserved in *Preserves*? Most obviously, apple descendants of one that grew in the orchard of Woolsthorpe Manor, Lincolnshire, and, as legend has it, landed on the head of Isaac Newton. Thus was born a new and general theory of how objects relate to the ground and how the ground holds everything that sits upon it. Also preserved is a warm myth of empirical insight, helped too by associated National Trust promotional material, in which an iconic male scientist comes to a universal understanding through surprisingly simple encounters with ripened fruit. Borland places no signs on these jars to tell us that these are from the 'Flower of Kent' variety that did their seminal late seventeenth-century falling. The apples themselves are thoroughly transformed in the jelly-making process, made into sets of slightly different orange hues, set in the 30 jars and each sealed with tinfoil. There is something here about preserving a passing moment that suggests a question about legacy, longevity and memory. The work is a meditation on the varieties of growth, decay (falling) and transubstantiation that are possible around any living organism—here an apple tree—and the knowledge that can be extracted from some of those varieties. An uncollected rotting apple in the grass, jelly-making as a kitchen craft or the spark for a universal theory of gravity.

A somewhat different encounter between the other-than-human and the human suspended in gloopy gel is caught in *Girl Grasping Eel* (1997). The final work, a photograph, has a visceral directness somewhat unusual in Borland's work (and

indeed she herself has described it as 'a striking image but not a great deal more'[26]).
After some time, as ever, the work opens up in vivid and complex ways. The
layout is simple, with the setting seemingly in a hygienic space (an aquarium or
fish counter perhaps), as a human hand grabs and seems to hold still the muscular
slipperiness of the eel's body. Its head and tail disappear behind the hand and into
the picture's back plane. Ian Hunt sees this 'strange work' as marking Borland's
increasing interest in the mid-1990s in 'gloopy stuff', where gels, solutions, amniotic fluids abound.[27] In terms of its formal arrangement the most obvious parallel
is Richard Serra's *Hand Catching Lead* (1968). While Serra's work has a sense of
folly and Sisyphean frustration, Borland's work, as a photograph, rests in redo-
lent poise. The pressure one can see in the fingertips imply a sustained effort, as if
gravity and slime combine to resist the human hold.

Hunt implies there is a sense of what one might term 'touching the other' which,
for him, produces 'an effect of overcoming a threshold, and perhaps enjoying
in imagination the visceral touch of live eel'.[28] To touch the other is to sense the
uncanny as a shudder-inducing difference. I agree with Hunt that the work resists
metaphoric reading, at least partly, which is common in other works. As he says:

> The sheer physicality overwhelms any possibility that the eel could simply 'stand
> for' anything, rich as a snaky slimy thing is in associations. The pointed use
> of a girl (as with the voices of adolescents used to read *The Monster's Mono-
> logue* from *Frankenstein*) prohibits any easy act of identification with the act
> of touching; it creates a curious sense of removal in the midst of immediacy.[29]

But then if we ignore the strong sexual imagery and associations here, what
remains? The eel certainly looks phallic, an impression exaggerated by the absence
of head and tail so it becomes a portion of tubular muscle rather than a creature
in its own right. Significantly, the title tells us the gender of the hand's owner (not
otherwise obvious from the photograph itself). And it is not a woman but a girl.
So the unsettling nature of the photograph starts to grow the longer we remain
engaged with it. Uncanniness can be both a fast and slow sense experience. The
work raises the spectre of the animal other as specimen, lifted for a spell into the
open air but soon to return (dead or alive) to its strange liquid world. In this sense
the eel is like a number of amniotic specimens that feature in Borland's work, from
spirit leaves to DNA cells to floating jelly fish. Here the threshold has indeed been
crossed in the heavy grasp in which the animal is held.

At the start of this chapter we introduced the idea that sits behind some of
Borland's work, concerning the close relationship between human knowledge
and the plant world. Clear alignments can be made between the interdisciplinary
projects of Borland and Michael Marder's sense of plant life speaking of the

'in-between'. He writes: 'Plants are the weeds of metaphysics: devalued, unwanted in its carefully cultivated garden, yet growing in-between the classical metaphysical categories of the thing, the animal and the human—for, the place of the weed is, precisely, in-between.'[30] Also at the outset, we looked at a major ecbolic work, *Medicine Cabinet (Desiccated)* (2006), with its ten dried and pressed plants, the last one of which is *Pennyroyal (Mentha pulegium)*. These plant-based works offer a bridge, a convergence, between two of our chosen themes—suspension and extraction—and here they merge.

Winter Garden (2001) speaks directly to Marder's sense of the in-between. The work consists of 12 hand-blown glass vessels, with each one containing a bleached sprig of Penny Royal preserved in an alcohol solution. Reflecting the development and first siting of the work in Australia, Borland used the Anglophone name of a local plant traditionally used by Aboriginal Australians as an abortifacient, or ecbolic plant. As Marsha Meskimmon notes,

> the bleached branches floating in the softly curved vessels are like still-born foetuses within the womb, the harvest of a winter garden. On this reading, woman is the fertile earth awaiting fulfilment in maternity and any interference with this process equates the womb with barren ground; the matrix becomes the tomb.[31]

The in-between nature of *Winter Garden* is exemplified in the way it merges the idea of colonial acquisition and museum classification, caught in the fact that European glasshouses were called 'winter gardens'—a place for displaying 'the native'.[32] The individual vials in *Winter Garden* are, as Meskimmon writes 'exquisite white specimens' that invoke 'female corporeal presence without resort to any simplistic rendering of the body of woman'. It speaks of processes not objects, of 'bodies of evidence, bodies of knowledge, the bodies of individuals and the composite body politic. Its strategies might well be understood as an aesthetics of the in-between'.[33]

Ecbolic Garden, (Fig. 13.4) installed in the Lisson Gallery, London, in 2001, drew on Borland's researches, being based on the sixteenth-century apothecaries garden at Glasgow University, a place with close connections to the neighbouring Glasgow Cathedral. Borland discovered that the Scottish vicar, Mark Jameson, was a benefactor of at least two hospitals in Glasgow and owned a copy of Leonhart Fuch's *De Historia Stirpium Commentarii Insignes* (Significant Notes on the History of Plants) of 1542).[34] She drew on other related research that revealed that many of the plants grown there were, at the time, considered ecbolic (including wild parsnip, tongue savoury, forking larkspur, juniper, calendula and pennyroyal). The likelihood was that local prostitutes bought these plants, introducing a clear

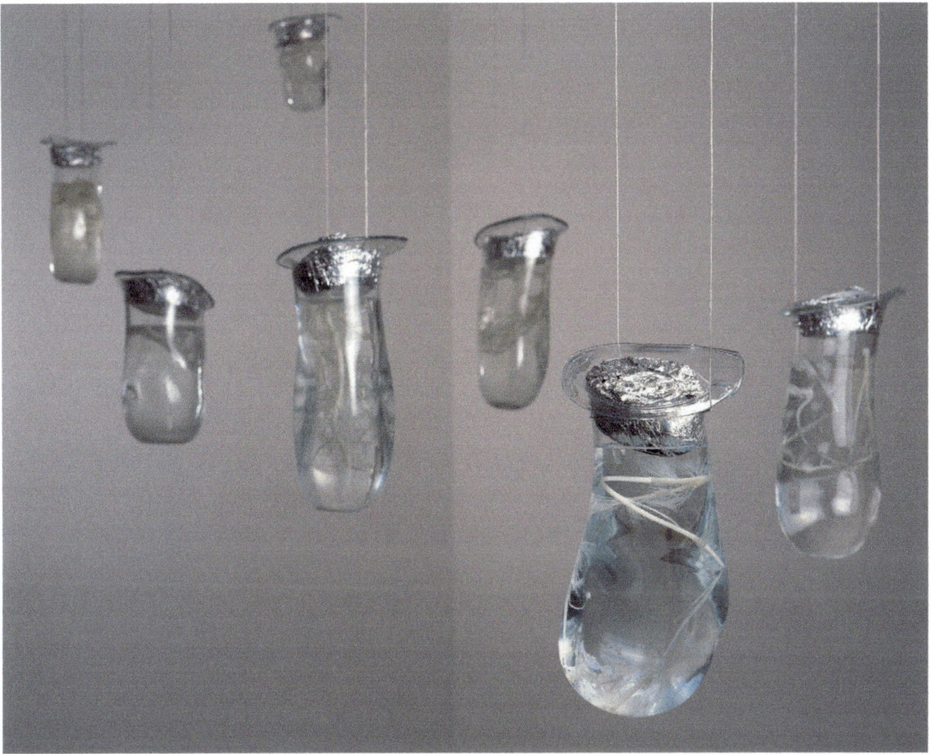

FIGURE 13.4. Christine Borland, *Ecbolic Garden, Winter* (detail) 2001, hand-blown glass vessels, bleached plant specimens, Kew solution, foam, tinfoil, wires. Installation dimensions variable. Centre for Life Science, Inverness. © the artist and Patricia Fleming Projects, Glasgow, 2001.

gender-labour-plant dynamic that was naturally attractive to Borland's sensibilities (and has found form in other projects by her). Again, she placed a leaf from each plant in a glass vessel initially filled with bleach, then with an alcohol solution. The colour drained from the leaves and, as with *Spirit Collection: Hippocrates*, only the leaf's skeletal ghost remains. Four years before *Medicine Cabinet*, Borland made *The History of Plants, According to Women, Children and Students* (2002) (Fig. 13.5) by engaging women in hand-colouring one hundred botanical etchings of these same ten ecbolic plants from Fuchs's book, *Significant Notes of the History of Plants*. She arranged for the women to use colouring techniques that echoed sixteenth-century publishing practices. What does it mean for a woman to hand-colour an image of a plant that cuts short pregnancy? Knowing what we do about the historical context of this work, how do we read the twisting extensions of each uprooted plant laid out across the page, delicate leaves in greens and

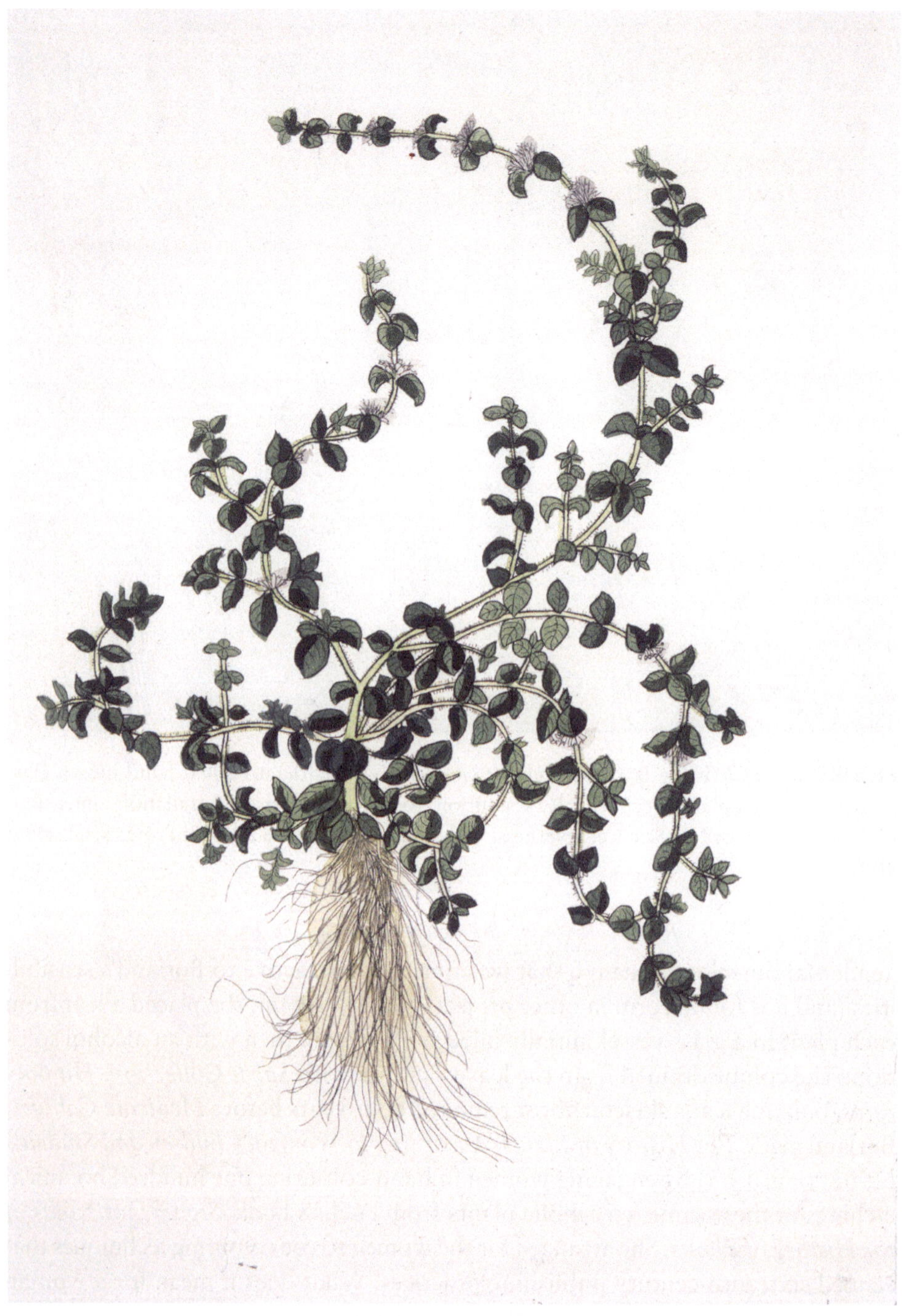

FIGURE 13.5. Christine Borland, 'Pennyroyal—Mentha pulegium', from *History of Plants According to Women, Children and Students* (2002/2006), hand-coloured etching, 61 × 47 cm. © the artist and Patricia Fleming Projects, Glasgow, 2006.

browns, deathly in life yet alive in the frame? Borland has instructed other women to birth instructional images of non-birth.

The Extracted

Extraction is a kind of absorption, a taking and moving over of an element from one host to another. Humans have developed a number of uses of natural material to enable such extraction or absorption for their benefit and survival. Humans have also given histories to the plant kingdom, whether the plants wanted it or not. Some plants and vegetables have become so close to the human sphere that they seem fully integrated technologies—cotton is surely one among many. Its ubiquity in our clothing and ancillary health and domestic worlds give it the impression of something akin to skin and almost as intimate. Cotton also signals the stores of its cultivation and production, particularly as a past of colonial and slave histories. Such stories have featured in other works by Borland (such as *English Family China*, 1998) as well as in similar textile material like wool (*Blanket Used on Police Firing Range, Berlin: Repaired*, 1993) and silk, a natural material that features in the rest of this section. Throughout her research and work, Borland has thought about the relationship between a common material such as cotton and a more specialized, less familiar one—sphagnum moss. She has used or referenced this moss in a number of more recent works, for example *To the Power of Twelve* (2018) a major installation at Mount Stuart on the Isle of Bute, that in particular draws on moss's history as a substitute for cotton in the medicinal and health sphere. Sphagnum moss as an absorbent material has been familiar in ancient societies as also in recent scholarly histories. In this context, the rarity and seemingly more feral nature of sphagnum moss allows a different tone to come into Borland's work rather than using the more familiar cotton, which, to reiterate, seems a technological produce at least as much as a natural substance. Underpinning Borland's employment of sphagnum moss is also something of a survivalist aesthetic of 'make-do-and-mend'. Those in need of an absorbent material to staunch blood and protect wounds would reach for moss as a readily available natural substitute. As we have seen with the ecbolic plants that Borland uses in other works, a folkloric and herbalist knowledge base seeps into the possible meanings of Borland's use of sphagnum moss.

A more direct form of extraction is apparent in a final series of works we look at here. Animals rather than plants or the ground form the extractive source. It is entirely consistent with the kind of posthumanism I mobilize here that hierarchies are flattened and borders are erased between types of materiality that spring from the biosphere and zoosphere. Further, it is useful to note that

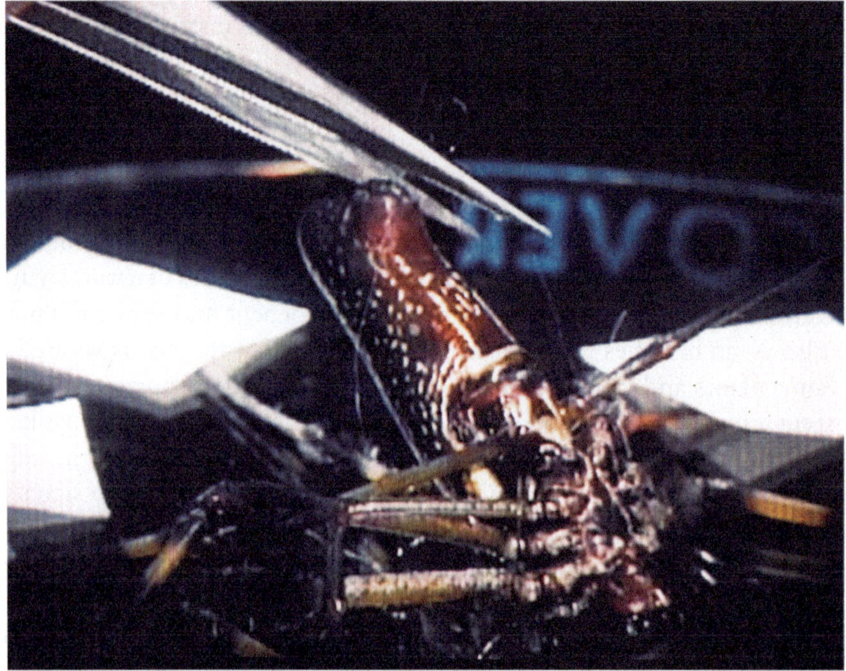

FIGURE 13.6. Christine Borland, *Nephila-Mania*, 2001, (still from video projection), The Fabric Workshop and Museum, Philadelphia. © the artist and Patricia Fleming Projects, Glasgow, 2001.

the way in which Borland engages with animal extraction raises ethical challenges, but is not explicitly founded in 'animal arts activism'. Before looking at the works, we might be reminded of one of the working notebooks of Charles Darwin, where he reached for a non-hierarchical appreciation for animals that he aligned explicitly to other forms of enslavement. 'Animals whom we have made our slaves we do not like to consider our equals.—(Do not slave-holders wish to make the black man other kind —animals with affections, imitation, fear of death, pain, sorrow for the dead—respect.'[35] *Bullet Proof Breath* and *Nephila-Mania* (both 2001) prompt such sentiments, whether or not deliberately intended by the artist.

Bullet Proof Breath is an editioned work comprising a plexiglass vitrine in which is placed a blown-glass object in the form of lungs, entwined in spider silk. The film *Nephila-Mania* (Fig. 13.6) forms a pair with *Bullet Proof Breath*, centring on how spiders' silk is extracted for material research purposes within the defence industry. These two works form a nexus of persistent conjunctions that appear in much of Borland's work, specifically animals and violent technologies, expressed through the intersection of body armour and human anatomy. Borland's study of the relations between weaponry, clothing or textiles and the human body started in the early 1990s, for example, *American Cotton* (1992) constituted a bullet laid in cotton wool, like a sample, showing how far it penetrated the wool structure when shot from a gun. Other works (such as *Apples with Holes* (1991) and *Blanket Used on Police Range, Berlin: Repaired* and *Shoes with .38mm Holes* (both 1993) also developed out of her research into ballistics and the seemingly soft and vulnerable materialities of cloth and human tissue could be damaged by or conversely protected from the projective violence of metal bullets. Research into bullet-proof substances has a long history, to which Borland was drawn. This included episodes in which laboratory experimenters would shoot into dead women's bodies, with their torsos wrapped in the bullet-proof fabric to see from what calibre of bullet and distance would provide some protection.[36] Violence, the military and gender were thematically condensed with peculiar intensity again in Borland's work.

Borland's research intensive project began with her identifying and initiating a collaboration with researchers in DuPont Central Research and Development Station, Delaware, who were looking at the webs constructed in silk by spiders and seeing whether through recombinant genetics research such fabric could be made artificially in the laboratory, and would have the same qualities.[37] The Golden Orb Weaver spider had been identified by these researchers as the best producer of silk for the kind of purposes the military and others had in mind. It was native to Papua New Guinea and openly on display at the Smithsonian National Zoo, Washington. Among many fascinating aspects to the spiders' intricate work, scientists have noted in the wild that damaged webs are darned by spiders (mirroring the repair work that Borland instigated for a piece such as *Blanket Used on Police Range, Berlin: Repaired*). On the process of silk extraction, or what is called the 'silking' of the spider, this is done by first knocking it unconscious (carbon dioxide is blown at it by the lab scientist), who then takes tweezers to the abdomen of the taped-down spider to pull the start of a silk thread. This is then attached to a rotating mechanical spindle, which runs its course until the silk is fully run out. For Borland's piece, the spiders were not wild but sourced from a commercial company, Carolina Biological Suppliers, so she followed the same route that other experimenters went down to source their animals. In replicating such acquisitions in her creative practice she reproduced some of the tricky ethical tactics that were vividly present in a work such as *From Life* (1994), for which she obtained human bones of dubious provenance through a mail order catalogue.

In writing about Borland's spider web film, Katrina Brown quotes Henry James, in an incisive passage where he invokes Denis Diderot's analogy between human consciousness and a spider's web. James writes: 'Experience is never limited, and it is never complete: it is an immense sensibility, a kind of huge spider-web of the finest silken threads suspended in the chamber of consciousness and catching every air-borne particle in its tissue'.[38] I would suggest that the direct analogy works not only for interpreting *Bullet Proof Breath* as an individual work but also perspicaciously illuminates Borland's overall strategies as an artist; the way she withholds judgement, collaborates with experts beyond her field, follows her intuition, and while keeping forensically close to empirical evidence, always resolves a work by means of circumstantial poetics, rather than reason.[39]

Of the three types of animals proposed by Gilles Deleuze and Félix Guattari (pack animals, pets and state animals), these spiders are clearly in the final class—state animals plundered for genetics research and the military–medical narratives of modern technocracy. Borland does not share many other artists' interest in the pack animal or the pet. Spiders exemplify one point on the extreme scale of unnatural extraction that has as its other opposite in the scale the medicinal extraction of plant chemicals. Humans co-opt, it is clear, with varying degrees of force.

Conclusion

Borland's other-than-human specimens are as extensive as their human counterparts—animal bones, medicinal plants and transfigured fruit, among other things. Borland entreats us to see these specimens differently. Donna Haraway reflected on the etymology of the word 'speces'—as 'seeing'—thus binding the visual and the specimen and leading us towards an idea of 'extended seeing', which for Haraway

> takes us to seeing again, to *respecere*, to the act of respect. To hold in regard, to respond, to look back reciprocally, to notice, to pay attention, to have courteous regard for, to esteem: all of that is tied to polite greeting, to constituting the polis, where and when species meet. To knot companion and species together in encounter, in regard and respect, is to enter the world of becoming with, where who and what are is precisely what is at stake.[40]

So looking and gazing bind together, in 'specare', the notions of species, specimen and respect. To respect is no more and no less than to see properly, to pay attention and to care for—perfect concepts for all of Borland's work.

I think it is enough to say that the figuration is centred on the human, the identified or anonymous human body, but in a way that is so shattered and distributed across the material-cultural realm as to border on the unrecognizable. Borland draws on an outer circle of moral categories in her work, not only from the marginalized or forgotten human (the bones and body parts of an Asian woman, the embryos and genetic code, the vestiges of identities removed from once unwilling and now silenced medical patients, the diseased and disabled, children), but also from the animal and vegetable world and, in certain works, of stones and gems. Borland's inclusion of animal, vegetable and mineral into her circle of attention is to speak of respect, of care and of attention. And I am reading this work not only within the sphere of human care but within an ecology of distributed attentiveness. Following Stengers,

> [t]he idea of ecology is incompatible, moreover, with neutrality: in an ecological situation, there is no neutral position from which an arbiter could assess rights and duties, nor is there any central and highest position from which a ruler could assign to each protagonist its part in a harmonious whole.[41]

Assuredly Borland is working with materialism and immaterialism through considerable attention to the animal and plant worlds. Anthropocentric domination and violence are tonal values within many pieces, but her intentions seem impelled more towards making such domination and violence strange and uncomfortable. As decades have passed since her earliest pieces, it becomes easier to appreciate that the bones, bodies, bullets and tragic stories pulled into her own discursive fields were not placed there to shock, like so much of 1990s British art of the time. As the shock value subsides (partly as even more provocative and transgressive artworks have taken their place) a truer sense of her purpose and contribution, unhinged from a human-only ethics, becomes easier to see.

ACKNOWLEDGEMENTS

The author would like to acknowledge the cooperation of the artist Christine Borland, and bibliographic advice from Craig Richardson.

NOTES

1. Ralph Waldo Emerson, *The Conduct of Life: Fate*, 1860, in *The Prose Works of Ralph Waldo Emerson* (Boston: Fields, Osgood, 1870), *ix*.
2. Aristotle, 'The History of Animals', in *The Animals Reader: The Essential Classic and Contemporary Writings*, ed. Linda Kalof and Amy Fitzgerald, trans. D'Arcy Wentworth Thompson (Berg, 2007), 6.
3. See Cary Wolfe, *What Is Posthumanism?*, Posthumanities 8 (Minneapolis: University of Minnesota Press, 2010), 99.
4. In email correspondence with the author, 19 December 2018.

5. Philippe Descola, *Beyond Nature and Culture: Forms of Attachment* (Chicago: University of Chicago Press, 2013), 30.

6. In email correspondence with the author, 19 December 2018.

7. The centrality of this much-quoted principle and the broader pedagogical connections between Environmental Art at GSA and the Artist Placement Group is discussed in David Harding, 'Public Art: Contentious Term and Contended Practice', in *Decadent*, ed. D. Harding, and Pavel Büchler, 9–19 (Glasgow: Foulis Press, 1997). The original phrase would seem to have originated in the period 1970–71, as part of an APG Manifesto either in an APG preview article in *Studio International* (issue 927, November 1970), or at their exhibition at Städtische Kunsthalle, Düsseldorf, June 1971, [online] available at https://aajpress.wordpress.com/2012/11/15/exhibition-the-individual-and-the-organisation-artist-placement-group-1966-79-raven-row-london-27-september-16-december-2012/ (accessed 4 May 2020).

8. For a summary of recent medical literature on the 'human microbiome' see Ron Sender, Shai Fuchs and Ron Milo, 'Are We Really Vastly Outnumbered? Revisiting the Ratio of Bacterial to Host Cells in Humans', *Cell* 164, no. 3 (January 2016): 337–40. On organic symbiosis and its theoretical implications, see Lynn Margulis, *Symbiotic Planet: A New Look at Evolution* (New York: Basic Books, 1998), Alphonso Lingis, 'Animal body, Inhuman Face', *Social Semiotics* 7, no. 2 (1997): 113–14 and Pramod K. Nayar, *Posthumanism* (Cambridge: Polity Press, 2013).

9. For seminal contributions, see Jane Bennett, *Vibrant Matter: A Political Ecology of Things* (Durham, NC: Duke University Press, 2010); Rosi Braidotti, *The Posthuman* (Polity, 2013); Cary Wolfe, *What Is Posthumanism?* (Minneapolis: University of Minnesota Press, 2010); Katherine Hayles, *How We Became Posthuman: Virtual Bodies in Cybernetics, Literature, and Informatics* (Chicago: University of Chicago Press, 1999); Timothy Morton, *Ecology without Nature: Rethinking Environmental Aesthetics* (Harvard: Harvard University Press, 2007); Donna J. Haraway, *When Species Meet* (Minneapolis: University of Minnesota Press, 2007); Matthew Hall, *Plants as Persons: A Philosophical Botany* (Albany: State University of New York Press, 2011); Michael Marder, 'Vegetal Anti-Metaphysics: Learning from Plants', *Continental Philosophy Review* 44, no. 4 (1 November 2011): 469–89, among others.

10. Haraway, *When Species Meet*, 32.

11. Mary Midgley, *Evolution as a Religion* (London: Routledge, 1985).

12. Ref. the artist Pinar Yoldas in Suzanne Anker, 'The Beginnings and the Ends of Bio Art', *Artlink* 34, no. 3 (2014): 16.

13. Gillian Beer, *Darwin's Plots: Evolutionary Narrative in Darwin, George Eliot and Nineteenth-Century Fiction*, 3rd ed. (Cambridge: Cambridge University Press, 2009), 45.

14. Fiona Bradley, ed., *Christine Borland: Preserves* (Edinburgh: Fruitmarket Gallery, 2006), 4.

15. Ian Hunt, 'Interior Structures', in *Christine Borland: Preserves*, ed. Fiona Bradley (Edinburgh: Fruitmarket Gallery, 2006), 65.

16. Isabelle Stengers, 'Comparison as a Matter of Concern', *Common Knowledge* 17, no. 1 (2011): 61.

17. Haraway, *When Species Meet*, 2.

18. In email correspondence with the author, 19 December 2018.

19. I acknowledge Hunt's essay, 'Interior Structures' for highlighting this particular aspect.

20. Christine Borland and Craig Richardson, 'Interview: Living Subjects', in *Christine Borland: Preserves*, ed. Fiona Bradley (Edinburgh: Fruitmarket Gallery, 2006), 146.

21. Charles Esche, ed., 'Escape from the Traps of Art', in *Christine Borland* (Glasgow: Tramway, 1994), 6.

22. Michael Marder, 'Vegetal Anti-Metaphysics: Learning from Plants', *Continental Philosophy Review* 44, no. 4 (1 November 2011): 484.

23. Ibid., 469.

24. Borland and Richardson, 'Interview: Living Subjects', 150.

25. OED definition

26. Borland and Richardson, 'Interview: Living Subjects', 150.

27. Hunt, 'Interior Structures', 67.

28. Ibid., 67.

29. Ibid., 67.

30. Marder, 'Vegetal Anti-Metaphysics', 487.

31. Marsha Meskimmon, 'Corporeal Theory with/in Practice: Christine Borland's Winter Garden', *Art History* 26, no. 3 (1 June 2003): 445.

32. Ibid., 447.

33. Ibid., 442.

34. See J. H. Dickson and W. W. Gauld, 'Mark Jameson's "Physic Plants, A Sixteenth Century Garden for Gynaecology in Glasgow?"', *Scottish Medical Journal* 32 (1987): 60–62.

35. From Notebook B (B231), in Beer, *Darwin's Plots*, 55.

36. Interestingly, one of the anatomists and collaborators in late nineteenth-century research was one Dr Leonard C. Borland. See Sławomir Łotysz, 'Tailored to the Times: The Story of Casimir Zeglen's Silk Bullet-Proof Vest', *Arms & Armour* 11, no. 2 (1 October 2014): 170.

37. The background for this section draws primarily from the exhibition catalogue *Christine Borland: Bullet Proof Breath* (2002), in particular a set of 'Notes' by the artist on the detail of her engagement with DuPont and the Smithsonian National Zoo and so on. See 54–63.

38. From 'Art of Fiction', Partial Portraits, 1888, in Katrina M. Brown, 'What Makes for the Fullness and Perfection of Life, for Beauty and Happiness Is Good. What Makes for Death, Disease, Imperfection, Suffering Is Bad', in *Progressive Disorder* (Dundee : London: Dundee Contemporary Arts; Book Works, 2001), 26.

39. For more on my overview of Borland's art, see Andrew Patrizio, 'Pre-War, at War, Post-War', in *Christine Borland: I Say Nothing* (Glasgow: Culture and Sport, Glasgow, 2018).

40. Haraway, *When Species Meet*, 19.

41. Stengers, 'Comparison as a Matter of Concern', 61.

REFERENCES

Anker, Suzanne. 'The Beginnings and the Ends of Bio Art'. *Artlink* 34, no. 3 (2014): 16–17.

Beer, Gillian. *Darwin's Plots: Evolutionary Narrative in Darwin, George Eliot and Nineteenth-Century Fiction.* 3rd ed. Cambridge: Cambridge University Press, 2009.

Bennett, Jane. *Vibrant Matter: A Political Ecology of Things.* Durham, NC: Duke University Press, 2010.

Borland, Christine, and Craig Richardson. 'Interview: Living Subjects'. In *Christine Borland: Preserves*, ed. Fiona Bradley, 142–53. Edinburgh: Fruitmarket Gallery, 2006

Bradley, Fiona, ed. *Christine Borland: Preserves.* Edinburgh: Fruitmarket Gallery, 2006.

Braidotti, Rosi. *The Posthuman.* Cambridge: Polity, 2013.

Brown, Katrina M. 'What Makes for the Fullness and Perfection of Life, for Beauty and Happiness Is Good. What Makes for Death, Disease, Imperfection, Suffering Is Bad'. In *Progressive Disorder*. ed. Katrina Brown, 7–28. Dundee: Dundee Contemporary Arts; London: Book Works, 2001.

Descola, Philippe. *Beyond Nature and Culture: Forms of Attachment.* Chicago: University of Chicago Press, 2013.

Dickson, J. H., and W. W. Gauld. 'Mark Jameson's "Physic Plants, A Sixteenth Century Garden for Gynaecology in Glasgow?"'. *Scottish Medical Journal* 32 (1987): 60–62.

Esche, Charles, ed. 'Escape from the Traps of Art'. In *Christine Borland*, 5–12. Glasgow: Tramway, 1994.

Hall, Matthew. *Plants as Persons: A Philosophical Botany.* SUNY Series on Religion and the Environment. Albany: State University of New York Press, 2011.

Haraway, Donna J. *When Species Meet.* Minneapolis: University of Minnesota Press, 2007.

Harding, David. 'Public Art: Contentious Term and Contended Practice'. In *Decadent*, ed. D. Harding and Pavel Büchler, 9–19. Glasgow: Foulis Press, 1997.

Hayles, Katherine. *How We Became Posthuman: Virtual Bodies in Cybernetics, Literature, and Informatics.* Chicago: University of Chicago Press, 1999.

Hunt, Ian. 'Interior Structures'. In *Christine Borland: Preserves*, ed. Fiona Bradley, 64–75. Edinburgh: Fruitmarket Gallery, 2006.

Kalof, Linda, and Amy Fitzgerald, eds. *The Animals Reader: The Essential Classic and Contemporary Writings.* London: Berg, 2007.

Łotysz, Sławomir. 'Tailored to the Times: The Story of Casimir Zeglen's Silk Bullet-Proof Vest'. *Arms & Armour* 11, no. 2 (1 October 2014): 164–86.

Marder, Michael. 'Vegetal Anti-Metaphysics: Learning from Plants'. *Continental Philosophy Review* 44, no. 4 (1 November 2011): 469–89.

Meskimmon, Marsha. 'Corporeal Theory with/in Practice: Christine Borland's Winter Garden'. *Art History* 26, no. 3 (1 June 2003): 442–55.

Midgley, Mary. *Evolution as a Religion.* London: Routledge, 1985.

Morton, Timothy. *Ecology without Nature: Rethinking Environmental Aesthetics.* Harvard: Harvard University Press, 2007.

Patrizio, Andrew. 'Pre-War, at War, Post-War'. In *Christine Borland: I Say Nothing*. Glasgow: Culture and Sport, Glasgow, 2018.

Sender, Ron, Shai Fuchs and Ron Milo. 'Are We Really Vastly Outnumbered? Revisiting the Ratio of Bacterial to Host Cells in Humans'. *Cell* 164, no. 3 (January 2016): 337–40.

Stengers, Isabelle. 'Comparison as a Matter of Concern'. *Common Knowledge* 17, no. 1 (2011): 48–63.

Tarantino, Michael. *Christine Borland: Bullet Proof Breath*. Toronto: Art Gallery of York University, 2002.

Wolfe, Cary. *What Is Posthumanism?* Posthumanities 8. Minneapolis: University of Minnesota Press, 2010.

Afterword
Specimen—What's at Stake?

Ludmilla Jordanova

There's a great deal to say about 'specimen', both the concept and the thing. The word has powerful resonances, as is clear from a recent novel, *The Specimen* by Martha Lea, published in 2013. A thrilling tale set in the mid-nineteenth century, it touches on contemporary scientific work on the natural world, as well as the deceptions, as these are presented, of spiritualism. There is a certain ambiguity as to who or what is 'the specimen', at least in my reading. Things in jars, flora, fauna and fossils might be the obvious candidates, but members of the extraordinary cast of characters, including a dwarf *patissier*, a hirsute woman and a ventriloquizing medium, as well as an assortment of scientific and medical figures, could also be 'specimens'. Lea touches on an array of issues such as gender, disability, collecting and the thirst for knowledge, that may also be found in the foregoing chapters. Her novel too may be read as a form of critique. But it is not only that. For example, the book is a commodity, published by a distinguished Edinburgh press, Canongate, just as medical and natural history specimens, and art works that riff on them, are also commodities and have been for some time. Commodities require an infrastructure in order to circulate. In the cases of anthropology, medicine, natural history, chemistry and so on, that infrastructure was elaborate, and included long-distance trade, exchanges between members of networks, sales and auctions, catalogues, other publications and institutions, such as museums, specialist organizations and sale rooms. The very idea of a specimen invites us to ask who is collecting it, from whom and why, what relationships give rise to collections and their forms of display, as well as who is viewing it. It is a formidably complex topic with significant roots in the deep past.

One of the most notable shifts of recent decades has been the refurbishment and redisplay of collections of natural history and medical specimens that were, not so long ago, perceived as old-fashioned, even obsolete. This sea change is part and parcel of a much larger trend in museums and galleries, which itself forms part of yet bigger transformations in leisure time, access to collections, and the desire of governments to reach audiences that are more numerous and diverse than hitherto. The art world, itself commoditized at local, national and international levels, has been a key player in all these phenomena. Examples include the vogue, now well established, for 'art and science', and 'art and medicine' projects. As a result, the notion of a specimen was bound to be explored and subjected to scrutiny, by artists, curators, critics and scholars. Curiosity about specimens is one aspect of the intense public interest in the human body, in human–animal relationships, and in science and medicine in general. The current success of science museums and science centres, for example, with their commitment to education as well as entertainment, testifies to the point. These are trends that deserve careful study. It is no coincidence that major funding bodies, the Wellcome Trust being a pre-eminent example, are not only supporting the acquisition and display of artworks that engage with scientific and medical phenomena, but also supporting research into the trends I have sketched in.

In order to probe these trends further we need many kinds of reflective practice, and from different vantage points, economic, political and social as well as cultural. In the worlds of museums and galleries, as in those of critics, scholars and commentators, there is room to talk a lot more about money: the cost of commissions; the role of government grants; the impact of big funders, such as the Wellcome Trust; the financial models used by the various organizations that display works of art, specimens and related artefacts. There is also room for the insights derived from audience research to be further integrated into our understanding of the fashion for what we can call the 'and' phenomenon: art *and* science; art *and* medicine. Critical commentary is needed because 'and' yokes domains together without expressing the nature of their relationships, and because the two key terms remain separate. 'In' and 'as' are intriguing alternatives, that is, we may want to think more in terms of blending than of juxtaposition. At the same time, it may be misleading to speak simply of 'science' given that this takes so many different forms - for instance, there is no single 'scientific method' - and that the very concept came into being relatively recently. Further, in many ways, natural history remains a separate field or, rather, a clutch of fields. It is telling that in London the Science Museum and the Natural History Museum are adjacent to each other but possess quite distinctive characteristics.

The interest in specimens forms one subset of the trends I have sketched in. It neatly focuses on something specific, or rather on many things, each specific in its own way. But matters are not quite so simple, as the notion of a type specimen reveals, since it stands for an entire species. Specimen, then, always refers on to some larger group for which it acts as an example. Human remains neatly make the point, where one skull, say, is taken to represent a whole people, what in some periods was construed as a 'race'.

Collections take many forms, and it is hard to think of a category of matter, whether inert, organic or fashioned by human beings, that has not been collected at some time or place. Motivations for assembling items have no doubt been mixed. While we may be drawn to pass retrospective judgement upon them, using our own categories and moral commitments, it is also helpful to recognize that motives too have their histories, that they were deeply rooted in other times and places and invite careful consideration. After all, artists, curators and critics often find inspiration in assemblages that are in some way alien or challenging to their own sympathies and preoccupations.

Engaging with collections in this spirit, opens up our understanding of the nature of authoritative knowledge and of the shifting forms of knowledge itself. Since disciplines are constantly being formed and reformed, an interdisciplinary approach, not constrained by present-day divisions, is particularly attractive. There are many ways of bringing the humanities, social sciences, medicine and the natural sciences together, and of fully integrating creative practice into any project. In displaying their collections, institutions are far more inventive and innovative than ever before. In 2019, London's Science Museum opened its new Medicine Galleries, a complete redisplay of the Wellcome collections in its care, although only a tiny percentage of this vast collection can be shown to visitors. There is a major work by Marc Quinn, *Self-Conscious Gene*, arrays of diverse objects, and much digital material—'specimens' indeed. Given the large numbers of visitors received by the museum, and their diversity—for example, in terms in age, background and educational level—displays need to be sensitive, accessible and informative. Since the collections cover huge historical spans, such an enterprise is also a form of public history. Public history—all the ways in which items from the past as well as the understanding and interpretation of earlier times are brought to non-specialist audiences—may seem far away from the contemporary arts, with their edgier concerns and aesthetic sensibilities. But there are opportunities for productive collaborations here, not least because 'public history' also refers to a relatively young discipline that assesses and critiques the histories that appear in the media, museums, books and so on. It addresses the nature of audiences, the representation of difficult subjects, memory and memorialization, as well as broad ethical and political issues: all of these areas come up in *Post-Specimen Encounters*.

A good example of the themes of this book is the representation of the foetus. William Hunter (1718–1783), the eighteenth-century Scottish surgeon turned physician, and a great collector of books, medals, paintings and prints as well as specimens, springs to mind here. His obstetric atlas, published in 1774, with its huge hyperrealist images, is well known. In addition to the drawings and the prints, three-dimensional casts were made from the female bodies he dissected. Examples of all these categories were displayed in 2018 in Glasgow and New Haven, Connecticut, along with other types of object from his collections in order to reveal their remarkable scope. There is no substitute for the meticulous research undertaken by the Hunterian Art Gallery in Glasgow, in conjunction with the Yale Centre for British Art, which provides inspiration for historians, curators, commentators and artists. Hunter's work on gestation also resonates with contemporary concerns, especially about the control of women's bodies, as in the fierce conflicts over abortion legislation being played out in many parts of the world in which specimens and photographs of them are prominent. Somehow 'art and medicine' doesn't quite capture the forms of visual culture and the violence of the current conflicts occasioned by reproduction. It is to be expected that artists enter the fray, just as they are active with respect of ecological crises, the Anthropocene, and human–animal relations. We can also anticipate that their reactions are likely to be surprising, thought provoking and, on occasion, difficult to view.

When considering specimens, critiques of science and medicine and artistic interventions, it is sobering to recognize just how vociferous climate-change deniers are; how active the anti-vaccination and anti-abortion movements are, and how profitable the industries are that exploit people's insecurities about their health and appearance. The simple fact is that 'specimen' has meanings that are uncomfortably close to home. Tissue acquired through biopsy is a specimen, as are samples of water, ice, soil and so on that are being used to assess environmental changes. Put like this our continued existence, both individual and collective depends on specimens, on their careful handling, their accurate analysis and their rigorous interpretation. In a post-truth world, it is necessary to hope at the very least, that specimens well used will contribute to survival.

Biographies

GEMMA ANDERSON is an artist and researcher at the University of Exeter and Associate Lecturer in Drawing at Falmouth University. She is the author of *Drawing as a Way of Knowing in Art and Science* (Intellect Press, 2017). She has collaborated on a number of art/science projects including the 'Cornwall Morphology and Drawing Centre' with the Natural History Museum, London. Her work has been exhibited at the Victoria & Albert Museum, the Freud Museum and the Wellcome Collection, London.

IRENE BROWN is an artist and Head of Fine Art at Newcastle University. Brown is a sculptor and site-specific installationist. Her research and practice are engaged with wonder, focusing on the history and philosophy of science, specifically cabinets of curiosity, investigating the threshold between aesthetic and scientific realms. She is co-editor of and author of *Wonder in Contemporary Artistic Practice* (Routledge, 2015). Brown works directly in response to place, usually a museum or heritage site, using a broad range of media.

CHRISTY DUCKER is a poet and teacher of creative writing. Her first full-length collection, *Skipper*, was published in 2015 and includes work commended by the Forward Prize judges. Her pamphlet, *Armour* (2011) was a PBS Pamphlet Choice. In 2015, her Creative Practice PhD was awarded the Ella Ritchie Prize for Thesis of the Year. From 2017–20, she was REA Fellow at the University's Institute for Creative Arts Practice.

MARION ENDT-JONES is a Lecturer in Arts Management and Museology at the University of Manchester. She has published on the revival of interest in cabinets of curiosities in surrealism, contemporary art and contemporary exhibitions as well as the role of wonder and curiosity in museums and galleries more generally. She is the curator of *Coral: Something Rich and Strange at Manchester Museum* (2013–2014) and her book *Coral* is forthcoming as part of Reaktion Book's Animal series.

LUDMILLA JORDANOVA is Emeritus Professor of History and Visual Culture at Durham University, where she was Director of the Centre for Visual Arts and Culture between 2015 and 2019. Her books include *Sexual Visions* (1989), *Nature*

Displayed (1999), *The Look of the Past* (2012), and *Physicians and Their Images* (2018). The third edition of *History in Practice* was published in 2019. She is currently working on several projects, on portraiture, the ethical dimensions of historical practice, and the artist John Collier (1850–1934). She is a Trustee of the Science Museum Group (2011–21).

Edward Juler is Lecturer in Art History at Newcastle University. He is the author of *Grown but Not Made: British Modernist Sculpture and the New Biology* (Manchester University Press, 2015). He has published widely on British sculpture, biocentric modernism, Surrealism and the work of Karl Blossfeldt. He has contributed to the *Edinburgh Companion to the Critical Medical Humanities* (Edinburgh University Press, 2016) and, more recently, to *No Two Alike: Karl Blossfeldt, Francis Bruguière, Thomas Ruff* (Verlag fur moderne Kunst GmbH, 2018). His articles have been published by, among others, *History of Photography*, *Interdisciplinary Science Reviews* and the Tate.

Rahma Khazam is a Paris-based researcher, art historian and art critic affiliated to Institut ACTE, Sorbonne Paris 1. Her research spans the fields of contemporaneity, modernism, image theory and speculative realism and has been published in exhibition catalogues, edited volumes and academic journals. She received the International Association of Art Critics (France) Award for Art Criticism in 2017. She recently completed an edited volume on the work of the artist Franck Leibovici.

Nadia Lichtig is an artist, writer and musician born in Munich (Germany) and living in Montpellier (France). As an artist, Nadia Lichtig uses a wide range of media such as photography, painting, performance and installation. Each medium is approached not as a field to be mastered, but as a source of possibilities to question our ability to decipher the present.

John Mack is Professor of World Art Studies in the Sainsbury Research Unit at the University of East Anglia. Prior to that he had a curatorial career at the British Museum where he was Keeper of Ethnography. His area of speciality is in the arts and cultures of Equatorial Africa including the islands of the western Indian Ocean. Amongst many publications, his most recent book is *The Artfulness of Death in Africa* (2019).

Gavin Parkinson is Professor of Modern Art at The Courtauld Institute of Art, London, and was editor of the Ashgate and Routledge series Studies in Surrealism. He has published numerous essays and articles; his books include *Enchanted Ground: André Breton, Modernism and the Surrealist Appraisal of Fin-de-Siècle*

Painting (Bloomsbury, 2018) and *Futures of Surrealism* (YUP, 2015) among others. His book *Robert Rauschenberg and Surrealism: Art, 'Sensibility' and War in the 1960s* is forthcoming from Bloomsbury.

ANDREW PATRIZIO is Chair of Scottish Visual Culture at the University of Edinburgh. His most recent book is *The Ecological Eye: Assembling an Ecocritical Art History* (Manchester, 2019). Other publications and curatorial projects include *Contemporary Scottish Sculpture* (1999), *Christine Borland* (1990); *Stefan Gec* (2002); *Anatomy Acts* (Medical Book of the Year from the Royal Society of Medicine, 2006); *Ilana Halperin. STEINE* (Berlin, 2012); and *The Scottish Endarkenment: Art and Unreason. 1945 to the Present.*

ALISTAIR ROBINSON is Director of the Northern Gallery for Contemporary Art, Sunderland UK, having held positions at the Victoria & Albert Museum and National Museum of Photography. He is the author of *Museum and Gallery Studies* (Routledge, 2018); *Rank: Picturing the Social Order 1516–2009* (Art Editions North) and monographs upon many artists published with Kerber, Distanz, Phillip Wilson and other publishers. He is currently undertaking research into the philosophies underpinning museum collections in museums of modern art across Europe.

RICHARD TALBOT studied at Goldsmiths' College and at Chelsea School of Art, and was awarded the Rome Scholarship in Sculpture in 1980. His work includes large-scale drawings, sculpture, and more recently, video/installation. His research and studio practice are centred on contemporary drawing, but he brings to this a particular interest in the theory, history and practice of perspective.

JANE WILDGOOSE is an artist and researcher who investigates the history of collecting, while reflecting on the emotional charge that may linger in objects in collections. She is Keeper of her own collection, The Wildgoose Memorial Library, which is dedicated to memory and remembrance. She is a Visiting Senior Research Fellow in the Centre for Life-Writing Research at King's College London. She is a contributor to the Opening the Cabinet of Curiosities project at the Victoria and Albert Museum.

Index